D0418954

The
TRAVELLER'S
DAYBOOK

The
TRAVELLER'S
DAYBOOK

*A Tour of the World
in 366 Quotations*

FERGUS FLEMING

Atlantic Books
London

First published in Great Britain in 2011 by Atlantic Books,
an imprint of Atlantic Books Ltd.

This edition published in Great Britain in 2012 by Atlantic Books.

Copyright in notes and selection of excerpts © Fergus Fleming, 2011

The moral right of Fergus Fleming to be identified as the author of this work
has been asserted by him in accordance with the Copyright,
Designs and Patents Act of 1988.

All rights reserved. No part of this publication may be reproduced, stored in
a retrieval system, or transmitted in any form or by any means, electronic,
mechanical, photocopying, recording, or otherwise, without the prior permission
of both the copyright owner and the above publisher of this book.

The permissions to quote from material in copyright contained on pp. 455–68
form part of this copyright page.

Every effort has been made to trace or contact all copyright-holders.
The Publishers will be pleased to make good any omissions or rectify any
mistakes brought to their attention at the earliest opportunity.

All images are courtesy of iStock, Shutterstock or public domain.

1 2 3 4 5 6 7 8 9 10

A CIP catalogue record for this book is available from the British Library.

ISBN: 978 1 84887 812 9

Designed by carrdesignstudio.com
Printed and bound in Great Britain by the MPG Books Group

Atlantic Books
An imprint of Atlantic Books Ltd
Ormond House
26–27 Boswell Street
London
WC1N 3JZ

www.atlantic-books.co.uk

CONTENTS

Introduction 6

JANUARY...11

FEBRUARY.......................................49

MARCH 85

APRIL...123

MAY..159

JUNE 197

JULY 235

AUGUST..273

SEPTEMBER 311

OCTOBER 347

NOVEMBER 385

DECEMBER.....................................421

Sources and Acknowledgements 455

Index 469

INTRODUCTION

An invitation to edit an anthology of travel writing is a rare privilege. Of all literary genres, travel is one of the most rewarding and diverse. The very act of moving from A to an unknown B seems to bring out the best in authors. Some travel in order to write, some write because they have travelled, while others have such eye-opening experiences that it doesn't matter if they can write well or not. Even in the dullest, most dutiful Victorian tome you can usually detect some stirring of the soul. To be let loose in a travel section of a library – and in this case to be paid for it! – is a splendid thing.

The challenge set by my publishers was to compile a calendar of extracts written on – or, failing that, within the vicinity of – each of the 366 days of the year, including the elusive 29 February. The task was both frustrating and stimulating: frustrating because many of the best travel writers do not supply dates; and stimulating because it introduced me to a host of others who do. Take the Marquis de Beauvoir, a soigné, globe-trotting teenager of the nineteenth century who began one paragraph with the words: 'When we left the harem, we went to see the tigers.' Or Lafcadio Hearn, a Greek-American in Meiji-era Japan who conjured the magic of sea-demons lurking off its western coast. There is a beautiful melancholy to Joseph Roth's description of Berlin's parks in the 1920s. And then the irrepressible Nicolas Bouvier, who feared his car had shot its pistons in a Turkish desert, only to find that the knocking came from a landscape of tortoises engaged in their autumn amours. Perhaps my favourite is Archer Crouch, a Victorian engineer who laid submarine cables off the West African coast and was so intimidated by the exploits of greater explorers that he dared not put his name to his journal: his high point, endearingly, was the discovery of a small monument to forgotten soldiers who had died in an out-of-the-way place that nobody had heard of.

Credit for this book must first of all be given to the writers who have made it possible. At Atlantic Books I would like to thank Anthony Cheetham, who came up with the idea for the book; Richard Milbank, who asked me to write it; Sarah Norman and Sachna Hanspal, who ensured its smooth passage through to press; and Mark Hawkins-Dady for his attention to the text. I would also like to thank my agent Gillon Aitken; and the staffs at the Bodleian Library, the British Library, the Kensington and Chelsea Libraries, the London Library and the Royal Geographical Society. I would like further to dedicate this book to the memory of an old friend and colleague, Alan Lothian, who died on 12 September 2010.

FF, London, 2011

JANUARY

∞

1 JANUARY

ALL BY MYSELF, 1900

Isabelle Eberhardt (1877–1904) was a young Swiss woman, disturbed and prey to addictions, who sought adventure in the Sahara dressed as a man. On the coast of Sardinia, she contemplated in her diary a nomadic future.

I sit here all by myself, looking at the grey expanse of murmuring sea... I am utterly *alone* on earth, and always will be in this Universe so full of lures and disappointments... *alone*, turning my back on a world of dead hopes and memories...

I shall dig in my heels and go on acting the lunatic in the intoxicating expanse of desert as I did last summer, or go on galloping through olive groves in the Tunisian Sahel, as I did last autumn...

Right now, I long for one thing only: to lead that life again in Africa... to sleep in the chilly silence of the night below stars that drop from great heights, with the sky's infinite expanse for a roof and the warm earth for a bed, in the knowledge that no one pines for me *anywhere on earth*, that there is no place where I am being missed or expected. To know that is to be free and unencumbered, a nomad in the great desert of life where I shall never be anything but an outsider. Such is the only form of bliss, however bitter, the Mektoub [Fate] will ever grant me, but then happiness of the sort coveted by all of frantic humanity, will never be mine.

ISABELLE EBERHARDT, *THE PASSIONATE NOMAD*.

2 JANUARY

NORDIC AUGURIES, 1895

On this date, the Norwegian explorer Fridtjof Nansen (1861–1930) welcomed the start of the year aboard his ship the *Fram*. Unique among polar vessels, the *Fram* had a rounded hull that allowed it to rise above the floes rather than be crushed by them. In 1893 Nansen had embedded his ship in the Arctic pack and let it drift with the ice, ostensibly to collect scientific data but also to provide a springboard for an attempt to ski to the North Pole.

Never before have I had such strange feelings at the commencement of the New Year. It cannot fail to bring some momentous events, and will possibly become one of the most remarkable years in my life, whether it leads me to success or to destruction. Years come and go unnoticed in this world of ice, and we have no more knowledge here of what these years have brought to humanity than we know of what the future ones have in store. In this silent nature no events ever happen; all is shrouded in darkness; there is nothing in view save the twinkling stars, immeasurably far away in the freezing night, and the flickering sheen of the aurora borealis. I can just discern close by the vague outline of the *Fram*, dimly standing out in the desolate gloom, with her rigging showing dark against the host of stars. Like an infinitesimal speck, the vessel seems lost amidst the boundless expanse of this realm of death. Nevertheless under her deck there is a snug and cherished home for thirteen men, undaunted by the majesty of this realm. In there, life is freely pulsating, while far away outside in the night there is nothing save death and silence, only broken now and then, at long intervals, by the violent pressure of the ice as it surges along in gigantic masses. It sounds most ominous in the great stillness, and one cannot help an uncanny feeling as if supernatural powers were at hand.

FRIDTJOF NANSEN, *FARTHEST NORTH*, VOLUME II.

3 JANUARY

MANDARIN JUSTICE, 1879

A semi-invalid in her native Britain, Isabella Bird (1831–1904) found the only cure for her ailments was to travel, which she did obsessively. In a letter to her younger sister Henrietta she described a law court in Canton. She had previously made a tour of a Chinese prison – 'foul with horror' – and was ill-disposed towards the country's legal system.

In a high backed armchair of dark wood such as one might see in any English hall sat the man who has the power of life and death in his hands, a young looking man in the usual black satin cap with a blue brocade robe and a sleeved cloak of dark blue satin lined with white fur over it. He spoke loudly and with much rapidity and emphasis and often beat his foot impatiently on the floor. He spoke in the Mandarin tongue, and put his questions through an interpreter who stood at his left, a handsomely dressed old man who wore a chain with a dependent ivory comb, with which he frequently combed a small and scanty grey moustache. Notaries attendant with scarlet crowned hats, city guards, and a small rabble of men and boys stood behind and down the sides. The open hall, though high, was shabby and extremely dirty with unswept broken pavement, strewn at one side with potsherds and disfigured by a number of more or less broken black pots and other rubbish making it look rather like a shed in an untidy nursery garden than a judgement hall. There are certain inscriptions on the pillars one of which is said to be an exhortation to mercy. Different pieces of bamboo used for the *bastinado* [beating] were ranged against the wall and there were other things at which I looked once and no more for a shuddering dread came over me that they were for use in the 'Question by Torture'.

ISABELLA BIRD, *LETTERS TO HENRIETTA*.

4 JANUARY

LEAVING SICILY, 1921

His books, his behaviour and his German wife – Frieda von Richthofen – all having been given a frosty reception in wartime Britain, the novelist and poet D.H. Lawrence (1885–1930) departed for more forgiving climes in November 1919. The couple settled on the east coast of Sicily, where they made brief forays to Sardinia, northern Italy, Austria and southern Germany. Here Lawrence describes their dawn departure to catch a ferry to the mainland.

Under the lid of the half-cloudy night sky, far away at the rim of the Ionian sea, the first light, like metal fusing. So swallow the cup of tea and the bit of toast. Hastily wash up, so that we can find the house decent when we come back. Shut the door-windows of the upper terrace, and go down. Lock the door: the upper half of the house made fast.

The sky and sea are parting like an oyster shell, with a low red gape. Looking across from the verandah at it, one shivers. Not that it is cold. The morning is not at all cold. But the ominousness of it: that long red slit between a dark sky and a dark Ionian sea, terrible old bivalve which has held life between its lips so long. And here, at this house, we are ledged so awfully above the dawn, naked to it.

Fasten the door-windows of the lower verandah. One won't fasten at all. The summer heat warped it one way, the masses of autumn rain warped it another. Put a chair against it. Lock the last door, and hide the key. Sling the knapsack on one's back, take the kitchenino [canteen] in one's hand, and look round. The dawn-red widening, between the purpling sea and the troubled sky. A light in the capucin convent across there. Cocks crowing, and the long, howling, hiccupping, melancholy bray of an ass. 'All females are dead, all females – och! och! och! – hoooo! Ahaa! – there's one left.' So he ends on a moaning grunt of consolation. – This is what the Arabs tell us an ass is howling when he brays.

Very dark under the great carob tree as we go down the steps. Dark still the garden. Scent of mimosa, and then of jasmine. The lovely mimosa tree invisible. Dark the stony path. The goat whinnies out of her shed. The broken Roman tomb which lolls right over the garden track does not fall on me as I slip under its massive tilt. Ah dark garden, dark garden, with your olives and your wine, your medlars and mulberries and many almond trees, your steep terraces ledged high up above the sea, I am leaving you, slinking out. Out between the rosemary hedges, out of the tall gate, on to the cruel steep stony road. So under the dark, big eucalyptus trees, over the stream, and up towards the village. There, I have got so far.

D.H. LAWRENCE, *D.H. LAWRENCE AND ITALY.*

5 JANUARY

NIGHT OPENS SLOWLY LIKE A YAWN, 1933

On an idiosyncratic journey through what was then the South American colony of British Guiana, the novelist Evelyn Waugh (1903–66) recorded the splendour of a jungle dusk.

That ride remains one of the most vivid memories of the cattle trail. Checked and annoyed as I was, the splendour of the evening compensated for everything. Out on the savannah there is no twilight; the sun goes down blazing on the horizon, affording five or ten minutes of gold and crimson glory; then darkness. In the forest night opens slowly like a yawn. The colours gradually deepened, the greens pure and intense to the point of saturation, the tree trunks and the bare earth glowing brown; the half shades, the broken and refracted fragments of light all disappeared and left only fathomless depths of pure colour. Then dusk spread; distances became incalculable and obstacles detached themselves unexpectedly and came suddenly near; and while it was almost night in the trail the tops of the trees were still ablaze with sunlight, till eventually they too darkened and their flowers were lost. And all the pattering and whistling and chattering of the bush at night broke out loudly on all sides, and the tired little horse – who was doing a double journey and, being always on the move – suddenly pricked his ears and raised his head and stepped out fresh as though his day were only just beginning.

EVELYN WAUGH, *NINETY-TWO DAYS*.

6 JANUARY

A WINTER'S NIGHT IN VERMONT, 1892

On a bright January afternoon the English novelist and 'poet of Empire' Rudyard Kipling (1865–1936) caught a train from New York to Vermont. Several hours later, he stepped from the warmth of his carriage into the chill of a New England night. The contrast took him aback.

Thirty degrees below freezing! It was inconceivable till one stepped out into it at midnight, and the first shock of that clear, still air took away the breath as does a plunge into sea-water... The night was as keen as the edge of a newly-ground sword; breath froze on the coat-lapels in snow; the nose became without sensation, and the eyes wept bitterly... But for the jingle of the sleigh-bells the ride might have taken place in a dream, for there was no sound of hoofs upon the snow, the runners sighed a little now and again as they glided over an inequality, and all the sheeted hills round about were as dumb as death. Only the Connecticut River kept up its heart and a lane of black water through the packed ice; we could hear the stream worrying round the heels of its small bergs. Elsewhere there was nothing but snow under the moon – snow drifted to the level of the stone fences or curling over their tops in a lip of frosted silver; snow banked high on either side of the road, or lying heavy on the pines and the hemlocks in the woods, where the air seemed, by comparison, as warm as a conservatory. It was beautiful beyond expression, Nature's boldest sketch in black and white, done with a Japanese disregard of perspective, and daringly altered from time to time by the restless pencils of the moon.

RUDYARD KIPLING, *LETTERS OF TRAVEL*.

7 JANUARY

RUIN IN MADRID, 1938

In the winter of 1937–8 the English writer Laurie Lee (1914–97) travelled on foot over the snowbound Pyrenees to fight for the Republicans in the Spanish Civil War. After first being taken for a spy (*see* 2 December) he was sent to Madrid, then a target for Franco's German bombers.

The experience of being in Madrid again, contrasting its present cold desolation with the easy days of my earlier visit, made me want to search out some of the places I'd known.

I found the Puerta del Sol smothered in a pall of greyness, and I remembered the one-time buzz of the cafés, the tram bells, the cries of the lottery-ticket sellers, the high-stepping servant girls with their baskets of fresh-scrubbed vegetables, the parading young men and paunchy police at street corners.

Now there was emptiness and silence – the cafés closed, a few huddled women queuing at a shuttered shop. Poor as it had been when I'd known it, there had always been some sense of holiday in the town, a defiant zest for small treats and pleasures, corner stalls selling popcorn, carobs, sunflower seeds, vile cigarettes, and little paper packets of bitter sweets. Nothing now, of course, no smell of bread, oil, or the reek of burnt fish that used to enliven the alleyways round the city centre – just a fusty aroma of horses, straw, broken drains and fevered sickness.

LAURIE LEE, *A MOMENT OF WAR.*

8 JANUARY

SHE HATED PARIS, 1876

Isabel Burton (1831–96), wife of the British explorer, linguist and orientalist Richard Burton, was no stay-at-home herself. In January 1876, while passing through Paris *en route* to meet her husband in India, she poured scorn on the French capital, still showing the scars of its siege during the Franco-Prussian War (1870–1) and the suppression of the revolutionary Commune in the war's aftermath.

From Boulogne we went to Paris, which I found terribly changed since the Franco-German War. The marks of the terrible siege were still burnt upon its face; and this applied not only to the city itself, but to the people. The radical changes of the last five years, and the war and the Commune, had made a new world of Paris. The light, joyous character of the French was no doubt still below the surface, but the upper crust was then (at least so it struck me) one of sulkiness, silence, an economy run mad, a rage for lucre, and a lust *pour la revanche*... I am afraid that I am one of the very few women who do not like Paris. I never liked it, even in its palmy days; and now at this time I liked it less than ever. I was so glad to leave at the end of the week, and to move out of the raw, white fog sunwards... I could not help feeling glad these *braves* had never reached Berlin; they would have made Europe uninhabitable. France was charming as an empire or as a monarchy, but as a brand-new republic it was simply detestable.

ISABEL BURTON, *THE ROMANCE OF ISABEL LADY BURTON*, VOLUME II.

9 JANUARY

THE FAKIR OF BENARES, 1913

While in India, the English novelist E.M. Forster (1879–1970) was advised to visit a fakir in the northern city of Benares, on the River Ganges, whom his friend William Rothenstein described as 'a majestic bearded Bengali'. Neither the city nor its fakir quite lived up to expectations.

Let me add a line about this queer city. I have now been three times to the riverside, which is the most interesting part of it, and am losing my first feeling of disappointment. According to Hindu religion, it is a merit to build but none to repair, and the whole river front is either in ruins or else under the hands of contractors. The mess is unbelievable – temples tumbling, staircases leading nowhere, stacks of wood for funeral pyres, sacred wells, trees, shrines; and scrambling up and down the chaos, or perched on stone platforms in the midst of it, are the holy men and other worshippers, while the river itself swarms with bathers, muddled up with landing stages and boats. Most visitors see all this from midstream, but it is only when you go among it that it can be understood in the least, and consequently I have enjoyed this morning's visit more than the others. I managed to find the Fakir to whom Rothenstein gave me an introduction. Yesterday I tried in vain, and was only shown a bed of spikes on which they assured me he usually sat, but he was out for a walk just now. Having gathered that he was not the sort who sits on spikes, I felt doubtful, but they were confident, and pointed out his house close by. The door was locked but of course it had a hole in it through which I put my card, giving my address and saying I would call again.

E.M. FORSTER, *THE HILL OF DEVI AND OTHER INDIAN WRITINGS*.

10 JANUARY

A SANTA BARBARA WEDDING, 1836

In 1834 a wealthy young Bostonian named Richard Henry Dana (1815–82) found his eyesight affected by measles. Advised that a sea journey would improve matters, he quit his studies at Harvard University and enrolled as an ordinary seaman on the *Pilgrim,* bound for California, at that time still a Mexican province. There, at Santa Barbara, he described a local wedding dance.

The great amusement of the evening – which I suppose was owing to its being carnival – was the breaking of eggs filled with cologne, or other essences, upon the heads of the company. One end of the egg is broken and the inside taken out, then it is partly filled with cologne, and the whole sealed up. The women bring a great number of these secretly about them, and the amusement is to break one upon the head of a gentleman when his back is turned. He is bound in gallantry to find out the lady and return the compliment, though it must not be done if the person sees you. A tall, stately Don, with immense grey whiskers, and a look of great importance, was standing before me, when I felt a light hand on my shoulder, and turning round, saw Donna Angustia (whom we all knew, as she had been up to Monterey, and down again, in the *Alert*), with her finger upon her lip, motioning me gently aside. I stepped back a little, when she went up behind the Don, and with one hand knocked off his *sombrero*, and at the same instant, with the other, broke the egg upon his head, and springing behind me, was out of sight in a moment. The Don turned slowly round, the cologne running down his face, and over his clothes, and a loud laugh breaking out from every quarter.

RICHARD HENRY DANA, *TWO YEARS BEFORE THE MAST.*

11 JANUARY

ICE ON THE DELAWARE, 1879

One of the United States' finest poets and a keen observer of Nature, Walt Whitman (1819–92) spent much of his time either in the woods or on the water. He liked to take the steam ferry across the Delaware River, particularly at night, and sometimes spent hours on end crossing back and forth, drawing inspiration from the experience. 'I don't know anything more *filling*,' he wrote one winter's evening, 'than to be on the wide firm deck of a powerful boat, a clear, cool, extra-moonlight night, crushing proudly and resistlessly through this thick, marbly, glistening ice.'

Fine trips across the wide Delaware tonight. Tide pretty high, and a strong ebb. River, a little after 8, full of ice, mostly broken, but some large cakes making our strong-timber'd steamboat hum and quiver as she strikes them. In the clear moonlight they spread, strange, unearthly, silvery, faintly glistening, as far as I can see. Bumping, trembling, sometimes hissing like a thousand snakes, the tide-procession, as we wend with or through it, affording a grand undertone, in keeping with the scene. Overhead, the splendor indescribable; yet something haughty, almost supercilious, in the night. Never did I realize more latent sentiment, almost *passion,* in those silent interminable stars up there. One can understand, such a night, why, from the days of the Pharaohs or Job, the dome of heaven, sprinkled with planets, has supplied the subtlest, deepest criticism on human pride, glory, ambition.

WALT WHITMAN, *SPECIMEN DAYS IN AMERICA.*

12 JANUARY

PLAGUE IN TRIPOLI, 1786

As the sister of the British consul, Miss Tully lived in Tripoli for ten years from 1783 (*see* 3 July). Her letters and diary entries described conditions in Libya, one of the Ottoman Empire's so-called Barbary Regencies. Three years into her stay, she recounted the oppression of waiting (yet again) for the plague to strike.

———

Imprisoned in the midst of increasing pestilence, your kind wishes for a happy new year can effect [sic] us but in a small degree. The plague seems likely to repeat all the horrors of the last year. Nobody is prepared to meet this second attack, though all were told, at the time the infection seemed to cease here, that a fresh and more severe disease was brooding within the mountains of Geurianno, which can be seen hence with our glasses, and whence we have now received it. I have mentioned that the Arabs dig their dwellings within these mountains, and thus concealed in the bowels of the earth, they have for a long time escaped the pestilence; but it has now reached them, and in those airless tombs of the living, it finds everything to accelerate its deadly strokes. The frightened Arabs, abandoning their retreats, crowd to the surrounding places, and carry new destruction with them. Owing to their hourly emigrating here, the plague increases from day to day; and its devastation is greater, in consequence of the people considering the infection as being over.

Miss Tully, *Narrative of a Ten Years' Residence at Tripoli in Africa.*

13 JANUARY

STURT'S STONY DESERT, 1845

Short-sighted and disaster-prone, Charles Sturt (1795–1869) was one of Australia's most endearing explorers. His 1844–5 expedition, which started in Adelaide, was to be his third and last attempt to investigate the continent's unmapped interior. He described his experiences by way of a series of letters to his wife, 'Dearest Charlotte', in his personal journal. In this example, he recorded the latest setback suffered by himself and his faithful servant Joseph Harris.

There we stood, Dearest, Joseph and I on a sand hill, being more than 200 miles to the westward of the Darling, nearly abreast of Moreton Bay in point of latitude... but there was no change in the terrible, for it was terrible, desert we had entered. It appeared as if we were the last of creation amid the desolation and destruction of the world. There was a solemn stillness around, not a living thing to be seen, not an ant, not a cricket, or a grasshopper. The horizon was unbroken from north all round to north again, nor was there a shadow of hope in that dreary and monotonous wilderness. I could not however neglect the horse on which our safety depended, so I turned back, after having gone about 67 miles. Just as we turned to go back a parrot flew over our heads with loud cries of alarm; it went thro' the air with a zig-zag flight, and appeared to be just as much at a loss as a bird that has been driven out to sea by a gale. It passed us and went to the north. 'That bird, Sir,' said Joseph, 'does not seem to know where to go.' 'No,' said I, 'He does not indeed, and if he cannot see a place on which to rest, how shall we find one?' 'Oh Sir,' said the poor boy, 'I was never in such a place as this before. It is a dreadful place indeed.'

CHARLES STURT, *JOURNAL OF THE CENTRAL AUSTRALIAN EXPEDITION, 1844–5.*

14 JANUARY

THE LURE OF THE ORIENT, 1928

Writing from a village in French-administered Syria, Freya Stark (1893–1993) described her fascination with the Middle East. Although born in Britain, her heart was in the Orient and she would later travel widely throughout the region, exploring an urge that found release only in the wilderness. 'The beckoning counts,' she famously wrote, 'and not the clicking latch behind you.'

The East is getting a firm grip. What it is I don't know; not beauty, not poetry, none of the usual things. This place is a grand scene with all the details neglected. Of course it is not the genuine Orient, only the semi-European fringe full of French ideas second-hand and second-rate, and European clothes and furniture peculiarly unadapted to the casual Eastern silhouette. And yet I feel I want to spend years at it – not here, but further inland, where I hope to go as soon as I get enough Arabic for the absolutely necessary amount of conversation.

The village is kind, at least the Christian part, for we all live in separate compartments and have little to do with such people as Druse, or Greek Orthodox, though we may live next door. My landlady speaks of the Druses as Napoleon used to be spoken of to naughty children in England.

FREYA STARK, *OVER THE RIM OF THE WORLD.*

15 JANUARY

BROWNSHIRTS AT THE HOFBRAUHAUS, 1938

On his eve-of-war trek from London to Istanbul (*see* 9 December), Patrick Leigh Fermor (1915–2011) investigated the Hofbrauhaus in Munich. In 1923 it had been the scene of Hitler's abortive 'Beer Hall Putsch'. Now, with the Nazis in power, it was redolent of menace.

———•+•———

I had expected a different kind of town, more like Nuremberg, perhaps, or Rothenburg. The neo-classical architecture in this boreal and boisterous weather, the giant boulevards, the unleavened pomp – everything struck chill to the heart. The proportion of Storm Troopers and S.S. in the streets was unusually high and still mounting and the Nazi salute flickered about the pavement like a *tic douloureux*. Outside the Feldherrnhalle, with its memorial to the sixteen Nazis killed in a 1923 street fight nearby, two S.S. sentries with fixed bayonets and black helmets mounted guard like figures of cast-iron and the right arms of all passers-by shot up as though in reflex to an electric beam. It was perilous to withhold this homage. One heard tales of uninitiated strangers being physically set-upon by zealots. Then the thoroughfares began to shrink. I caught a glimpse down a lane of Gothic masonry and lancets and buttresses and further on copper domes hung in convolutions of baroque. A Virgin on a column presided over a slanting piazza, one side of which was formed by a tall, Victorian-Gothic building whose great arched undercroft led to a confusion of lesser streets. In the heart of them stood a massive building; my objective, the Hofbrauhaus. A heavy arched door was pouring a raucous and lurching party of Brownshirts onto the trampled snow.

I was back in beer territory. Halfway up the vaulted stairs a groaning Brownshirt, propped against the wall on a swastika'd arm, was unloosing, in a staunchless gush down the steps, the intake of hours. Love's labour lost.

PATRICK LEIGH FERMOR, *A TIME OF GIFTS*.

16 JANUARY

CHAMELEONS IN ROSETTA, 1817

Having been deposited in the Egyptian town of Rosetta while her husband Giovanni (*see* 12 March) went in search of antiquities, Sarah Belzoni (1783–1870) had little to do but record the arrival and departure of the plague and attempt to tame the local wildlife. On a January day she described her success with pet chameleons of which, at one point, she kept a multitude for export to Britain.

One cameleon [sic] lived with me eight months, and most of that time I had it fixed to the button of my coat: it used to rest on my shoulder, or on my head. I have observed, when I have kept it shut up in a room for some time, that on bringing it out in the air it would begin drawing the air in, and on putting it on some marjorum it has had a wonderful effect on it immediately: its colour became most brilliant... [Their colour change] proceeds in a great degree from the temper they are in: a little thing will put them in a bad humour: if in crossing a table, for instance, you stop them and attempt to turn them another road, they will not stir, and are extremely obstinate: on opening the mouth at them it will set them in a passion: they begin to arm themselves by swelling and turning black, and will sometimes hiss a little, but not much... In Rosetta I had between fifty and sixty... their chief food was flies: the fly does not die immediately on being swallowed, for upon taking the cameleon up in my hands it was easy to feel the fly buzzing, chiefly on account of the air they draw in their inside: they swell much and particularly when they want to fling themselves off a great height, by filling themselves up like a balloon: on falling they get no hurt, except on their mouth, which they bruise a little, as that comes first to the ground... I have held a glass in one hand while the cameleon rested its two fore paws on the edge of it, the two hind ones resting on my other hand. It stood upright while drinking, holding its head up like a fowl... They will drink mutton broth.

Giovanni Belzoni, *Narrative of the Operations and Recent Discoveries in Egypt and Nubia.*

17 JANUARY

SHAME AND PENICILLIN IN ABADAN, 1951

In 1951 the Welsh poet Dylan Thomas (1914–53) was invited to describe the beneficial effect that Anglo-Persian Oil (now BP) exerted on the Arabian Gulf. The mild-mannered radio talk he eventually gave for public consumption was nothing like this letter to an American friend.

——•——

I am writing this in a tasty, stifflipped, liverish, British Guest House in puking Abadan on, as you bloody well know, the foul blue boiling Persian buggering Gulf. And lost, God blast, I gasp between gassed vodkas, all crude and cruel fuel oil, all petroleum under frying heaven, benzola, bitumen, bunkers and tankers, pipes and refineries, wells and derricks, gushers and superfractionators and Shatt-el-Arab and all. Today I was taken to see a great new black-towered hissing and coiling monster. It cost eight million pounds. It is called a Cat-Cracker.

Abadan is inhabited almost entirely by British – or so it seems. There are thousands of young Britishers in the bachelor quarters, all quietly seething. Many snap in the heat of their ingrowing sex and the sun, and are sent back, baying, to Britain. Immediately, their places are taken by fresh recruits: young wellgroomed pups with fair moustaches and briar pipes, who, in the soaking summer, soon age, go bristled about, chain-smoke damp hanging fags, scream blue on arak, toss themselves trembly all sleepless night in the toss-trembling bachelors' quarters, answer the three-knock knock at the midnight door, see before them in the hot moonlight wetmouthed Persian girls who ask, by custom, for a glass of water, invite the girls in, blush, stammer, grope, are lost. These old-young men are shipped back also, packed full with shame and penicillin. And the more cautious stay on, boozed, shrill, hunted, remembering gay wonderful London so white-skinned and willing.

I visited oil-fields in the mountains last week. By night, the noise of frustrated geologists howled louder than the jackals outside my tent. Utterly damned, the dishonourable, craven, knowledgeable, self-pitying jackals screamed and wailed in the abysses of their guilt and the stinking garbage pails. 'Rosemary', 'Jennifer', Margery', cried the nearmale un-sleepers in their near-sleep. And the hyenas laughed like billyho deep down in their dark diseased throats. O evergreen, gardened, cypressed, cinema'd, oil-tanked, boulevarded, incense-and-armpit cradle of Persian culture, rock me soft before lorn hotel-bedtime...

A lonely country. And so is stricken Persia, mosque and blindness, fountains and mudhuts, Cadillac and running sore, pomegranate and Cat-Cracker. Beer in an hotel bar costs ten shillings a bottle; whiskey, one pound a nip. There is no nightlife. Shiraz sleeps at nine. Then, through the dark, the low camel bells ring, jackals confess their unworthiness to live in an ignoble fury of siren howls and utter their base and gutter-breathed gratitude to the night that hides their abominable faces; insomniac dogs rumpus in the mountain villages; the Egyptian deputy-Minister of Education, who has the next hotel room, drunkenly gallumphs with a thin, hairy secretary; dervishes plead under my bed; there are wolves not far away... The moon does what she does, vermin persist, camels sail, dogs defy, frogs gloat, snow-leopards drift.

DYLAN THOMAS, *COLLECTED LETTERS*.

18 JANUARY

A PLAGUE OF HAWKS, 1845

Misery followed misery for poor Charles Sturt (*see* 13 January) as he ventured deeper into the arid Australian interior.

You cannot indeed conceive the dreadful heat in this exposed and stony region. Every article we have went to ruin before it, the teeth of our combs fell off, the handles of our razors split, every box warped, and every nail was loosened. Our tires fell off the wheels, and the drays rattled all over. The soles of the men's shoes were fairly burnt off, and citric acid melted in the bottle in which it was kept...

One day as we were crossing a plain on a most sultry day, when the wind was blowing in our faces as if from a furnace, a flight of large hawks came down upon us from the upper sky in hundreds. I suppose they did not know what we were and fancied they were to have a fine feast. At first we saw two or three dark specks in the sky coming towards us, which as they came nearer turned out to be a kind of large hawk. Behind them were other specks to an immeasurable distance, until at length every part of the sky was alive with them. They approached so near that I went at them several times with a whip, and if they really had made an attack upon us, I do believe their numbers would have prevailed against our strength. They flew right into our faces in such rapid succession as to perplex one, but at length having satisfied their curiosity I suppose, they soared up aloft again and disappeared. What they were doing in the upper air it is difficult to say, and in such immense numbers. All I know is that they were enough to frighten a timid man.

CHARLES STURT, *JOURNAL OF THE CENTRAL AUSTRALIAN EXPEDITION, 1844–5.*

19 JANUARY

A SORDID PARADISE, 1939

During a cruise through the West Indies, Clementine Churchill (1885–1977) wrote sharply to her husband Winston about the state of affairs on the supposedly paradisiacal islands. However, as her closing words suggested – 'And, Oh, Winston, are we drifting into War?' – he probably had other things on his mind.

We have now reached Barbados, & soon I think I shall come home. These islands are beautiful in themselves but have been desecrated & fouled by man.

These green hills covered with tropical bush & trees rise straight out of the sea & fringing the coasts are hideously dilapidated crazy houses, unpainted for years with rusty corrugated iron roofs – Trade stagnating, enough starchy food to keep the population alive but under nourished – Eighty per cent of the population is illegitimate, seventy per cent (in several islands) have syphilis and yaws. The homes of the labourers are small sheds full of holes stuffed with rags or patched with old tin – There is no sanitation of any sort, not even earth latrines; in some places the women have to walk 3 miles to get water – In many places the proportion of doctors to the population is one doctor to 30,000 persons. Labourers wages are 1/- a day for men & 6d. for women – There is much unemployment & no system of insurance – And this is a sample of the British Empire on which the Sun never sets!

CLEMENTINE AND WINSTON CHURCHILL, *SPEAKING FOR THEMSELVES.*

20 JANUARY

SNAKES IN AN EGYPTIAN GARDEN, 1889

In 1889 the British traveller and poet Sir Wilfrid Scawen Blunt (1840–1922) settled in Egypt. The house he built for himself at Sheykh Obeyd, on the desert's edge, remained his spiritual home for decades.

I don't know how sufficiently to describe the delight of life here... Day has gone by like day, each full of interest. This morning we began pulling down an outhouse to clear the land for a new building; thirty men and boys have been working at the job in high good humour, and certainly they are neither lazy nor unintelligent. In the midst of the demolition a large cobra jumped out and put up its hood in the middle of them, but they knocked him over with their picks before he could do any harm. He measured exactly six feet in length, and by general advice he was cut up at once into four portions and thrust down the throat of a sick camel they had with them for a cure. Four other smaller snakes were also killed, but these were of a harmless kind. They tell me a horned viper was also seen in the garden, a fortnight before I came, but this is unusual except in the extreme heat of the summer. Lizards, of course, are plentiful. I have seen one with rudimentary legs only, making its way along the ground as snakes do, its feet hardly helping it.

WILFRID BLUNT, *My Diaries*, VOLUME I.

21 JANUARY

A WHALE IN THE WAY, 1962

In November 1961 the Swiss traveller Michel Mermod (born 1936) left Peru in the *Genève,* a boat he had built himself and in which he would eventually spend five years sailing single-handed round the world. Not far into the journey he met his first peril.

———•·•———

There, dead ahead of us, is a whale. *Genève* is heading straight for it! There is no time to free the tiller and take avoiding action... The boat is making her four knots, and this speed is more than enough to ensure that the shock will crack the hull wide open...

There is nothing I can do, and the feeling of helplessness is dreadful. If the creature is asleep it *must* be woken up. I jump on to the top of the cabin, cursing, swearing, screaming: 'Get out of the way, you bastard, get out of the way!'

And that wakes it! I can see its little eye fixing me. But the distance diminishes relentlessly and we are almost on top of it. I stop shouting; I don't move; I hold my breath.

Slowly, very slowly, the whale dives. Its huge head seems to sink just ahead of my prow. But it is too late: we are bound to strike. The rear part of its body now stands straight up in the air. I crouch on the deck, my fists clenched, nails digging in, waiting for the moment when the keel strikes its back. The tail, at my level beats the air in all directions and vanishes into the sea. A great jet of spray strikes me. A few seconds more. We haven't touched, we've got away with it.

Suddenly I drown in my own fear. Trembling, I collapse into the cockpit, my legs knocked from under me.

MICHEL MERMOD, *THE VOYAGE OF THE GENÈVE.*

22 JANUARY

ABOVE THE JAPANESE LINES, 1941

In 1941 the US journalist Martha Gellhorn (1908–98) visited Hong Kong to report on the Sino-Japanese War. In January she boarded a plane belonging to the China National Aviation Corporation (CNAC) and flitted unseen over the Japanese lines to the temporary Chinese capital of Chungking.

———•·•———

It was four-thirty in the morning and cold, and a heavy wind blew through the dark hangar and against the passengers as they crossed the Hong Kong airfield to the plane. Lights went on at the edge of the field, and we saw the Douglas DC-2, huge and silver-colored, with great black letters on the wings: CNAC in English letters on the right wing, CNAC in five-foot-high Chinese characters on the left wing. We could not see the humped green mountains that rise 3,000 feet to border the field. The eight passengers found seats in the unlighted cabin and fastened their safety belts. The weather report said the ceiling was 500 feet, visibility two miles, and storms ahead. It was perfect weather for the China National Aviation Corporation. No U.S. transport line would allow its planes to leave that mountain-girdled field in such weather. We took off, sliding and swaying into the wind. We were going to fly at night over the Japanese lines, and over sharp unbroken mountain ranges with peaks 9,200 feet high and no plateaus for forced landings. It was 770 miles to Chungking.

The plane circled up, higher and higher above the safe territory of Hong Kong. The hills around the harbor were beaded with light. There were brightly lighted ships, and floating points of light on the sampans. The city lights and the lights on the water jumped and slanted as the DC-2 climbed. Then the city was gone and white furry cloud wrapped the plane. The Chinese passengers pulled up their blankets and looked very small and quiet in their chairs, and slept. You could feel the forward pull of the plane, and you could feel the wind. We climbed to 13,000 feet above Hong Kong. The red and green wing lights went off.

Now at this great height and flying blind, we were ready to head north across the Japanese lines. The flash from the exhausts flickered against the propellers and over the wings and lighted up the drifting cloud. Then the shape of the cloud changed. It was no longer loose and soft; it had a texture like stone and it rose in a wall before the plane, and it was like flying against the side of a sandstone mountain. The wing letters blurred and finally we could see nothing. The plane moved, with sharp side drops and down plunges, in absolute darkness.

At five, we entered a storm. The Chinese passengers still slept. It was very cold. The American officer, who was making this trip for the first time too, looked at me and we both laughed because there was nothing else to do. We naturally did not believe anything could happen to this plane. Once you are in a plane you are part of it, and you give it confidence, feeling that the pilot and co-pilot and the radio operator and the passengers and the plane are all one thing: an indestructible whole. Accidents have happened, but you never think it will be now, not you, not to this plane, not to this solid unit of machine and men that is roaring through a hailstorm. So we fastened our safety belts again to keep from being battered against the seat in front or flung to the floor, and the DC-2 bucked in the wind.

MARTHA GELLHORN, *THE FACE OF WAR*.

23 JANUARY

ENNUI IN NEW ZEALAND, 1907

The writer Katherine Mansfield (1888–1923) spent almost four years studying in London before returning to her native New Zealand. Barely had she set foot on home territory than she vowed to leave it. 'London!' she exclaimed in her journal. 'To write the word makes me feel that I could burst into tears... *London* – it is life.' Amidst a rainy southern summer, she gave vent to her depression.

Oh, this monotonous, terrible rain. The dull, steady, hopeless sound of it. I have drawn the curtains across the windows to shut out the weeping face of the world – the trees swaying softly in their grief and dropping silver tears upon the brown earth – the narrow, sodden, mean, draggled wooden houses, colourless save for the dull coarse red of the roof – and the long line of grey hills, impassable, spectral-like...

Sometimes, through the measured sound of the rain comes the long, hopeless sound of a foghorn far out at sea. And then all life seems but a crying out drearily, and a groping to and fro in a foolish, aimless darkness. Sometimes – it seems like miles away – I hear the sound of a door opening and shutting.

And I listen and think and dream until my life seems not *one* life, but a thousand million lives, and my soul is weighed down with the burden of past existence, with the vague, uneasy consciousness of future strivings.

And the grey thoughts fall on my soul like the grey rain upon the world, but I cannot draw the curtain and shut them out.

KATHERINE MANSFIELD, *JOURNAL*.

24 JANUARY

THE POISONER OF MECCA, 1807

In January 1807 the Spanish adventurer Domingo Badia y Leblich (1766–1818) became the first European to see Mecca in more than a century. Although disguised impeccably as a Muslim pilgrim named Ali Bey, he still had to run the gauntlet of the keeper of the sacred well of Zemzem.

This wretch observes the same conduct to all the Pachas [Pashas] and important personages who come here. Upon the slightest suspicion, or the least caprice that may arise in the mind of the Scherif [Governor of Mecca], he orders, the others obey, and the unhappy stranger ceases to exist. As it is reckoned impious not to accept the sacred water presented by the chief of the well, this man is arbiter of the lives of every one, and has sacrificed many victims.

From time immemorial the Scherifs of Mecca have had a poisoner at their court; and it is remarkable that they do not try to conceal it, since it is well known, in Egypt and Constantinople, that the Divan [governing council] has several times sent to Mecca, Pachas, or other persons, to be sacrificed in this manner.

This was the reason why the Mogrebins or Arabs of the West, who are entirely devoted to me, hasted to warn me to be upon my guard upon my arrival in the city. My servants wished this traitor at the devil; but I myself treated him with the greatest marks of confidence. I accepted his water and his entertainments with an unalterable serenity and coolness. I took the precaution, however, to keep three doses of vitriolated zinc, a much more active emetic than tartar emetic, always in my pocket, to take the instant I should perceive the least indication of treason.

DOMINGO LEBLICH, *TRAVELS OF ALI BEY*, VOLUME II.

25 JANUARY

NUDITY ON THE NILE, 1616

The Italian traveller Pietro Della Valle (1586–1652) visited Cairo in 1616. He sent frequent despatches to a friend in Naples, one of which included this description of a journey up the Nile during which he was astonished by the locals' lack of decorum.

The agility of the peasants in swimming pleased me greatly, and when, as very often happens, they go across the river, either alone or with the animals they have with them, they straight away, whether males or females, take off their shirt which for the most part is all they wear, and made of blue cloth, broad, reaching down to the feet, sewn at the sides like dresses, with very wide sleeves. And if over the shirt they wear another long gown, usually the same shape, they take this off as well, and having tied their clothes together on their heads, they swim through the river merrily at marvellous speed, putting on their clothes again, though soaked, as soon as they have reached the other side. We saw nothing else on the river all day, and what seemed to me more strange, since it is contrary to the custom of the Turks who are of the same religion, was that I have never seen a country where, for just as many of the women as of the men, less concern is taken over showing one's private parts than here. They appear half-naked, or rather completely so: people pass by, and look, and they do not care at all.

PIETRO DELLA VALLE, *THE PILGRIM*.

26 JANUARY

LIBERIAN TIME, 1935

The English author Graham Greene (1904–91) entered Liberia in 1935 on a 350-mile journey through West Africa, accompanied by his cousin Barbara Greene. Neither of them had ever left Europe before, and they were unprepared for the tempo of African travel.

I was vexed by the delay at Kailahun [in Sierra Leone]. I had not yet got accustomed to the idea that time, as a measured and recorded period, had been left behind on the coast. In the interior there was no such thing as time; the best watches couldn't stand the climate. Sooner or later they stopped. My own watch and my cousin's were the first to go, and afterwards, one by one, I used up the six cheap watches I had brought with me for 'dashes' from Marks and Spencer's. Only one reached the coast and it had long since ceased to record the 'real' time; when it got dark I simply put the hands at six-thirty. If I wanted to get up earlier in the morning I put the hands on. Perhaps this was what [Henry Morton] Stanley had in mind when he heard Big Ben strike as he lay dying and exclaimed at the strangeness, 'So that is Time!'

But on the lorry from Kailahun I still believed that I could plan my journey by time-table. I thought that we were going to Monrovia, the [Liberian] capital, straight from Bolahun and that we would be there within a fortnight; I would not have admitted the possibility that in four weeks we should be in a place I had never heard of, in the middle of the Republic, watching an old skinny woman who had made lightning in her village carry water back on her head to her fellow-prisoners in the horrible little gaol at Tapee-Ta.

GRAHAM GREENE, *JOURNEY WITHOUT MAPS*.

27 JANUARY

THE SHOCK OF THE WEST, 1898

Sidney Whitman, a British correspondent for the *New York Herald*, had just returned from an assignment to Mesopotamia and was shocked by the spiritual meanness of London when contrasted with so-called primitive villages of the Middle East.

———•+•———

It was a strange, for the moment an almost unaccountable, sight to behold the crowds of people flocking into the City of a morning from the suburbs. This haste, this eagerness, as if their very life depended upon catching a train, constantly struck one as unnatural after living for weeks along the banks of the Tigris and the Euphrates, staying in villages in which conditions were so primitive – a contrast almost beyond comprehension. What could be the driving motive that impelled these people to this feverish activity, this restlessness? Why, hunger, to be sure, the grim necessities of the battle of life, a struggle to be continued without intermission from youth to the grave, and, when done, leaving little to take note of except, perhaps, that a mutton chop more or less would be called for at their particular luncheon haunt. And the background: Tooting Bec, Clapham, and Brixton in the South, Pentonville and Hackney in the North, and the East End with its miles of slums and its paupers; or to take those parts more familiar to middle-class life, Marylebone and Bloomsbury, with their interminable, dull, featureless roads and terraces, the rows of houses in their dread monotony, veritable soul-killing mausoleums of the living: what Ruskin termed 'streets in hell'... Surely life should have some wider and nobler scope, aim, and application than the mere gratification of the appetite to live.

SIDNEY WHITMAN, *TURKISH MEMORIES*.

28 JANUARY

NIGHTINGALE ON THE NILE, 1850

Florence Nightingale (1820–1910) had yet to win fame as a nurse in the Crimean War when she took a holiday in Egypt – an experience she described in letters home to her family. In one episode, having visited the southern stretches of the Nile, she shot the rapids on her way back to Cairo.

If going *up* the Cataracts was strange, it was nothing to coming *down*. We set off before sunrise, as it is necessary to have no breath of wind... Our boat is the largest that has ever been up the Cataracts, and we came down a passage which is very rarely used, as the tossing rapid would swamp a smaller boat. It was widened for Ibrahim Pacha's* steamer... Truly it was a sight worth seeing how she gradually accelerated her speed as she approached the rapid, which, foaming and tossing, with scarcely two feet on either side our oars, seemed as if no boat could live in it, then took the leap like a racehorse, so gallantly, and went riding down the torrent as if she enjoyed it. Three times her bows dived under water (I don't mean that the waves broke over the boat, – that they did all the time, and half filled her with water, and all our biscuit, too, which was of more consequence), but sometimes she dived under water up to the kitchen, and rose again; twice she struck, but gallantly triumphed over all her enemies, and long before I have written this one line we were at the bottom, and swung around at the end of the rapid – the first time this feat has been tried.

FLORENCE NIGHTINGALE, *LETTERS FROM EGYPT*.

* Ibrahim Pasha (1789–1848), Egyptian military leader and son of modern Egypt's foundational ruler Muhammad Ali.

29 JANUARY

DRUGSTORE DAYS IN AMERICA, 1947

French intellectual Simone de Beauvoir (1908–86) flew to the United States in 1947, equipped with a letter of introduction from her lover Jean-Paul Sartre. Hailed by New York columnists as the 'prettiest existentialist', she would soon establish herself as a feminist trailblazer. For the moment, though, she was largely happy just to record the wonder of America as it appeared to a war-worn European.

———•••———

Breakfast in the corner drugstore is a celebration. Orange juice, toast, *café au lait* – an unadulterated pleasure. Sitting on my revolving stool, I participate in a moment of American life. My solitude does not separate me from my neighbors, who are also eating alone. Rather, it's the pleasure I feel that isolates me from them. They are simply eating; they're not on vacation.

The truth is that it's all a holiday for me. The drugstores especially intrigue me. I stop at one on any pretext. To me, they are the essence of American exoticism. I was not really able to imagine them. I hesitated between the tedious vision of a pharmacy and – because of the word 'soda fountain' – the image of a magical fountain spewing out billows of pink and white ice cream. The fact is, drugstores are the descendants of the old general stores in colonial towns and the encampments of the Far West, where the pioneers of past centuries found cure-alls, ointments, tools – all the necessities of life. They are at once primitive and modern – that's what gives them this specific American poetry. All the objects seem related: the same great bargains, the same unpretentious cheerfulness. The glossy paperback books, the tubes of toothpaste, and the boxes of candies have the same colors: one has the vague impression that reading these books will leave a sweet taste in your mouth, and that the candy will have stories to tell. I buy soap, creams, and toothbrushes. Here the creams are creamy, the soaps are soapy: this honesty is a forgotten luxury. As soon as you stray from this norm, the quality of the products becomes more dubious. Certainly, the stores on Fifth Avenue will satisfy the most exacting tastes, but those furs, those suits of such international elegance are reserved for the international capitalist. As for the more popular shops, at first their abundance and sparkling variety are astonishing. But if the men's shirts are attractive, the ties are doubtful, the women's handbags and shoes are quite ugly, and in this profusion of dresses, blouses, skirts, and coats, a Frenchwoman would have trouble finding anything that didn't offend her taste. And then one soon perceives that beneath their multicolored paper wrappers, all the chocolates have the same peanut taste, and all the best-sellers tell the same story. So why choose one toothpaste over another? In this useless profusion, there's an aftertaste of deception. There are a thousand possibilities, but they're all the same. A thousand choices, but all equivalent. In this way, the American citizen can squander his obligatory domestic freedom without perceiving that this life itself is not free.

SIMONE DE BEAUVOIR, *AMERICA DAY BY DAY*.

30 JANUARY

A BAPTISM OF SOLITUDE IN THE SAHARA, 1953

In a 1953 magazine article the American author Paul Bowles (1910–99) explained the unique qualities that can imprint the Sahara on a person's soul.

Immediately when you arrive in the Sahara, for the first or the tenth time, you notice the stillness. An incredible, absolute silence prevails outside the towns; and within, even in busy places like the markets, there is a hushed quality in the air... Then there is the sky, compared to which all other skies seem faint-hearted efforts. Solid and luminous, it is always the focal point of the landscape. At sunset, the precise, curved shadow of the earth rises into it swiftly from the horizon, cutting it into light section and dark section. When all daylight is gone, and the space is thick with stars, it is still of an intense and burning blue, darkest directly overhead and paling towards the earth, so that the night never really grows dark.

You leave the gate of the fort or the town behind, pass the camels lying outside, go up into the dunes, or out onto the hard, stony plain and stand awhile, alone. Presently you either shiver and hurry back inside the walls, or you will go on standing there and let something very peculiar happen to you, something that everyone who lives there has undergone and which the French call *le baptême de la solitude*. It is a unique sensation, and it has nothing to do with loneliness, for loneliness presupposes memory. Here, in this wholly mineral landscape lighted by stars like flares, even memory disappears; nothing is left but your own breathing and the sound of your heart beating. A strange, and by no means pleasant, process of reintegration begins inside you, and you have the choice of fighting against it, and insisting on remaining the person you have always been, or letting it take its course. For no one who has stayed in the Sahara for a while is quite the same as when he came.

PAUL BOWLES, *TRAVELS*.

31 JANUARY

DEATH IN THE SKY, 1986

Space was, indeed, the final frontier for seven NASA astronauts who perished on 28 January when the Space Shuttle *Challenger* exploded shortly after lift-off. The dead included Christa McAuliffe, a schoolteacher, who had won a competition to go on what she described as the 'ultimate field trip'. The tragedy was recorded a few days later by Alistair Cooke, the veteran American-based newsman (1908–2004) whose weekly radio broadcasts, *Letter from America,* were an institution in his native Britain.

'Three engines running normally. Three good cells. Three good ABU's. Velocity 2,257 feet per second. Altitude 4.3 nautical miles... three engines now at 104 percent. *Challenger*, go with throttle up.' Commander Dick Scobee: 'Roger, go with throttle up.'

That was the last word from *Challenger*'s commander, and would be the last word from any of them. There came a moment that, to a normal ignoramus like me, was at the same time most beautiful and most baffling. A colossal, never-before-seen fireworks display. The puzzle was the tone of NASA's public relations officer, the man calling off the technical progress of the flight. He went on intoning in the same professional, emotionless way: 'One minute, fifteen seconds. Velocity 2,900 feet per second, altitude nine nautical miles, down-range distance seven nautical miles.' The longest pause. Was he not seeing what we saw? This huge spray of colour against the very blue sky? He was not. It was not his job to look at the monitor. He was watching a maze of ticking numbers, the lightning calculations done from the thousand sensors, as they're called, that the shuttle feeds into the telemetry. So, while the enormous horror of the fireball was sinking into our numbed minds, he was saying his last words: 'Obviously a major malfunction. We have no down link.' Surely the most leaden understatement of the year, for 'the shuttle has totally disintegrated in an instant, and we have no word from the crew.'

ALISTAIR COOKE, *REPORTING AMERICA.*

FEBRUARY

1 FEBRUARY

SINGING IN THE ARCTIC, 1822

In 1822, while searching for a North West Passage, Captain George Lyon (1795–1832) of HMS *Hecla* described his first encounter with the Eskimos – or Inuit – of Foxe Basin.

A distribution of ornaments being made to the ladies, we were soon established on a good footing, and visited each hut in its turn. Our astonishment was unbounded, when, after creeping through some long low passages of snow, to enter the different dwellings we found ourselves in a cluster of dome-shaped edifices, entirely constructed of snow, which, from their recent erection, had not been sullied by the smoke of the numerous lamps that were burning, but admitted the light in most delicate hues of verdigris green and blue, according to the thickness of the slab through which it passed. The natives were evidently in their best apparel, and made a very neat appearance; the darkness of their deer-skin dresses affording a strong contrast to the brilliancy of their habitations. To attempt giving a description of all we saw in one visit would be ridiculous; suffice it to say, we were very much pleased, and determined on spending the ensuing day with our new friends, of whom about fifty persons of both sexes accompanied us on board, and we were now as familiar as old acquaintances. As we walked I assisted in singing to them some songs and choruses, and met with unbounded applause, in such ditties especially as terminated in 'Tol de riddle loll', which never failed to excite loud screams of admiration, and a vast deal of jumping.

GEORGE LYON, *PRIVATE JOURNAL*.

2 FEBRUARY

A HELL-SHIP BENEATH THE SOUTHERN CROSS, 1949

En route from the United States to Hong Kong aboard the SS *President Cleveland*, the American satirist S.J. Perelman (1904–79) waxed vitriolic on the horrors of cruise-ship travel. In a letter to his mistress, Leila Hadley, he explained just how awful life could get.

Now is the horrid hour when the grave yawns and the grisly gaiety of organized fun aboardship takes over. As I sit down to write this, every man jack of the passengers is plummeting around the corridors on a scavenger hunt – which, as a former organizer of parties, will probably curl up your toes with loathing. Retired bank presidents, their jowls flushed with hypertension, sprint by my door searching for unbearably quaint items like a lady's garter on toast, corseted dowagers invade the junior pursers' cabins on the pretext of promoting an Upmann cigar wrapper – jeez, it's a veritable Sodom and Gomorrah, a hell-ship beneath the unwinking Southern Cross...

This ship is really pretty droll – a luxury liner (in reality an attack transport capable of being converted within a week into its original purposeful self) which cost $23,000,000 and is now toting 340 first class and 270 Orientals across the drink. Everything is being done (at least in first class) to assure the customer that this is his home away from home. The food is very good, the service obsequious – possibly not as much so as on European vessels, a source of aggravation to some of the plutocrats here – and on the whole all efforts are bent to deceive the wayfarer into forgetting all that nasty old water outside the hull. Personally I prefer the previous way I girdled this ocean, viz., a cargo ship which gave you some sense of accomplishment, and a mite fewer of those elderly ladies with the cast-iron permanents from Shaker Heights [in Ohio] and Paoli [in Pennsylvania].

S.J. Perelman, *Don't Tread on Me.*

3 FEBRUARY

DRUMMING ON THE BANKS OF THE LUALABA, 1877

Between 1874 and 1877 the journalist and explorer Henry Morton Stanley (1841–1904) crossed Africa east to west, from Zanzibar to the Congo coast, and in doing so became the first European to traverse the continent. It was a feat achieved in the face of countless obstacles, both human – as here on the Lualaba, one of the Congo's headstreams – and topographical. By the time he reached the mouth of the Congo River he had lost 242 of the 356 men with whom he had set out.

It seems that we edged a little too much to the left bank in our eagerness to avoid all channels that might take us to the right. The Barundu, of whom we heard yesterday, sighted us, as we passed a gap between the islands, and instantly manned eighteen large war-canoes. But as we had obtained a start of them we pulled desperately down river among the islands, leading them a chase of eight miles or so, when they returned.

Livingstone called floating down the Lualaba a fool-hardy feat. So it has proved, indeed, and I pen these lines with half a feeling that they will never be read by any man; still, as we persist in floating down according to our destiny, I persist in writing, leaving events to an all-gracious Providence. Day and night we are stunned with the dreadful drumming which announces our arrival and presence on their waters. Either bank is equally powerful. To go from the right bank to the left bank is like jumping from the frying-pan into the fire. As we row down amongst these islands, between the savage countries on either side of us, it may well be said that we are 'running the gauntlet.'

H.M. STANLEY, *THROUGH THE DARK CONTINENT*, VOLUME II.

4 FEBRUARY

BOMBING FISH IN HAITI, 1927

Aeronaut and deep-sea diver William Beebe (1877–1962) spent five months in 1927 studying the marine life of Haiti on behalf of the New York Zoological Society. In the second month of his visit he took advantage of the US Air Force's annual bombing practice to collect a few specimens.

When the last plane had dropped its load, it grape-vined downwards in steep side banks, waved 'all clear' to us, and rushed across the bay. We started our engines full speed and soon caught sight o' the white bellies of floating fish. Some were dead, many were only stunned and we reaped a harvest. Almost all were large and of widely differing species; great rosy red snappers – the best of pan-fish, many-colored anglefish, groupers, trigger-fish with their poisonous triggers set at full cock as futile protection against this unthinkable danger, trunkfish whose shelter within their armored box was of no avail.

There were porcupine fish who at the shock had valiantly inflated themselves behind their *chevaux-de-frise* of spines and so died, and there were mackerel – masters of the bay – whose sharp teeth and wonderful speed aided them not at all against this holocaust of vibration. And finally, here and there, like variegated water-lilies, floated butterfly-fish in gay pigments and patterns, with the colored eye-spots at the far end of their bodies appearing more alert and perceptive than their real vacant orbs. I thought of the hundreds of fish which must have sunk to the bottom, and the unending lines of influence which spread and spread – the news somehow going abroad of the wonderful manna at hand. For days and weeks to come, strange, beautiful, ugly and weird beings would continue to swim or crawl or creep toward the dead things which had given up their lives to make a bombman's holiday.

WILLIAM BEEBE, *BENEATH TROPIC SEAS*.

5 FEBRUARY

AT THE THRESHOLD OF WILD TRAVEL, 1905

In 1905 Gertrude Bell (1868–1926) left her native Scotland for a journey through the Ottoman provinces of Lebanon, Syria and Palestine. Fluent in Arabic, Farsi and Turkish, she would later travel further into Arabia than any other European woman before her. She recorded her anticipation in Jerusalem, at the start of her trip.

To those bred under an elaborate social order few such moments of exhilaration can come as that which stands at the threshold of wild travel. The gates of the enclosed garden are thrown open, the chain at the entrance of the sanctuary is lowered, with a wary glance to right and left you step forth, and, behold! the immeasurable world. The world of adventure and of enterprise, dark with hurrying storms, glittering in raw sunlight, an unanswered question and an unanswerable doubt hidden in the fold of every hill. Into it you must go alone, separated from the troops of friends that walk the rose alleys, stripped of the purple and fine linen that impede the fighting arm, roofless, defenceless, without possessions. The voice of the wind shall be heard instead of the persuasive voices of counsellors, the touch of the rain and the prick of the frost shall be spurs sharper than praise or blame, and necessity shall speak with an authority unknown to that borrowed wisdom which men obey or discard at will. So you leave the sheltered close, and, like the man in the fairy story, you feel the bands break that were riveted about your heart as you enter the path that stretches across the rounded shoulder of the earth.

GERTRUDE BELL, *THE DESERT AND THE SOWN*.

6 FEBRUARY

THE COMFORT OF A GULL, 1962

After three months on the Pacific (*see* 21 January), solo navigator Michel Mermod became mesmerized by the shapelessness of the ocean. A seabird kept him company for a while, sheering off before he landed at the Marquesas Islands, in French Polynesia, on 11 February.

This is another world. No right-angles, no verticals, no horizontals. Everything is continuous movement, sea, sky, clouds. Nothing begins or ends anywhere, everything is infinite. Was yesterday not today, and will not tomorrow be just the same?

Our mother, the night, covers us with her cloak and points the way for this sailing boat which, alone in the dark, leaves a luminous green wake astern...

The bird is still there, faithful after many miles... Its cry, at the same time both sharp and harsh, often shatters the silence. It hardly moves its wings in flight, but glides quickly between the waves, slipping from one trough to the next, skimming the broken water on the crests. Sometimes it pulls out a fish with its beak or its feet, and now and again it settles on the surface for a few seconds, having carefully sought out a piece of smooth, unruffled water. These must be its only moments of rest. Once or twice at night I have got up surreptitiously to look on the deck, but the bird has not been there. Its constant company warms my loneliness a little and, lost as I am in the middle of this immensity, although I feel just as small, I no longer feel as if I were a solitary creature swallowed up in nothingness.

MICHEL MERMOD, *THE VOYAGE OF THE GENÈVE*.

7 FEBRUARY

COBBLERS AND CICADAS IN RIO, 1847

Thomas Henry Huxley (1825–95), like his countryman and fellow scientist Charles Darwin, began his career with a voyage of exploration. Between 1846 and 1850 he circumnavigated the globe aboard the converted survey ship HMS *Rattlesnake,* where for the first part of the voyage he was overseen by the ship's naturalist, John MacGillivray. The two men found they shared an interest not only in collecting specimens but also in drinking vast quantities of alcohol, the Sherry Cobbler (a tropical cocktail) being their favourite tipple.

All my rambles at Rio were in the company of the Naturalist and therefore had or pretended to have a more or less naturalistic tendency. However, singular to relate, our investigations always took in the end a chemical turn, to wit, the examination of the nature and properties of a complex liquid called Sherry Cobbler. Oh Rio, thou Sodom-and-Gomorrah in one, town of stinks and beastliness, thou shalt be saved not because of one man, but because of the excellence of the iced drink of the man. We have a tradition, McG. and I, that one evening we consumed nine pigeons and eighteen Sherry Cobblers! Can these things be?

Cobblers or no cobblers, however, our liege lady Nature was not neglected... There are two things that forcibly strike anyone going into the country here. 1st the enormous number, variety and beauty of the butterflies, 2nd the noise of the cicadas. These fellows are as big as a man's thumb and fly about the trees like locusts. They emit a very acute loud continuous note, and when numbers of them are together it is really deafening. Singularly enough they seem to agree to short intervals of silence, then the note begins, at first weakly, then swelling into a grand chorus and gradually dying away again.

Thomas Henry Huxley, *Diary of the Voyage of H.M.S. Rattlesnake.*

8 FEBRUARY

'VISIT ITALY', 1944

In the penultimate year of the Second World War US journalist Martha Gellhorn (*see* 22 January) followed the Allied forces as they ground their way north through Italy. In February she recorded a sardonic and rueful encounter with a French driver.

———•+•———

The French soldier driving the jeep had large dark sad eyes. He was small, thin and dirty and he looked ill. The windshield and the top of the jeep were down and the snow had changed to hail. The road circling up the mountains was narrow and slippery. Wind blew across the gray stone sides of the mountains and over the snow peaks and drove the hail into our faces.

The little jeep driver was having a bad time, as was everyone else on the road. From time to time we would pass a completely unnecessary sign; a skull-and-bones painted on a board with underneath the phrase in French, 'The enemy sees you.' No one needed to be warned. There you were, on a roller-coaster road freezing to death, and if the enemy couldn't see you, he was blind; he was sitting right across there, on that other snow mountain.

The jeep driver spoke with sudden bitter mockery. '*Visitez l'Italie!*' he said.

There used to be tourist posters in France, in all the railroad stations, showing a sunstruck and enchanting glimpse of country with a dark-haired girl eating grapes or maybe just laughing, and the posters urged 'Visit Italy.'

Now we were visiting Italy. It was a small, peculiar and unhealthy piece of Italy – the French front. It was a bulge of mountains; the French held these mountains, and opposite them on higher mountains, were the Germans. The mountains to the right were occupied by the Poles, and to the left, around Cassino, were the Americans. The Italian front is very curious anyhow. One day we figured there were twenty races and nationalities stretched across Italy from the Mediterranean to the Adriatic, all fighting the Germans. The French held the highest mountains of all: this front. It was colder here than anywhere else – though it was cold enough everywhere – and no one believed this wind would ever blow at less than gale force, and just when you began to hope that spring might come it would snow again.

Before he came to this naked road, the jeep driver had been a barman in Casablanca. Now he said, through stiff, cold lips: 'Have you ever had an Alexander cocktail, mademoiselle?'

We passed a burned American tank, rounded a curve and saw two trucks which had plunged down a ravine and were hanging almost perpendicularly against the side of the mountain. An Alexander is a horrible, sweet drink made with crème de cacao.

'Yes, indeed,' I said, holding a tin hat in front of my face as a shield against the hail.

'I do not mean to brag,' the Frenchman said, 'but I made the best Alexanders in Casablanca.'

Then we were silent because it was too hard to talk. Perhaps he was thinking of his bar, or the small café he hoped to have in France after the war. I was thinking about that wonderful phrase, 'Visit Italy.'

MARTHA GELLHORN, *THE FACE OF WAR.*

9 FEBRUARY

A HENNA TATTOO IN ADEN, 1938

Freya Stark (*see* 14 January) was travelling through Arabia when she halted at a remote town in what was then the British Colony of Aden. Unable to resist the locals' blandishments, she succumbed to the soothing balm of a henna tattoo.

Being settled with cushions as supports all round me, I handed my hands over beginning with the right one 'for blessing'. The specialist dips her forefinger in the paste which hangs down in a thin drip with which she traces out rings and stars and trees and anything she fancies on your hand. It is no joke. I went at 1 p.m. And came out at five. Meanwhile the ladies came round, pressed glasses of tea in my free hand, looked at the process, and told the gossip. A feeling of leisure hung over the harem: one could not imagine anyone being in a hurry ever. When all was done, I was arranged on cushions full length and told I could sleep while one of the ladies did my feet and the rest had coffee in one corner. I lay with closed eyes, just feeling the little cold drops on my foot: henna is supposed to be very cooling, and they asked if I felt chilled by it. I dozed, and woke to find the work finished, a lovely sun with rays shining on each instep – 'taken', the lady said, 'from a printed book'. My hands had three little branches, and one up the middle finger, besides other small patterns and circles, and the first joint of the palm a solid block of henna: this elaborate affair is for women who 'have a man', the others can have a simple band or so; but though I pleaded age and spinsterhood I was not to be let so lightly off.

FREYA STARK, *OVER THE RIM OF THE WORLD*.

10 FEBRUARY

THE COMFORTS OF CIVILIZATION, 1931

In October 1930 Evelyn Waugh (*see* 5 January) arrived in Ethiopia for the coronation of Emperor Haile Selassie. He subsequently zig-zagged down the length of Africa, eventually catching a steamer home to England from Cape Town in March 1931. After a difficult passage through the Belgian Congo he paused at the southern town of Elizabethville – modern Lubumbashi – to review his sense of affront.

I had some difficulty explaining, to the satisfaction of the immigration officer whose permission was necessary before I could leave the Congo, why I diverged so much from the itinerary outlined in my certificate of entry. In the end, however, he understood my difficulties and gave me leave to depart. In the meantime, I worked, rested, and enjoyed the comfort and tranquillity of Elizabethville. How reassuring are these occasional reconciliations with luxury. How often in Europe, after too much good living, I have begun to doubt whether the whole business of civilized taste is not a fraud put upon us by shops and restaurants. Then, after a few weeks of gross, colonial wines, hard beds, gritty bath-water, awkward and surly subordinates, cigars from savage Borneo or the pious Philippines, cramped and unclean quarters, and tinned foodstuffs, one realizes that the soft things of Europe are not merely rarities which one has been taught to prefer because they are expensive, but thoroughly satisfactory compensations for the rough and tumble of earning one's living – and a far from negligible consolation for some of the assaults and deceptions by which civilization seeks to rectify the balance of good fortune.

Evelyn Waugh, Remote People.

11 FEBRUARY

UNDERNEATH THE SPREADING ZAMANG TREE, 1802

Alexander von Humboldt (1769–1859) was a German naturalist, whose travels through South America produced the most comprehensive study of flora and fauna the world had yet seen. In Venezuela he encountered a vast and magical tree.

Beyond the village of Turmero, towards Maracay, you can observe on the distant horizon something that seems to be a tumulus covered in vegetation. But it is not a hill, nor a group of trees growing close together, but one single tree, the famous *zamang de Guayre*, known through the country for the enormous extent of its branches, which form a semi-spherical head some 576 feet in circumference. The zamang is a fine species of the mimosa family whose twisted branches are forked. We rested a long time under this vegetable roof. The branches extend like an enormous umbrella and bend towards the ground. Parasitical plants grow on the branches and in the dried bark. The inhabitants, especially the Indians, venerate this tree, which the first conquerors found in more or less the same state as it is today. We heard with satisfaction that the present owner of the zamang had brought a lawsuit against a cultivator accused of cutting off a branch. The case was tried and the man found guilty.

ALEXANDER VON HUMBOLDT, *JAGUARS AND ELECTRIC EELS*.

12 FEBRUARY

COWARD'S ORIENTAL CRUISE, 1930

While visiting the Far East in 1930, the actor-playwright Noël Coward (1899–1973) cadged a lift on a Royal Navy cruiser from Shanghai to Hong Kong. Perhaps fittingly, it was between these two outposts of empire that he wrote the song 'Mad Dogs and Englishmen'.

I've never in my life enjoyed anything so much. We took four days and did gunnery practice, and kept watch on the bridge all night, drinking lovely ship's cocoa and made ourselves very popular. We were shown over the ship from stem to stern as you might say, and Oh God, a really up to date warship in motion is beyond words exciting. Sitting in a gun turret alone is enough to wreck you! Talk about the poetry of Higher Mathematics, one small lever is touched and enormous guns come rushing up at you out of a pit, load themselves and fire themselves and retire down to their hole again as quick as buggery! It really was splitarsingly loverly. And all the ritual of saluting the sun, and playing 'Last Post' and sailors having special roaring tunes played by the ship's band for every job they do!...

HK is I think the most beautiful place I've ever seen, specially at night with an enormous black mountain rearing itself out of the sea, covered with lights. And the most lovely harbour with thousands of ships of all sizes and sampans and junks farting 'ither and thither for all the world like tainy [sic] insects...

NoËL COWARD, *LETTERS*.

13 FEBRUARY

WHITE FLOWERS IN TAHITI, 1914

The Engish poet Rupert Brooke (1887–1915) had been touring America and the South Seas for almost a year when he landed on Tahiti. After several weeks he was so enchanted by island life that he decided to stay a while longer. In a letter to his friend (and later fiancée) Cathleen Nesbitt he described the moment when, six days previously, he bade farewell to the monthly ship.

Europe slides from me, terrifyingly. There are but one or two things that prevent me letting time flow over me here till I turn to white sand and scented dust and little bright fish: a friend or two, a certain worthless Irish lady [Nesbitt], the thought of some enemies I want to smash, the ever-rare memory of primroses and English hedges, a thought of running a theatre...

Will it come to you having to come and fetch me?

The boat's ready to start. The brown lovely people in their bright clothes are gathered on the old wharf to wave her away. Everyone has a white flower behind their ear... Do you know the significance of a white flower worn over the ear?

A white flower over the *right* ear means

I am looking for a sweetheart

A white flower over the *left* ear means

I have found a sweetheart

And a white flower over each ear means

I have one sweetheart and am looking for another.

A white flower over each ear, my dear, is dreadfully the most fashionable way of adorning yourself in Tahiti.

Bon voyage, to the travellers! Good luck to everybody else! Tonight we will put scarlet flowers in our hair and sing strange slumberous South Sea songs to the concertina and drink red French wine and dance obscure native dances and bathe in a soft lagoon by moonlight...

RUPERT BROOKE, *THE LETTERS OF RUPERT BROOKE.*

14 FEBRUARY

THE DUST OF CAWNPORE, 1858

In 1858 the Irish journalist W.H. Russell (1820–1907) arrived at Cawnpore (Kanpur), a military outpost that had seen appalling bloodshed the previous year during the Indian 'Mutiny'. Incensed not only by the massacre of the surrendering garrison but also by the dismemberment of their wives and children, the British had exacted stern retribution. As labourers toiled to reconstruct roads and bridges, it appeared to Russell as if the whole town had been turned to dust – and the old way of empire with it.

The dust of the whole neighbourhood for miles around, as these people go to and return from their labour, is distressing. All the country about Cawnpore is covered with the finest powdered dust, two or three inches deep, which rises into the air on the smallest provocation. It is composed of sand, pulverised earth, and the brick powder and mortar of the dilapidated houses; whatever, in fact, can turn to dust. As the natives shuffle along, their pointed slippers fling up suffocating clouds of this unpleasant compound, and when these slippers are multiplied by thousands, the air is filled with a floating stratum of it, fifteen or eighteen feet high, and extending over the whole of the station. Even in the old days, when the roads were watered, Cawnpore had a bad notoriety for dust. What an earthquake to shake to pieces, what a volcano to smother with lava and ashes, has this mutiny been! Not only cities, but confidence and trust have gone, never to be restored!

WILLIAM HOWARD RUSSELL, *MY INDIAN MUTINY DIARY.*

15 FEBRUARY

GREASE AND DIRT IN THE ARCTIC, 1896

Following their extraordinary attempt to ski to the North Pole (*see* 2 January), Fridtjof Nansen and his companion Hjalmar Johanssen retreated over the floes to the remote archipelago of Franz-Josef Land, where they spent the winter in a rough shelter built of stone, earth and ice that they called 'The Hole'. They lived almost exclusively off raw meat and blubber – a diet that kept scurvy at bay but encased them in grease and gave them constipation and piles – until they were rescued by a British expedition in June, completely by chance.

Our legs suffered most; for there our trousers stuck fast to our knees, so that when we moved they abraded and tore the skin inside our thighs till it was all raw and bleeding. I had the greatest difficulty in keeping these sores from becoming altogether too ingrained with fat and dirt, and had to be perpetually washing them with moss, or a rag from one of the bandages in our medicine-bag, and a little water, which I warmed in a cup over a lamp. I have never before understood what a magnificent invention soap really is. We made all sorts of attempts to wash the worst of the dirt away; but they were all equally unsuccessful. Water had no effect upon all this grease; it was better to scour oneself with moss and sand. We could find plenty of sand in the walls of the hut, when we hacked the ice off them. The best method, however, was to get our hands thoroughly lubricated with warm bears' blood and train-oil, and then scrub it off again with moss. They thus became as white and soft as the hands of the most delicate lady, and we could scarcely believe that they belonged to our own bodies. When there was none of this toilet preparation to be had, we found the next best plan was to scrape our skin with a knife.

If it was difficult to get our own bodies clean, it was a sheer impossibility as regards our clothes. We tried all possible ways; we washed them both in Eskimo fashion and in our own; but neither was of much avail. We boiled our shirts in the pot hour after hour, but took them out only to find them just as full of grease as when we put them in. Then we took to wringing the train-oil out of them. This was a little better; but the only thing that produced any real effect was to boil them, and then scrape them with a knife while they were still warm. By holding them in our teeth and our left hand and stretching them out, while we scraped them all over with the right hand, we managed to get amazing quantities of fat out of them; and we could almost have believed that they were quite clean when we put them on again after they were dry. The fat which we scraped off was, of course, a welcome addition to our fuel.

In the meantime our hair and beard grew entirely wild. It is true we had scissors and could have cut them; but as our supply of clothes was by no means too lavish, we thought it kept us a little warmer to have all this hair, which began to flow down over our shoulders. But it was coal-black like our faces, and we thought our teeth and the whites of our eyes shone with an uncanny whiteness now that we could see each other again in the daylight of the spring. On the whole, however, we were so accustomed to each other's appearance that we really found nothing remarkable about it, and not until we fell in with other people and found that they were not precisely of that opinion, did we begin to recognise that our outer man was, perhaps, open to criticism.

Fridtjof Nansen, Farthest North, Volume II.

16 FEBRUARY

STARTING FOR TARTARY, 1935

In 1935 the British explorer Peter Fleming (1907–71) undertook a 3,500-mile trek from China to India accompanied by the Swiss traveller Ella Maillart. His journey began here.

———•••———

I was sitting by myself in a dining-car on the Peking–Hankow Railway in the late afternoon of February 16th, 1935. We were running south through Hopei, not very fast. Outside, in the clear, mild sunlight, a brown plain, chequered into little fields, stretched far away to a jagged rim of hills. Although the fields were naked and the rare trees bare, a faint green patina of spring lay along the ground; there was no ice anywhere. High up in the blue sky skeins of geese were flying east. Here and there a peasant, wadded and bulbous in his winter clothes, was breaking the ground behind a team of ponies woolly and blunt-headed like puppies. Carts on huge solid wheels lurched along rut-scarred roads. From behind the mud walls of a farm unseen winnowers threw up a lovely rhythmic series of golden jets which spread into fine golden clouds, then settled slowly. A cluster of dark trees on a mound embossed with graves sheltered the tired dust of generations. Ancient and symmetrical walls enclosed a little city. 'Sifflez!' said a notice-board (unavailingly) as we approached a bend; the Peking–Hankow Railway was built by French engineers. The sun, stooping towards the horizon, began to set in a diffuse yellow haze.

In this moment, which I remember very clearly, I as it were woke up. The eleventh hour preparations which had for long absorbed not only my energies but my imagination were either finished or for ever shelved. The eleventh hour was over. We were off.

Peter Fleming, *News from Tartary*.

17 FEBRUARY

THE GREAT NOISE OF LONDON, 1810

Louis Simond (1767–1831) landed in Falmouth, Cornwall, on Christmas Eve 1809 for an extended tour of Britain. Before emigrating to the United States during the eighteenth century, Simond had been a French subject, and he was keen to see how Britain compared to both his native and adopted lands. The evening din made by London society was one of the many spheres in which he considered Britain to be the winner.

————•+•————

From six to eight the *noise* of wheels increases; it is the dinner hour. A multitude of carriages, with two eyes of flame staring in the dark before each of them, shake the pavement and the very houses, following and crossing each other at full speed. Stopping suddenly, a footman jumps down, runs to the door, and lifts the heavy knocker – gives a great knock – then several smaller ones in quick succession – then with all his might – flourishing as on a drum, with an art, and an air, and a delicacy of touch, which denote the quality, the rank, and the fortune of his master.

For two hours, or nearly, there is a pause; at ten a *redoublement* comes on. This is the great crisis of dress, of noise, and of rapidity – a universal hubbub; a sort of uniform grinding and shaking, like that experienced in a great mill with fifty pair of stones; and, if I was not afraid of appearing to exaggerate, I should say that it came upon the ear like the fall of Niagara, heard at two miles distance! This crisis continues undiminished till twelve or one o'clock; then less and less during the rest of the night – till, at the approach of day, a single carriage is heard now and then at a great distance.

Louis Simond, *An American in Regency England*.

18 FEBRUARY

ST CATHERINE'S MONASTERY, 1971

In 1971 the English writer Eric Newby (1919–2006) was travelling through the Sinai Peninsula when he visited the desert monastery of St Catherine, an institution of such ancient piety that it had been granted the written protection of the Prophet Mohammed.

Extraordinary, too, were the congeries of buildings linked by a labyrinth of passages. Exploring them was like a dream in which one floated through narrow tunnels in the immensely thick walls (the lower courses made up of enormous blocks of granite), constructed by Justinian's men and repaired by those of General Kléber, sent there for this purpose at the time of Napoleon's expedition to Egypt, with on either side the workshops of the Jebelliyeh craftsmen dead and gone, who also worked on the fabric; past chapels closed because there was no one to serve them any more; up winding staircases; along balconies supported by flimsy bamboo laths and crumbling plaster; into vaults and windowless courtyards, in which the apparatus for distilling raki from dates lay long abandoned. (Apparently the principal reason for this distillation was to gain income by selling it to pilgrims. Records of monkish drunkenness are rather rare.)

On under trellises of vines, into bakeries furnished with wooden moulds to embellish the bread with the outline of St Katherine and huge wooden troughs excavated from trunks of trees (How did they come here, and where did they come from? Were they dragged overland from Lebanon?); into a disused refectory with a vaulted roof and embrasures cut through it to let in light, its walls covered with graffiti done when this was, temporarily, a Crusader officers' mess. Outside, growing against one of the curtain walls in a little enclosure, was a plant that resembled a raspberry. A notice, gratifyingly in English, stated that it was the Burning Bush. It seemed impossible that all this could exist within a space of 280 by 250 feet.

ERIC NEWBY, *A TRAVELLER'S LIFE*.

19 FEBRUARY

A NORWEGIAN IN NEW YORK, 1882

When 'America Fever' swept Norway in the early 1880s, the young novelist Knut Hamsun (1859–1952) was one of the many infected. Writing in 1882 to his friend Torger Kyseth, he described his first impressions of the New World.

Torger, you should have been with me in New York and seen all the splendour there. The railway goes up in the air over the people's roofs, and there are thousands of telegraph and telephone wires stretching between the buildings; the bridge from New York to Brooklyn is about ¾ of a Norwegian mile long; there the railway is to go; but above that fine steel wires are formed into a net, and that is where the pedestrians are to go. That bridge is the world's biggest engineering undertaking, and it is so high that when you walk across you come up into a different layer of air, and there is a terrible wind blowing. And you should have been there to have seen the buildings. I saw buildings in New York that were 13 storeys, two of which were underground. One day I went to the 'New York Post Office' with a letter to Frosland. When I got there I was hoisted up to the 4th storey by a kind of seesaw device. I wanted to walk down, but it seemed unending. The Post Office is also a pretty impressive building; it occupies a whole block of the city and is absolutely square. The new town hall in Chicago is similarly and takes up practically the whole block in New Street; it is the most *beautiful* building I have seen. The granite blocks are so highly polished that we went and looked at our reflections in them.

KNUT HAMSUN, *SELECTED LETTERS*, VOLUME I.

20 FEBRUARY

THE FAMISHED ROAR OF AUTOMOBILES, 1909

The artist-provocateur Filippo Tommaso Marinetti (1876–1944) diced with death on a drunken car journey with friends, an experience he found so profound that he incorporated it into his 'Manifesto of Futurism', which appeared in 20 February 1909's edition of *Le Figaro*.

As we listened to the old canal muttering its feeble prayers and the creaking bones of sickly palaces under their damp green beards, under the windows we suddenly heard the famished roar of automobiles.

'Let's go!' I said. 'Friends, away! Let's go! Mythology and the Mystic Ideal are defeated at last. We're about to see the Centaur's birth and, soon after, the first flight of Angels... We must shake the gates of life, test the bolts and hinges. Let's go! Look, there on the earth, the very first dawn! There's nothing to match the splendour of the sun's red sword, slashing for the first time through our millennial gloom!'

We went up to the three snorting beasts, to lay amorous hands on their torrid breasts. I stretched out on my car like a corpse on its bier, but revived at once under the steering wheel, a guillotine blade that threatened my stomach.

The raging broom of madness swept us out of ourselves and drove us through streets as rough and deep as the beds of torrents. Here and there, sick lamplight through window glass taught us to distrust the deceitful mathematics of our perishing eyes.

I cried, 'The scent, the scent alone is enough for our beasts.'

And like young lions we ran after Death, its dark pelt blotched with pale crosses as it escaped down the vast violet living and throbbing sky...

And on we raced, hurling watchdogs against doorsteps, curling them under our burning tyres like collars under a flatiron. Death, domesticated, met me at every turn...

FILIPPO MARINETTI, *MANIFESTO OF FUTURISM*.

21 FEBRUARY

SECRET ORCHARDS ON THE CÔTE D'AZUR, 1934

Rudyard Kipling (*see* 6 January) was, in 1934, staying in the south of France when he wrote this letter to his architect friend Herbert Baker.

———•·•———

The almonds almost crazy with bloom, and the bees, who have come in to plunder, quite so. They are banded, rather savage, ladies who have been losing their tempers over the ragged and frost-bitten rosemary outside our windows. But, if you get over the side of the hill where it drops steeply to the Cannes road you come into a sheltered world and higher temperatures. We strayed into one of these *enclaves* the other day by means of walking along an aqueduct which went everywhere, openly or underground. At last we found ourselves amongst timeless terrace-works of old orange trees, heavy with fruit, and not a breath to trouble them. We had to climb a series of these tiers, each about six feet high and each stiller and older than the last. Then – without explanation – we found ourselves on a terrace of three sides, set with some orange trees; a loquat; and a peach in fullest bloom. That was all right, but underneath this display were some brilliantly-hued cocks and hens and a Nun pigeon on most vivid grass, adorned with low wild irises in flower. It sounds mad, but under the daylight and the slashing shadows of the loquat-trees, it all composed like a most marvellous piece of *cloisonnée* lacquer-work. And we praised Allah and climbed up and out, into a raw wind and an ash-coloured landscape on the naked side of the hill. It was like coming out of the Garden of Armida to the landscape round the Dark Tower.

RUDYARD KIPLING, UNPUBLISHED LETTER, RIBA ARCHIVE (LONDON).

22 FEBRUARY

LAST WORDS FROM PETROPOLIS, 1942

Austrian playwright Stefan Zweig (1881–1942) had been on the move almost continually since the First World War. Driven from Europe by the Nazis, he ended up in Brazil, where he and his wife Elizabeth committed suicide on 23 February 1942 in the town of Petropolis. Zweig's valedictory note, written the evening before, signalled both an end to his wanderings and the start of a new journey.

Before parting from life of my own free will and in my right mind I am impelled to fulfil a last obligation: to give heartfelt thanks to this wonderful land of Brazil which afforded me and my work such kind and hospitable repose. My love for the country increased from day to day, and nowhere else would I have preferred to build up a new existence, the world of my own language having disappeared for me and my spiritual home, Europe, having destroyed itself.

But after one's sixtieth year unusual powers are needed in order to make another wholly new beginning. Those that I possess have been exhausted by long years of homeless wandering. So I think it better to conclude in good time and in erect bearing a life in which intellectual labour meant the purest joy and personal freedom the highest good on earth.

I salute all my friends! May it be granted them to see the dawn after the long night! I, all too impatient, go on before.

STEFAN ZWEIG, *THE WORLD OF YESTERDAY*.

23 FEBRUARY

A NOVICE IN THE COLD, 1851

From 1850 to 1851 Dr Elisha Kent Kane (1820–1857) served aboard the *Advance*, a ship sponsored by US philanthropist Henry Grinnell to join the search for the English explorer Sir John Franklin, who had disappeared five years earlier in the North West Passage. During the long Arctic nights they filled the time with amateur dramatics. Unlike the British, who had decades of Arctic experience, the Americans were relative greenhorns in the cold.

Caught a cold last night in attending the theatre. A cold here means a sudden *malaise* with insufferable aches in back and joints, hot eyes, and fevered skin. We all have them, coming and going, short-lived and long-lived: they leave their mark too. This Arctic work brings extra years upon a man. A fresh wind makes the cold very unbearable. In walking to-day my beard and mustache became one solid mass of ice. I inadvertently put out my tongue, and it instantly froze fast to my lip. This being nothing new, costing only a smart pull and a bleeding abrasion afterward, I put up my mittened hands to 'blow hot' and thaw the unruly member from its imprisonment. Instead of succeeding, my mitten was itself a mass of ice in a moment: it fastened on the upper side of my tongue and flattened it out like a batter-cake between the two disks of a hot griddle. It required all my care, with the bare hands, to release it, and that not without laceration.

ELISHA KENT KANE, *THE U.S. GRINNELL EXPEDITION.*

24 FEBRUARY

THREE RUSSIANS IN NAPLES, 1915

On this date, or thereabouts, the Russian composer and pianist Sergei Prokofiev (1891–1953) took a tour of Naples and its environs accompanied by two of his countrymen: the Ballets Russes impresario Sergei Diaghilev and his companion, the composer Léonide Massine. Prokofiev had been lured from St Petersburg by Diaghilev's insistence that he stage his latest ballet in Rome, an invitation he had accepted despite the fact that Europe was at war. It was an arduous business: the eighteen-day journey from Russia to Italy had entailed detours through Romania, Bulgaria and Greece; and when he got there Diaghilev ordered him to scrap half the music and change the story completely. By rights, Prokofiev should have been incensed; but the beauty of Italy, as recorded in his diary entry, seems to have soothed his soul; as did the opportunity to tell friends back home that Diaghilev was now so fat that he resembled 'a vertical hippopotamus'.

As for our aim of seeing all that Naples has to offer, Diaghilev, who has put on a lot of weight and now waddles rather than walks, tapped into surprising reserves of energy, and we were on our feet from morning till night. The noisy, vital city often made me think of Moscow, but its special charm was a labyrinth of narrow little lanes no more than ten feet wide or so and six storeys high, in which life seethed not so much in the houses as outside in the streets, the walls festooned from top to bottom with drying laundry. It was an extraordinary and curious sight. Vesuvius puffed out its cloud of white smoke. I was told that the last eruption had done serious damage to the former nobility of its conical form. A couple of times we lunched on the hill outside the city, from where we had staggeringly beautiful views over the town and the bay... One wonderful excursion we made was to Pompeii, walking through the dead streets and hearing the expositions of the guide. (Very interesting, and wherever one turned one's attention, there would be a sign announcing to the world that such and such a house was a brothel.) Our stay in Naples concluded with a trip to the island of Capri, about which I had heard much and which I was most interested to see. My first thought was that once I had achieved all my plans and got back here in a couple of months' time to write my ballet, Capri could be where I would base myself. But, wonderful though it is, Capri turned out to be so mountainous, so overpopulated and crowded, that I abandoned the idea. We arrived on a balmy and moonlit evening and walked along the cliffs; Diaghilev and Massine were like a pair of love-birds. We spent a day and a half on the island and then came back to Naples via lovely Sorrento, and thence back to Rome.

[P.S.]... Diaghilev is nervous whenever he is on the water, and would not allow the rowers to sing. There was a light breeze, and although the boat rocked only slightly, it was enough to frighten Diaghilev. When the oarsmen started to sing softly, Diaghilev stopped them, saying that this was no time to sing, seeing that any moment we might be drowned.

SERGEI PROKOFIEV, *DIARIES*.

25 FEBRUARY

BYRON IN MISSOLONGHI, 1824

The British poet, rake and philhellene Lord Byron (1788–1824) wrote to his publisher John Murray from Missolonghi, in western Greece, where he was helping Greek nationalists in their war for independence from Ottoman rule. He died there two months later, not in battle but of fever.

You will perhaps be anxious to hear some news from this part of Greece (which is the most liable to invasion); but you will hear enough through public and private channels. I will, however, give you the events of a week, mingling my own private peculiar with the public; for we are here jumbled a little together at present.

On Sunday (the 15th, I believe), I had a strong and sudden convulsive attack, which left me speechless, though not motionless – for some strong men could not hold me; but whether it was epilepsy, catalepsy, cachexy, or apoplexy, or what other *exy* or *epsy*, the doctors have not decided; or whether it was spasmodic or nervous, etc.; but it was very unpleasant, and nearly carried me off, and all that. On Monday, they put leeches to my temples, no difficult matter, but the blood could not be stopped till eleven at night (they had gone too near the temporal artery for my temporal safety), and neither styptic nor caustic would cauterise the orifice till after a hundred attempts...

On Saturday we had the smartest shock of an earthquake which I remember (and I have felt thirty, slight or smart, at different periods; they are common in the Mediterranean,) and the whole army discharged their arms, upon the same principle that savages beat drums, or howl, during an eclipse of the moon: – it was a rare scene altogether – if you had but seen the English Johnnies, who had never been out of a cockney workshop before! – or will again, if they can help it; – and on Sunday we heard that the Vizier is come down to Larissa, with one hundred and odd thousand men.

LORD BYRON, *A SELF-PORTRAIT*, VOLUME II.

26 FEBRUARY

SELF-DOUBT IN THE SUDAN, 1865

Returning from the discovery of Lake Albert N'yanza (*see* 14 March), the English explorer Sam Baker (1821–93) and his wife Florence came to Gondokoro, an outpost on the Nile, now in southern Sudan, from where they hoped all would henceforth be plain sailing. In the great tradition of Victorian exploration they were, of course, disappointed. Baker, quite untypically, even began to wonder what it was all for.

We were told that some people had suggested that we might possibly have gone to Zanzibar, but the general opinion was that we had all been killed. At this cold and barren reply, I felt almost choked. We had looked forward to arriving at Gondokoro as to a home; we had expected that a boat would have been sent on the chance of finding us, as I had left money in the hands of an agent in Khartoum – but there was literally nothing to receive us, and we were helpless to return. We had worked for years in misery, such as I have but faintly described, to overcome the difficulties of this hitherto unconquerable exploration; we had succeeded – and what was the result? As I sat beneath a tree and looked down upon the glorious Nile that flowed a few yards beneath my feet, I pondered upon the value of my toil. I had traced the river to its great Albert source, and as the mighty stream glided before me, the mystery that had ever shrouded its origin was dissolved. I no longer looked upon its waters with a feeling approaching to awe, for I knew its home, and had visited its cradle. Had I overrated the importance of the discovery? And had I wasted some of the best years of my life to obtain a shadow? I recalled to recollection the practical question of Commoro, the chief of Latooka, – 'Suppose you get to the great lake, what will you do with it? What will be the good of it? If you find that the large river does flow from it, what then?'

SAMUEL BAKER, *THE ALBERT N'YANZA*, VOLUME II.

27 FEBRUARY

AMERICAN LIGHTS, 1947

When Simone de Beauvoir (*see* 29 January) visited Los Angeles in 1947 she was left cold by Hollywood. The studios seemed little different from those in France and a group of strikers, huddled morosely over a fire at the studio gates, lent a sour note to her visit. But she was taken by the profusion and beauty of the city lights. It was not just that she came from a continent that had been blacked out for many years, but that in the United States lights did more than illuminate – they seemed to have life, a life reflected (on all sides) in this Hawaiian-themed restaurant and which, in her imagination, achieved cosmic significance.

Los Angeles is far from possessing the beauty of New York or the depth of Chicago, and I understand why some French people spoke to me about it with such distaste: without friends, I'd be lost. But it can be enjoyable as a kaleidoscope – with a shake of the wrist, the pieces of colored glass give you the illusion of a new rosette. I surrender to this hall of mirrors... The French consul has invited me to dinner with N and M. In the entrance hall there is an exhibition of Hawaiian jewelry, shell necklaces, leis, and softly colored seeds. I have never seen such an enchanting restaurant: it's as beautiful as the Palais des Mirages in the Musée Grevin. Greenhouses with luxuriant plants, aquariums, aviaries where birds colored like butterflies swoop, all bathed in a murky, submarine light. The tables are glass pedestals in which the gleaming ceiling is reflected; the prismatic pillars are faceted mirrors in which space is infinitely multiplied. We dine under a straw hut at the end of a lake, in a forest, in the middle of an enormous diamond. The waitresses' costumes are a modest version of Hawaiian dress. In cylindrical glasses, which hold nearly a pint, we are served zombies (cocktails made from seven kinds of rum poured on top of each other: the amber liquid is layered from dark brown to light yellow). The meal transports us, unexpectedly, to China. The dishes don't have that overly visual aspect that often discourages the palate in America; instead, they look very appealing. And if French cooking is 'thoughtful', as Colette says, this cuisine seems the fruit of a thousand years of meditation.

At midnight we are alone on top of a hill. We sit on the ground and smoke in silence. Los Angeles is beneath us, a huge, silent fairy-land. The lights glitter as far as the eye can see. Between the red, green, and white clusters, big glowworms slither noiselessly. Now I am not taken in by the mirage: I know that these are merely streetlamps along the avenues, neon signs, and headlights. But mirage or no mirage, the lights keep glittering; they, too, are a truth. And perhaps they are even more moving when they express nothing but the naked presence of men. Men live here, and so the earth revolves in the quiet of the night with this shining wound in its side.

SIMONE DE BEAUVOIR, *AMERICA DAY BY DAY*.

28 FEBRUARY

MIDNIGHT MARCH TO OUDH, 1858

Much to his relief, on this day in 1858 the journalist W.H. Russell left the killing fields of Cawnpore (*see* 14 February) to accompany the military columns to the region of Oudh (modern Awadh). Everything in Cawnpore had been 'blighted, burnt and ruined', he wrote, whereas Oudh was supposed to be 'the garden of India'.

The column started in the early hours to avoid the worst of the heat. How to find one's way was no easy matter. The ground looked pitch-black, and was covered with cooking-places, and my horse went plunging from one to another, and dancing amid red-hot ashes in a most unseemly manner. My friend Stewart, mounted on a camel, came to guide me to the head of the column, which we reached, after wandering through a wilderness of bazaars and natives for nearly an hour. We got out on the road; where in silence and order, the Rifle Brigade was plunging with steady tramp through the dust. As the moon sank in the heavens, the line of our march became more like some dream of the other world, or some recollections of a great scene at the theatre than anything else. The horizontal rays just touched the gleaming arms and heads of the men, lighted up the upper portions of the camels and the elephants, which resembled islands in an opaque sea, whilst the plain looked like an inky waste, dotted with star-like fires. The sun soon began to make his approach visible, and an arc of greyish-red appeared in the east, spreading but not deepening, till the Far-Darter himself rose like a ball of fire in the hazy sky.

WILLIAM HOWARD RUSSELL, *My Indian Mutiny Diary*.

29 FEBRUARY

THE LAST COCOA IN ANTARCTICA, 1916

Ernest Shackleton (1874–1922) left Britain in 1914 with the ambition of leading the first expedition to cross from one side of Antarctica to the other. Before he even reached the continent his ship was crushed in the Weddell Sea, forcing him to lead his men north over the floes to safety. As they dragged their boats over the ice they rapidly became accustomed to short and unfamiliar rations.

On Leap Year day, February 29, we held a special celebration, more to cheer the men up than for anything else. Some of the cynics of the party held that it was to celebrate their escape from woman's wiles for another four years. The last of our cocoa was used today. Henceforth water, with an occasional drink of weak milk, is to be our only beverage. Three lumps of sugar were now issued to each man daily...

Lees, who was in charge of the food and responsible for its safekeeping, wrote in his diary: 'The shorter the provisions the more there is to do in the commissariat department, contriving to eke out our slender stores as the weeks pass by. No housewife ever had more to do than we have in making a little go a long way.'

By this time blubber was a regular article of our diet – either raw, boiled, or fried. 'It is remarkable how our appetites have changed in this respect. Until quite recently almost the thought of it was nauseating. Now, however, we positively demand it. The thick black oil which is rendered down from it, rather like train oil in appearance and cod liver oil in taste, we drink with avidity.'

ERNEST SHACKLETON, *SOUTH*.

MARCH

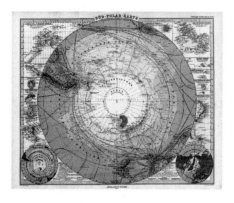

1 MARCH

GOETHE IN NAPLES, 1787

On a tour through Italy the German poet, dramatist and general polymath Johann Wolfgang von Goethe (1749–1832) summed up, in his journal, his first impressions of Naples. A bit of a windbag on occasions, he was luckily interrupted mid-flow by a young woman to whom he had taken a fancy.

How shall I describe a day like today? – a boat trip; some short drives in a carriage; walks on foot through the most astonishing landscape in the world; treacherous ground under a pure sky; ruins of unimaginable luxury, abominable and sad; seething waters; caves exhaling sulphur fumes; slag hills forbidding all living growth; barren and repulsive areas; but then, luxuriant vegetation, taking root wherever it can, soars up out of all the dead matter, encircles lakes and brooks, and extends its conquest even to the walls of an old crater by establishing there a forest of noble oaks.

Thus one is tossed about between the acts of nature and the acts of men. One would like to think, but feel too incompetent. Meanwhile the living merrily go on living. We, of course, do not fail to do the same, but people of culture, who belong to the world and know its ways, and are also warned by grave events, are inclined to reflections. As I was lost in contemplation of an unlimited view over earth, sea and sky, I was called back to myself by the presence of an amiable young lady who is accustomed to receive attentions and is not indifferent to them.

JOHANN WOLFGANG VON GOETHE, *ITALIAN JOURNEY*.

2 MARCH

FROSTBITE AT MINUS FORTY, 1912

Having arrived at the South Pole on 17 January, only to find he had been pre-empted by Amundsen (*see* 14 December), the English explorer Robert Falcon Scott (1868–1912) had written: 'Now for the run home and a desperate struggle. I wonder if we can do it.' More than a month later, it looked as if he couldn't. The party had already lost one man to exhaustion, its progress was hampered by sledge-loads of geological samples, and now they were falling behind schedule with the Antarctic winter hard on their backs. 'Things looking *very* black,' Scott wrote a day later, 'we preserve every semblance of good cheer, but one's heart sinks...'

Lunch. Misfortunes rarely come singly. We marched to the (Middle Barrier) depot fairly easily yesterday afternoon, and since that have suffered three distinct blows which have placed us in a bad position. First we found a shortage of oil; with most rigid economy it can scarce carry us to the next depot on this surface (71 miles away). Second, Titus Oates disclosed his feet, the toes showing very bad indeed, evidently bitten by the late temperatures. The third blow came in the night, when the wind, which we had hailed with some joy, brought dark overcast weather. It fell below −40° in the night, and this morning it took 1½ hours to get our foot gear on, but we got away before eight. We lost cairn and tracks together and made as steady as we could N. by W., but have seen nothing. Worse was to come – the surface is simply awful. In spite of strong wind and full sail we have only done 5½ miles. We are in a *very* queer street since there is no doubt we cannot do the extra marches and feel the cold horribly.

ROBERT FALCON SCOTT, *JOURNALS*.

3 MARCH

ICED *CRÈME DE MENTHE* IN MONROVIA, 1935

On about this date Graham Greene and his cousin Barbara finally reached the Liberian capital, Monrovia, after a month's trek through the jungle (*see 26 January*). Despite the rigours of the journey, the return to so-called civilization came as an unwelcome surprise. The icing on their disappointment was supplied by Monrovia's tiny colony of fever-ridden expats.

———•·•———

One couldn't expect them to do anything else but drink, beginning after breakfast with beer at each other's houses and ending with whisky at four in the morning. But what was worst was the iced *crème de menthe*. It was served everywhere automatically after lunch and dinner: it would have been thought eccentric not to like the sweet nauseating stuff, as it would have been thought curious not to enjoy at sundown, in the damp heat of the evening, while the backs of the hands and the armpits sweated all the time, the heavy clogging Tokay the Hungarian doctor kept. They had every reason to drink; you couldn't read much in a climate which rotted your books; you couldn't even deceive yourself that you were there for some good, ruling the natives, for it was the natives in this case who ruled you and presented, so far as the Cabinet Ministers were concerned, a depressing example of sobriety and attention to business; you couldn't womanise, for the range was too embarrassingly limited; there were no games to play, no strangers regularly bringing the gossip of one's own country; there was no ambition, for Liberia, whether to the diplomat or the storekeeper, was about the deadest of all ends; there was really nothing but drink and the wireless, and of the two drink was preferable.

GRAHAM GREENE, *JOURNEY WITHOUT MAPS*.

4 MARCH

TWO POETS IN CHINA, 1938

When the English authors W.H. Auden (1907–73) and Christopher Isherwood (1904–86) were commissioned to write a travel book about the Far East, they chose China as their subject. They arrived in late February 1938 in a country in disarray: not only was it riven by factionalism – Mao Zedong's Communists versus Chiang Kai-shek's Nationalists – but it had been invaded by Japan the previous year. Before boarding a train at Canton, the two writers had acquired visiting cards bearing the phonetic names 'Au Dung' and 'Y Hsiao Wu', which they were assured were essential for travel in the interior.

Along the road near the line hundreds of coolies squatted humbly in the dust: these, it appeared, never aspired to get on the platform at all. Only, at the very last moment, when everybody of any consequence was already on board, they might be allowed to scramble over the fence and mingle in one desperate fighting rush for the few remaining places in a cattle-truck. Many of them, obviously, would be left behind. Several would very likely break an arm or a leg.

The station building was small, shabby, and crammed with soldiers. It smelt very bad indeed. A group of police officers in smart black-and-silver uniforms challenged us smilingly. But they didn't want to see our tickets, or even our passports; they merely demanded from each of us a visiting-card. These cards, somebody told us later, are the perquisites of the officials who collect them; they like to show them to their wives, and boast about the interesting people they have met.

W.H. AUDEN AND CHRISTOPHER ISHERWOOD, *JOURNEY TO A WAR*.

5 MARCH

THE DOMAIN OF SEÑOR REBOLLEDO, 1880

In 1879 Edward Whymper (1840–1911), conqueror of the Alps, turned his attention to the Andes of Ecuador. On approaching one of the more tantalizing heights, Mount Antisana, he discovered that it was owned by a local grandee. So was almost everything else in the vicinity. In fact, Señor Rebolledo's domain seemed limitless.

———•—•—

I was surprised – not having met a soul in the course of the day – to see a grave and very unshaven man approaching, well mounted on a fast ambler; by dress, as well as demeanour, evidently no common wayfarer. He drew rein, and there was scarcely time to wonder who was this distinguished stranger before another horseman cantered round the farthest corner, and another, and then they came by twos and threes, until I saw thirty or more, rising and falling over the undulating ground like buoyant ships on a breezy sea; jovial, wild-looking fellows, picturesquely attired in sombreros and with legs encased in hairy buskins, all riding powerful horses, and sitting like men born in the saddle. As they came up, they halted at a respectful distance behind their lord. I sent Verity forward to make enquiries; and then, after formally saluting, each party went its way.

I was not aware until the train had swept past that we had met Señor Rebolledo, the owner of Antisana, of the farms of Piñantura, Antisanilla, Antisana and all the intervening country, and other large estates; the proprietor of a princely domain, unlimited on the Amazonian side. If one asked how far it extended, they answered 'As far as you can go to the East' – it had no boundaries in that direction.

EDWARD WHYMPER, *TRAVELS AMONGST THE GREAT ANDES*.

6 MARCH

SNOW ON THE YANGTZE, 1938

Having caught a train from Canton (*see* 4 March), the literary duo Auden and Isherwood journeyed through wartime China to the edge of the Yangtze River. On the opposite bank stood Hankow, which, following the Japanese invasion in 1937, was now the country's temporary capital.

Early next morning we arrived at Wuchang. The thermometer had dropped during the night, and we staggered out of the station into a driving blizzard. The causeway and the stone stairs down to the ferry were slippery with ice. Coolies jostled blindly against us, with the averted, snot-smeared, animal faces of the very humble, the dwellers in Society's smallest crevices, the Insulted and Injured. Auden's paper umbrella had broken in the storm; it wrapped itself round his head like a grotesque kind of hat. Slithering and cursing, we crowded into the hold of the listing steamer and stood, jammed too tight to move, amidst straw baskets, rifles, soldiers, peasants, and sacks. This was not the moment to fuss about infection or lice. On the distant shore, the buildings of Hankow stood grim and black against the low clouds; before us swept the Yangtze, a terrible race of yellow waves and tearing snow. We had arrived, it seemed, at the very end of the world.

W.H. Auden and Christopher Isherwood, *Journey to a War*.

7 MARCH

BLOOD-RED SINAI, 1922

En route from Sicily to the United States via an easterly route, D.H. Lawrence (*see* 4 January) passed through the Suez Canal. In a letter to his mother-in-law he transformed this businesslike and oft-reviled short cut into a channel of harsh beauty and biblical significance.

In the distance little sharp sandhills, so rosy gold and sharp, and the horizon sharp as a knife edge, so clear – then a couple of lonely palms, lonely and forlorn in the strong light, small, like people who have not grown tall – then again only sand, gold-pink, and sharp sandhills, so sharp and defined and clear, not like reality, like a dream. Slowly came the evening, and we so still, one would have thought we no longer moved. A thousand gulls flew about, like a snowstorm, and a great black bird of prey, alone and cruel, so large, among thousands of white, screaming fast-moving seabirds... Next morning we were just in the Red Sea – There stood Mount Sinai, red as old, dried blood, naked as a knife, and so sharp, so unnaturally sharp, defined like a 'poinard' [dagger] that was dipped in blood, and has long since dried again, and is a bit 'rusted', and always there, like something dreadful, between man and his lost Paradise. All is Semitic and cruel – naked, sharp, no tree, no leaf, no life: the murderous will and iron of idea and ideal – iron, will, and ideal – so stand these terrible shores of this Red Sea, that is hot as an oven, without air.

D.H. LAWRENCE, *LETTERS*, VOLUME IV.

8 MARCH

HUNTING OUT *YAGÉ* IN LIMA, 1956

In 1956 the American 'Beat' writer William Burroughs (1914–97) searched feverishly through South America for *yagé,* a drug that he hoped would reveal a higher, blissful plane of existence. In his diary he describes the penultimate turn of his journey to nirvana. When he finally got hold of the stuff it induced only a state of mild paranoia.

From Bogota I flew down to Lima, since I intended to visit the Peruvian Amazon. Lima is in a coastal desert. The city and the area immediately surrounding it is irrigated by the River Rimac. Outside the irrigated area, the landscape is dead and empty as the moon. It never rains in Lima, but during the Winter months – (their Winter is our Summer) – a heavy mist comes down from the Andes and covers the city.

You see vultures everywhere, roosting on buildings and statues in the center of town, always wheeling overhead as if they were waiting for all Lima to die.

There is a high incidence of T.B. in Lima, and bloody spit all over the streets. Lima is full of open vistas, wide streets, parks and vast, rubble strewn lots. A peculiar languor permeates the city. At all hours boys and young men loll in the parks, sleeping on the grass, or just lying there doing nothing. In the poorer quarters of the city, sanitary facilities are evidently inadequate. In any vacant lot you see people lined up along adobe walls relieving themselves. A city of great open spaces, enchanted languor, weed grown parks, vultures wheeling in a violet sky, and boys spitting blood in the street.

The Wholesale Market – Mercado Mayorista – covers several blocks. In all South American towns the market is the center of life. The Lima market is full of little bars and Chinese restaurants open twenty-four hours a day. The Peruvian folk music is on the juke boxes. Boys play these tunes and dance with each other or alone. Peruvians love to dance. Fights continually break out for no apparent reason. Ramming a broken glass into your opponent's face seems to be standard practice in Peruvian bars. Everyone does it.

The national drink of Peru is pisco, a raw cane whisky. After drinking this stuff for a week I came down with neuritis, and had to take a course of vitamin B injections. After that I switched to cognac.

Lima has an extensive Chinatown with restaurants that serve real Chinese food. There are also good Italian restaurants, and the native Creole dishes are quite tasty. Food is good and cheap. You do not feel the influence of Spain in Lima. There are, of course, Spanish colonial buildings in Lima, but the atmosphere of the city is not Spanish. Lima is pure South America, a city like no other place on earth.

After spending a week in Lima, I flew to Pucallpa which is on the Ucayali River, a large tributary of the Amazon. Pucallpa is an end of the road town like Mocoa. In most small, South American towns they never have what you want in the shops. If the place is insufferably hot there are no cold drinks. A river town will stock no fish hooks. A place infested with mosquitoes never heard of citronella. There is something intentional in this, a determination to be stupid and jerkwater, a negative hostility, a deep self depreciation. But Pucallpa has what you want. Alert, intelligent personnel in shops and restaurants.

I stayed at the Hotel Pucallpa and the manager was extremely helpful when I told him I was interested in yagé.

WILLIAM BURROUGHS, *The Yage Letters*.

9 MARCH

AVALANCHE IN THE INDUS, 1974

In November 1974 the Irish traveller Dervla Murphy (born 1931) took her six-year-old daughter Rachel on a journey by foot and horseback through the Indus Gorge into the Karakoram Mountains of northern Pakistan. It was four months before they returned to civilization, during which time she became accustomed to the telltale sounds of avalanches and *au fait* with their consequences.

The regular habits of avalanches astonish me. As we were walking around the invisible lake we heard today's first 'gun-shot', followed after the usual moment of tense silence by a terrific rumbling boom – the loudest we have heard – seeming to come from the far side of a mountain on the west shore of the lake. I looked at my watch: it was 11.58. It is quite extraordinary how the first avalanche each day is heard between 11.55 and 12.05. Deep grooves and long brown earth-stains were visible on the steeper snowy slopes and while coming from Skardu we had noticed fresh blood stains on the white path – a curiously melodramatic combination of colours. After about two miles we came to the scene of the accident, where the stains continued up a snowy slope to an expanse of bare scree. At one point high on the snow there was a wide patch of crimson, from which the victim had rolled down to the path, bringing a small rock-fall with him. Later we heard that he had been traversing the scree, searching for a lost sheep, when a rock hit him on the head. But like a true Balti he picked himself up, tied his shirt around the wound and walked four miles to hospital – where he found no one on duty, because this is Sunday. So he tightened the tourniquet and walked another eight miles home. A few months among the Baltis make one realize how perilously effete we Westerners have become. After a few more generations of pampering and motor-transport our bodies will no longer be capable of normal functioning.

DERVLA MURPHY, *WHERE THE INDUS IS YOUNG.*

10 MARCH

SLOW TRAINS IN ITALY, 1921

The British author and socialite Agnes Castle returned from a visit to Italy in such high dudgeon that she felt compelled to write to the papers: her diatribe appeared in the *Daily Express* some time in March 1921. Although it conjures a faintly ridiculous image of an outraged dowager in search of her wardrobe, Castle's report had ominous relevance for travellers. In the aftermath of the First World War, Italy's disorganized, strike-ridden railways were indeed a mess; but the resulting programme to make the trains run on time brought its own perils (*see* 31 July).

This Italy is a strange, sloppy country as we find it to-day... You cannot even find the exact hour of a train. Everything fluctuates, nothing is fixed. Your train may start to meet a train which, with luck, may leave the station two hours after the time marked in the guide-book.

Your luggage, labelled and registered for Genoa, goes to Rome, because it is too much trouble to unload it at the intermediate station. But no one is surprised at your luggage having gone to Rome. It happens every day, you are told. It will be returned, perhaps the day after tomorrow, anyhow near that date. And eighteen other trunks have gone on with yours. How can you be so unreasonable as to complain?

AGNES CASTLE, QUOTED IN JAMES MCMILLAN (ED.), *THE WAY IT WAS*.

11 MARCH

A DOG'S CHANCE, BUT NO MORE, 1912

The situation facing Robert Falcon Scott and his Antarctic team (*see* 2 March) had deteriorated. By now Titus Oates was a serious drag on the party, his frostbitten feet delaying them by valuable hours, not only while on the march but in the simple act of putting his boots on every morning. It was impossible to abandon him, but at the same time he was holding them back. They were covering at best six miles a day, they had seven days' food left, and it was fifty-five miles to their next depot. The mathematics was depressingly simple. 'With great care we might have a dog's chance, but no more,' Scott wrote. Already, as this extract shows, he and his men were contemplating suicide.

Titus Oates is very near the end, one feels. What we or he will do, God only knows. We discussed the matter after breakfast; he is a brave fine fellow and understands the situation, but he practically asked for advice. Nothing could be said but to urge him to march as long as he could. One satisfactory result to the discussion; I practically ordered Wilson to hand over the means of ending our troubles to us, so that any one of us may know how to do so. Wilson had no choice between doing so and our ransacking the medicine case. We have 30 opium tablets apiece and he is left with a tube of morphine. So far the tragical side of our story.

ROBERT FALCON SCOTT, *JOURNALS*.

12 MARCH

A CRUSH OF MUMMIES, 1817

Giovanni Belzoni (1778–1823), or 'The Great Belzoni' as he advertised himself, was 6' 7" tall, a native of Padua, and had worked variously as a circus strongman and a hydraulic engineer before discovering a passion for archaeology. In 1815 he embarked for Egypt where, among other achievements, he removed a colossal head of Rameses II and shipped it to the British Museum. (It is still there.) On a mid-March day he stumbled through a catacomb of mummies near Thebes.

After the exertion of entering into such a place, through a passage of fifty, a hundred, three hundred, or perhaps six hundred yards, nearly overcome, I sought a resting-place, found one, and contrived to sit; but when my weight bore on the body of an Egyptian, it crushed it like a band-box. I naturally had recourse to my hands to sustain my weight, but they found no better support; so that I sunk altogether among the broken mummies, with a crash of bones, rags, and wooden cases, which raised such a dust as kept me motionless for a quarter of an hour, waiting till it subsided again. I could not remove from the place, however, without increasing it, and every step I took I crushed a mummy in some part or other. Once I was conducted from such a place to another resembling it, through a passage of about twenty feet in length, and no wider than that a body could be forced through. It was choked with mummies, and I could not pass without putting my face in contact with that of some decayed Egyptian; but as the passage inclined downwards, my own weight helped me on; however, I could not avoid being covered with bones, legs, arms, and heads rolling from above. Thus I proceeded from one cave to another, all full of mummies piled up in various ways, some standing, some lying, and some on their heads.

GIOVANNI BELZONI, *NARRATIVE OF THE OPERATIONS AND RECENT DISCOVERIES IN EGYPT AND NUBIA.*

13 MARCH

AMBUSHED BY COPTS, 1850

When the French novelist Gustave Flaubert (1821–80) visited Egypt in 1850 he took a trip up the Nile. Writing to his friend Louis Bouilhet he described how, at Gebel-el-Teir, the boat was waylaid by a band of predatory monks.

On the summit of a mountain overlooking the Nile there is a convent of Copts, who have the habit, as soon as they see a boatload of tourists, of running down, throwing themselves in the water, and swimming out to ask for alms. Everyone who passes is assailed by them. You see these monks, totally naked, rushing down their perpendicular cliffs and swimming towards you as fast as they can, shouting: '*Baksheesh, baksheesh, cawadja christiani!*' And since there are many caverns in the cliff at this particular spot, echo repeats: '*Cawadja, cawadja!*' loudly as a cannon. Vultures and eagles were flying overhead, the boat was darting through the water, its two great sails bulging. To drive off the Christian monks one of our sailors, the clown of the crew, began to dance a naked, lascivious dance, offering them his behind as they clung to the sides of the boat. The other sailors screamed insults at them, repeating the names of Allah and of Mohammed. Some hit them with sticks, others with ropes; Joseph rapped their knuckles with his kitchen tongs. It was a chorus of blows, yells, and laughter. As soon as they were given money they put it in their mouths and returned home via the route they had come. If they weren't received with a good beating, the boats would be assailed by such hordes of them that capsizing would be almost inevitable.

GUSTAVE FLAUBERT, *SELECTED LETTERS.*

14 MARCH

ON THE SHORES OF ALBERT N'YANZA, 1864

Sam Baker was – apart from the rare moment of introspection (*see* 26 February) – the perfect caricature of a Victorian explorer. Bearded, booted and armed to the teeth, he strode beneath his pith helmet in search of the source of the Nile, collecting big-game trophies whenever he could. Reaching his goal, the shores of Lake Albert N'yanza, prompted a surge of jubilation.

The day broke beautifully clear, and having crossed a deep valley between the hills, we toiled up the opposite slope. I hurried to the summit. The glory of our prize burst suddenly upon me! There, like a sea of quicksilver, lay far beneath the grand expanse of water – a boundless sea horizon on the south and south-west, glittering in the noon-day sun; and on the west, at fifty or sixty miles distance, blue mountains rose from the bosom of the lake to a height of about 7,000 feet above its level...

After a toilsome descent of about two hours, weak with years of fever, but for the moment strengthened by success, we gained the level plain below the cliff. A walk of about a mile through flat sandy meadows of fine turf interspersed with trees and bush, brought us to the water's edge ... It was with extreme emotion that I enjoyed this glorious scene. My wife who had followed me so devotedly, stood by my side, pale and exhausted – a wreck upon the shores of this great Albert Lake that we had so long striven to reach. No European foot had ever trod upon its sand, nor had the eyes of a white man ever scanned its vast expanse of water. We were the first; and this was the key to the great secret that even Julius Caesar yearned to unravel, but in vain. Here was the great basin of the Nile that received every drop of water, even from the passing shower to the roaring mountain torrent that drained from Central Africa towards the north. This was the great reservoir of the Nile!

SAMUEL BAKER, *THE ALBERT N'YANZA*, VOLUME II.

15 MARCH

FIRES IN A DESERT GORGE, 1894

At the age of forty-four, the French novelist and naval officer Pierre Loti (1850–1923) visited the Holy Land in an attempt to regain the Christian faith of his youth. His pilgrimage began in Jordan, where he took a camel caravan through the desert.

Our encampment tonight is in the mountains, in one of the deep, almost vertical gorges where travellers usually stop because they are sheltered from the storms and feel protected as if by battlements from nocturnal surprise.

Between the rocks, a slash of open sky reveals the seven stars of David's Chariot [The Great Bear], and the Ramadan moon hangs above them, a semi-circle of startling red. The night, always wondrous, has just fallen, bringing with it an astonishing transparency and clarity of vision – yet, also, the uncertainty of dreams.

The whole caravan is here... groups of people are clustered near and far, right up to the shadowy corridors that led us here. They're everywhere, camped on pedestals of rock – and their fires glimmer on dark faces, white teeth, shining sabres, elaborate burnouses, majestic figures and the monkey antics of naked children.

It's baking day, when we make loaves for the next week – unleavened bread, hard as rocks, cooked on cinders – which necessitates, as usual, great pyres of perfumed wood.

So great a blaze is needed for our bread, flames so high and so red, that the overhanging granite walls seem to catch fire, glowing with the cinders that rise to a sky that has now become dark – a shadowy trench at the bottom of which lies a paler moon, faint, sinking and blue.

We fill this corner of wilderness, where previously the air was sweet and pure, with a complexity of smells: the odour of Bedouins, the musk of camels, the stink of ourselves, the perfume of our Turkish pipes and the incense from the fire.

PIERRE LOTI, *VOYAGES*.

16 MARCH

FLAMINGOES ON MARS, 1956

On assignment for the *Sunday Times,* the British author Ian Fleming (1908–64) investigated Inagua, the most southerly of the Bahama islands. Fleming often wove elements of his journalism into his books and this was no exception – the Inaguan scenery featured prominently in his 1958 James Bond novel *Dr No.*

Only the light and the sky redeem this dreadful lake. Dreadful? Well, its base is marl mud, very fine in texture and the colour of a corpse. The lake is only two to three feet deep for the whole of its area and the bottom is pockmarked every few feet with sharp limestone coral excrescences. The shores and cays are thick with mangroves, scraggly and leggy, from which came the rotten-egg smell of the marsh gas in which we lived for two days. And yet it was also wonderful. The great mirrored expanse of water through which we pushed for ten miles in flat-bottomed boats, the mirages, the silence, the sense of being on Mars. And then the birds.

Flamingoes? Every horizon was shocking pink with them, hundreds of them, thousands of them, reflected double in the blue-green glass of the lake, talking away and going about their business in huge congregations that literally owned this world across which we were moving like water-boatmen across a pond.

IAN FLEMING, *TALK OF THE DEVIL.*

17 MARCH

I MAY BE SOME TIME, 1912

Disaster followed disaster as Scott and his party limped back from the Pole (*see* 2 and 11 March). They had already lost one man to exhaustion. Now Scott had to record the death of another, the injured Captain Oates, who left the tent so as not to hinder the party; he prefaced his departure with an understatement that has since achieved near-mythical status. Few travellers have written so coolly, so clearly and with such flair in so desolate a spot or so desperate a plight as Scott. His diary, a small, lined book of a size that would fit in a breast pocket, was written in pencil – the only writing tool that worked in sub-zero temperatures. There were just five, increasingly brief, entries after this one.

Friday, March 16 or Saturday 17. – Lost track of dates but think the last correct. Tragedy all along the line. At lunch, the day before yesterday, poor Titus Oates said he couldn't go on; he proposed we should leave him in his sleeping-bag. That we could not do, and induced him to come on... and we made a few miles. At night he was worse and we knew the end had come.

Should this be found I want these facts recorded. Oates' last thoughts were of his Mother, but immediately before he took pride in thinking that his regiment would be pleased with the bold way in which he met his death. We can testify to his bravery. He has borne intense suffering for weeks without complaint, and to the very last was able and willing to discuss outside subjects. He did not – would not – give up hope to the very end. He was a brave soul. This was the end. He slept through the night before last, hoping not to wake; but he woke in the morning – yesterday. It was blowing a blizzard. He said, 'I am just going outside and may be some time.' He went out into the blizzard and we have not seen him since.

I take this opportunity of saying that we have stuck to our sick companions to the last. In the case of Edgar Evans, when absolutely out of food and he lay insensible, the safety of the remainder seemed to demand his abandonment, but Providence mercifully removed him at this critical moment. He died a natural death, and we did not leave him till two hours after his death. We knew that poor Oates was walking to his death, but though we tried to dissuade him, we knew it was the act of a brave man and an English gentleman. We all hope to meet the end with a similar spirit, and assuredly the end is not far.

I can only write at lunch and then only occasionally. The cold is intense, −40° at midday. My companions are unendingly cheerful, but we are all on the verge of serious frostbites, and though we constantly talk of fetching through I don't think any one of us believes it in his heart.

We are cold on the march now, and at all times except meals. Yesterday we had to lay up for a blizzard and to-day we move dreadfully slowly. We are at No.14 pony camp, only two pony marches from One Ton Depot. We leave here our theodolite, a camera, and Oates' sleeping-bags. Diaries, &c., and geological specimens carried at Wilson's special request, will be found with us or on our sledge.

ROBERT FALCON SCOTT, *JOURNALS*.

18 MARCH

IN THE COUNTRY OF THE MOON, 1917

The poet John Masefield (1878–1967) was visiting Amiens on behalf of the Red Cross when he wrote to Margaret Bridges, daughter of the Poet Laureate Robert Bridges, describing the detritus – human and material – that still littered the battlefield of the Somme.

The battlefield is a bedevilled and desolate and awful place, still heaped, here and there, with dead Germans, and all littered and skinned and gouged, till it looks like the country of the moon. Here there is a heap of picks, there a coil of wire, here a body or a leg, then a bomb or two, a rifle, a smashed helmet, a few dozen cartridges, then some boots with feet in them, a mess of old coats and straps and leather work, all smashed and smothered in a litter of mud and mess, and great big stinking pools and old dud shells, burnt trees, and powdered bricks and iron. It cannot be described nor imagined; but I suppose the place once looked like the Chilterns, and now, at a distance, it looks like Dartmoor under rain, and nearby like Sodom and Gomorrah.

Near the ruins of Hamel there is a little dwarf evergreen which somehow hasn't been destroyed. A soldier has put a notice on it: 'Kew Gardens. Please do not touch.'

JOHN MASEFIELD, *LETTERS TO MARGARET BRIDGES*.

19 MARCH

LOST SOULS OF LISBON, 1942

As a member of Britain's Secret Intelligence Service, Malcolm Muggeridge (1903–90) spent long periods abroad during the Second World War. In 1942 he went to Portugal, a country whose neutrality made it a haven for spies and drifters of every denomination.

Here in Lisbon is the last vestige in Europe of our old way of life now precariously existing. It is like the owner of some ancestral mansion moving when ruined into the lodge with one or two of his pictures, a piece of plate or so, one aged servant in threadbare livery. Here are cafés, neon signs, money haggling, *petit déjeuner* with pats of butter brought in on a tray, jangling trams and taxi cabs and newspapers of all the nations. One deep and significant change may, however, be noted – the pound sterling has lost its magical properties; rub, rub at the lamp, and no all-powerful, obsequious djinn appears, at best only a reluctant slut who must be coaxed for any service at all.

With this important exception, an entirely familiar scene. There are even some remnants of the enormous regiment of dwellers abroad, income tax avoiders, makers of afternoon tea in pension bedrooms, readers of the Continental *Daily Mail*, enjoyers of the Mediterranean or other sun, driven at last, like rabbits when the hay is being cut, to this one remaining, dwindling, sanctuary. Alas, alas, poor souls; poor parasites, soon to be quite crushed out of existence.

MALCOLM MUGGERIDGE, *LIKE IT WAS*.

20 MARCH

ON THE SEA OF CORTEZ, 1940

Between March and April of 1940 the American novelist John Steinbeck (1902–68) sailed on a research trip to the Gulf of California – or, as he preferred to call it, the 'Sea of Cortez'. These were the best months for investigating the shoreline, when the notoriously volatile stretch of water was at its most dependable, and the local children helped collect specimens.

There is a small ghost shrimp which lives on these flats, an efficient little fellow who lives in a burrow. He moves very rapidly, and is armed with claws which can pinch painfully. He retires backwards into his hole so that to come at him from above is to invite his weapons. The little boys solved the problem for us. We offered ten centavos for each one they took. They dug into the rubble and old coral until they got behind the ghost shrimp in his burrow, then, prodding, they drove him outraged from his hole. Then they banged him good to reduce his pinching power. We refused to buy the banged-up ones – they had to get us lively ones. Small boys are the best collectors in the world. Soon they worked out a technique for catching the shrimps with only an occasionally pinched finger, and then the ten centavo pieces began running out and an increasing cloud of little boys brought us specimens. Small boys have such sharp eyes, and they are quick to notice deviation. Once they know you are generally curious, they bring amazing things. Perhaps we only practice an extension of their urge. It is easy to remember when we were small and lay on our stomachs beside a tide pool and our minds and eyes went so deeply into it that size and identity were lost, and the creeping hermit crab was our size and the octopus a monster. Then the waving algae covered us and we hid under a rock at the bottom and leaped out at fish. It is very possible that we, and even those who probe space with equations, simply extend this wonder.

JOHN STEINBECK AND EDWARD RICKETTS, *SEA OF CORTEZ*.

21 MARCH

A DOVER WELCOME, 1973

In 1973 a midnight ferry from Calais deposited the Iowa-born Bill Bryson (born 1951) on English soil. The Dover boarding-house where eventually he found a room was so alien that the memory was still fresh in his mind when he recounted it almost a quarter of a century later.

———

I don't remember its name, but I well recall the proprietress, a formidable creature of late middle years called Mrs Smegma, who showed me to a room, then gave me a tour of the facilities and outlined the many complicated rules for residing there – when breakfast was served, how to turn on the heater for the bath, which hours of the day I would have to vacate the premises and during which period a bath was permitted (these seemed, oddly, to coincide), how much notice I should give if I intended to receive a phone call or remain out after 10 p.m., how to flush the loo and use the loo brush, which materials were permitted in the bedroom waste-basket and which had to be carefully conveyed to the outside dustbin, where and how to wipe my feet at each point of entry, how to operate the three-bar fire in the bedroom and when that would be permitted (essentially, during an Ice Age). This was all bewilderingly new to me. Where I came from, you got a room in a motel, spent ten hours making a mess of it, and left early the next morning. This was like joining the Army.

BILL BRYSON, *NOTES FROM A SMALL ISLAND*.

22 MARCH

HOME OF THE BLIZZARD, 1912

In 1911 Douglas Mawson (1882–1958) led an Australian expedition to Adélie Land, a corner of Antarctica about which little was known. He had been invited to join Robert Falcon Scott's race to the South Pole but had demurred: Adélie Land, he explained, was more interesting. It certainly was. Buffeted by winds that flowed remorselessly from the interior, Mawson's coastal base enjoyed blizzards more severe and more continuous than anywhere else on earth.

———·—·——

Whatever has been said relative to the wind-pressure exerted on inanimate objects, the same applied, with even more point, to our persons; so that progression in a hurricane became a fine art. The first difficulty to be encountered was a smooth, slippery surface offering no grip for the feet. Stepping out of the shelter of the Hut, one was apt to be immediately hurled at full length down wind. No amount of exertion was of any avail unless a firm foothold had been secured. The strongest man, stepping on to ice or hard snow in plain leather or fur boots, would start sliding away with gradually increasing velocity; in the space of a few seconds, or earlier, exchanging the vertical for the horizontal position. He would then either stop suddenly against a jutting point of ice, or glide along for twenty or thirty yards till he reached a patch of rocks or some rough sastrugi [wind-blown waves of ice].

Of course we soon learned never to go about without crampons on the feet... [But] before the art of 'hurricane-walking' was learnt, and in the primitive days of ice-nails and finnesko [soft, insulated travelling boots], progression in high winds degenerated into crawling on hands and knees. Many of the more conservative persisted in this method, and, as a compensation, became the first exponents of the popular art of 'board-sliding'. A small piece of board, a wide ice flat and a hurricane were the three essentials for this new sport.

Wind alone would not have been so bad; drift snow accompanied it in overwhelming amount. In the autumn overcast weather with heavy falls of snow prevailed, with the result that the air for several months was seldom free from drift. Indeed, during that time, there were not many days when objects a hundred yards away could be seen distinctly. Whatever else happened, the wind never abated, and so, even when the snow had ceased falling and the sky was clear, the drift continued until all the loose accumulations on the hinterland, for hundreds of miles back, had been swept out to sea. Day after day deluges of drift streamed past the Hut, at times so dense as to obscure objects three feet away, until it seemed as if the atmosphere were almost solid snow.

Picture drift so dense that daylight comes through dully, though, maybe, the sun shines in a cloudless sky; the drift is hurled, screaming through space at a hundred miles an hour, and the temperature is below zero, Fahrenheit. You have then the bare, rough facts concerning the worst blizzards of Adélie Land. The actual experience of them is another thing.

Shroud the infuriated elements in the darkness of a polar night, and the blizzard is presented in a severer aspect. A plunge into the writhing storm-whirl stamps upon the senses an indelible and awful impression seldom equalled in the whole gamut of natural experience. The world a void, grisly, fierce and appalling. We stumble and struggle through the Stygian gloom; the merciless blast – an incubus of vengeance – stabs, buffets and freezes; the stinging drift blinds and chokes... It may well be imagined that none of us went out on these occasions for the pleasure of it.

Douglas Mawson, *Home of the Blizzard*, Volume I.

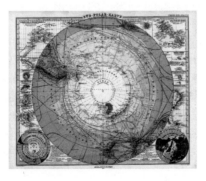

23 MARCH

AUSTRIAN RAIL, 1919

In 1919, having spent the previous two years in Switzerland (*see* 6 May), the playwright Stefan Zweig returned to his Austrian homeland. He found a nation impoverished by war and teetering on the edge of collapse. 'At that time,' he wrote, 'a visit to Austria called for preparations similar to those of an Arctic expedition.'

Through the broken windows... blew the soot and cinders of the miserable lignite with which the locomotives were fuelled. It smudged the floor and walls, but its stench at least tempered the smell of iodoform, a reminder of the sick and wounded who had been transported in these skeleton cars during the war. That the train moved at all was a miracle, even if a wearisome one; every time the unlubricated wheels shrieked a little less shrilly we were afraid that the work-worn engine had given up the ghost. Distances which used to take an hour now required four or five, and when dusk set in we remained in darkness. The electric bulbs had either been smashed or stolen, so that whoever searched for anything had to feel his way about with matches; and if we did not freeze it was because we had been crowded together throughout, with six or eight people in each compartment. New passengers had been crowding in from our very first stop, and more continued to come, all of them weary with hours of waiting. The corridors were jammed and some people even spent the semi-wintry night on the steps of the cars. Everyone held on to his baggage anxiously and hugged his package of provisions close; no one dared separate himself from a possession for a single minute in the darkness. From the midst of peace I was riding back into the horror of war which I thought to be over.

STEFAN ZWEIG, *THE WORLD OF YESTERDAY*.

24 MARCH

DISAPPOINTMENT IN THE INDIES, 1949

Shortly after the Second World War, the satirist S.J. Perelman (*see* 2 February) passed through the Banda Islands in eastern Indonesia. In a letter to his mistress, Leila Hadley, he was dismayed at the mix of mouldering colonial grandeur and abject poverty.

———•———

Altogether, Banda is what you might get if you took forty or fifty Southern mansions, pillars and all, and popped them down on a pin-point in the Pacific. About half are untenanted, roofs fallen in and tropical mold staining the walls. The other half shelter vast families of indolent, apathetic natives and half-castes who can barely summon up enough steam to grate the large white sweet potatoes and catch the fish swarming around on which they subsist. There hasn't been a vitamin on Banda since Constantinople fell to the Turks. All the kids are spindly-legged, their mothers are hags at thirty, and the diseases, from the terrifying one called framboisia, through elephantiasis, trachoma, and leprosy, are as luxuriant as the foliage. Nobody there can be persuaded to eat a vegetable; the one vacuous medical officer and the venal Eurasian controleur who represents government have no interest in bettering the lot of the population. It's a pretty dispiriting picture. If ever Nature smiled on any corner of the earth, it's Banda; there's every conceivable fruit and flower at your elbow, bananas, mangoes, coconuts, cotton, what-not. And amid it all these indescribably lovely houses, all floored with Dutch tiles worth fortunes, some of them still containing bits of their original furniture, rotting away.

S.J. PERELMAN, *DON'T TREAD ON ME*.

25 MARCH

THE GREAT SOUTHERN OCEAN, 1938

In 1938, at the age of 19, Eric Newby (*see* 18 February) quit his job in an advertising agency to enlist aboard the *Moshulu,* a Scandinavian vessel bound for Australia and one of the few sailing ships still in commercial use. He recorded his experiences as the *Moshulu* rounded Cape Horn.

———

The wind was immense. It no longer blew in the accepted sense of the word at all; instead it seemed to be tearing apart the very substance of the atmosphere. Nor was the sound of it any longer definable in ordinary terms. It no longer roared, screamed, sobbed or sang according to the various levels on which it was encountered. The power and noise of this wind was now more vast and all-comprehending, in its way as big as the sky, bigger than the sea itself, making something that the mind balked at, that it took refuge in blankness...

The barometer fell and fell, 746, 742, 737 millimetres. The sun went down astern, shedding a pale watery yellow light on the undersides of the deep black clouds hurrying above the ship. It was extremely cold, colder than it had ever been, blowing a strong gale force 9. Big seas were coming aboard. I felt very lonely. The ship that had seemed so huge and powerful was nothing now, a speck in the Great Southern Ocean... She was running before seas that were being generated in the greatest expanse of open ocean, of a power and size unparalleled because there was no impediment to them as they drove eastwards round the world. She was made pigmy too by the wind, the wind that was already indescribable... that had only now begun to blow...

At this moment, for the first time I felt certain of the existence of an infinitely powerful and at the same time merciful God. Nearly everyone in the ship felt something of this, no one spoke of it. We were all of us awed by what we saw and heard beyond the common experience of men.

Eric Newby, *The Last Grain Race.*

26 MARCH

ARCTIC MONOTONY, 1894

In 1894, during his record-breaking drift on the *Fram* (*see* 2 January), Fridtjof Nansen railed against life in the Arctic pack-ice.

We are lying motionless – no drift. How long will this last? Last equinox how proud and triumphant I was; the whole world looked bright; but now I am proud no longer.

The sun mounts up and bathes the ice-plain with its radiance. Spring is coming, but brings no joys with it. Here it is as lonely and cold as ever. One's soul freezes. Seven more years of such life – or say only four – how will the soul appear then? And she... ? If I dared to let my longings loose – to let my soul thaw. Ah! I long more than I dare confess.

I have not courage to think of the future... And how will it be at home, when year after year rolls by and no one comes?

I know this is all a morbid mood; but still this inactive, lifeless monotony, without any change, wrings one's very soul. No struggle, no possibility of struggle! All is so still and dead, so stiff and shrunken under the mantle of ice. Ah!... the very soul freezes. What would I not give for a single day of struggle – for even a moment of danger.

Still I must wait, and watch the drift; but, should it take a wrong direction, then I will break all the bridges behind me and stake everything on a northward march over the ice. I know nothing better to do. It will be a hazardous journey, a matter, may be, of life or death. But have I any other choice?

It is unworthy of a man to set himself a task and then give in when the brunt of the battle is upon him. There is but one way, and that is *Fram* – forwards.

FRIDTJOF NANSEN, *FARTHEST NORTH*, VOLUME I.

27 MARCH

ENGLISH LADY, TURKISH BATH, 1717

In 1717 Lady Mary Wortley Montagu (1689–1762) travelled overland to Constantinople where her husband had been appointed ambassador. His appointment was not a success, but his wife's letters found lasting fame. Here, writing to a friend at home, she describes a visit some time in late March to a bath-house in Sofia.

———·—·———

I was in my travelling habit, which is a riding dress, and certainly appeared very extraordinary to them. Yet there was not one of them that showed the least surprise or impertinent curiosity, but received me with all the obliging civility possible. I know no European court where the ladies would have behaved themselves in so polite a manner to a stranger. I believe, in the whole, there were two hundred women, and yet none of those disdainful smiles or satirical whispers that never fail in our assemblies when anybody appears that is not dressed exactly in fashion. They repeated over and over to me: 'Guzelle, pek guzelle', which is nothing but 'charming, very charming'. The first sofas were covered with cushions and rich carpets, on which sat the ladies, and on the second their slaves behind them, but without any distinction of rank by their dress, all being in the state of nature, that is, in plain English, stark naked, without any beauty or defect concealed. Yet there was not the least wanton smile or immodest gesture among them. They walked and moved with the same majestic grace which Milton describes of our general mother. There were many amongst them as exactly proportioned as ever any goddess was drawn by the pencil of Guido or Titian, and most of their skins shiningly white, only adorned by their beautiful hair divided into many tresses, hanging on their shoulders, braided either with pearl or ribbon, perfectly representing the figures of the Graces.

I was here convinced of the truth of a reflection I had often made, that if it was the fashion to go naked, the face would be hardly observed.

I perceived that the ladies with finest skins and most delicate shapes had the greatest share of my admiration, though their faces were sometimes less beautiful than those of their companions. To tell you the truth, I had wickedness enough to wish secretly that Mr Gervase [a portrait painter] could have been there invisible. I fancy it would have very much improved his art to see so many fine women naked, in different postures, some in conversation, some working, others drinking coffee or sherbert, and many negligently lying on their cushions while their slaves (generally pretty girls of seventeen or eighteen) were employed in braiding their hair in several pretty manners. In short, 'tis the women's coffee house, where all the news of the town is told, scandal invented etc. They generally take this diversion once a week, and stay there at least four or five hours, without getting cold by immediate coming out of the hot bath into the cool room, which was very surprising to me. The lady that seemed the most considerable amongst them entreated me to sit by her and would fain have undressed me for the bath. I excused myself with some difficulty, they being however all so earnest in persuading me, I was at last forced to open my shirt and show them my stays, which satisfied them very well, for I saw they believed I was so locked up in that machine, that it was not in my power to open it, which contrivance they attributed to my husband. I was charmed with their civility and beauty, and should have been very glad to pass more time with them, but Mr Wortley resolving to pursue his journey the next morning early I was in haste to see the ruins of St Justinian's church, which did not afford me so agreeable a prospect as I had left, being little more than a heap of stones.

LADY MARY WORTLEY MONTAGU, *THE COMPLETE LETTERS*, VOLUME I.

28 MARCH

THE WILDNESS OF NIGHT, 2006

During a series of journeys in search of Britain's remaining wild places, the author Robert MacFarlane (born 1976) discovered that his quest depended as much upon time and season as place. Near Buttermere, in the Lake District, he stood poised for a spot of noctambulism.

———••——

Noctambulism is usually taken to mean sleepwalking. This is inaccurate: it smudges the word into somnambulism. Noctambulism means walking at night, and you are therefore etymologically permitted to do it asleep or awake. Generally, people noctambulise because they are in search of melancholy, or rather a particular type of imaginative melancholy. Franz Kafka wrote of feeling like a ghost among men – 'weightless, boneless, bodiless' – when he walked at night.

I had found another reason for being out at night, however, and that is the wildness which the dark confers on even a mundane landscape. Sailors speak of the uncanniness of seeing a well-known country from the sea; the way that such a perspective can make the most homely coastline seem strange. Something similar happens to a landscape in darkness. Coleridge once compared walking at night in his part of the Lake District to a newly blind man feeling the face of a child: the same loving attention, the same deduction by form and shape, the same familiar unfamiliarity. At night, new orders of connection assert themselves: sonic, olfactory, tactile. The sensorium is transformed. Associations swarm out of the darkness. You become even more aware of landscape as a medley of effects, a mingling of geology, memory, movement, life. The landforms remain, but they exist as presences: inferred, less substantial, more powerful. You inhabit a new topology. Out at night, you understand that wildness is not only a permanent property of land – it is also a quality which can settle on a place with a snowfall, or with the close of day.

ROBERT MACFARLANE, *THE WILD PLACES*.

29 MARCH

DEATH IN THE ANTARCTIC, 1912

On this day Robert Falcon Scott wrote the final entry in his journal (*see* 17 March). The Antarctic weather remained so unremittingly bad afterwards that Scott's body, along with those of his two remaining companions, Edward Wilson and Henry 'Birdie' Bowers, was not discovered until eight months later. Inside the tent Wilson and Bowers lay peacefully in their sleeping bags. Scott, however, had not gone quietly: he was half out of his bag, his arms frozen in defiance and his journal lying nearby. The rescuers collapsed the tent, piled it with a cairn of snow, erected a cross fashioned from the dead men's skis, and fled Antarctica as soon as they could. Scott's expedition was a tragedy that defined a continent, an age and, quite possibly, a nation.

Since the 21st we have had a continuous gale from W.S.W. and S.W. We had fuel to make two cups of tea apiece and bare food for two days on the 20th. Every day we have been ready to start for our depot *11 miles* away, but outside the door of the tent it remains a scene of whirling drift. I do not think we can hope for any better things now. We shall stick it out to the end, but we are getting weaker, of course, and the end cannot be far.

It seems a pity, but I do not think I can write more.

R. Scott

Last Entry

For Gods Sake look after our people

ROBERT FALCON SCOTT, *JOURNALS*.

30 MARCH

A TRAIN JOURNEY TO MADRID, 1937

In 1937 the American journalist Martha Gellhorn (*see* 22 January) was one of many foreigners who flocked to support the Republican cause in the Spanish Civil War – albeit wielding the pen rather than the sword. Having crossed the border at the Pyrenees she caught a train for Barcelona.

I was in a wooden carriage with six boys who were eating garlic sausage and bread made of powdered stone. They offered me their food, they laughed, they sang. Whenever the train stopped, another man, perhaps their officer, stuck his head in the carriage and exhorted them. I gathered that he was exhorting them to behave beautifully. They did behave beautifully, but I do not know what they said, as I spoke no Spanish.

Barcelona was bright with sun and gay with red banners, and the taxi driver refused money; apparently everything was free. Apparently everyone was everyone else's brother too. Since few people have lived in such an atmosphere, even for a minute, I can report that it is the loveliest atmosphere going. I was handed round like a package, with jollity and kindness; I rode on trucks and in jammed cars. And finally, by way of Valencia, we came at night to Madrid, which was cold, enormous and pitch-black, and the streets were silent and perilous with shell holes... I had not felt as if I were at war until now, but now I knew I was. It was a feeling I cannot describe; a whole city was a battlefield, waiting in the dark. There was certainly fear in that feeling, and courage. It made you walk carefully and listen hard and it lifted the heart.

MARTHA GELLHORN, *THE FACE OF WAR*.

31 MARCH

ATHENS THROUGH AN ELBOW, 1936

In 1936 the Surrealist jack-of-all-trades Jean Cocteau (1889–1963) and his secretary Marcel Khill emulated the fictional character Phileas Fogg by going around the world in eighty days. Khill played the part of Fogg's manservant Passepartout. Cocteau, meanwhile, sustained the role of semi-repentant opium addict. Among their first stops was Athens.

We find a bank open. Our poor dollars become thousands of drachmae and, at the bank-door, Passepartout, seized by an inspiration and inaugurating what is to become our settled method of journeying, leaps onto the running-board of an ancient motor-bus. A noisy, jerky old vehicle, filled with government officials. He worms his way up to the front portion but I can not manage to follow him there. The bus with a rattle like old iron bears us away with Passepartout standing, bent double, in the front and myself sitting uncomfortably in a rear seat next to four Greeks who are engaged in an impassioned argument about a handful of silky-looking seeds which they try their teeth on and stuff in their pockets, bring them out again, show them and then repeat the same process. They interrupt each other only to wink at a young typist half sitting, half upright, further down the vehicle. She is wearing glasses and resting her hand on her hip.

In the triangle formed by her arm and torso a landscape flies past that resembles a suburb of Toulon. I doze off, but am wakened by sudden jerks.

All at once my eyes open wide. What do I see? In the frame made by this female body I see a small broken cage, very long and low like those children weave with grasses to imprison grasshoppers in. It stays suspended in the air and is surrounded by space. What is it? My heart starts beating. Could this little gutted cage be... but it is the Parthenon!

JEAN COCTEAU, *My Journey Round the World.*

APRIL

∞

1 APRIL

DICKENS ON A RIVER BOAT, 1842

In 1842 the English novelist Charles Dickens (1812–70) made a tour of the United States. A series of ungenerous observations – exemplified by this description of a journey by river boat on the Ohio from Pittsburgh to Cincinnati – won him few friends in his host nation.

At dinner, there is nothing to drink upon the table, but great jugs full of cold water. Nobody says anything, at any meal, to anybody. All the passengers are very dismal, and seem to have tremendous secrets weighing on their minds. There is no conversation, no laughter, no cheerfulness, no sociality, except in spitting; and that is done in silent fellowship round the stove, when the meal is over. Every man sits down, dull and languid; swallows his fare as if breakfasts, dinners, and suppers, were necessities of nature never to be coupled with recreation or enjoyment; and having bolted his food in a gloomy silence, bolts himself, in the same state. But for these animal observances, you might suppose the whole male portion of the company to be the melancholy ghosts of departed book-keepers, who had fallen dead at the desk; such is their weary air of business and calculation. Undertakers on duty would be more sprightly beside them; and a collation of funeral-baked meats, in comparison with these meals, would be a sparkling festivity.

The people are all alike, too. There is no diversity of character. They travel about on the same errands, say and do things in exactly the same manner, and follow in the same dull cheerless round. All down the long table, there is scarcely a man who is anything different from his neighbour.

CHARLES DICKENS, *AMERICAN NOTES AND PICTURES FROM ITALY*.

2 APRIL

A BREAKFAST FIT FOR A FRENCH MARQUIS, 1867

In 1865 the nineteen-year-old Marquis de Beauvoir (1846–1929) left France with a group of aristocrat friends on a voyage round the world. Two years later, after many adventures, they reached China. At Peking they were invited by China's *de facto* ruler, the Imperial Regent Prince Kung, to breakfast. More than 150 dishes were served and there was no escaping them.

[I will] tell you of what has given us great pleasure, a gracious invitation to breakfast with His Imperial Highness Prince Kung, uncle of the Emperor, regent of the Empire, Son of Heaven, and descendant of Fire.

We give our horses to grooms dressed in sky blue, wearing black velvet boots, and find ourselves before three red-buttoned dignitaries in foxskin jackets, with official hats covered with red silk fringes and adorned with a long plume of peacock's feathers, pearl-grey silk robes with gold buttons, and white satin boots. It would take a table of logarithms to calculate the number of regular and mechanical bows made in the courtyard. We bow, you bow, they bow, till you wonder when etiquette will allow you to raise your head. Besides, in China, you must always give a little forced laugh in saying good morning, with oh's! and ah's! in a crescendo scale... A sojourn of ten weeks in China has accustomed us to Celestial good manners, and I assure you that you would have taken us all for descendants of Fire, so skilful are we in drawing our closed hands within our sleeves, then with much gravity and ceremony raising them joined together to our foreheads...

You cannot imagine how gracious they were pleased to be; at one moment I had more than twenty different viands at once on my plate... [and] the excellent Minister of Public Instruction – with extreme politeness – put into my mouth, with his chopsticks, quarters of orange dipped in sugar, while the Minister of Commerce – rivalling him in good will – insinuated between my teeth, on the left side, slices of ham preserved in ginger.

MARQUIS DE BEAUVOIR, *THE CONCLUSION OF A VOYAGE ROUND THE WORLD*.

3 APRIL

BLACK SAVANNAH, 1947

Simone de Beauvoir's experience of New York (*see* 29 January) and the United States' East Coast left her unprepared for the antagonism she encountered on visiting the racially segregated South. There, with her companion 'N', she explored the suburbs of Savannah, Georgia.

In the middle of the flowering azaleas, the dormant old houses, and the playing children, the statues of the great slave owners who created the city and fought for it are fixed in glory. But around this dead Savannah, there's another, living city where the grandchildren of slaves live inglorious lives of poverty and hatred: a black belt around the white city. For miles and miles, the bus followed avenues lined with wretched shacks, where unfriendly dark faces turned toward us; we felt the bite of those looks. But the black belt fascinates us; we decide to try to walk in these hostile streets. Children playing in the road look at us with surprise; the men standing on the porches, the women leaning out of the windows and staring at us, are frighteningly impassive. This is not Lenox Avenue or Harlem; there is hatred and rage in the air. Brightly colored wash is drying in yards behind wooden or rusty iron fences. The houses are very small, squeezed up against one another, brown like the earth. The streets and squares are merely vacant lots. With every step our discomfort grows. As we go by, voices drop, gestures stop, smiles die: all life is suspended in the depths of those angry eyes. The silence is so stifling, the menace so oppressive that it's almost a relief when something finally explodes. An old woman glares at us in disgust and spits twice, majestically, once for N, once for me. At the same moment, a tiny girl runs off crying, 'Enemies! Enemies!' It seems a long way back to the squares with flowering baskets.

SIMONE DE BEAUVOIR, *AMERICA DAY BY DAY*.

4 APRIL

A JAPANESE SCHOLAR, 1891

In 1891 a sixteen-year-old Japanese student wrote a short essay on 'European and Japanese Customs'. It was recorded by his teacher, Lafcadio Hearn (1850–1904), a Greek-born American who settled in Japan during the Meiji Restoration – a period of tumult, beginning in 1867, in which the nation was transformed by the wholesale adoption of Western customs and practices.

Europeans wear very narrow clothes and they wear shoes always in the house. Japanese wear clothes which are very *lenient* and they do not *shoe* except when they walk *out-of-the-door*.

What we think very strange is that in Europe every wife loves her husband more than her parents. In Nippon there is no wife who more loves not her parents than her husband.

And Europeans walk out in the road with their wives, which we utterly refuse to, except on the festival of Hachiman.

The Japanese woman is treated by man as a servant, while the European woman is respected as a master. I think these customs are both bad.

We think it is very much trouble to treat European ladies; and we do not know why ladies are so much respected by Europeans.

LAFCADIO HEARN, *GLIMPSES OF UNFAMILIAR JAPAN*, VOLUME II.

5 APRIL

FLYING WITH THE FÜHRER, 1932

When Adolf Hitler made a propaganda flight around Germany in 1932, the year before he became chancellor, the British journalist Sefton Delmer (1904–79) wangled his way onto the passenger list. As the plane left Berlin's Tempelhof airport, Delmer was struck by how dreary a figure Hitler cut when out of the public eye.

———•—•———

The whole lot of them... seemed to be bent on attracting Hitler's attention to themselves with some act betokening National Socialist zeal for Führer and fatherland. 'Auwi' [Prince August Wilhelm] held up the front page of the *Völkischer Beobachter* for Hitler to admire the impressive typographic display of his latest speech. Goebbels leaned forward to tell him with a great cackle of laughter a piquant piece of news which Goebbels clearly thought extremely funny, but which left Hitler mirthless. Schaub [Hitler's assistant] came over to offer sandwiches. Hitler declined them. And it was with a purely mechanical gesture that he leafed through a file of newspaper cuttings that Goebbels thrust forward for him to read.

Soon Hitler had sunk into morose apathy. He just sat there, staring gloomily out of the window his chin cradled in his right hand, wads of cotton wool in his ears. The only movement he made was to shift position from time to time or to scratch the back of his neck. It was an entirely new picture of Hitler for me, and a complete contrast to the glad-hand extrovert who had said goodbye to Magda Goebbels and the others at Tempelhof... Never again have I seen such a contrast between the public and the private figure as in Hitler.

The man I was looking at now was a tired and not very successful salesman flying with his samples to a client who had no great wish to see him and whom he himself had no wish to see. I began to wonder whether this was the real Adolf Hitler I was looking at now... Was the other Hitler just an act, the product of a terrific effort of will and imagination?

SEFTON DELMER, *TRAIL SINISTER*.

6 APRIL

A SOUTH SEA WELCOME, 1768

During a voyage of exploration to the South Pacific, the French navigator Louis de Bougainville (1729–1811) was irritated to find that wherever he went a Briton had almost always beaten him to it. At the island of Tahiti, however, precedence was the last thing on his mind.

The pirogues [canoes] were full of females; who, for agreeable features, are not inferior to most European women; and who in point of beauty of the body might, with much reason, vie with them all. Most of these fair females were naked; for the men and the old women that accompanied them, had stripped them of the garments which they generally dress themselves in. The glances which they gave us from their pirogues, seemed to discover some degree of uneasiness, notwithstanding the innocent manner in which they were given; perhaps, because nature has everywhere embellished their sex with a natural timidity; or because even in those countries, where the ease of the golden age is still in use, women seem least to desire what they most wish for. The men, who were more plain, or rather more free, soon explained their meaning very clearly. They preferred us to choose a woman, and to come on shore with her; and their gestures, which were nothing less than equivocal, denoted in what manner we should form an acquaintance with her. It was very difficult, amidst such a sight, to keep at their work four hundred young French sailors, who had seen no woman for six months. In spite of all our precautions, a young girl came on board, and placed herself upon the quarter-deck, near one of the hatch-ways, which was open, in order to give air to those who were heaving at the capstan below it. The girl carelessly dropped a cloth, which covered her, and appeared to the eyes of all beholders, such as Venus showed herself to the Phrygian shepherd, having, indeed, the celestial form of that goddess. Both sailors and soldiers endeavoured to come to the hatch-way; and the capstan was never hove with more alacrity than on this occasion.

At last our cares succeeded in keeping these bewitched fellows in order, though it was no less difficult to keep the command of ourselves. One single Frenchman, who was my cook, having found means to escape against my orders, so returned more dead than alive. He had hardly set his feet on shore, with the fair one whom he had chosen, when he was immediately surrounded by a crowd of Indians, who undressed him from head to feet. He thought he was utterly lost, not knowing where the exclamations of those people would end, who were tumultuously examining every part of his body. After having considered him well, they returned him his clothes, put into his pockets whatever they had taken out of them, and brought the girl to him, desiring him to content those desires which had brought him on shore with her. All their persuasive arguments had no effect; they were obliged to bring the poor cook on board, who told me, that I might reprimand him as much as I pleased, but that I could never frighten him so much, as he had just now been frightened on shore.

LOUIS DE BOUGAINVILLE, *A VOYAGE ROUND THE WORLD*.

7 APRIL

WONDERFUL SAN FRANCISCO, 1950

In 1950 the poet Dylan Thomas (*see* 17 January) applied for a post at the University of California at Berkeley. After a preliminary interview he brimmed with enthusiasm about the San Francisco sights, sounds and tastes in a letter to his wife, Caitlin; but alas the university rejected him as being too unstable.

But oh, San Francisco! It is and has everything... The wonderful sunlight there, the hills, the great bridges, the Pacific at your shoes. Beautiful Chinatown. Every race in the world. The sardine fleets sailing out. The little cable-cars whizzing down the city hills. The lobsters, clams, & crabs. Oh, Cat, what food for you. Every kind of seafood there is. And all the people are open and friendly... Everyone connected with the Universities is hard-up. But that doesn't matter. Seafood is cheap. Chinese food is cheaper & lovely. Californian wine is good. The iced bock beer is good. What more? And the city is built on hills; it dances in the sun for nine months of the year: & the Pacific Ocean never runs dry...

I love you, Caitlin.

You asked me about the shops. I only know that the shops in the big cities, in New York, Chicago, San Francisco, are full of everything you have ever heard of and also full of everything one has never heard of or seen. The foodshops knock you down. All the women are smart, as in magazines – I mean, the women in the main streets; behind, lie the eternal poor, beaten, robbed, humiliated, spat upon, done to death – and slick & groomed. But they are not as beautiful as you. And when you & me are in San Francisco, you will be smarter & slicker than them, and the sea & sun will make you jump over the roofs & the trees, & you will never be tired again. Oh, my lovely dear, how I love you. I love you for ever & ever.

DYLAN THOMAS, *COLLECTED LETTERS*.

8 APRIL

ON THE GOLD TRAIL THROUGH PANAMA, 1850

One day in April 1850, while toiling through the jungles of Panama, the British actor, adventurer and artist Frank Marryat (1826–55) encountered a mule train carrying gold from Peru. His ultimate destination was the gold fields of California, and the American prospectors whom he had already met along the way – all of them armed to the teeth – struck him as a much tougher proposition than this effete and leisurely procession from the South American interior.

Pass on filth, squalor and poverty, and make way as you should for wealth, for here, with tinkling bells and gay caparisons, comes a train of mules laden with gold – pure gold from Peru; as each mule bears his massive bars uncovered, glittering beneath the cordage which secures them to the saddle, you can touch the metal as they pass. Twenty of these file by as we draw on one side, and after them, guarding so much wealth, are half a dozen armed natives with rusty muskets slung lazily on their backs; but behind them on an ambling jennet [a small horse], is a well 'got up' Don, with muslin shirt and polished jack-boots, richly-mounted pistols in his holsters, and massive silver spurs on his heels, smoking his cigarette with as much pomposity as if the gold belonged to him, and he had plenty more at home. This gentleman, however, is in reality a clerk in an English house at Panama, and when he returns to that city, after shipping the gold on board the English steamer, and getting a receipt, he will change this picturesque costume for a plaid shooting-coat and continuations, and be a Don no longer.

FRANK MARRYAT, *MOUNTAINS AND MOLEHILLS*.

9 APRIL

ON THE TOP OF THE WORLD, 1909

On this date in 1909 Robert Peary (1856–1920) became the first man to reach the North Pole – or so he claimed. His was not the first claim, however (*see* 20 April), and it has since been suggested that he fell several score miles short of the mark.

We were now at the end of the last long march of the upward journey. Yet with the Pole actually in sight I was too weary to take the last few steps. The accumulated weariness of all those last days and nights of forced marches and insufficient sleep, constant peril and anxiety, seemed to roll across me all at once. I was actually too exhausted to realize at the moment that my life's purpose had been achieved. As soon as our igloos had been completed and we had eaten our dinner and double-rationed the dogs, I turned in for a few hours of absolutely necessary sleep, Henson and the Eskimos having unloaded the sledges and got them in readiness for such repairs as were necessary. But, weary though I was, I could not sleep long. It was, therefore, only a few hours later when I woke. The first thing I did after awaking was to write these words in my diary: 'The Pole at last. The prize of three centuries. My dream and goal for twenty years. Mine at last! I cannot bring myself to realize it. It seems all so simple and commonplace.'...

East, west, and north had disappeared for us. Only one direction remained and that was south. Every breeze which could possibly blow upon us, no matter from what point of the horizon, must be a south wind. Where we were, one day and one night constituted a year, a hundred such days and nights a century. Had we stood in that spot during the six months of the arctic winter night, we would have seen every star of the northern hemisphere circling the sky at the same distance from the horizon with Polaris (the North Star) practically overhead.

ROBERT E. PEARY, *THE NORTH POLE*.

10 APRIL

AN UNDERTASTE OF BLOOD AND SWEAT, 1922

On visiting Ceylon (now Sri Lanka) in 1922, *en route* to Australia, D.H. Lawrence (*see* 4 January) gave vent to his irritation at things oriental. His aim in travelling had been to escape the confines of the Old World – and the stuffiness of Britain in particular. He should, in theory, have embraced the exoticism of places such as Ceylon. Instead, their unfamiliarity filled him with horror and self-doubt; as he wrote soon after his arrival: 'We make a mistake forsaking England and moving out into the periphery of life. After all, Taormina [in Sicily], Ceylon, Africa, America – as far as we go, they are only the negation of what we ourselves stand for and are: and we're rather like Jonahs running away from the place we belong.'

No, the East doesn't get me at all. Its boneless suavity, and the thick, choky feel of the tropical forest, and the metallic sense of palms and the horrid noises of the birds and the creatures, who hammer and clang and rattle and cackle and explode all the livelong day, and run little machines all the livelong night; and the scents that make me feel sick, the perpetual nauseous overtone of cocoanut and cocoanut fibre and oil, the sort of tropical sweetness which to me suggests an undertang of blood, hot blood, and thin sweat: the undertaste of blood and sweat in the nauseous tropical fruits; the nasty faces and yellow robes of the Buddhist monks, the little vulgar dens of the temples: all this makes up Ceylon to me, and all this I cannot bear. Je m'en vais. Me ne vo'. I am going away. Moving on.

D.H. LAWRENCE, *LETTERS*, VOLUME IV.

11 APRIL

DETESTABLE TIERRA DEL FUEGO, 1833

In 1832 HMS *Beagle* was working its way round the coast of South America. Its captain, Robert Fitzroy, had been ordered to do no more than chart the region, but, being of an inquiring bent and interested in natural history, he had taken a supernumerary aboard. His name was Charles Darwin (1809–82) – a young man recommended for his enthusiasm and for being the 'grandson of Dr. Darwin the poet'. Writing from Tierra del Fuego, on the continent's southern tip, Darwin described conditions in a letter to J.S. Henslow, his old Cambridge tutor and the very man who had recommended him.

It is some time since we have been at a civilized port, nearly all this time has been spent in the most Southern part of Tierra del Fuego. – It is a detestable place, gales succeed gales with such short intervals that it is impossible to do anything... The Fuegians are in a more miserable state of barbarism, than I had expected ever to have seen a human being. – In this inclement country they are absolutely naked, & their temporary houses are like what children make in summer, with boughs of trees. – I do not think any spectacle can be more interesting, than the sight of Man in his primitive wildness. – It is an interest, which cannot well be imagined, until it is experienced. I shall never forget, when entering Good Success Bay, the yell with which a party received us. They were seated on a rocky point, surrounded by the dark forest of beech; as they threw their arms wildly round their heads & their long hair streaming they seemed the troubled spirits of another world. – The climate in some respects, is a curious mixture of severity & mildness; as far as regards the animal kingdom the former character prevails.

CHARLES DARWIN, *THE BEAGLE LETTERS*.

12 APRIL

A GREAT COLD IN SIBERIA, 1990

The Polish journalist Ryszard Kapuściński (1932–2007) made a tour of Russia between 1989 and 1991, shortly after the collapse of the Soviet Union. Travelling east on the Trans-Siberian Express, he stopped at the city of Yakutsk, where a young schoolgirl related the peculiarities of a 'great cold'.

One can recognize a great cold, she explains to me, by the bright, shining mist that hangs in the air. When a person walks, a corridor forms in this mist. The corridor has the shape of that person's silhouette. The person passes, but the corridor remains, immobile in the mist. A large man makes a huge corridor, and a small child – a small corridor. Tanya makes a narrow corridor because she is slender, but, for her age, it is a high one – which is understandable; she is after all the tallest in her class. Walking out in the morning, Tanya can tell from these corridors whether her girlfriends have already gone to school – they all know what the corridors of their closest neighbours and friends look like.

Here is a wide, low corridor, with a distinct, resolute line – the sign that Claudia Matveyevna, the school principal, has already gone.

If in the morning there are no corridors that correspond to the stature of students from the elementary school, it means the cold is so great that classes have been cancelled and the children are staying home.

Sometimes one sees a corridor that is very crooked and then abruptly stops. It means – Tanya lowers her voice – that some drunk was walking, tripped, and fell. In a great cold, drunks frequently freeze to death. Then such a corridor looks like a dead-end street.

RYSZARD KAPUŚCIŃSKI, *IMPERIUM.*

13 APRIL

ANTARCTIC SKIES, 1934

In 1934 Admiral Richard Byrd (1888–1957) of the US Navy spent the winter alone at Bolling Advance Base, a meteorological station on Antarctica's Ross Ice Shelf (or Barrier). He was enthralled by the way the atmosphere distorted as the long polar night approached.

These are the best times, the times when neglected senses expand to an exquisite sensitivity. You stand on the Barrier, and simply look and listen and feel. The morning may be compounded of an unfathomable, tantalizing fog in which you stumble over sastrugi [wind-blown waves of ice] you can't see, and detour past obstructions that don't exist, and take your bearings from tiny bamboo markers that loom as large as telephone poles and hang suspended in space. On such a day, I could swear that the instrument shelter was as big as an ocean liner. On one such day I saw the blank north-eastern sky become filled with the most magnificent Barrier coast I have ever seen, true in every line and faced with cliffs several thousand feet tall. A mirage, of course. Yet, a man who had never seen such things would have taken oath that it was real. The afternoon may be so clear that you dare not make a sound, lest it fall in pieces. And on such a day I have seen the sky shatter like a broken goblet, and dissolve into iridescent tipsy fragments – ice crystals falling across the face of the sun. And once in the golden downpour a slender column of platinum leaped up from the horizon, clean through the sun's core; a second luminous shadow formed horizontally through the sun, making a perfect cross. Presently two miniature suns, green and yellow in colour, flipped simultaneously to the ends of each arm. These are parhelia, the most dramatic of all refraction phenomena; nothing is lovelier.

RICHARD BYRD, *ALONE*.

14 APRIL

NOTHING TO SEE IN THE HOLY LAND, 1936

Noël Coward (*see* 12 February) wrote frequently to his friend Gladys Calthrop while touring the Mediterranean in 1936. His impressions of the Middle East were varied. Of Egypt he wrote: 'I am *very very gracious* about everything and drink a great deal of fucking awful coffee.' As for Palestine (then a British Protectorate), he wasn't much impressed by the people who lived there, the quarrels they pursued or the places they fought over. The great man of the theatre summed up the Holy Land in a message sent from Government House, Jerusalem.

Well Cock,

I flew here yesterday and it's a fair fucker except for the Arabs and Jews fighting and me having to faire the gentil promenade surrounded by armed guards... Really, the way everyone's gone on to me about the Holy Land. There isn't anything to see except places where Jesus might have done whatever it was but no one is sure because Jerusalem the G[olden] having been razed to the ground 11 times and no nonsense everything has been built over and over again on everything else and there are far too many churches. The Wailing Wall's a bit of all right tho'... This afternoon I bathed in the Dead Sea or rather sat in it because you can't do anything else and it feels most silly.

NOËL COWARD, *LETTERS*.

15 APRIL

THE SINKING OF THE *TITANIC*, 1912

In 1912 Harvey Collyer sold his grocery store in England and headed for Idaho, where he had bought an orchard and whose climate he hoped would be good for his wife Charlotte's health. Unfortunately he booked a cabin on the White Star liner RMS *Titanic*. He went down with the ship, but his wife Charlotte escaped with their daughter Marjorie and wrote the following account for an American women's magazine.

Loose ice was floating in the water. It was very cold. We had gone perhaps half a mile when the Officer ordered the men to cease rowing. No other boats were in sight and we did not even have a lantern to signal with. We lay there in silence and darkness in that utterly calm sea. I shall never forget the terrible beauty of the *Titanic* at that moment. She was tilted forward head down with her first funnel partly under the water. To me she looked like an enormous glow worm for she was alight from the rising waterline clear to her stern – electric light blazing in every cabin, lights on all her decks and lights to her mast head. No sound reached us except the music of the band which I seemed strange to say to be aware of for the first time... They were playing *Ragtime*, and they kept it up to the very end... At that distance it was impossible to recognise anyone on board, but I could make out groups of men on every deck. They were standing with arms crossed upon their chests and with lowered heads. I am sure that they were in prayer. On the boat deck that I had just left perhaps fifty men had come together. In the midst of them was a tall figure. This man had climbed upon a chain or a coil of rope so that he was raised far above the rest, his hands were stretched out as if he were pronouncing a blessing...

The end was very close. It came with a deafening roar that stunned me. Something in the very bowels of the *Titanic* exploded and millions of sparks shot up to the sky. This red spurt was fan shaped as it went up but the sparks dispersed in every direction in the shape of a fountain of fire.

Two other explosions followed dull and heavy as if below the surface. The *Titanic* broke into two before my eyes. The fore part was already partly under the water. It wallowed over and vanished instantly. The stern reared straight on end and seemed poised on the ocean for many seconds. They seemed minutes to us. It was only then that the electric lights on board went out.

Before the darkness came I saw hundreds of human bodies clinging to the wreck or jumping into the water. Cries more terrible than I have ever heard rung in my ears. I turned my face away but I looked round the next moment and saw the other half of the ship slip below the surface as easily as a pebble in a pond. I shall always remember that last moment as the most hideous of the whole disaster.

QUOTED IN D. HYSLOP ET AL., *TITANIC VOICES*.

16 APRIL

HERMITICALLY SEALED IN TIBET, 1907

While visiting a monastery in Tibet the Swedish explorer Sven Hedin (1865–1952) was fascinated by the confined existence of its Lama Rimpoche, or Holy Monk.

———·•·———

Every morning a bowl of tsamba [roasted barley flour], and perhaps a small pat of butter, were shoved in to him. He got water from a spring that bubbled in the interior of the cave. Every morning the empty bowl was withdrawn and refilled. Every sixth day he got a pinch of tea, and twice a month a few sticks, which he could ignite with a fire-steel. Should the lama who brought him his daily food address him through the opening, he would bring down upon himself eternal damnation. He was therefore silent. Should the immured man speak to the serving-brother, he would sacrifice all credit for his years of solitary meditation. If the serving-brother found the bowl untouched when he pulled it out, he understood that the recluse was either ill or dead. He would then push the bowl back in again and walk away in dejection. If the bowl remained untouched the following day, and altogether for six days, the cave was broken open; for then it was safe to assume that the recluse had died. The dead man was then carried out and his body destroyed by fire, like those of the saints...

I could hardly tear myself away from the place. In there, only a few feet away from me, was a man, possessed of will-power compared to which all else became insignificant. He had renounced the world; he was already dead; he belonged to eternity. The soldier going towards inevitable death is a hero; but he does it once. The Lama Rimpoche's physical life persisted through decades, and his suffering lasted until death liberated him. He had an unquenchable longing for death. The Lama Rimpoche fascinated me irresistibly.

SVEN HEDIN, MY LIFE AS AN EXPLORER.

17 APRIL

THE GARDEN OF EDEN, 1958

While in pursuit of buried treasure on the Seychelles, author Ian Fleming (*see* 16 March) visited the pristine forest of the Vallée de Mai on the island of Praslin – home to the Coco de Mer palm and also, by repute, the Garden of Eden.

The great trunks of the trees rise straight as gun-barrels to the green shell-bursts a hundred feet above your head and above them again the broken patches of blue sky seem to belong to quite a different, a more modern world of familiar people and familiar shapes. Here, down below, you have seen none of it before and you gaze with curiosity at these elephantine vegetables, many of them over 600 years old, and think how odd it must have been then.

Everyone who has visited the Vallais de Mai has been struck by the strange sense of original sin that hangs in this secret place. It comes partly from the grotesque impudicity of the huge fruit of the female tree – the largest fruit in the world – and from the phallic shape of the inflorescence of the male, but also from the strong aroma of animal sweat the trees exude. The natives will not go there at night-time. When it is dark, they say that the trees march down to the sea to bathe and then march back up the valley and make massive love under the moon. I can well believe it...

In due course, after indulging in a riot of strange thoughts, I found my way out on to the well-beaten mud path. Where I came out there was a piece of paper on the ground. It was a page from a child's exercise book – clearly a message to me from Eve. Repeated ten times down the page in a clear, young hand, were the words, 'Le chagrin la menait et elle versait des torrents de larmes amères.' ['Regret overcame her and she wept torrents of bitter tears.'] Puzzling over the significance of these melancholy words I walked thoughtfully down the mountain and back into the world.

IAN FLEMING, *TALK OF THE DEVIL*.

18 APRIL

RAPIDS ON THE URUBAMBA, 1960

The US naturalist Peter Matthiessen (born 1927) was travelling down the Rio Urubamba in Peru when he braved the whitewater canyon of Pongo de Mainique. He and his companions, including some of the local Machiguenga people, were aboard a balsa-wood raft, *Happy Days,* whose only safety feature was a few lianas strung fore and aft.

———•——

I was sitting in the fore part of the raft, behind Toribio and Alejandro. Then came the small cargo rack, and behind it Andres; I turned to look at him and he peered at me non-committally, like a beaver. We were just hanging on now, psychically as well as physically. Behind Andres, Raul and Agostino commenced to moan, and I faced forward again: the channel was narrowing, and ahead the water had turned white.

The Indians were yelling something and Andres called to me, his voice a little strained. 'Look out now,' he said. 'Hang on with all you've got.' I got a death grip on the lianas. Alejandro was staring forward at the waves, and even the back of his head looked surprised. The waves had not looked very high at first, but this was because we had seen only the crests of them; the waterfall between the raft and the waves had not been apparent in the rain. 'Alejandro,' I said, 'Be ready now.' He nodded rapidly and flashed a kind of smile in a quick half-turn of his head. This was all he had time for. The Machiguengas were yipping and grunting, and Raul was making a special sound of his own that came from somewhere in his pelvis, a sound a man might make when, having been confronted with the imminence of his own death, he was then punched in the stomach. The next moment, forsaking their paddles, they howled as one and sprang for the lianas, for there was nothing more they could do; we seemed to slide sideways down the waterfall, and then we were looking up from the bottom of a hole, with the waves caving in on us from impossible heights.

PETER MATTHIESSEN, *THE CLOUD FOREST.*

19 APRIL

THE VIEW FROM BELOW, 1927

The zoologist William Beebe was nearing the end of his stay in Haiti (*see* 4 February) when he paused on the seabed for a moment's contemplation. A pioneer of underwater exploration, he was perpetually fascinated by the play of colours beneath the waves.

Toward the end of the dive I sat on white sand and watched the surface above me. The sea breeze had sprung up and it was fairly rough. The view from beneath was of green, wrinkled, translucent ceiling cloth, never still for a moment, crinkling and uncrinkling, waving and flapping as in a breeze, or rather cross breezes. It was decidedly green in comparison with the ever more blue distance, – turquoise green in the sunlight, changing toward greenish glaucous in shadow. As to the distance, I can never get away from the idea of the most diluted, ethereal ultramarine, and yet my mind knows that a dozen other colors are somehow in it.

As to the opacity of the ceiling, I thought it absolute until I threw my head back as far as I dared, and saw, almost directly overhead, facets of clarity, appearing and vanishing, showing me an instant's patch of sky, a momentary glimpse of friends or boat – of that world to which it seemed at this moment inconceivable that I belonged. But anywhere except straight above me, the ceiling of the bay was watered gauze.

WILLIAM BEEBE, *BENEATH TROPIC SEAS.*

20 APRIL

POLAR FEAT, POLAR FRAUD, 1908

Frederick Cook (1865–1940) was Robert Peary's compatriot and rival in the race for the North Pole (*see* 9 April). He claimed to have reached it in 1908, a full year ahead of Peary, a victory that was at first hailed by the geographical community. But in the absence of proof, and with several other cases of deception laid at his door, he was swiftly dismissed as a cheat. Some still say that Cook beat Peary; others insist that they were both frauds.

As we lifted the midnight's sun to the plane of the midday sun, the shifting Polar desert became floored with a sparkling sheen of millions of diamonds, through which we fought a way to ulterior and greater glory.

Our leg cramps eased and our languid feet lifted buoyantly from the steady drag as the soul arose to effervescence. Fields of rich purple, lined with running liquid gold, burning with flashes of iridescent colors, gave a sense of gladness long absent from our weary life. The ice was much better. We still forced a way over large fields, small pressure areas and narrow leads. But, when success is in sight, most troubles seem lighter. We were thin, with faces burned, withered, frozen and torn in fissures, with clothes ugly from overwear. Yet men never felt more proud than we did, as we militantly strode off the last few steps to the world's very top.

FREDERICK COOK, *MY ATTAINMENT OF THE POLE*.

21 APRIL

ALONE IN ANTARCTICA, 1934

By now the polar night had descended on the Bolling Advance Base, and Richard Byrd was far less keen on the beauties of Antarctica than he had hitherto been (*see* 13 April). His mission – ostensibly to gather meteorological data – was rapidly turning into a personal trial of introspection and endurance.

The morning is the hardest time. It is hard enough anywhere for a man to begin the day's work in darkness; where I am it is doubly difficult. One may be a long time realizing it, but cold and darkness deplete the body gradually; the mind turns sluggish; and the nervous system slows up in its responses. This morning I had to admit to myself that I was lonely. Try as I may, I find I can't take my loneliness casually; it is too big. But I must not dwell on it. Otherwise I am undone.

At home I usually awaken instantly, in full possession of my faculties. But that's not the case here. It takes me some minutes to collect my wits; I seem to be groping in cold reaches of interstellar space, lost and bewildered. The room is a non-dimensional darkness, without shadow or substance; even after all these days I sometimes ask myself: Where am I? What am I doing here? I discover myself straining, as if trying to hear something in a place where no sound could possibly exist. Ah, yes. Tick-tick, tick-tick-tick, tick. The busy, friendly voices of the register and the thermograph on the shelves, each distinct and dramatic – sounds I can understand and follow, even as a mariner emerging from the darkness of the boundless ocean can recognize and follow a coast by the bell buoys offshore.

RICHARD BYRD, *ALONE*.

22 APRIL

THE SEEDY SIDE OF RANGOON, 1936

Pausing at Rangoon on the next stage of his global circumnavigation (*see* 31 March), Jean Cocteau was drawn inexorably to the seedier side of town. He embarked on a night-time journey, hauled by a rickshaw driver who trotted 'almost airborne between the shafts'.

———————

Not infrequently a tall woman knotting her chignon with a maidenly gesture turns round to reveal the hairy face of a young Sikh. The Sikhs, of whom there are quite a number, and who were once a warrior race, counterbalance the Chinese invasion. While the latter offer the barber even their armpits, chests and legs, the Sikhs have not even the right to have the hair on their faces or heads cut. Later, on the road which brings us back from the Chinese quarter into the Sikh quarter, the people will scatter the ground with sleeping corpses. These masculine Amazons sleep on the ground, anywhere, in front of the bungalows, their limbs intertwined like sea-horses and spillikins...

The arrows of fatigue riddle these unarmed and entangled heaps of warriors. They sleep, their profiles turned upwards, a hand stretched away from their bodies, their long hair let down, They sleep with their eyes open. The whites of their eyes star their nocturnal faces and a red trickle of betel juice oozes from the corner of their parted lips.

It is next to impossible for our coolie to avoid them and find a passage for the rickshaw wheels. A wheel passes over an arm, a leg, without waking the strange heap riveted to the ground. And everywhere the insidious poppy spreads its deep, forbidden odour.

JEAN COCTEAU, *MY JOURNEY ROUND THE WORLD*.

23 APRIL

ON THE BERLIN OVERGROUND, 1922

The Austrian writer Joseph Roth (1894–1939) found Berlin's public transport system a never-ending source of fascination and conjecture. In 1922 he explained the allure of the S-Bahn (*Stadtbahn*), the overground railway.

Sometimes a ride on the S-Bahn is more instructive than a voyage to distant lands. Experienced travellers will confirm that it is sufficient to see a single lilac shrub in a dusty city courtyard to understand the deep sadness of all the hidden lilac trees anywhere in the world...

It's a curious thing, how much the people who live in houses bordering the S-Bahn resemble one another. It's as though there were a single extended family of them, living along the S-Bahn lines and overlooking the viaducts.

I have come to know one or two apartments near certain stations really quite well. It's as if I'd often been to visit there, and I have a feeling I know how the people who live there talk and move. They all have a certain amount of noise in their souls from the constant din of passing trains, and they're quite incurious because they've gotten used to the fact that every minute countless other lives will glide by them, leaving no trace.

There is always an invisible, impenetrable strangeness between them and the world alongside. They are no longer even aware of the fact that their days and their doings, their nights and their dreams, are all filled with noise. The sounds seem to have come to rest on the bottom of their consciousness, and without them no impression, no experience the people might have, feels complete.

JOSEPH ROTH, *WHAT I SAW.*

24 APRIL

SAILING SOLO ROUND THE WORLD, 1895

In 1898 the Canadian-born Joshua Slocum (1844–1909) became the first person to sail single-handed around the globe – and he did so in the *Spray,* a ship he had built himself. He began his remarkable journey on this April day in 1895 from the eastern US seaboard.

I had resolved on a voyage around the world, and as the wind on the morning of April 24, 1895, was fair, at noon I weighed anchor, set sail, and filled away from Boston, where the *Spray* had been moored snugly all winter. The twelve-o'clock whistles were blowing just as the sloop shot ahead under full sail. A short board was made up the harbor on the port tack, then coming about she stood seaward, with her boom well off to port, and swung past the ferries with lively heels. A photographer on the outer pier at East Boston got a picture of her as she swept by, her flag at the peak throwing its folds clear. A thrilling pulse beat high in me. My step was light on deck in the crisp air. I felt that there could be no turning back, and that I was engaging in an adventure the meaning of which I thoroughly understood. I had taken little advice from any one, for I had a right to my own opinions in matters pertaining to the sea. That the best of sailors might do worse than even I alone was borne in upon me not a league from Boston docks, where a great steamship, fully manned, officered, and piloted, lay stranded and... broken in two over a ledge. So in the first hour of my lone voyage I had proof that the *Spray* could at least do better than this full-handed steamship, for I was already farther on my voyage than she.

JOSHUA SLOCUM, *SAILING ALONE AROUND THE WORLD.*

25 APRIL

THE SHOCKING STATE OF WALATA, 1352

Ibn Battuta (1304–68/9) was a Moroccan scholar who went on pilgrimage to Mecca in 1325, aged twenty-one, and thereafter just kept on going. For almost thirty years he travelled the length and breadth of the Islamic world before returning to his homeland. On the final leg of his odyssey he dipped down into the Sahara, spending most of April and June 1352 in the town of Iwalatan (Walata, in present-day Mauretania). Having accumulated a veritable flock of wives during his transglobal voyages he was surprisingly prudish when he saw how Saharan Muslims carried on.

The women are of surpassing beauty, and are shown more respect than the men. The state of affairs amongst these people is indeed extraordinary. Their men show no signs of jealousy whatever; no one claims descent from his father, but on the contrary from his mother's brother. A person's heirs are his sister's sons, not his own sons. This is a thing which I have seen nowhere in the world except among the Indians of Malabar. But those are heathens; *these* are Muslims...

The women there have 'friends' and 'companions' amongst the men outside their own families, and the men in the same way have 'companions' amongst the women of other families. A man may go into his house and find his wife entertaining her 'companion' but he takes no objection to it. One day at Iwalatan I went into the qadi's house, after asking his permission to enter, and found him with a young woman of remarkable beauty. When I saw her I was shocked and turned to go out, but she laughed at me, instead of being overcome by shame, and the qadi said to me 'Why are you going out? She is my companion.' I was amazed at their conduct, for he was a theologian and a pilgrim to boot. I was told that he had asked the sultan's permission to make the pilgrimage that year with his 'companion' (whether this one or not I cannot say) but the sultan would not grant it.

IBN BATTUTA, *TRAVELS IN ASIA AND AFRICA*.

26 APRIL

JAPANESE TINDERBOX, 1867

In 1865, the 19-year-old Marquis de Beauvoir left France with a group of aristocratic friends on a voyage around the world. Two years later, after many adventures, they reached Yokohama, Japan. There, they were awoken one night by a fire in a neighbouring property. The marquis and his party were dismissive of local attempts at fire-fighting – the blaze was finally extinguished by men from an English ship – but were in awe of Japanese house builders.

At three o'clock in the morning we are awoke suddenly by the sound of a most infernal din, and, while rubbing our eyes, are dazzled by a great glare. There is a fire in the town. The street is filled with the noise of carts and wheels, and we hear nothing but loud exclamations of 'ohaiho!' Bodies of Japanese firemen are hastening forwards, and (how polite these people are!) saying good morning to each other in this noisy fashion as they pass under our windows... The brigade wear high iron helmets ornamented with horns, bronze masks, cuirasses, gauntlets, thigh-pieces, and the whole panoply of knightly armour, and with great noise work a pump, which throws an imperceptible stream of water something like that in a certain fountain at Brussels... The officers wear gilt or silver helmets, as if they were on the stage; and the captain, perched on the top of a church porch, directs his cohorts by means of a kind of *vexillum* [banner] with a gilt handle, a great pasteboard machine which serves as a rallying signal...

This town is a perfect tinderbox, built as it is entirely of wood, with braziers and quantities of lanterns in every house. Last November, during a violent gale of wind, it was entirely burnt down, and as it is a town of shopkeepers you may suppose what a disaster that was. But the Japanese are not of a melancholy turn of mind; three days after the fire they began to rebuild; and, by the way, it is very interesting to see them building a house! In some parts of the world people begin building at the foundation;

here it is just the contrary! First, the roof is made upon the ground and covered with little wooden tiles, two fingers wide and as thin as paper; then this is raised and supported on four posts, and in less than no time the many-folded transparent screen which serves as a wall, is slipped into double grooves, and you have a charming house, finished to minuteness in its smallest details and built without a single nail! In the whole of Japan there are only three or four general varieties of plans of houses, the basis of all is the mat. Each mat is about six feet long by three broad; so you have houses of six, twelve, eighteen, or twenty-four mats, all perfect marvels of joiner's work, of elegance and cleanliness.

MARQUIS DE BEAUVOIR, *THE CONCLUSION OF A VOYAGE ROUND THE WORLD*.

27 APRIL

BAIKONUR, STAIRWAY TO THE STARS, 2000

Alan Lothian (1947–2010), a Scottish writer working for the European Space Agency, gave his friends an unofficial glimpse into his mission to Baikonur, Kazakhstan, site of Russia's space launch facility. The night before departure he had stayed up later than was wise and when packing forgot some of the essentials.

Land at Baikonur, which turns out to be about 5,000 sq km of industrial wasteland set like a jewel amidst about five billion sq km of ballsachingly flat, boring and frequently radio-active Kazakh steppe. Stagger out of plane into icy wind and whimper with regret for forgotten coat. Queue at customs shack where people shout at each other in Russian and Kazakh. Climb into dilapidated bus, where we meet thuggish-looking driver Boris (yes, Boris) and drive for forty-five mins on badly potholed road, passing assorted crumbling and rusting industrial architecture and abandoned vehicles before stopping at launch and assembly site for Rus space shuttle *Buran*, cancelled due to lack of roubles in 1988.

Huge rockets, shuttles moulder beneath leaking roof 200 feet high. Wind penetrates ribs as climb stairway to stars on nearby launch gantry, reached by way of rickety steel plates over weeping stained puddles. Regret absence of Sturdy Boots. Stairway to stars rusted through at about 120-foot level where wind in any case appalling beyond belief; descend, shivering and watch Italian airforce Tenente-Colonnello chase flying gold-braided hat through yet more rust and rubble. Charismatic Russian rocket scientist appears from nowhere and tells tales of Great Days and Present Woes, incompetently translated by girl Rus interpreter into English, which is then translated into Italian mainly by me.

All heartbreakingly sad, so retire as potential hypothermia case to bus and bottle of whisky self has wisely secreted in baggage. At least did not forget whisky.

ALAN LOTHIAN, PRIVATE CORRESPONDENCE.

28 APRIL

THE WHITE MAN'S FEET, 1877

During his transcontinental African expedition (*see* 3 February), Henry Morton Stanley took with him a small army of black porters and three white men, of whom the incautious Frank Pocock was, by this time, the last survivor – though not for long: he too would eventually perish under Stanley's command. But in April 1877 they were battling their way down the Congo.

Though I had kept one pair of worn-out shoes by me, my last new pair had been put on in the jungles of doleful Uregga, and now six weeks' rough wear over the gritty iron and clink-stone, trap, and granite blocks along the river had ground through soles and uppers, until I began to feel anxious. As for Frank, he had been wearing sandals made out of my leather portmanteaus, and slippers out of our gutta-percha pontoon; but climbing over the rocks and rugged steeps wore them to tatters in such quick succession, that it was with utmost difficulty that I was enabled, by appealing to the pride of the white man, to induce him to persevere in the manufacture of sandals for his own use. Frequently, on suddenly arriving in camp from my wearying labours, I would discover him with naked feet, and would reprove him for shamelessly exposing his white feet to the vulgar gaze of the aborigines! In Europe this would not be considered indelicate, but in barbarous Africa the feet should be covered as much as the body; for there is a small modicum of superiority shown even in clothing the feet.

H.M. STANLEY, *THROUGH THE DARK CONTINENT*, VOLUME II.

29 APRIL

THE DEPARTURE OF THE *KON-TIKI*, 1947

The previous day, the Norwegian adventurer Thor Heyerdahl (1914–2002) and five fellow Scandinavians had left Peru on a balsa-wood raft called *Kon-Tiki*. Their goal – in which they were eventually successful – was to prove that Polynesia could have been settled in pre-Columbian times by South Americans using similar vessels.

At the moment the steering arrangements were our greatest problem. The raft was built exactly as the Spaniards described it, but there was no one living in our time who could give us a practical advance course in sailing an Indian raft. The problem had been thoroughly discussed among the experts on shore, but with meagre results. They knew just as little about it as we did. As the south-easterly wind increased in strength it was necessary to keep the raft on such a course that the sail was filled from astern. If the raft turned her side too much to the wind, the sail suddenly swung round and banged against cargo and men and bamboo cabin, while the whole raft turned round and continued on the same course stern first. It was a hard struggle, three men fighting with the sail and three others rowing with the long steering oar to get the nose of the wooden raft round and away from the wind. And as soon as we got her round the steersman had to take good care that the same thing did not happen again the next minute.

The steering oar, nineteen feet long, rested loose between two tholepins on a huge block astern. It was the same steering oar our native friends had used when we floated the timber down the Palenque in Ecuador. The long mangrove-wood pole was as tough as steel, but so heavy that it would sink if it fell overboard. At the end of the pole was a large oar-blade of firwood lashed on with ropes. It took all our strength to hold this long steering oar steady when the seas drove against it, and our fingers were tired out by the convulsive grip which was necessary to turn the pole so that the oar-blade stood straight up in the water. This last problem was solved by our lashing a cross-piece to the handle of the steering oar, so that we had a lever to turn. And meanwhile the wind increased.

By the late afternoon the trade wind was already blowing at full strength. It quickly stirred up the ocean into roaring seas which swept against us from astern. Now we fully realized for the first time that here was the sea itself coming to meet us; it was bitter earnest now, our communications were cut. Whether things went well now would depend entirely on the balsa raft's good qualities in the open sea. We knew that from now onwards we should never get another on-shore wind or chance of turning back. We had got into the real trade wind, and every day would carry us farther and farther out to sea. The only thing to do was to go ahead under full sail; if we tried to turn homewards we should only drift farther out to sea stern first. There was only one possible course, to sail before the wind with our bows towards the sunset. And, after all, that was just the object of our voyage, to follow the sun in its path, as we thought *Kon-Tiki* and the old sun-worshippers must have done when they were chased out to sea from Peru.

THOR HEYERDAHL, *THE KON-TIKI EXPEDITION.*

30 APRIL

TIFFIN UNDER THE CAMPHOR-TREE, 1938

Having recently visited the front during the Sino-Japanese War, Auden and Isherwood (*see* 4 March) now went to the hill station of Kuling in the hope of interviewing Chiang Kai-shek, the leader of China's Nationalist forces. They were unimpressed by what they saw, describing him as lounging in a deckchair surrounded by bankers and German military advisers. But their hotel, 'Journey's End', made up for the great man's shortcomings.

Our rooms were large and the beds very comfortable. Each bedroom was provided with a Bible and a volume of pornographic French literature. If you stayed at Journey's End long enough you could work through twenty of them at least. 'You'll have tiffin under the camphor-tree; it keeps off the insects,' said the headmaster (for surely this was a preparatory school?) or the abbot (for perhaps, after all, it was a monastery)...

So we had tiffin under the camphor-tree, aware, in a trance of pleasure, of the smell of its leaves; of the splash of the stream over the stones; of the great gorge folding back, like a painting by Salvator Rosa, into the wooded hills behind the house. There were snipe to eat, and rainbow trout. It was all far, far too beautiful to be real. 'If I make the sign of the Hammer and Sickle,' I said, 'everything will disappear.' And Auden agreed: 'It's the Third Temptation of the Demon.' One could arrive for the weekend and stay fifteen years – eating, sleeping, swimming; standing for hours in a daze of stupefied reverence before the little Ming tomb in the garden; writing, in the porch, the book that was altogether too wonderful to finish and too sacred ever to publish.

W.H. AUDEN AND CHRISTOPHER ISHERWOOD, *JOURNEY TO A WAR*.

MAY

1 MAY

THE START OF THE NEAPOLITAN SUMMER, 1944

Stationed in Naples as a British intelligence officer in the penultimate year of the Second World War, Norman Lewis (1908–2003) was desk-bound for much of the time and so had ample opportunity to record the seasonal changes in Neapolitan life.

Today the arrival of summer was announced by the cry of the seller of venetian blinds – sad to the point of anguish in our narrow street – *s'e 'nfucato 'o sole* (the sun's turned fiery). Immediately, as if in response to a signal all Naples had awaited, the tempo of life changed and slowed down. As the melancholy howl was heard, first in the distance, then coming closer, people seemed to move cautiously into the shade, and those who hadn't already let down their blinds did so. Fans came out, girls walked about shading their eyes, and the seller of black-market cigarettes immediately under our window unfolded a Communist newspaper and held it over his head. We are told that after today stray dogs are liable to be picked up by the municipal catchers and knocked over the head.

Whitsun draws near – the Easter of Roses, as they call it in Naples. On Saturday the general hope and expectation is that the blood of San Gennaro [the patron saint of Naples] will liquefy in a satisfactory manner. It is believed by Neapolitans of all political creeds and degrees of religious conviction that the fortunes of the city depend on this phenomenon, and many advertisements have appeared in the newspapers paid for by commercial firms or political parties wishing the community 'a good and prosperous miracle'.

NORMAN LEWIS, *NAPLES '44.*

2 MAY

A LETTER FROM AFGHANISTAN, 1934

The English traveller Robert Byron (1905–41) was on a prolonged trip through Central Asia when he came to the border between Persia and Afghanistan. Faced with two routes to his ultimate destination, India, he chose the shortest and notoriously most hazardous one. Byron, who wrote to his mother at every opportunity – and later used these letters, along with his journals, to write his classic travel book, *The Road to Oxiana* – explained why he felt compelled to travel and, perhaps unnecessarily, why his mother shouldn't be worried by a journey she'd never have heard of had he not told her.

You must *not* fuss if you don't hear for 6 or 8 weeks or even 12 weeks, if we go on. You must promise not to fuss when you get this letter – I shall know. It won't be fair if you do – because although not exactly formidable, it will be a fairly difficult journey and if I have the additional worry of thinking you are worrying, it will be more than I can bear and I probably *shall* get ill, in which case it will be all your fault... You must remember that I don't travel merely out of idle curiosity or to have adventures (which I loathe). It is a sort of *need* – a sort of grindstone to temper one's character and get rid of the cloying thoughts of Europe. It is how I develop. I have become quite a different person from what I was when I went away, and the change is for the better.

ROBERT BYRON, *LETTERS HOME.*

3 MAY

A TRANSPARENT CATHEDRAL, 1838

While on a sketching tour of Italy in 1838, the English poet and artist Edward Lear (1812–88) based himself for a while in Rome. Despite his claims to have no truck with papal pomp and frippery, he was nevertheless mightily impressed by the illuminations he saw when, on returning from a painting trip, he became embroiled in the celebrations for Holy Week.

I returned in time for Holy Week – but I did not like its ceremonies at all; I hate crowds & bustle. The grandest of all is on Thursday at noon when the Pope comes into the great gallery of St. Peter's & the Piazza is full of people kneeling while he blesses them. The illumination is also *wonderful*. About dusk men (400) are slung by ropes (!!!) all over the dome and colonnades of St. Peter's – where they put little paper lamps in regular places – till the evening grows darker – every line, column & window becomes gradually marked by dots of light! It has the exact appearance of a transparent church – with light seen through pricked holes... – about 9 o'clock, by an astonishing series of signals, the whole fabric blazes with hundreds of torches; immense iron basins full of oil & shavings are suspended *between* the little lamps, & these all at once burst out into light! I can only compare it to a stupendous diamond crown in the dark night. It is the most beautiful thing in the world of its sort.

EDWARD LEAR, *LEAR'S ITALY*.

4 MAY

OUR MAN IN FREETOWN, 1942

During the Second World War, while working for the Secret Intelligence Service, Graham Greene (*see* 26 January) was sent to Sierra Leone. He was not an accomplished spy, though in the circumstances that mattered little: in Sierra Leone there was nothing to spy on. He came to loathe the place, but in a letter to his mother written shortly after his arrival, he described the capital, Freetown, with guarded optimism.

Last night I had my first film in a long time. I went on board one of the naval ships and saw the full length Disney *The Reluctant Dragon*... One sat on deckchairs on deck, and though the sound was a bit off, it was quite delightful with the lights of Freetown over the water.

Freetown always looks its best from the water. On shore after the rain the plague of house flies has come back to my part. And at night there are far too many objects flying and crawling for my liking. Wherever one wants to put one's hand suddenly, to turn on a switch or what not, there always seems to be a gigantic spider. Whenever one kills something which has flopped on the floor the ants come out and get to work, stripping the corpse and then heaving and pushing the skeleton towards the door. Last night I counted a slow procession of four black hearse-like corpses: you couldn't see the ants underneath. And I never get quite used to seeing a vulture sitting complacently on my roof as I come home.

GRAHAM GREENE, *A LIFE IN LETTERS*.

5 MAY

A CROSSROAD IN MAINE, 1850

In 1850 the Concord Railroad and the Boston & Maine Railroad met at a point in the Maine wilderness. The 45-year-old New England author Nathaniel Hawthorne (1804–64), himself a resident of Concord, Massachusetts, found the junction mesmerizing.

On the Concord rail is the train of cars, with the locomotive puffing, and blowing off its steam, and making a great bluster in that lonely place, while along the other railroad stretches the desolate track, with the withered weeds growing up betwixt the two lines of iron, all so desolate. And anon you hear a low thunder running along these iron rails; it grows louder; an object is seen afar off; it approaches rapidly, and comes down upon you like fate, swift and inevitable. In a moment, it dashes along in front of the station-house, and comes to a pause, the locomotive hissing and fuming in its eagerness to go on. How much life has come at once into this lonely place! Four or five long cars, each, perhaps, with fifty people in it, reading newspapers, reading pamphlet novels, chattering, sleeping; all this vision of passing life! A moment passes, while the luggage-men are putting on the trunks and packages; then the bell strikes a few times, and away goes the train again, quickly out of sight of those who remain behind, while a solitude of hours again broods over the station-house, which, for an instant, has thus been put in communication with far-off cities, and then remains by itself, with the old, black, ruinous church, and the black, old farm-house, both built years and years ago, before railroads were ever dreamed of.

NATHANIEL HAWTHORNE, *COMPLETE WORKS*, VOLUME IX.

6 MAY

ESCAPE FROM AUSTRIA, 1917

When Stefan Zweig's pacifist play *Jeremiah* was published at Easter 1917, the Austrian wartime authorities banned its production. Luckily, the Zürich Stadttheater offered to stage it and invited him to attend the premiere. To his surprise Zweig (*see* 22 February) was given permission to leave the country and a few weeks later he caught a train to neutral Switzerland. The memory, if not the exact date, of his stop at the border town of Buchs remained imprinted on his mind.

———•·•———

It is hard to make intelligible what the transition from a walled-in and half-starved country at war to a neutral zone signified at that time. It took but a few minutes from one station to another, but in the very first second one was sensible of such a change as that of suddenly stepping from a closed suffocating room into invigorating and snow-filled air, of something like a giddiness which trickled palpably from the brain through all one's nerves and senses... Passengers leaped from the train and found there – their first surprise! – at the buffet all the things which they had long forgotten as belonging to the commonplaces of life; there were golden oranges, bananas; chocolate and ham, things which we were used to getting only by slinking to back doors, were frankly displayed; there was bread and meat, obtainable without bread cards or meat cards – and truly like hungry beasts they attacked the cheap magnificence. There was a post and telegraph office from which one could write and wire uncensored to the four corners of the world. There lay French, Italian, and English newspapers which one could buy, and read with impunity. Here the interdicted was available, while five minutes distant the available was interdicted. The whole paradox of European wars became almost physically clear to me through this contiguity. In the tiny village beyond, the posters and signs of which one could read from here with the naked eye, men had been taken out of every little house or hut and shipped to the Ukraine and Albania, to murder and be murdered, while here, within eyeshot, men of like age sat with their wives peacefully before their ivy-framed doors, smoking their pipes. I found myself asking whether the fish in this frontier rivulet were belligerents on the right bank and neutral on the left. In the moment of crossing the border I was already thinking differently, more freely, more actively, less servilely, and on the very next day I had evidence that not only our mental state but our physical organism as well declines within a world at war; the guest of relatives, after dinner I drank nonchalantly a cup of black coffee and smoked a Havana cigar when suddenly I became dizzy and experienced violent palpitations. After many months of *ersatz* supplies my body and my nerves proved unequal to real coffee and real tobacco; the change from the abnormality of war to the normality of peace called for a corporal adjustment, too.

That unsteadiness, that agreeable dizziness, carried over to the mental plane. Every tree struck me as more beautiful, every mountain boulder, every prospect as more gracious; for, inside a country at war the rhythmical calm of a meadow appears to the gloomy eye to be insolent indifference on Nature's part, each purple sunset recalls spilled blood; while here, where peace reigned normally, the noble aloofness of Nature had again become natural and I loved Switzerland as I had never loved it before.

STEFAN ZWEIG, *THE WORLD OF YESTERDAY*.

7 MAY

THE TURKISH INTERIOR, 1907

While travelling through southwestern Anatolia in 1907, Gertrude Bell (*see* 5 February) visited Lake Bey-Sheher (Beyşehir). She was struck by the difference between the Turkish coast, with its bustling community of Greek traders, and the more sombre cast of the hinterland.

A melancholy land, in spite of its lakes and mountains, though I like it. You leave the bright and varied coast line which was Greece, full of vitality, full of the breath of the sea and the memory of an active enterprising race, and with every step into the interior you feel Asia, the real heart of Asia.

Monotonous, colourless, lifeless, unsubdued by a people whose thoughts travel no further than to the next furrow, who live and die and leave no mark upon the great plains and the barren hills – such is Central Asia, of which this country is a true part. And that is why the Roman roads make so deep an impression on one's mind. They impressed the country itself, they implied a great domination, they tell of a people that overcame the universal stagnation. It was very hot and still; clouds of butterflies drifted across the path and there was no other living thing except a stork or two in the marshy ground and here and there a herd of buffaloes with a shepherd boy asleep beside them. At the end of the lake a heavy thunderstorm gathered and crept along the low hills to the east and up into the middle of the sky.

GERTRUDE BELL, *THE LETTERS OF GERTRUDE BELL*, VOLUME I.

8 MAY

WATCHING PAINT DRY IN ST HELENA, 1966

Towards the end of his circumnavigation (*see* 6 February) Michel Mermod stopped at the island of St Helena. Once an important staging post in the Atlantic – and memorable as the location of Napoleon's final exile – it was now a neglected outpost of the British Empire, redolent of decline and depression. 'At every corner of the street,' he wrote, 'one meets boredom, face to face.'

Throughout my visit, I follow with fascination a scene which perfectly illustrates life on St Helena. On the very first day I notice two men in the main thoroughfare, stooping over the delicate and laborious task of repainting the white lines marking a parking place for a couple of dozen vehicles. I am not quite sure what attracted my attention; perhaps the high degree of concentration on the part of the two workmen, or perhaps their calculated slowness? I stop for a moment to observe them, and almost at once appreciate my initial misunderstanding. I am not dealing with anything as vulgar as workmen from the Public Transport Department, but with two artists! On the terrace of Jamestown they are painting, with masterful skill and for all posterity, the geometrical outlines of a parking place. Comfortably seated on the ground, they wield a dextrous and delicate brush. Their labours are often interrupted by long periods of meditation, during which they wait to be inspired afresh...

Day after day I note this same restrained enthusiasm. A week later, about two-thirds of the work is done. I should be wrong, though, to accuse these men of any misdemeanour... I am sure it is not congenital idleness which causes them to spin the job out. On the contrary, they are acting out of courtesy, wishing as far as possible to spare their boss the dramatic and almost insoluble worry of finding them something else to do.

MICHEL MERMOD, *THE VOYAGE OF THE GENÈVE*.

9 MAY

APPROACHING THE CHINA COAST, 1936

In May 1936, having left Burma behind (*see* 22 April), Jean Cocteau approached Hong Kong during his self-imposed challenge to circle the globe in eighty days.

The sailors have draped a snake-skin over the rails to dry. Eighty centimetres wide, six metres long, it forms the ideal foreground for an approach to China. The beiges, yellows, blacks, spots and geometric interlacing that adorn it give us a preview of all the opium-den rush mats and that characteristic gold smudge that patinates the most insignificant objects in use among the Chinese.

It is almost cold. The sea no longer has anything Japanese about it. It unfurls the grey scrolls of a wrinkled skin round the ship and as if under the pallor of enormous jelly-fish move black inky clouds which, cleft by the keel, are transformed into a fringe of violet ink that will become phosphorescent at night...

Dark islands with a single great white break at their edge, and lighthouses. Suddenly we became aware that it was dark, for Hongkong loomed up at an unexpected spot, visible through its lights alone, so oddly disposed all the way up the mountain that each light assumed the disturbing importance of a signal. This celestial mountain, gleaming with large constellations, could belong to no other coastline in the world, and Chinese night, composed of shadow, semi-darkness, mists and haloes, is unlike night anywhere else.

JEAN COCTEAU, *MY JOURNEY ROUND THE WORLD.*

10 MAY

UNDERCOVER TO SINAI, 1816

In 1816 the Swiss traveller Johann Burckhardt (1784–1817), known among other things for the discovery of ancient Petra, made an expedition to Mount Sinai. Like many other Westerners who investigated Islamic lands, he went in disguise. And like most of them he was eventually found out – though not quite yet.

———·•·———

Wishing to penetrate into a part of the country occupied by other tribes, it became important to conceal my pursuits, lest I should be thought a necromancer, or in search of treasures. In such cases many little stratagems must be resorted to by the traveller, not to lose entirely the advantage of making memoranda on the spot. I had accustomed myself to write when mounted on my camel, and proceeding at an easy walk; throwing the wide Arab mantle over my head, as if to protect myself from the sun, as Arabs do, I could write under it unobserved, even if another person rode close by me; my journal books being about four inches long and three broad, were easily carried in a waistcoat pocket, and when taken out could be concealed in the palm of the hand; sometimes I descended from my camel, and walking a little in front of my companions, wrote down a few words without stopping. When halting I lay down as if to sleep, threw my mantle over me, and could thus write unseen under it. At other times I feigned to go aside to answer a call of nature, and then crouched down, in the Arab manner, hidden under my cloak.

JOHANN BURCKHARDT, *Travels in Syria and the Holy Land*.

11 MAY

A SMALL TOWN IN UKRAINE, 1887

The Russian author Anton Chekhov (1860–1904) stopped at the Ukrainian town of Slavyansk while on pilgrimage to the 'Holy Mountains' monastery of Svyatogorsk, on the banks of the Donetz River. Conditions had been rudimentary so far, hence his joy on encountering 'Yakov Andreyich' – his private name for a chamber-pot.

The town is something like Gogol's Mirgorod.* There is a barber shop and a watchmaker, so presumably in a thousand years there will be a telephone. Circus posters are painted on walls and fences, alongside of them are burdocks and excrement; pigs, cows and sundry domesticated creatures promenade on green, dusty streets. Houses peep out cordially and affectionately, like good-humoured grannies; the pavements are soft, the streets wide, and the air is fragrant with lilac and acacia; the singing of nightingales, the croaking of frogs, barking, a harmonica, a woman's squeal – all that is heard from far.

I put up at Kulikov's hotel, and paid 75 copecks for a room. After sleeping on wooden couches and in troughs it was delightful to see a bed with a mattress, a wash basin and – oh magnanimity of Fate! – beloved Yakov Andreyich... Green boughs and westerly breezes push through the wide-open window. Stretching and screwing up my eyes like a tomcat, I order food and for 30 copecks I am served a mighty portion, larger than the biggest chignon, of roast beef, that is equally entitled to be called not only roast beef but also a chop, a beefsteak, and a little meat pillow with which I would certainly have cushioned my side had I not been as hungry as a dog.

ANTON CHEKHOV, *LETTERS*.

* Mirgorod is a town in Ukraine, but is also the title of a volume of short stories (1835) revolving around provincial life by Nikolai Gogol, himself a Ukrainian.

12 MAY

WELTSCHMERZ IN ROME, 1904

After a winter in Rome, the Bohemian-born Austrian poet Rainer Maria Rilke (1875–1926) began to pine for northern climes. Too sickly was the place for his liking, too monotonous its seasons, too bland its blooms, too fixed and backward-looking its society.

The Judas-tree flowered, flowered, and flowered, even from its trunk gushed the coagulated tripes of its bursting unfruitful blossom, and in a few weeks everything, anemones and clover and syringa and windflower, everything was drenched with the mauve of its mauve, God knows why – from laziness, from adaptation to circumstance, from lack of original idea. And even now the red roses, dying, take on this corpse-like mauve, and the strawberries have it if they lie for a day, and the sunsets belch it up, and it spreads over the clouds morning and evening. And the skies in which such cheap tints come and go, are sick and as though silted up; they are not everywhere, they do not, as the skies of the moor, the sea, and the plains do, play *round* things, they are not an endless beginning of the distance, they are finish, curtain, end, – and behind the last trees, which stand flat as stage-scenery against the indifferent photo-background, – everything stops. They are so rightly the skies above the Past; skies empty, deserted, sapped dry, sky-husks from which the last sweetness has long been drained. And as the sky is, so are the nights, and as the nights are, so is the voice of the nightingales. Where the nights are wide their note is deep, and they draw from it an infinite distance and carry it to an end. Here the nightingale is really only a lewd little bird with a frivolous song and an easily satisfied longing. In two nights you have grown accustomed to her call and you remark it with an inward reserve, as though you were afraid of injuring your own memories by any greater response, memories of nightingale-nights which are quite, quite, different.

RAINER MARIA RILKE, *SELECTED LETTERS*.

13 MAY

ON A TUNISIAN WATERFRONT, 1943

In 1943, the travel writer Norman Lewis (*see* 1 May) served in the British Intelligence Corps in North Africa. His unit, which could charitably be described as eccentric, was never quite sure why it had been posted to any particular place, let alone what it was meant to do when it got there. They gazed across a Tunisian seafront, as the last part of North Africa fell into Allied hands.

Lank, sad-eyed warehouses dominated the waterfront at La Goulette. The sun had flayed the paint from all the facades, and bleached out all the words where the advertisements had once been, leaving nothing but naked silvered wood, lurching cranes and abandoned tackle; hawsers, pulleys, chains insisted that this was a working port, but the ships had gone elsewhere. Air-raid shelters stood like concrete wigwams among the bomb craters. A Renault car had been sliced almost in half and pushed to the water's edge, and the once bright red stains on its ripped upholstery had turned black. In the exact centre of this desolation the French had erected a wonderfully decorated iron *pissoir* and this was visited throughout the day by tattered but scrupulous Arabs carrying cans of water for their ritual ablutions. When not washing their private parts they sat fishing over the edge of the quay for small, obscene-looking fish that crawled rather than swam among the seaweed clogging the piers. Oil from a spill in La Marsa slithered over the sea-water, stifling the waves under its coat of many colours. The place smelt of baked bladderweed, oil and dust. The bombs had torn a gap in the harbour wall and through it Tunis showed its small ivory teeth along the horizon, and when the hot breeze puffed over us from the direction of Rades, which was only four kilometres away, it often brought with it the noise of trumpets and drums. Otherwise the war had passed us by.

NORMAN LEWIS, *JACKDAW CAKE*.

14 MAY

WHO WILL PLAY FOR US TO DANCE?, 1927

Returning from the Congo (*see* 7 September), the French novelist André Gide (1869–1951) overheard the following conversations among his fellow-passengers. They capture exquisitely the casual prejudices of the age.

———·•·———

There are some children on board – from eleven to fourteen years old. The eldest, who is by far the most affected of the lot, declared to one of the little girls that when he grew up, he intended to be a 'literary critic or else pick up cigarette ends in the street. All or nothing. No medium. That's my motto.' I was hidden in the corner of the saloon, sheltered behind a number of *L'Illustration*, and listened to them indefatigably. How difficult it is to be natural at that age – for a white at any rate! One's single idea is to astonish other people – to make a show.

A little later I came across the same boy, leaning against the bulwarks, with a companion rather younger than himself; they were talking to a Swede.

'We French detest other nations – all of us French... don't we George?... Yes, it's a peculiar thing about the French that they can't endure other nations... Unless we allow that they have qualities – Oh! then, if we allow them qualities, we do it thoroughly.' (This last remark obviously made for the sake of his interlocutor, who looked very much amused – and no wonder.)

'I call a musician,' he said to the little girl, 'a person who understands what he plays. I don't call a person a musician who bangs on the piano just like people kicking niggers.' And, as he added, with an air of authority, that they should 'be put an end to' – not the niggers, perhaps, and certainly not the people who kick them, but the bad musicians – the little girl exclaimed indignantly:

'But then who will play for us to dance?'

ANDRÉ GIDE, *TRAVELS IN THE CONGO*.

15 MAY

HOSTAGE IN BURMA, 1824

The wife of a Baptist missionary in Burma, Ann Judson (1789–1826) found her fortitude tested on the outbreak of war: she was taken hostage when British East India Company forces invaded the kingdom in 1824, and after a British fleet sailed up to threaten Rangoon. It was an experience she described in a letter to her brother in the United States. Although Ann died in 1826, her husband Adoniram remained in harness until 1850. On the republication of her letters, the couple became minor celebrities in nineteenth-century America.

Government immediately ordered every person in Rangoon who wears a hat, to be taken prisoner, which was accordingly done. In the course of the succeeding night, Mr. Hough and myself were chained, and put into close confinement, under armed keepers. In the morning the fleet was in sight of the town, and our keepers were invited to massacre us the moment the first shot was fired upon the town. But when the firing commenced, our murderers were so effectually panic struck, that they all slunk away into one corner of the prison, speechless, and almost breathless. The next shot made our prison tremble and shake, as if it would be immediately down upon our heads. Our keepers now made for the prison door: we used every exertion to persuade them to remain, but all to no purpose; they broke open the door and fled. In a few moments after, the firing ceased; and we expected the troops were landing, and that we should be soon released; when, horrible to relate, about fifteen Burmans rushed into the prison, drew us out, stripped us of everything but pantaloons; our naked arms were drawn behind us, and corded as tightly as the strength of one man would permit; and we were almost literally carried through the streets upon the points of their spears, to the seat of judgement, and were made to sit upon our knees, with our bodies bending forward, for the convenience of the executioner, who was ordered that moment to behead us. None of us understood the order but Mr. Hough. He requested the executioner to desist a moment, and petitioned the Ray-woon to send him on board the frigate, and promised to use his influence to prevent any further firing upon the town. The linguists seconded the proposal, and pleaded that we might be reprieved for a few moments...

At this moment, several shots were sent very near us: the government people fled from the seat of judgement, and took refuge under the banks of a neighbouring tank. All the others fled from the town, but kept us before them: we were obliged to make our way as fast as possible, for the madness and terror of our attendants allowed no compliments.

We were soon overtaken by the government people, fleeing on horseback.

About a mile and a half from the town they halted, and we were again placed before them. Mr. Hough and the linguists renewed their petition. After a few moments his irons were taken off, and he was sent on board the frigate, with the most awful threatenings to himself and us, if he did not succeed.

The remainder of us were obliged again to resume our march. Finally, a part of us were confined in a strong building, at the foot of the golden pagoda. I, with two others, was taken into the pagoda, and confined in a strong building, and left under the care of a door-keeper. After dark this fellow, by the promise of a present, was induced to remove us into a kind of vault, which had but a small aperture, and was without windows: it afforded only sufficient air for the purpose of respiration...

The next morning early, we were searched for by our blood thirsty enemies, who, upon finding we were not in the room where they left us, concluded that we had escaped and fled. We expected every moment to be discovered, when to our great relief, we heard them cry out, 'The English are coming!' and they fled.

ANN JUDSON, *MEMOIR*.

16 MAY

GHOSTS OF BROTHELS PAST, 2002

In 2002 the US-based author Ariel Dorfman (born 1942) made a journey of rediscovery to Chile, the country where he had spent much of his youth.

We are standing in the midst of the ruins of Pampa Union, a town that did not produce even one ounce of nitrate, a town that produced instead pleasure and indulgence and illusions, a town of brothels and bars, opium dens and gambling joints, a town only visited now by the whirlwinds and the shifting sands.

I know about this town... a town that sprouted in the desert in 1912 to serve (and service) the twenty-seven surrounding nitrate communities, only to disappear forty years later like a fata morgana, a mirage devoured by the desert. A mere twenty residences of Pampa Union officially strutted the title of whorehouse, but in fact there were over two hundred of them... The town became so corrupt that at one point the authorities had to dismiss the whole police force. But none of the policemen left. They stayed on in Pampa Union and the next day there you could find them, each former officer of the law, administering a brothel.

I wander among the crumbling walls of this place of perdition... I stand inside what must have been a large reception hall, maybe a saloon. Almost square in its middle, the twisted stump of a tree blooms, germinating from who knows what hidden well of water, what hidden memory of past voluptuousness. I kick through the debris toward the back, where a series of brick and stucco delineate the cubbyhole rooms where love was dispensed by the hour to desperate men... I warily step over the scraps of what must have been a protecting wall, straight into the sun again. I wonder where they held the cockfights, how the liquor was delivered, who escorted the drunks out at dawn, what sort of post-coital card games were still being played as the sun came up.

ARIEL DORFMAN, *DESERT MEMORIES*.

17 MAY

'AWAY WE GO, AWAY, AWAY', 1839

When his expedition through Western Australia came to grief, the explorer George Grey (1812–98) decided to split the party. He himself made it home but the other group, which included a young Englishman, Frederick Smith, was not so lucky. Among the rescue team was an Aborigine named Warrup, who gave the following account of finding Smith's body.

The others continue returning; we go away, away; in the forest we see no water; we see no footsteps; we see some papers – the papers put by Mr Mortimer we see: still we go onwards, along the sea away, along the sea away, along the sea away: through the bush away, through the bush away; then along the sea away, along the sea away. We see white men – three of them we see. They cry out, 'Where is water?' Water we give them – brandy and water we give them. We sleep near the sea.

Away, away go we (I, Mr Roe and Kinchela), along the shore away, along the shore away, along the shore away. We see a paper, the paper of Mortimer and Spofforth. Away we go, away, away, along the shore away, away, away, a long distance we go. I see Mr Smith's footsteps ascending a sandhill, onwards I go regarding his footsteps. I see Mr Smith dead. We commence digging the earth.

Two sleeps had he been dead; greatly did I weep, and much I grieved. In his blanket folding him, we scraped away the earth.

We scrape the earth into the grave, we scrape the earth into the grave, a little wood we place in it. Much earth we heap upon it – much earth we throw up. No dogs can dig there, so much earth we throw up. The sun had just inclined to the westward as we laid him in the ground.

GEORGE GREY, *JOURNALS OF TWO EXPEDITIONS OF DISCOVERY*, VOLUME II.

18 MAY

GODS IN THE RAIN, 1916

Writing in 1916, T.E. Lawrence (1888–1935) described an incident during Britain's campaigns against Ottoman forces in the Middle East. 'Lawrence of Arabia', as he was known in Britain (though not so much in Arabia), was at the ancient site of Carchemish, on the Turkish–Syrian border, when he and his Kurdish companions were hit by a violent storm. Very rarely does warfare combine such extremes of antiquity, meteorology and melody.

There was a torrential burst of rain which hissed down in sheets, and rattled over the shingle in our court-yard like the footsteps of a great crowd of men; then there would come a clap of thunder, and immediately after a blue flash of lightning which made our open door and window livid gaps in the pitch-black wall... through which we caught odd glimpses of the sculpture outside shining in the rain and dazzle of light. I remember particularly the seven foot figure of a helmeted god striding along an inscription towards the doorway: – and the dripping jaws of the two lions of the pedestal which seemed in the alternate glare and shadow of the flashes to be grinning at us through the window. The musicians did not stop, but changed their song for a wild improvisation which kept time with the storm. The pipe shrilled out whenever the thunder pealed and fell down again slow and heavy for the strained silences in between. One did not realise that they were men playing independently: the rhythm seemed so born of the bursts of wind and rain, so made to bind together the elements of the night into one great thunder-song.

T.E. LAWRENCE, *LETTERS*.

19 MAY

THE BLUE GROTTO, 1831

The German composer Felix Mendelssohn (1809–47) was travelling through Italy when he stopped for a day on the island of Capri. As he explained in a letter to his sisters, he was keener on its depths than its heights.

Next day we went to Capri. This place has something Eastern in its aspect, with the glowing heat reflected from its rocky white walls, its palm trees, and the round domes of the churches that look like mosques. The sirocco was burning, and rendered me quite unfit to enjoy anything; for really climbing up five hundred and thirty-seven steps to Anacapri in this frightful heat, and then coming down again, is toil only fit for a horse. True, the sea is wondrously lovely, looking down on it from the summit of the bleak rock, and through the singular fissures of the jagged peaks...

But above all, I must tell you of the blue grotto... The colour is the most dazzling blue I ever saw, without shadow or cloud, like a pane of opal glass; and as the sun shines down, you can plainly discern all that is going on under the water, while the whole depths of the sea, with its living creatures are disclosed. You can see the coral insects and polypuses clinging to the rocks, and far below, fishes of different species meeting and swimming past each other... Every stroke of the oars echoes strangely under the vault, and as you row round the walls, new objects come to light. I do wish you could see it, for the effect is singularly magical. On turning towards the opening by which you entered, the daylight seen through it seems bright orange, and by moving even a few paces, you are entirely isolated under the rock, in the sea, with its own peculiar sunlight: it is as if you were actually living under the water for a time.

FELIX MENDELSSOHN, *LETTERS FROM ITALY AND SWITZERLAND.*

20 MAY

A CELEBRITY IN TOMSK, 1890

In 1890 Anton Chekhov (*see* 11 May) forsook his comfortable Moscow life for an overland voyage to the far eastern island of Sakhalin – a penal settlement for Russia's most dangerous criminals and dissidents. In a letter from the Siberian city of Tomsk, he related the first stages of his journey. Tomsk itself he considered a deplorable spot, noting that the 'most notable thing about Tomsk is that governors come here to die'.

I've been as hungry as a horse all the way. I filled my belly with bread in order to stop thinking of turbot, asparagus and suchlike. I even dreamt of buckwheat kasha. I dreamt of it for hours on end.

I bought some sausage for the journey in Tyumen, if you can call it a sausage! When you bit into it, the smell was just like going into a stable at the precise moment the coachmen are removing their foot bindings; when I started chewing it, my teeth felt as if they had caught hold of a dog's tail smeared with tar. Ugh! I made two attempts to eat it and then threw it away...

Oh Lord, my expenses are mounting up! Thanks to the floods I had to pay all the coachmen almost twice and sometimes three times as much as usual, for they had to work hellishly hard, it was like penal servitude. My suitcase, a nice little trunk, has proved not to be very suitable for the journey: it takes up too much room, bashes me continually in the ribs as it rattles about, and worst of all, is threatening to fall to pieces. 'Don't take trunks on a long journey' well-meaning people told me, but I only remembered this when I had got halfway. What to do? Well, I have decided to let my trunk take up residence in Tomsk, and have bought myself some piece of shit made of leather, but which has the advantage of flopping on the floor of a tarantass [carriage] and adopting any shape you like. It cost me 16 roubles...

Stop press! I have just been informed that the Assistant Chief of Police wants to see me. What can I have done?!?

False alarm. The policeman turned out to be a lover of literature and even a bit of a writer; he came to pay his respects. He's gone home to collect a play he's written; apparently he intends to entertain me with it... He'll be back in a moment and again interrupt my writing to you...

Stop press! The policeman has returned. He didn't read me his play, although he did bring it with him, but regaled me instead with a story he had written. It wasn't bad, a bit too local though. He showed me a gold ingot, and asked me if I had any vodka. I cannot recall any occasion on which a Siberian has not, on coming to see me, asked for vodka. This one told me he had got himself embroiled in a love affair with a married woman, and showed me his petition for a divorce addressed to the highest authority. Thereupon he suggested a tour of Tomsk's houses of pleasure.

I've now returned from the houses of pleasure. Quite revolting. Two a.m.

ANTON CHEKHOV, *A JOURNEY TO THE END OF THE RUSSIAN EMPIRE*.

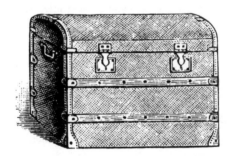

21 MAY

A DARK LEAP IN MEXICO, 1840

Frances Calderón de La Barca (1804–82), a Scottish woman married to a Spanish aristocrat, accompanied her husband when he was appointed ambassador to Mexico. Her letters provided an illuminating picture of life in what had, twenty years before, been a Spanish colony. The state of the roads left a particularly vivid impression.

To make our situation more disagreeable, we had scarcely set off, before a terrible storm of thunder and rain again came on with more violence than the night preceding. It grew perfectly dark, and we listened with some alarm to the roaring torrents, over which, especially over one, not many leagues from Sopayuca, where we were to spend the night, it was extremely doubtful whether we could pass. The carriage was full of water, but we were too much alarmed to be uneasy about trifles. Amidst the howling of the wind and the pealing of thunder, no one could hear the other speak. Suddenly, by a vivid flash of lightning, the dreaded barranca [ravine] appeared in sight for a moment, and almost before the drivers could stop them, the horses had plunged in.

It was a moment of mortal fear such as I shall never forget. The shrieks of the drivers to encourage the horses, the loud cries of Ave Maria! the uncertainty as to whether our heavy carriage could be dragged across, the horses struggling and splashing in the boiling torrent, and the horrible fate that awaited us should one of them fail or falter!... certainly no one breathed until we were safe on the other side. We were then told that we had crossed within a few feet of a precipice over which a coach had been dashed into fifty pieces during one of these swells, and of course every one killed.

FRANCES CALDERÓN DE LA BARCA, *LIFE IN MEXICO*.

22 MAY

TOWARDS THE HEART OF DARKNESS, 1890

Writing in 1890 from Freetown, Sierra Leone, the Polish author Józef Korzeniowski (aka Joseph Conrad, 1857–1924) described his departure for the Congo in a letter to his cousin Karol Zagorski. The vague disquiet underlying his excitement presages the novella, *Heart of Darkness*, that he would later write about life in the Congo, at that time the personal fiefdom of King Leopold II of the Belgians.

If only you knew the devilish haste I had to make! From London to Brussels, and back again to London! And then again I dashed full tilt to Brussels! If you had only seen all the tin boxes and revolvers, the high boots and the tender farewells; just another handshake and just another pair of trousers! – and if you knew all the bottles of medicine and affectionate wishes I took away with me, you would understand in what a typhoon, cyclone, hurricane, earthquake – no! – in what a universal cataclysm, in what a fantastic atmosphere of mixed shopping, business, and affecting scenes, I passed two whole weeks. But the fortnight spent at sea has allowed me to rest and I am impatiently waiting for the end of this trip... As far as I can make out from my 'lettre d'instruction' I am destined to the command of a steamboat, belonging to M. Delcommune's exploring party, which is being got ready. I like this prospect very much, but I know nothing for certain as everything is supposed to be kept secret. What makes me rather uneasy is the information that 60 per cent of our Company's employees return to Europe before they have completed even six months' service. Fever and dysentery! There are others who are sent home in a hurry at the end of a year, so that they shouldn't die in the Congo. God forbid! It would spoil the statistics which are excellent, you see!

JOSEPH CONRAD, *COLLECTED LETTERS*, VOLUME I.

23 MAY

GOBLINS OF THE DEEP, 1947

By now Thor Heyerdahl's balsa-wood raft the *Kon-Tiki* was almost a month into its Pacific voyage (*see* 29 April), and its crew had reached a state of near fantastical communion with the sea and its inhabitants.

About two o'clock on a cloudy night, on which the man at the helm had difficulty in distinguishing black water from black sky, he caught sight of a faint illumination down in the water which slowly took the shape of a large animal. It was impossible to say whether it was plankton shining on its body, or if the animal itself had a phosphorescent surface, but the glimmer down in the black water gave the ghostly creature obscure, wavering outlines. Sometimes it was roundish, sometimes oval or triangular, and suddenly it split into two parts which swam to and fro under the raft independently of one another. Finally there were three of these large shining phantoms wandering round in slow circles under us. They were real monsters, for the visible parts alone were some five fathoms long, and we all quickly collected on deck and followed the ghost dance. It went on for hour after hour, following the course of the raft. Mysterious and noiseless, our shining companions kept a good way beneath the surface, mostly on the starboard side, where the light was, but often they were right under the raft or appeared on the port side. The glimmer of light on their backs revealed that the beasts were bigger than elephants, but they were not whales, for they never came up to breathe. Were they giant rayfish which changed shape when they turned over on their sides? They took no notice at all if we held the light right down on the surface to lure them up, so that we might see what kind of creature they were. And like all proper goblins and ghosts, they had sunk into the depths when the dawn began to break.

THOR HEYERDAHL, *THE KON-TIKI EXPEDITION*.

24 MAY

SEA MONSTER AT NOON, 1947

The goblins and ghosts of the previous day (*see* 23 May) now materialized into a real monster as the *Kon-Tiki* ploughed on through the Pacific. It was a whale shark, at fifty feet long the world's largest known fish, both rare and dangerous.

Knut had been squatting there, washing his pants in the swell, and when he looked up for a moment he was staring straight into the biggest and ugliest face any of us had ever seen in the whole of our lives. It was the head of a veritable sea monster, so huge and hideous that if the Old Man of the Sea himself had come up he could not have made such an impression on us. The head was broad and flat like a frog's, with two small eyes right at the sides, and a toadlike jaw which was four or five feet wide and had long fringes hanging drooping from the corners of the mouth. Behind the head was an enormous body ending in a long thin tail with a pointed tail fin which stood straight up and showed that this sea monster was not any kind of a whale. The body looked brownish under the water, but both head and body were thickly covered with small white spots. The monster came quietly, lazily swimming after us from astern. It grinned like a bulldog and lashed gently with its tail. The large round dorsal fin projected clear of the water and sometimes the tail fin as well... In front of the broad jaws swam a whole crowd of zebra-striped pilot fish in fan formation, and large remora fish and other parasites sat firmly attached to the huge body and travelled with it through the water.

The monster was so large that when it began to swim in circles round us and under the raft its head was visible on one side while the whole of its tail stuck out on the other. And so incredibly grotesque, inert and stupid did it appear when seen full-face that we could not help shouting with laughter, although we realized that it had strength enough in its tail to smash both balsa logs and ropes to pieces if it attacked us.

THOR HEYERDAHL, *THE KON-TIKI EXPEDITION*.

25 MAY

THE SEAS OF FORGETFULNESS, 1946

The Algerian-born French writer Albert Camus (1913–60) had an ambivalent relationship with the sea. 'That's the way the sea is, and that's why I love it!' he wrote. 'A call to life and an invitation to death!' Returning from a trip to the United States he meditated on the ocean's vastness and profundity.

Marvellous night on the Atlantic. This hour when the sun has disappeared and the moon has just barely been born, when the west is still luminous and the east is already dark. Yes, I've loved the sea very much – this calm immensity – these wakes folded under wakes – these liquid routes. For the first time a horizon that measures up to the breath of a man, a space as large as his audacity. I've always been torn between my appetite for people, the vanity and the agitation, and the desire to make myself the equal of these seas of forgetfulness, these unlimited silences that are like the enchantment of death. I have a taste for worldly vanities, my fellows, for faces but, out of step with this century, I have an example in myself which is the sea and anything in this world which resembles it. O sweetness of nights where all the stars sway and slide above the masts, and this silence in myself, this silence which finally frees me from everything.

ALBERT CAMUS, *AMERICAN JOURNALS*.

26 MAY

LIFE ON ELEPHANT ISLAND, 1916

Having finally escaped the Antarctic floes (*see* 29 February), Ernest Shackleton deposited his crew on a remote lump of rock called Elephant Island, while he and five others sailed to the whaling outpost of South Georgia for help. Those left behind built shelters from their overturned boats and stoically awaited his return.

From all parts there dangles an odd collection of blubbery garments, hung up to dry, through which one crawls, much as a chicken in an incubator. Our walls of tent canvas admit as much light as might be expected from a closed Venetian blind. It is astonishing how we have grown accustomed to inconveniences, and tolerate, at least, habits which a little time back were regarded with repugnance. We have no forks, but each man has a sheath knife and a spoon, the latter in many cases having been fashioned from a piece of box lid. The knife serves many purposes. With it we kill, skin, and cut up seals and penguins, cut blubber into strips for the fire, very carefully scrape the snow off our hut walls, and then after a perfunctory rub with an oily penguin skin, use it at meals. We are as regardless of our grime and dirt as is the Eskimo. We have been unable to wash since we left the ship, nearly ten months ago. For one thing we have no soap or towels, only bare necessities being brought with us; and, again, had we possessed these articles, our supply of fuel would only permit us to melt enough ice for drinking purposes. Had one man washed, half a dozen would have had to go without a drink all day. One cannot suck ice to relieve the thirst, as at these low temperatures it cracks the lips and blisters the tongue. Still, we are all very cheerful.

ERNEST SHACKLETON, *SOUTH.*

27 MAY

REFLECTIONS ON ARABIA, 1946

At the end of his second journey across the Empty Quarter of Saudi Arabia, the English writer-explorer Wilfred Thesiger (1910–2003) took a dhow to Bahrain. The boat was becalmed for several days, during which he had time to examine the philosophy that underpinned his lifestyle.

———•—•———

I was sailing on this dhow because I wanted to have some experience of the Arab as a sailor... [also] to escape a little longer from the machines which dominated our world... All my life I had hated machines. I could remember how bitterly at school I had resented reading the news that someone had flown across the Atlantic or travelled through the Sahara in a car. I had realised even then that the speed and ease of mechanical transport must rob the world of all diversity.

For me, exploration was a personal venture. I did not go to the Arabian desert to collect plants nor to make a map; such things were incidental. At heart I knew that to write or even to talk of my travels was to tarnish the achievement. I went there to find peace in the hardship of desert travel and the company of desert peoples. I set myself a goal on these journeys, and, although the goal itself was unimportant, its attainment had to be worth every effort and sacrifice. Scott had gone to the South Pole in order to stand for a few minutes on one particular and almost inaccessible spot on the earth's surface. He and his companions died on their way back, but even as they were dying he never doubted that the journey had been worth while. Everyone knew that there was nothing to be found on the top of Everest, but even in this materialistic age few people asked, 'What point is there in climbing Everest? What good will it do anyone when they get there?' They recognized that even today there are experiences that do not need to be justified in terms of material profit.

No, it is not the goal but the way there that matters, and the harder the way the more worth while the journey. Who, after all, would dispute that it is more satisfying to climb to the top of a mountain than to go there in a funicular railway? Perhaps this is one reason why I resented modern inventions; they made the road too easy. I felt instinctively that it was better to fail on Everest without oxygen than to attain the summit with its use. If climbers used oxygen, why should they not have their supplies dropped to them by aeroplanes, or landed by helicopter? Yet to refuse mechanical aids as unsporting reduced exploration to the level of a sport, like big-game shooting in Kenya when the hunter is allowed to drive up to within sight of the animal but must get out of the car to shoot it. I would not myself have wished to cross the Empty Quarter in a car. Luckily this was impossible when I did my journeys, for to have done the journey on a camel when I could have done it in a car would have turned the venture into a stunt.

At last a puff of wind stirred the water and did not immediately die away. The mate shouted to the sleeping crew. They trimmed the sail, stamping and singing as they hauled. The breeze freshened.

WILFRED THESIGER, *ARABIAN SANDS*.

28 MAY

FIREFLIES IN THE TOWN OF PISTOLS, 1845

During his lifetime, the English art critic John Ruskin (1819–1900) was widely acclaimed as the Great Mage of nineteenth-century aesthetics. On his travels he wrote daily to his father, the following letter being posted from the Tuscan town of Pistoia, northwest of Florence. It was his first visit to Italy, the nation from which he drew his inspiration and with which he enjoyed a love–hate relationship, sometimes cursing its inadequacies, at other times praising its perfection.

I have had a heavenly drive from Pisa – one vista of vine and blue Apennine convents and cypresses – and I have just come in from an evening walk among the stars and fireflies. One hardly knows where one has got to, between them, for the flies flash, as you know, exactly like stars on the sea, and the impression to the eye is as if one were walking on water. I was not at the least prepared for their intense brilliancy. They dazzled me like fireworks, and it was very heavenly to see them floating over field beyond field under the shadowy vines.

This is a wonderful place. It is odd. I never knew till tonight where *pistols* got their name from. It is the most untouched middle age town in Tuscany, and its churches are quite perfect – or at least free from any intentional injury – on the outside. *Inside* they are whitewashed & barbarized of course, but one may thank heaven here for *any side*.

JOHN RUSKIN, *RUSKIN IN ITALY*.

29 MAY

SURFING IN THE SOUTH SEAS, 1769

While serving as naturalist aboard the *Endeavour*, Joseph Banks (1743–1820) recorded a hitherto unknown sport when the ship stopped at Tahiti. As with other Polynesian customs such as tattooing (*see* 5 July) it would soon make its way round the world.

We saw the Indians amuse or exercise themselves in a manner truly surprizing. It was in a place where the shore was not guarded by a reef, as is usualy the case, consequently a high surf fell upon the shore, and a more dreadfull one I have not often seen: no European boat could have landed in it, and I think no Europaean who had by any means got into it could possibly have saved his life, as the shore was coverd with pebbles and large stones. In the midst of these breakers 10 or 12 Indians were swimming who whenever a surf broke near them they divd under it with infinite ease, rising up on the other side; but their chief amusement was being carried on by an old canoe, with this before them they swam out as far as the outermost breach, then one or two would get into it and opposing the blunt end to the breaking wave were hurried in with incredible swiftness. Sometimes they were carried almost ashore but generally the wave broke over them before they were half-way, in which case they divd and quickly rose on the other side with the canoe in their hands, which was towd out again and the same method repeated. We stood admiring this very wonderful scene for full half an hour, in which time no one of the actors attempted to come ashore but all seemd most highly entertaind with their strange diversion.

JOSEPH BANKS, *THE 'ENDEAVOUR' JOURNAL*, VOLUME I.

30 MAY

DEATH IN ROME, 1817

Writing on this day to his publisher John Murray, Lord Byron (*see* 25 February), the bad boy of English Romanticism, described a visit to Rome in 1817.

———————

The day before I left Rome I saw three robbers guillotined. The ceremony – including the *masqued* priests; the half-naked executioners; the scaffold; the soldiery; the slow procession, and the quick rattle and heavy fall of the axe; the splash of the blood, and the ghastliness of the exposed heads – is altogether more impressive than the vulgar and ungentlemanly dirty 'new drop', and dog-like agony of infliction upon the sufferers of English sentence. Two of these men behaved calmly enough, but the first of the three died with great terror and reluctance, which was very horrible. He would not lie down; then his neck was too large for the aperture, and the priest was obliged to drown his exclamations by still louder exhortations. The head was off before the eye could trace the blow; but from an attempt to draw back the head, notwithstanding it was held forward by the hair, the first head was cut off close to the ears: the other two were taken off more cleanly. It is better than the oriental way, and (I should think) than the axe of our ancestors. The pain seems little; and yet the effect to the spectator, and the preparation to the criminal, are very striking and chilling. The first turned me quite hot and thirsty, and made me shake so that I could hardly hold the opera-glass (I was close, but determined to see, as one should see everything, once, with attention); the second and third (which shows how dreadfully soon things grow indifferent), I am ashamed to say, had no effect on me as a horror, though I would have saved them if I could.

LORD BYRON, *BYRON: A SELF-PORTRAIT*, VOLUME II.

31 MAY

SAN FRANCISCO'S DIZZY LABYRINTH, 1936

When Jean Cocteau reached California on his round-the-world voyage (*see* 31 March) he was unstinting in his praise for San Francisco. By night, he said, it was 'the most beautiful city in the world'.

San Francisco is a scenic railway. Broad, impressive, precipitous streets. On the seaward side they slope down with all the violence of toboggans plunging into the water. The heart stops a beat, flutters, leaps up. The hotel lift had already bisected it, gently, like a metal wire cutting through butter. And all this dizzy labyrinth of rearing and plunging streets, all this procession of Chinese and Italian quarters, all these dance halls, warehouses in which yellow planks of sequoia are piled up, all those plots of waste land and all those blocks of flats whose pyramidical bases sustain fortresses and cathedrals, all these facades furrowed by lightning-flashes that are fire-escapes, the whole of this fabulous castle of cards, comes to its climax in Tower Hill, an esplanade surrounded with railings and bearing the name Coit... In the middle of the esplanade an arrogant tower soars up against the sky. A cosmic sky, cuprous, fiery, a sky of planets which appear and disappear behind chasing clouds. Pink fires, red, absinthe-coloured, feathery clouds, like a squadron flying high, and heavy clouds that subside among the buildings and form a bluish sea of mist from which foundering vessels, liners, adrift with all their lights blazing, emerge. The panorama then changes. From being overloaded, confused, piled up, crenellated, feudal, it becomes the vast nocturnal bay at the end of which the Golden Gate Bridge, the most famous suspension bridge in the world, crosses the space with the exquisite audacity of gossamer.

JEAN COCTEAU, *My Journey Round the World*.

JUNE

∞

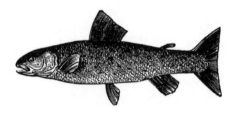

1 JUNE

WAITING FOR VESUVIUS, 1787

Johann Wolfgang von Goethe (*see* 1 March) was in Naples when he learned that Vesuvius had erupted and that all roads out of the city were closed. He was at first irritated – he had grown tired of the place and had planned to move on – but after a while resigned himself to patience and went to watch the beauty of the sparks and lava.

————•—•————

The servant I hired to bring me my passport said he was sorry to see me go, and told me that the great lava stream which has just issued from Vesuvius is moving towards the sea; it has already reached a point far down the steeper slopes and may well reach the shore in a few days... I was still settling bills, packing and doing this and that when night began to fall, and I hurried to the Molo to watch the lights and their trembling reflections in the agitated sea, the full moon in all its glory, the flying sparks of the volcano and, above all, the lava, which had not been there two nights ago, moving on its fiery, relentless way.

I thought of driving out to see it, but this would have been complicated to arrange and it would have been morning before I got there. Besides, I did not want impatience to spoil my present enjoyment, so I stayed where I was, sitting on the Molo, oblivious of the passing crowds, their explanations, stories, comparisons and senseless arguments about the direction the lava would take, until I could no longer keep my eyes open.

JOHANN WOLFGANG VON GOETHE, *ITALIAN JOURNEY*.

2 JUNE

THE PLEASANT PORT OF MIDDLE AGE, 1884

On 2 May 1884 Robert Louis Stevenson (1850–94) suffered a haemorrhage of the lung. It was the most dramatic manifestation to date of the tuberculosis that would eventually kill him. A month later, while recovering in the French spa of Royat, in the Auvergne, he wrote to his friend William Henley.

I earnestly desire to live. This pleasant middle age into whose port we are steering, is quite to my fancy. I would cast anchor here, and go ashore for twenty years, and see the manners of the place. Youth was a great time, but somewhat fussy. Now in middle age (bar lucre) all seems mighty placid. It likes me; I spy a little bright café in one corner of the port, in front of which I now propose we should sit down. There is just enough of the bustle of the harbour and no more; and the ships are close in, regarding us with stern-windows – the ships that bring deal from Norway and parrots from the Indies. Let us sit down here for twenty years, with a packet of tobacco and a drink, and talk of art and women. By the by, the whole city will sink, and the ships too, and the table, and we also; but we shall have sat for twenty years and had a fine talk; and by that time, who knows? exhausted the subject.

ROBERT LOUIS STEVENSON, *LETTERS*, VOLUME IV.

3 JUNE

HIGH HEELS IN VENICE, 1645

A man of curiosity and intelligence, John Evelyn (1620–1706) was a founder member of Britain's Royal Society as well as one of the nation's great diarists. While travelling for several years during the Civil War he was, in early June 1645, faintly appalled by the Venetian dress code during the city's Masquerade festivities.

———

Twas now Ascension Weeke, & the greate Mart or faire of the whole yeare now kept, every body at liberty, & jollie; the Noblemen stalking with their Ladies on Choppines about 10 foote high from the ground. These are high heeld shoos particularly affected by these proude dames, or as some say, invented to keep them at home, it being so difficult to walke with them... The truth is their Garb is very odd, as seeming allways in Masquerade, their other habite also totaly different from all Nations: They weare very long crisped haire of several strakes and Colours, which they artificially make so, by washing their heads in pisse, & dischevelling them on the brims of a broade hat that has no head, but an hole to put out their head by, drie them in the Sunn, as one may see them from above, out of their windos:... besides this they go very bare of their breasts & back, with knots of poynts richly tagg'd, about their shoulders & other places, of their body, which they usualy cover with a kind of yellow Vaile of Lawn very transparant. Thus attir'd they set their hands on the heads of two Matron-like servants or old women to support them, who are mumbling in their beades: Tis very ridiculous to see how these Ladys crawle in & out of their Gundolas by reason of their Choppines & what dwarfes they appeare when taken down from their Wooden scaffolds: Of these I saw neere 30 together stalking, halfe as high more, as the rest of the World.

JOHN EVELYN, *DIARY*.

4 JUNE

THE PROPRIETY OF PEKING, 1958

The People's Republic of China was less than ten years old when Malcolm Muggeridge visited Peking (Beijing). A keen observer of revolutions (*see* 19 March), he was much taken by the moral rigour of China's new Communist regime.

Then I went... to see the Forbidden City. It was very exquisite – the gleaming roofs, the bizarre shapes, the bright colours, but too strange and outlandish to move me much. For buildings, or any art, to make my heart stand still (as, for instance, Salisbury Cathedral and Chartres did) it has to be connected with what I understand and belong to. The wall and the massive gates and the towers were most impressive, but even then I could not populate the place, as I could, for instance, the ruined Roman cities in Transjordan. I could not bring this place to life, at all, and so, for me, it remained just a curiosity. In any case, I have never had much interest in the past. I find the present too absorbing.

In the afternoon I tramped about Peking. Peking streets are decidedly ramshackle, but still, as on the train, people are smiling and amiable and orderly. They are very innocent. Most of the filth that used to be in China was foreign imported. Now it's all gone – no opium, whore houses, gambling dens, drunkenness, striptease; nothing of that sort at all now. At nine o'clock everything closes. Never have I seen such propriety. I like it – no eroticism at all; total absence of... filth and sadism, which is to be seen wherever Freedom reigns and Western Values prevail.

MALCOLM MUGGERIDGE, *LIKE IT WAS*.

5 JUNE

AS I WALKED OUT, 1935

One summer morning in 1935 Laurie Lee (*see* 7 January) left his home in Slad, Gloucestershire, to discover the world. Travelling on foot, and earning his keep from the violin, he walked through Spain on the eve of its civil war.

The stooping figure of my mother, waist-deep in the grass and caught there like a piece of sheep's wool, was the last I saw of my country home as I left it to discover the world. She stood old and bent at the top of the bank, silently watching me go, one gnarled red hand raised in farewell and blessing, not questioning why I went. At the bend of the road I looked back again and saw the gold light die behind her; then I turned the corner passed the village school, and closed that part of my life for ever.

It was a bright Sunday morning in early June, the right time to be leaving home. My three sisters and a brother had already gone before me; two other brothers had yet to make up their minds. They were still sleeping that morning, but my mother had got up early and cooked me a heavy breakfast, had stood wordlessly while I ate it, her hand on my chair, and had then helped me pack up my few belongings. There had been no fuss, no appeals, no attempts at advice or persuasion, only a long and searching look. Then, with my bags on my back, I'd gone out into the early sunshine and climbed through the long wet grass to the road.

LAURIE LEE, *As I Walked Out One Midsummer Morning*.

6 JUNE

MADE IN CHINA, 1938

After Japanese forces overran Shanghai, early in the Sino-Japanese War, the literary travellers Auden and Isherwood (*see* 30 April) observed conditions in the International Settlement, the only part of the city not under Japanese control.

The Japanese have destroyed seventy per cent of China's industry. Some of the luckier concerns have been able to crowd into the International Settlement, and reopen there. Most of these factories are very small – two or three rooms crammed with machinery and operatives. The majority of the operatives are young boys who have been bought from their parents outright for twenty dollars: they work from twelve to fourteen hours a day. Their only wages are their food, and a sleeping-space in a loft above the work-room. There are no precautions whatever against accident or injury to health. In the accumulator factories, half the children have already the blue line in their gums which is a symptom of lead poisoning. Few of them will survive longer than a year or eighteen months. In scissors factories you can see arms and legs developing chromium-holes. There are silk-winding mills so full of steam that the fingers of the mill-girls are white with fungus growths. If the children slacken in their work the overseers often plunge their elbows into boiling water as a punishment. There is a cotton mill where the dust in the air makes T.B. almost a certainty... Accidents are invariably found to be due to the carelessness of the workers involved. There is no compensation and no insurance.

The Japanese [it is said] will exploit the Shanghai workers even more brutally than the Chinese owners have exploited them in the past. They will flood the markets with cheap goods and so gradually lower working-class standards of living all over the world.

W.H. AUDEN AND CHRISTOPHER ISHERWOOD, *JOURNEY TO A WAR*.

7 JUNE

THE LIFE OF A CALIFORNIAN SHEPHERD, 1869

While accompanying a herd of 2,500 sheep across the mountainous region of Yosemite, California, the Scottish-born naturalist John Muir (1838–1914) had ample time to reflect upon the life of a shepherd in the Wild West. It was thanks largely to Muir's environmental activism that the Yosemite wilderness was preserved as a National Park.

———•———

Coming into his dingy hovel-cabin at night, stupidly weary, he finds nothing to balance and level his life with the universe. No, after his dull drag all day after the sheep, he must get his supper; he is likely to slight this task and try to satisfy his hunger with whatever comes handy. Perhaps no bread is baked; then he just makes a few grimy flapjacks in his unwashed frying-pan, boils a handful of tea, and perhaps fries a few strips of rusty bacon. Usually there are dried peaches or apples in the cabin, but he hates to be bothered with the cooking of them, just swallows the bacon and flapjacks, and depends on the genial stupefaction of tobacco for the rest. Then to bed, often without removing the clothing worn during the day. Of course his health suffers, reacting on his mind; and seeing nobody for weeks or months, he finally becomes semi-insane or wholly so.

The shepherd in Scotland... has but a small flock to look after, sees his family and neighbours [and] has time for reading... The oriental shepherd, we read, called his sheep by name... But whatever the blessings of sheep-culture in other times and countries, the California shepherd, as far as I've seen or heard, is never quite sane for any considerable time. Of all Nature's voices baa is about all he hears. Even the howls and ki-yis of coyotes might be blessings if well heard, but he hears them only through a blur of mutton and wool, and they do him no good.

JOHN MUIR, *MY FIRST SUMMER IN THE SIERRA.*

8 JUNE

RETURN TO ALGIERS, 1902

Having been expelled as an embarrassment to the French colonial authorities, Isabelle Eberhardt (*see* 1 January) returned to Algiers in 1902 to pursue her self-destructive love affair with Africa. Claiming to scoff at death so long as it served a purpose, she died quite purposelessly in Algeria two years later, in a flash flood at Ain Sefra.

Life goes on, monotonous as ever, yet there is the hint of some future direction in the midst of all this dreadful emotional turmoil...

Now that the torrid heat of summer has suddenly come again, the notion that I am back in Africa is slowly sinking in. Soon I will feel completely at home, especially if my plan to go to Bou-Saada comes off... Oh, that journey! It will mean a brief return, not to the magnificent Sahara itself, but to a place nearby that has all the palm trees and sunshine one would want!

Remarks about Algiers

While the weather was cool, the shadows in the upper town's dark streets were grey and dark, to the point of gloominess. Now that there is a sudden sharp contrast between light and dark, it all looks African again, or Arab in any event.

No, the true African landscape is not to be found in any of the large cities, certainly not in those of the Tell [Algeria's coastal region]. African perspectives are hazy with a distant horizon. Vast space and emptiness, a blinding light, are what makes a landscape African! The architecture of Algiers boasts none of those traits. Its houses are all piled on top of each other and huddle fearfully at the bottom of culs-de-sac, in a city accustomed to raids and sieges.

The mindless noise of the crowds, where the only Arabs are those awful Kabyles in European garb, makes certain parts of the town look like places of ill repute where no one's life is safe.

The uninitiated European thinks those men in dirty burnouses over tattered European clothes, and those Moorish women are all part of the local colour. But that is precisely what is so un-Arabic about Algiers, for it is contrary to Arab custom. The truth is that Old Algiers is medieval, Turkish, Moorish, or what have you, but not Arabic and certainly not African!

In truly Arabic towns like the Ksours in the south, the magic of Africa and its poignant mystery are actually tangible. They lie in the wide open space, the small, low, tumbledown houses, either very white or in the same hue as their hazy environment, in all that light and bleakness.

The trouble with Algiers is its abject population. Any sort of contemplative streetlife, of the calm and fertile, gratifying sort I love so much, is out of the question there.

The savage hatred I feel for crowds is getting worse, natural enemies that they are of imagination and of thought. They make it impossible for me to feel *alive* here, the way I do in other places. Oh, how evil civilisation is! Why was it ever brought over here?

ISABELLE EBERHARDT, *THE PASSIONATE NOMAD*.

9 JUNE

A FORGOTTEN MONUMENT IN GAMBIA, 1887

In 1887, Archer Crouch helped lay a telegraph cable off the west coast of Africa. He recounted the experience so bashfully that he refused to name his employer, his ship, his co-workers, the people he met or, indeed, himself ('the author, in order to preserve uniformity on this point, assumes the name of Bertram'). Nobody but Crouch could have uncovered a monument as obscure as this, by the River Gambia.

In front of the barrack entrance, and at the foot of another great tree, is erected, in the midst of the soft turf, a stone monument of simple design and unpretentious appearance. On the front I read that the monument had been put up to the memory of four officers and two non-commissioned officers who died here of an epidemic in 1859. As the garrisons in Bathurst have never been very large, that must have been a large percentage of the whole number of the officers. It was erected by those of their companions in arms who survived them. At the base of the monument, in the extreme corner, is inscribed in small characters, 'Higgins fecit, Betton, Rutland, England'.

It seemed curious that these simple stones, carved, presumably, by some rustic artist in a small village in the heart of England, should, in spite of the heavy freight they must have cost, find their way over so many hundred miles of water to an almost equally obscure town on the Western Coast of Africa. If Higgins is yet alive, he will no doubt be gratified to hear that his work withstands alike the burning tropic sun and the pouring tropic rains, and still declares the hand that carved it, and the distant home from which it came.

ARCHER CROUCH, *ON A SURF-BOUND COAST*.

10 JUNE

NATURE BOY, 1949

'Beat' writer Jack Kerouac (1922–69) was at the start of his career as a novelist and staying in Denver when he wrote to his friend and fellow 'Beatnik' Allen Ginsberg with a wild and dreamlike vision of travel.

I decided someday to become a Thoreau of the Mountains. To live like Jesus and Thoreau, except for women. Like Nature Boy with his Nature Girl. I'll buy a saddlehorse for $30, an old saddle on Larimer St., a sleeping bag at Army surplus; frying pan, old tin can; bacon, coffee, beans, sourdough; matches etc.; and a rifle. And go away in the mountains forever. To Montana in the summers and Texas–Mexico in the winters. Drink my java from an old tin can while the moon is riding high. Also, I forgot to mention my chromatic harmonica... so I can have music. Thus, I'll wander the wild, wild mountains and wait for Judgment Day. I believe there will be a Judgment Day, but not for men... for *society*. Society is a mistake...

I want to be left alone. I want to sit in the grass. I want to ride my horse. I want to lay a woman naked in the grass on the mountainside. I want to think. I want to pray. I want to sleep. I want to look at the stars. I want what I want. I want to get and prepare my own food, with my own hands, and live that way. I want to roll my own. I want to smoke some deermeat and pack it in my saddlebag, and go away over the bluff. I want to read books. I want to write books. I'll write books in the woods. Thoreau was right; Jesus was right. It's all wrong and I denounce it and it can all go to hell. I don't believe in this society; but I believe in man, like Mann. So roll your own bones, I say.

Jack Kerouac, *Selected Letters*.

11 JUNE

THE BIRDS OF ALCOBACA, 1794

Author, politician, art-collector, builder of grand follies and general eccentric, William Beckford (1760–1844) was also one of the richest men in England. Among the many ways he devised of spending his fortune – in which he was outstandingly successful – was a project to travel through Europe in search of works of art. In 1794 he visited a Portuguese garden near Alcobaca, whose owner, a mad countess, had a passion for birds.

As far as the eye could stretch, extended a close bower of evergreens, myrtle, bay, and ilex, not to mention humble box, lofty, broad, and fragrant; on either side, arches of verdure most sprucely clipped, opened into large square plats of rare and curious flowers; and in the midst of each of these trim parterres, a fountain inclosed within a richly-gilded cage, containing birds of every variety of size, song and plumage; parroquets with pretty little flesh-coloured beaks, and parrots of the largest species, looking arch and cunning as they kept cracking and grinding walnuts and filberts between their bills black as ebony.

In one of these inclosures I noticed an immense circular basin of variegated marble, surrounded by a gilt metal balustrade, on which were most solemnly perched a conclave of araras [macaws] and cockatoos. Their united screechings and screamings upon my approach gave the alarm to a multitude of smaller birds, which issued forth in such clouds from every leaf and spray of these vaulted walls of verdure, that I ran off as if I had committed sacrilege, or feared being transformed by art-magic into a biped completely rigged out with beaks, claws, and feathers.

WILLIAM BECKFORD, *THE TRAVEL-DIARIES*.

12 JUNE

SAN FRANCISCO'S WALKING HOUSES, 1867

When the Marquis de Beauvoir (*see* 2 April) first saw San Francisco he was unimpressed. After the verdant charms of Japan, this 'yellow and hideous' gold-mining town came as an unpleasant contrast. But a surprise lay in store when he went for a stroll that evening.

———•·•———

Hardly had we gone a hundred paces along the quay, than we met a house – out for a walk; the Duc de Penthièvre and Fauvel had often told me of the facility with which Yankees could move an inhabited house across streets and fields; I believed them – but I could not realize it. Well, it is the first thing I have seen in this extraordinary country. It was a wooden house, with five windows to the front and three to the side, consisting of a ground floor, and one story; there were lights in several rooms: on the first story a worthy citizen, with a goat's beard, was smoking a long pipe; below, a household were supping with their children. All this time the house was advancing slowly; you may imagine that I stopped to see how it was all done. At some hundred yards off, a horse was working a capstan; some tackle and a cable pulled the whole thing along as it lay, or rather glided upon wooden rollers; so one horse was enough to move the dwelling-place of two families. They told me they were going to put the house at the corner of 277 Street and 48 Street, about two miles off. I could not get over it, for it was not one of those gipsy carts we see at home, and I had only to turn round to see that it was precisely similar to all those which formed the street in which we stood.

MARQUIS DE BEAUVOIR, *THE CONCLUSION OF A VOYAGE ROUND THE WORLD*.

13 JUNE

UNSPEAKABLE FOREIGNERS, 1765

The British author Tobias Smollett (1721–71) made a tour of France and Italy between 1763 and 1765. He complained throughout of dirt, vermin, poison, idleness, dissipation and incompetence, not to mention the horrors of the French national character. 'If a Frenchman is capable of real friendship,' he wrote, 'it must certainly be the most disagreeable present he can possibly make to a man of true English character... If he suffers a repulse from your wife, or attempts in vain to debauch your sister, or your daughter, or your niece, he will... make his addresses to your grandmother.' He recorded his experiences in a series of letters of which this, he was glad to say, was the last.

DEAR SIR, – I am at last in a situation to indulge my view with a sight of Britain, after an absence of two years; and indeed you cannot imagine what pleasure I feel while I survey the white cliffs of Dover, at this distance...

Our journey hither from Lyons produced neither accident or adventure worth notice; but abundance of little vexations, which may be termed the Plagues of Posting... Upon a just comparison of all circumstances posting is much more easy, convenient, and reasonable in England than in France. The English carriages, horses, harness, and roads are much better; and the postilions more obliging and alert. The reason is plain and obvious. If I am ill-used at the post-house in England, I can be accommodated elsewhere. The publicans on the road are sensible of this, and therefore they vie with each other in giving satisfaction to travellers. But in France, where the post is monopolized, the post-masters and postilions, knowing that the traveller depends entirely upon them, are the more negligent and remiss in their duty, as well as the more encouraged to insolence and imposition. Indeed the stranger seems to be left intirely at the mercy of those fellows, except in large towns, where he may have recourse to the magistrate or commanding officer. The post stands very often by itself in a lone country situation, or in a paltry village, where the post-master is the principle inhabitant; and in such a case, if you should be ill-treated by being supplied with bad horses; if you should be delayed on frivolous pretences in order to extort money; if the postilions should drive at a waggon-pace with a view to provoke your impatience; or should you in any shape be insulted by them or their masters; and I know not what redress you can have, except by a formal complaint to the comptroller of the posts, who is generally one of the ministers of state, and pays little or no regard to any such representations. I know an English gentleman, the brother of an earl, who wrote a letter of complaint to the Duc de Villars, governor of Provence, against the post-master of Antibes, who had insulted and imposed upon him. The duke answered his letter, promising to take order that the grievance should be redressed; and never thought of it after... Through the whole south of France, except in large cities, the inns are cold, damp, dark, dismal, and dirty; the landlords equally disobliging and rapacious; the servants awkward, sluttish, and slothful; and the postilions lazy, lounging, greedy, and impertinent. If you chide them for lingering, they will continue to delay you the longer: if you chastise them with sword, cane, cudgel, or horse-whip, they will either disappear entirely, and leave you without resource; or they will find means to take revenge by overturning your carriage.

Tobias Smollett, Travels through France and Italy.

14 JUNE

THE INSATIABLE HUNGER OF POLAR BEARS, 1854

In 1853 an American ship under the command of Dr Elisha Kent Kane (*see* 23 February) sailed up the west coast of Greenland. Among other goals Kane wanted to find the Open Polar Sea, a mythical body of water that was supposed to lie at the top of the globe. In mid-June 1854 he described the depredations made by polar bears on a cache of provisions he had laid down the previous year.

The final cache, which I relied so much upon, was entirely destroyed. It had been built with extreme care, of rocks which had been assembled by very heavy labour, and adjusted with much aid often from capstan-bars as levers. The entire construction was, so far as our means permitted, most effective and resisting. Yet these tigers of the ice seemed to have scarcely encountered an obstacle. Not a morsel of pemmican remained except in the iron cases, which, being round with conical ends, defied both claws and teeth. They had rolled and pawed them in every direction, tossing them about like footballs, although over eighty pounds in weight. An alcohol-case, strongly iron-bound, was dashed into small fragments, and a tin can of liquor mashed and twisted almost into a ball. The claws of the beast had perforated the metal, and torn it up as with a cold chisel.

They were too dainty for salt meats: ground coffee they had an evident relish for: old canvas was a favorite for some reason or other; even our flag, which had been reared 'to take possession' of the waste, was gnawed down to the very staff. They had made a regular frolic of it; rolling our bread-barrels over the ice-foot and into the broken outside ice; and, unable to masticate our heavy India-rubber cloth, they had tied it up in unimaginable knots.

ELISHA KENT KANE, *ARCTIC EXPLORATIONS*, VOLUME I.

15 JUNE

A BETTER CLASS OF COCKFIGHT, 1840

During her stay in Mexico Frances Calderón de la Barca applied herself diligently to a study of the country. If the roads were a disappointment (*see* 21 May) she had nothing but praise for a cockfight in the town of San Agustin, a short distance from the capital.

———··———

We went to the *gallos* [cockerels] about three o'clock. The plaza was crowded, and the ladies in their boxes looked like a parterre of different coloured flowers... The President and his suite were already there, also several of the foreign ministers.

Meanwhile the cocks crowed valiantly, bets were adjusted, and even the women entered into the spirit of the scene, taking bets with the gentlemen *sotto voce* in their boxes, upon such and such favourite animal. As a small knife is fastened to the leg of each cock, the battle seldom lasted long, one or other falling every few minutes in a pool of blood. Then there was a clapping of hands, mingled with the loud crowing of some unfortunate cock, who was giving himself airs previous to a combat where he was probably destined to crow his last... Unlike cockpits in other countries, attended by blacklegs and pickpockets and gentlemanly *roués*, by far the largest portion of the assembly in the pit was composed of the first young men in Mexico, and for that matter, the first old ones also. There was neither confusion, nor noise, nor even loud talking, far less swearing amongst the lowest of those assembled in the ring; and it is this quiet and orderly behaviour which throws over all these incongruities a cloak of decency and decorum, that hides their impropriety so completely, that even foreigners who have lived here a few years, and who were at first struck with astonishment by these things, are now quite reconciled to them.

Frances Calderón de La Barca, *Life in Mexico*.

16 JUNE

AN ISLAND OF STONE, 1804

Writing from Malta in mid-June 1804, the English poet Samuel Taylor Coleridge (1772–1834) described conditions on the island – a mixture of intimidating stone and abundant flora – in a letter to his wife Sara.

The whole island looks like one monstrous fortification. Nothing *green* meets your eye – one dreary, grey-white, – and all the country towns from the retirement and invisibility of the windows look like towns burnt out and desolate. Yet the fertility is marvellous. You almost see things grow, and the population is, I suppose, unexampled. The town of Valetta itself contains about one hundred and ten streets, all at right angles to each other, each having from twelve to fifty houses; but many of them very steep – a few *staired* all across, and almost all, in some part or other, if not the whole, having the footway on each side so staired. The houses lofty, all looking new. The good houses are built with a court in the centre, and the rooms are large and lofty, from sixteen to twenty feet high, and walls enormously thick, all necessary for coolness. The fortifications of Valetta are endless. When I first walked about them, I was struck all of a heap with their strangeness, and when I came to understand a little of their purpose I was overwhelmed with wonder. Such vast masses – bulky, mountain-breasted heights; gardens with pomegranate trees – the prickly pears in the fosses, and the caper (the most beautiful of flowers) growing profusely in the interstices of the high walls and on the battlements. The Maltese are a dark, light-limbed people. Of the women five tenths are ugly; of the remainder, four tenths would be ordinary but that they look so *quaint*, and one tenth, perhaps, may be called quaint-pretty.

SAMUEL TAYLOR COLERIDGE, *LETTERS*, VOLUME II.

17 JUNE

AN ASTHMATIC ON MOUNT ETNA, 1847

The poet and artist Edward Lear (*see* 3 May) arrived in Sicily on 10 May 1847, accompanied by his friend the Hon. John Proby. Little more than a month later, despite Lear's asthma and weak lungs, they were scaling the volcanic heights of Etna.

On Saturday, resolving to go up to the top of the mountain, we set off early & first went to the Val di Bove, a most awful chasm of valley below the crater – exceeding in grandeur and terror anything of the kind I ever saw; thence we returned to Nicolosi, & passed our Sunday there – going up in the evening through what is called the woody region of Etna to a little hut in the forest, where, well wrapped up in additional clothes, we supped & slept comfortably enough.

At midnight we started on mules & with a light, & after two hours climbing reached the snow, beyond which it is necessary to go on foot. Here the trouble begins: fancy two hours of climbing up & slipping down, over the steepest hill of frozen snow. I never was so disgusted. Sometimes I rolled back as far as 20 minutes had taken me up. It was impossible to keep one's footing, even with a spiked stick. By the aid of the guide, however, we reached the top of this horrible height, & rested in another hut called Casa Inglese. Then we crossed a plain of snow which surrounds the cone & began to climb that, an operation as difficult as the last, as it is nearly perpendicular & made up of fine ash & sulphur, into which you plunge up to your knees at each step.

This, however, is not the obstacle that prevents your progress, but rather the extreme rarity of the air which takes different effects on different persons. Some it stupefies, others it causes to vomit. Had it made me very ill, I should have turned back, but it only caused me to feel as if I were drowning, & made me lose my breath almost & my voice altogether. A sort of compulsive catching [of the breath] was very disagreeable, & at times was so violent that for a moment or two I lost the use of my limbs & fell down. Being on the ground, however, restored one's breathing, & so we got on by very slow degrees – climbing & falling alternately. The fatigue is certainly immense, but one is amply repaid by the extraordinary scene above – where you look on the whole island of Sicily just like a great pink map in the sky, with the sea around it so blue & the dark purple triangular shade of the mountains over that part furthest from the sun, which rose just before we got to the mouth of the crater...

We did not remain long there, as you may suppose on my telling you that the sulphur we sat on burned our clothes very much, & was horribly hot – yet one was too glad to bury one's hand in it, one's body & head being wrapped up in cloaks & plaids through all which one shivered in the icy wind, which blew like knives from the north (Etna, you know, is nearly as high as Mont Blanc). We came down ridiculously fast: you stick your heels in the ashy cone, slide down almost without stopping to the bottom, & with a spiked stick you shoot down the ice hill we had taken so long to surmount in 10 minutes.

Today, I feel greatly better for my excursion.

EDWARD LEAR, *LEAR'S ITALY*.

18 JUNE

A STROLL OUTSIDE GHENT, 1815

The Romantic writer and politician François-René, Vicomte de Chateaubriand (1768–1848), had frequently been at odds with French revolutionary fervour and with Napoleon. He had consequently spent several years abroad and in exile, including a spell in England. On Napoleon's resurgence in 1814 Chateaubriand left France once again, this time heading for Ghent in Belgium. And on this day, he took a country stroll that brought him, unwittingly, within earshot of a defining European event.

On 18 June 1815, I left Ghent about noon by the Brussels gate; I was going to finish my walk alone on the highroad. I had taken Caesar's *Commentaries* with me and I strolled along, immersed in my reading. I was over two miles from the town when I thought I heard a dull rumbling: I stopped and looked up at the sky, which was fairly cloudy, wondering whether I should walk on or turn back towards Ghent for fear of a storm. I listened; I heard nothing more but the cry of a moor-hen in the rushes and the sound of a village clock. I continued on my way: I had not taken thirty steps before the rumbling began again, now short, now drawn out and at irregular intervals; sometimes it was perceptible only through a trembling of the air, which was so far away that it communicated itself to the ground as it passed over those vast plains. The detonations, less prolonged, less undulating, less interrelated than those of thunder, gave rise in my mind to the idea of a battle. I found myself opposite a poplar planted at the corner of a hop-field. I crossed the road and leant against the trunk of the tree, with my face turned in the direction of Brussels. A southerly wind sprang up and brought me more distinctly the sound of artillery. That great battle, nameless as yet, whose echoes I was listening to at the foot of a poplar, and for whose unknown obsequies a village clock had just struck, was the Battle of Waterloo.

Vicomte de Chateaubriand, *The Memoirs of Chateaubriand*.

19 JUNE

HONEYMOON IN THE ALPS, 1867

The British mountaineer and man of letters Leslie Stephen (1832–1904) married Minny Thackeray on this date, an event presaged in a letter to his American literary friend Oliver Wendell Holmes. (Stephen never sent it, for fear of appearing drunk.) The honeymoon was to be in Stephen's favourite stamping ground, the Bernese Oberland of Switzerland – which, as he never tired of telling Holmes, was vastly superior to anything America could offer.

This is the last letter you will get from Leslie Stephen – at least it is not but it would be if I was Miss Thackeray – or say then it would be the last letter you would get from Minny Thackeray: but this is irrelevant; it is the last letter you will get from me before I am married...

I am quite certain that after months of London fog (not but what London has the finest climate in the world mind you) I shall be devilish glad to see once more the Jungfrau Monch & Eiger. Shall I be allowed to risk my (now) precious limbs in ascending any of these mountains? I don't know, but I must say I shall grudge the deprivation, even though it will be jolly loafing about the valleys. Think of smoking a pipe on the Wengern Alp, with masses of Alpine roses, & cows & strawberries & cream, & people blowing horns into your ears, & demanding centimes for their infernal inflictions! I could stand upon my head with delight & my mouth waters at the mere thought of it, & I shall be there D.V. (really something must be wrong, I am dropping piety about quite promiscuously) in a fortnight. Poor son of a degraded race, thinking I dare say of a trip to the White Mountains [of New Hampshire] or some such substitute for the genuine article, don't you envy me?

LESLIE STEPHEN, *LETTERS*, VOLUME I.

20 JUNE

THUNDER ON THE EASTERN SEABOARD, 1894

The Welsh-born W.H. Davies (1871–1940) was twenty-two years old when, one day in June, he sailed from Liverpool aboard an emigrant ship bound for New York. He had always wanted to be a writer but on arrival he found it simpler to be a vagrant. In 1907, however, on a whim, he wrote his autobiography and sent it to George Bernard Shaw for approval. It was published the same year.

The great Atlantic was as smooth as an inland river. Every one sought to escape the thoughts of home, and to do so, we often worked ourselves into a frenzy of singing and dancing. Sometimes our attention would be drawn to an iceberg on the port side, very innocent and beautiful to the passengers, but feared by mariners, who saw into its depths. And then a ship full sail; or another great Atlantic liner on the starboard bow. There was a total lack of ceremony aboard, strangers familiar with strangers, and the sexes doing each other little kindnesses, who had never met before and would probably never meet again, parting without even enquiring or giving each other a name. As we neared the coast we had a thunderstorm, and I was surprised and somewhat awed at the sound of its peals, and at the slower and larger flashes of lightning. Nature, it seemed, used a freer and more powerful hand in this country of great things than is her wont among our pretty little dales, and our small green hills. I thought the world was coming to an end, and in no way felt reassured when an American, noting my expression, said that it was nothing to what I would see and hear if I remained long in God's own country of free and law-abiding citizens.

WILLIAM HENRY DAVIES, *THE AUTOBIOGRAPHY OF A SUPER-TRAMP*.

21 JUNE

NOTES ON THE ECUADOREAN MULE, 1880

Continuing his treks in the Andes of Ecuador (*see* 5 March), Edward Whymper was on his way back to Quito, in preparation for an assault on Mounts Carihuairazo and Chimborazo, when he wrote this heartfelt observation on the character of South American mules. Despite his recalcitrant transport he successfully reached the peaks of both mountains, and in doing so claimed a world altitude record of 20,702 feet.

Little refreshed by slumber, we returned across the rickety bridge to Riobamba; without incident except a furious stampede of our animals, who took this way of showing that they had benefited by their sojourn in the forest. As a general rule, Ecuadorean mules display no eagerness to get either onward or upward, and upon flat, open ground, where there is plenty of room, each one seems to wish to be *last*; while on approaching narrow places, and ruts in greasy earth where only one can pass at a time, suddenly galvanized into life, they dash forward with outstretched necks, racing to get through *first*; and deaf to command, persuasion or entreaty outstrip the arrieros [muleteers], unheeding their shouts and 'lado's,' and rush at headlong speed, cannoning into each other and dislodging their loads. Then arises Hullabaloo! while the corners of packing-cases are splintered and their sides stove in, to the future dismay of consignor and consignee. After six months' experience of the manners and customs of the Ecuadorean mule, one began to understand why glass was dear in Quito.

EDWARD WHYMPER, *TRAVELS AMONGST THE GREAT ANDES OF THE EQUATOR*.

22 JUNE

THE POET AND THE TRAMPS, 1878

The US poet Walt Whitman (*see* 11 January) was staying with friends at Esopus, in New York State, when he took a day trip by coach and horses through the nearby countryside. Nature lover as he was, he paid due attention to his surroundings, but it was an encounter with a group of tramps that stirred him most. Writing to his daughter Mannahatta, he described the Gothic mystery of a young basket-seller with a corpse-like look in her eyes. The image struck him so forcefully that he remodelled it for an article in *Tribune* magazine and his later book *Specimen Days in America*.

I tell you it is very different country here from out west, or down in Jersey – the old stone fences, two feet thick – the scenery – the many splendid locust trees, often long rows of great big ones – the streams down the mountains, with waterfalls – 'Black Creek' – the Catskills in the distance – all did me good. It is lucky the roads are first rate (as they are here) for it is up or down hill or around something continually –

We pass'd many *tramps* on the roads – one squad interested me – it was a family of five (or six) in a small flat ricketty one-horse open wagon, with some poor household traps huddled together, some new baskets for sale (they were basket makers I suppose) & some three young children – the man driving, the woman by his side, thin & sickly, & a little babe wrapt in a bundle on her lap, its little feet & legs sticking out towards us as we went by –

On our return at sundown a couple of hours afterwards, we met them again – they had hauled aside in a lonesome spot near the woods, evidently to camp for the night – the horse was took out & was grazing peacefully near by – the man was busy at the wagon, with his baskets & traps, & the boy of 11 or so had gather'd a lot of dry wood & was building a fire on the open ground – As we went on a little on the road we encounter'd the woman with the little baby still in her arms, & her pretty-eyed 6 year old barefoot girl trotting behind, clutching her gown – the woman had two or three baskets she had probably been on to neighboring houses to sell – we spoke to her & bought a basket – she didn't look up out of her old sun-bonnet – her voice, & every thing seem'd queer, *terrified* – then as we went on, Al stopp'd the wagon & went back to the group to buy another basket – he caught a look of the woman's eyes & talked with her a little – says she was young, but look'd and talk'd like a *corpse*.

WALT WHITMAN, *SELECTED LETTERS*.

23 JUNE

AN AMERICAN IN OCCUPIED PARIS, 1940

The American war correspondent William Shirer (1904–93) was working in Berlin for CBS when he made a visit to Paris, newly occupied by the Nazis. Accompanied by a fellow Journalist, he took a 'Sentimental Journey' through a city where he had once spent happy years.

It was an exquisite June day, and we stopped to admire the view (my millionth, surely!) up the Tuileries to the Champs-Elysées, with the silhouette of the Arc de Triomphe on the horizon. It was as good as ever. Then through the Louvre and across the Seine. The fishermen were dangling their lines from the bank, as always. I thought: 'Surely this will go on to the end of Paris, to the end of time... men fishing in the Seine.' I stopped, as I have always stopped a thousand times, to see if – after all these years – I might witness one man at last having at least a bite. But though they jerked their lines out continually, no one caught a fish. I have never seen a fish caught in the Seine.

Then down the Seine to Notre-Dame. The sandbags had been removed from the central portal... Inside the Cathedral the light was too strong, with the original rose window and the two transept windows out. But from up the river as we had approached, the view of the facade, the Gothic in all its glory was superb...

And then... down the rue Bonaparte past the bookshops, the art shops, so civilized, past the house where Jess and I had lived in 1934. Across the Seine again... to stroll in the gardens of the Palais Royal, which we did, and they were as peaceful as ever before...

And thence to our hotel, filled with German soldiers, and outside, on the boulevard, a long column of German artillery roaring by.

WILLIAM SHIRER, *BERLIN DIARY*.

24 JUNE

ICELESS IN THEATRELAND, 1887

A glimpse of late-Victorian London life was provided by Ralph Blumenfeld (1864–1948), a US newspaperman who had just arrived in Britain and was thoroughly baffled by the place. Americans, before and since, have shared his bewilderment as to the nation's reluctant way with ice.

———•+•———

In front of us near Birdcage Walk, about twenty yards away, was a young woman most fashionably dressed. She was leading one of those silly, clipped black poodles, and was mincing her way along when suddenly and most appropriately in Birdcage Walk her bustle, shaped like a bird-cage, came rattling down from out of her voluminous skirts. She never deigned to turn, but walked on. Innocently – and stupidly – in spite of Sir John's restraining hand, I ran on, picked up the contraption, came upon the owner, and proffered it to her, but she turned on me furiously and said: 'Not mine!' and walked on. I shall know better next time.

Came home late after an evening at the Argyll Music Hall in Piccadilly... It was very warm in the theatre. I asked for a long drink of lemonade, which here is called 'lemon squash.' The waiter brought it, lukewarm. 'Will you get me some ice please?' I asked. 'Get you what, sir?' he asked in turn. 'Ice.' 'Why?' 'To make this stuff drinkable.' And then he burst into laughter. 'We don't keep it,' he said indulgently. I cannot understand how these people exist without ice. I have not seen a chip of it since I landed. As for ice cream, they barely know what it is except at expensive restaurants. The poor only get ale and winkles.

RALPH BLUMENFELD, *R.D.B.'s Diary*.

25 JUNE

TOO MUCH IN MASSACHUSETTS, 1957

In the summer of 1957 the newly wed poets Ted Hughes (1930–98) and Sylvia Plath (1932–63) stayed at her parents' home in Massachusetts. It was Hughes's first visit to the United States and the contrast it supplied with Britain provoked an ambivalent reaction, as described in this letter to his brother Gerald.

The houses are splendid here – each in its little grounds. The food, the general opulence is frightening. My natural instinct is to practise little private filthinesses – I spit, pee on shrubbery etc., and have a strong desire to sleep on the floor – just to keep in contact with a world that isn't quite as glazed as this one. But I'll learn my position. It's good too for me to be surrounded by a world from which I instinctively recoil. I mightn't waste quite so much energy here. For all this though there's something – a great deal – about what tiny bit I've seen, that I like. The birds are interesting – the robins are big as thrushes & shaped like them. The jays – which are everywhere, – are smaller than ours, and give the impression of being bright blue all over. They make a smacking rawk like ours. There are lots of others. Last night I saw fireflies – twinkling in and out like little aircraft on fire. There are skunks – though I haven't seen them. I'm going to get some fishing tackle and keep myself buried as deep in what these 86ft long Cadillacs cannot touch, as I can. I never saw so many cars & so huge. Those illustrations of the highways of the future – vast butterfly crossings with hundreds of cars like wingless airliners streaming in every direction through wooded countryside – that's what it's like just round here. But the real American phenomena [sic] is the kindness of these folk.

TED HUGHES, *LETTERS*.

26 JUNE

A PICNIC AT CLIVEDEN, 1887

Two days after his unhappy encounter with lukewarm lemonade at a London music hall (*see* 24 June), the American journalist Ralph Blumenfeld took a trip up the Thames Valley. The experience appears to have transformed him into a positive Anglophile.

———

A remarkable and enjoyable experience to-day such as could only be found in this delightful summer country... We met at Paddington at 10 a.m. Never have I seen anything like it. There must have been at least 5,000 people on the platforms waiting for trains. All of them, men and women, in white and all wearing 'boaters', and every woman carrying a coloured sunshade. I am told this scene is presented every Saturday and Sunday from eight until noon. We got out at Maidenhead, and took there a large steam launch and went up the river as far as the Duke of Westminster's picturesque estate called Cliveden, where we were especially permitted to land and picnic. The river was crowded with rowing boats and punts, and for long distances the banks were lined with house-boats, blooming with flowers. The house-boats appear to be the special summer resort of the well-to-do, who live on them throughout the summer. What struck me particularly was the athletic prowess of so many young women, who were astonishingly adept at rowing and punting, and seemed to be quite capable of handling their boats as well as the men. That I take it is the reason why English girls are so fresh complexioned and free in their movements. It is a fact that you see fewer white-lipped and waxen-cheeked girls than anywhere else, in spite of tight-lacing, which is as prevalent here as in France or the United States. But the women play tennis and go for long walks. They are not restricted by convention as in other countries.

RALPH BLUMENFELD, *R.D.B.'s DIARY*.

27 JUNE

A WHORE IN AMUR, 1890

In 1890, while on his journey to the Russian penal colony of Sakhalin (*see* 20 May), Anton Chekhov travelled through the Amur Valley, along the Russian–Chinese border. He was delighted by its space, climate and sense of freedom as well as the skill and adroitness of its Japanese prostitutes.

The Japanese start at Blagoveshchensk, or rather Japanese women, diminutive brunettes with big, weird hair-dos. They have beautiful figures and are, as I saw for myself, rather short in the haunch. They dress beautifully. The 'ts' sound predominates in their language. When, to satisfy your curiosity, you have intercourse with a Japanese woman, you begin to understand Skalkovsky, who is said to have had his photograph taken with a Japanese whore. The Japanese girl's room was very neat and tidy, sentimental in an Asiatic kind of way, and filled with little knick-knacks – no washbasins or objects made out of rubber or portraits of generals. There was a wide bed with a single small pillow. The pillow is for you; the Japanese girl puts a wooden support under her head in order not to spoil her coiffure. The back of her head rests on the concave part. A Japanese girl has her own concept of modesty. She keeps the light on, and if you ask her what is the Japanese word for such and such a thing she answers directly, and because she doesn't know much Russian points with her fingers or even picks it up, also she doesn't show off or affect airs and graces as Russian women do. She laughs all the time and utters a constant stream of 'ts' sounds. She has an incredible mastery of her art, so that rather than just using her body you feel as though you are taking part in an exhibition of high-level riding skill.

Anton Chekhov, *A Journey to the End of the Russian Empire*.

28 JUNE

WINGED RABBITS IN ICELAND, 1856

Emerging from a boisterous Icelandic wedding, the Earl of Dufferin (1826–1902) and friends were 'in the position of three fast young men about Reykjavik, determined to make a night of it'. It was midnight, the sun was shining, so they took a boat to a nearby island where they encountered their first puffins. The earl, who went on to become Governor General of Canada, found it all very confusing.

The grating of our keel upon the strand disturbed my reflections, and by the time I had unaccountably stepped up to my knees in the water, I was thoroughly awake, and in a condition to explore the island. It seemed to be about three-quarters of a mile long, not very broad, and a complete rabbit-warren; in fact, I could not walk a dozen yards without tripping up in the numerous burrows by which the ground was honeycombed: at last, on turning a corner, we suddenly came upon a dozen rabbits, gravely sitting at the mouths of their holes. They were quite white, without ears, and with scarlet noses. I made several desperate attempts to catch one of these singular animals, but though one or two allowed me to come pretty near, just as I thought my prize was secure, in some unaccountable manner it made unto itself wings, and literally flew away!... Red-nosed, winged rabbits! I had never heard or read of the species; and I naturally grew enthusiastic in the chase, hoping to bring home a choice specimen to astonish our English naturalists. With some difficulty we managed to catch one or two, which had run into their holes instead of flying away. They bit and scratched like tiger-cats, and screamed like parrots; indeed, on a nearer inspection, I am obliged to confess they assumed the aspect of birds, which may perhaps account for their powers of flight. A slight confusion still remains in my mind as to the real nature of the creatures.

EARL OF DUFFERIN, *LETTERS FROM HIGH LATITUDES*.

29 JUNE

FRIED FISH OF DESTINY, 1940

At the start of the Second World War the Spanish Surrealist Salvador Dalí (1904–89) left Paris for Bordeaux; but when the Nazis bombed it on 20 June 1940 he once again felt restless. By the end of June, give or take a few days (or perhaps weeks – a Surrealist's memoirs are, *ipso facto*, unreliable), he was in Lisbon, clutching a ticket for the United States.

So I arrive in Lisbon. Lisbon beneath the frenzied song of the crickets at that torrid period of the dogdays was a kind of gigantic frying-pan bubbling over with all the boiling oil of circumstances, in which was being cooked the future of thousands of migratory and fleeing fish, which the thousands of refugees of all sorts and nationalities had become. In that historic Place del Rossio which had once been fragrant with the stench of the burning flesh of the victims of the Inquisition, now again rose the ardent smoke of the new martyrs immolated by the red-hot iron pincers of visas and passports, with a smell which choked respiration and which was the very smell of the nauseating fried fish of destiny. Of the fish of that destiny I had to taste a piece of the tail, which the European actuality put perforce into my mouth. I chewed and rechewed it, but I did not swallow it, and the moment I felt my two feet braced solidly on the deck of the *Excambion* which was to take me to America I spat it with enraged repugnance and spite into that hand which I was going to abandon. It was in that right shoulder of the Iberian peninsula weighted down with the monumental sack of atavistic and pointless melancholy of the marvellous city of Lisbon that was performed the authentic and the most pitifully sad drama of the European war (with the theatre empty of spectators, and with neither glory nor pleasure). It was a solitary drama... that was being played in the oozing effusion of those hotel rooms where the refugees slept crowded together like rotting sardines, to which they returned every evening after a day of fruitless efforts, no longer discouraged, smiling with hatred and with the gangrene of hopeless bureaucratic proceedings already devouring the tissues, blue-tinged with death, of their donkeys' patience! It was the drama of those who were going to take advantage of the small comfort offered by the... ignominious bespattered watercloset for which they also had to stand in line in order at last basely to open the veins of their sole and ultimate liberty with a razor blade!

My sojourn in Lisbon still continues to appear to me as something utterly unreal. One had always the impression of meeting familiar faces in the street. One turned round, and so they were. 'Say, doesn't she look like [fashion designer] Schiaparelli? It was she. 'He's the spitting image of [filmmaker] René Clair.' It *was* René Clair! The painter Sert would be leaving the Zoological Park by streetcar just as the Duke of Windsor crossed the street and [pianist-composer] Paderewski sat down on a bench opposite to enjoy the sun. On the edge of the sidewalk, sitting on a newspaper, the famous banker, king of the bankers, would listen to the song of a cricket shut up in a golden cage, which he had just bought, and next to him the legless man who was observing him you would have sworn was Napoleon Bonaparte in person, so greatly did the bitter brow and the triangular nose resemble those of the Emperor. At the far end of the square, standing in line before the Navigation Company offices, the one you see from behind, wearing a brown suit, looks like Salvador Dalí...

SALVADOR DALÍ, *THE SECRET LIFE OF SALVADOR DALÍ*.

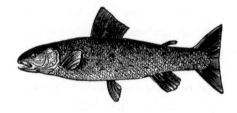

30 JUNE

TRULY FOREIGN TANGIER, 1867

While working as roving correspondent for the *Alta California* newspaper, the American author and humorist Mark Twain (1835–1910) was detailed in 1867 to accompany a shipload of US pilgrims bound for the Holy Land. The first truly foreign stop on their cruise was Tangier.

This is Royal!... Tangier is the spot we have been looking for all the time. Elsewhere we have found foreign-looking things and foreign-looking people, but always with things and people intermixed that we were familiar with before, and so the novelty of the situation lost a deal of its force. We wanted something thoroughly and uncompromisingly foreign – foreign from top to bottom – foreign from centre to circumference – foreign inside and outside and all around – nothing any where about it to dilute its foreignness – nothing to remind us of any other people or any other land under the sun. And lo! in Tangier we have found it. Here is not the slightest thing that ever we have seen save in pictures – and we always mistrusted the pictures before. We can not any more. The pictures used to seem exaggerations – they seemed too weird and fanciful for reality. But behold, they were not wild enough – they were not fanciful enough – they have not told half the story. Tangier is a foreign land if ever there was one; and the true spirit of it can never be found in any book save the Arabian Nights.

MARK TWAIN, *THE INNOCENTS ABROAD*.

JULY

∞

1 JULY

EARTHBOUND ON A DONKEY, 1935

The British explorer Peter Fleming and his Swiss companion Ella Maillart (*see* 16 February) were crossing the deserts and mountains of western China – the 'roof of the world' – when they approached the oasis of Keriya in Sinkiang province, north of Tibet. Fleming, who had experienced many modes of transport, felt a trifle let down by his donkey.

We went on, crawling timelessly across hard, dune-flecked desert, where tall wickerwork baskets, filled with stones and painted red, marked the track. For eleven days now I had ridden on a donkey and I was getting tired of it. There is something about a donkey which keeps your mind and spirits earthbound. On a horse, on a camel, even on a yak, your imagination soars without much difficulty; you are never for very long impervious to the romance of the road, such as it is. But the donkey, though perhaps on some beach of your childhood it provided an adventure which made you as breathless as your nurse, is a sublunary mount for the adult. Its mean stature, its demure and patient aspect, above all the tripping rhythm of its gait – all these combine to take the gilt off the golden road. After a few days on a donkey you come to see life from the ignoble, the unstimulating viewpoint of a sack of potatoes.

PETER FLEMING, *NEWS FROM TARTARY*.

2 JULY

A BOAT TRIP ON THE BOSPHORUS, 1860

The British aristocrat Lady Emilia Bithynia Maceroni Hornby (no less) spent several years in Constantinople during the mid-nineteenth century. Her letters home, such as this one dated simply 'July', give a portrait of the Ottoman capital at its most voluptuously sybaritic.

———•·•———

It is very sultry on the Bosphorus just now; all nature seems asleep, – very little stirring on land or sea; a few Greeks moving about in the high terraced gardens; here and there a caique slowly threading its way up the stream, or lightly gliding down, the cool *thud thud* of the oars sounding pleasantly enough. The pennants of the anchored ships are scarcely waving in the languid air, and even the restless sea-birds are quietly away somewhere, till sundown.

I rowed close in shore yesterday afternoon... Not a soul was visible even from the salaamlik, or male part, of the numerous water-palaces which I passed; not the murmur of a single voice sounded through the closely latticed and curtained windows of the women's apartments. Here and there, through an open door, I got delightful glimpses of cool gardens, with rows of orange and lemon trees, and rich parterres of flowers. Here and there by the stone steps sat a turbaned Turk of the old school, quietly fishing with a line wound round his hand, looking so cool and comfortable in his soft, flowered robe; then you float by the silent, mysterious caique-haus, where dark green water ebbs and flows and murmurs against rows of boats... Sometimes a rapid turn brings you close to the grey-stone causeway of some ancient house, before which sits a huge Black, silently smoking, who slowly turns his yellow eyes to mark you as your caique shoots past. The deep plunge of oars re-echoes against the lofty walls, and through the depths of the vast open hall beyond.

LADY HORNBY, *CONSTANTINOPLE DURING THE CRIMEAN WAR.*

3 JULY

FORBIDDEN SIGHTS IN TRIPOLI, 1783

Miss Tully (*see* 12 January), the British consul's sister, had barely arrived in Tripoli before she started taking notes. She describes here the extraordinary lengths to which the ladies of the court went to ensure that they might be heard and smelled – but never seen.

———

None of the ladies in the royal family ever walk in the streets, except when they go to their mosques, to fulfil a vow, or make an offering, which they frequently do on various occasions but with the greatest circumspection. They go out as late as eleven or twelve o'clock at night, attended by a considerable guard from the castle. A number of black female slaves and Moorish servants form a large body, in the very centre of which the princess or princesses walk, with their own particular attendants or ladies encircling them. The guard continually announces them as they go, to give timely notice of their approach. They have with them a great number of lights, and a vast quantity of burning perfume, which is carried in silver filagree vases, and also large silver ewers of rose and orange-flower water, to damp the burning perfume, which, during their walk, produces a thick cloud around them, composed of the finest aromatic odours. Either of these accompaniments, besides the vociferous cry of the guards, is fully sufficient to indicate the approach of the royal party, in time to leave the way clear for them; and this is particularly necessary, as their law decrees no less a punishment than death for any person who may be in the street and remain there while their ladies are passing by, or for any man who may look at them from a window. Of course, every place is perfectly free from spectators before they come near to it.

MISS TULLY, *LETTERS WRITTEN DURING A TEN YEARS' RESIDENCE AT THE COURT OF TRIPOLI.*

4 JULY

TROPICAL THIRST IN GHANA, 1958

In 1958 the Polish journalist Ryszard Kapuściński (*see* 12 April) reported from Accra, Ghana, during the rainy season. At the city's Hotel Metropol, a rickety two-storey construction built on a raft, he encountered a motley group of hard-up, hard-drinking ex-pats.

————

In the tropics drinking is obligatory. In Europe, the first thing two people say to each other when they meet is 'Hello. What's new?' When people greet each other in the tropics, they say 'What would you like to drink?' They frequently drink during the daytime, but in the evening the drinking is mandatory; the drinking is premeditated. After all, it is the evening that shades into night, and it is the night that lies in wait for anyone reckless enough to have spurned alcohol.

The tropical night is a hardened ally of all the world's makers of whiskey, cognac, liqueurs, schnapps and beers, and the person who denies them their sales is assailed by the night's ultimate weapon: sleeplessness. Insomnia is always wearing, but in the tropics it is killing. A person punished all day by the sun, by a thirst that can't be satisfied, maltreated and weakened, has to sleep.

He has to. And then he cannot... Time stands still. Sleep will not come. At six in the morning, the same invariable six in the morning all year round, the sun rises. Its rays increase the dead steam-bath closeness. You should get up. But you don't have the strength. You don't tie your shoes because the effort of bending over is too much... You are tormented by undefined longings, nostalgias, dusky pessimisms. You wait for the day to pass, for all of it, damn it to hell, finally to pass.

So you drink. Against the night, against the depression, against the foulness floating in the bucket of your fate. That's the only struggle you're capable of.

RYSZARD KAPUŚCIŃSKI, *THE SOCCER WAR*.

5 JULY

PATTERNS ON THE SKIN, 1769

When HMS *Endeavour* stopped at Tahiti, the main reason for so doing was to take astronomical sightings; but the naturalist Joseph Banks (1743–1820) used the stay to make his own observations. He was fascinated not only by the sport of surfing (*see* 29 May) but by the practice of tattooing. 'What can be a sufficient inducement to suffer so much pain is difficult to say,' he wrote, 'not one Indian (tho I have askd hundreds) would ever give me the least reason for it.' Nevertheless, the practice spread rapidly throughout the Royal Navy and thence the world.

This morn I saw the operation of *Tattowing* the buttocks performd upon a girl of about 12 years old, it provd as I have always suspected a most painfull one. It was done with a large instrument about 2 inches long containing about 30 teeth, every stroke of this hundreds of which were made in a minute drew blood. The patient bore this for about ¼ of an hour with most stoical resolution; by that time however the pain began to operate too strongly to be peacably endurd, she began to complain and soon burst out into loud lamentations and would fain have persuaded the operator to cease; she was however held down by two women who sometimes scolded, sometimes beat, and at others coaxd her... This was one side only of her buttocks for the other had been done some time before. The arches upon the loins upon which they value themselves much were not yet done, the doing of which they told causd more pain than what I had seen.

JOSEPH BANKS, *THE 'ENDEAVOUR' JOURNAL*, VOLUME II.

6 JULY

SEEKING SHADE IN TUSCANY, 1841

On a visit to Italy, the British author Frances Trollope (1779–1863) stayed at the Tuscan resort of Bagni di Lucca, famous for its thermal springs. Until recently she had been sweltering in Florence where, as she wrote, 'the very name of shade is refreshing'.

I cannot express to you one half of the pleasure I feel, at finding myself here... I had no idea that any spot so abounding in shade, so sheltered from the scorching sun, so freshened by the eternal coolness of the briskly-running stream... AND so perfectly free from mosquitoes... could have been found in July, on this side of the Alps... and the shade too, is not the thin straggling shade of olive-trees, but that of chestnut, beech, and oak... It is perfect enchantment!

[From the hills] you can look out upon a teeming landscape that seems to live and breathe at your feet, showing a vigour and richness of vegetation that only this downward view of it can show to the best advantage:... for as to turning aside from the high road to wander through the fields, as is the manner in England, the thing is impossible; you would get entangled, fettered, stifled, cribbed, confined, if you made the attempt – a gigantic growth of Indian corn would overwhelm you in one direction, hedge rows of vines would strangle you in another, if you attempted to make your way athwart the graceful-looking, but very sturdy impediment which they offer; and lupines, hemp, clover, and French-beans, tangled in their rank luxuriance, make traps and snares in all directions; so that a walk in the fields is absolutely impossible. But among the chestnut trees the case is different.'

FRANCES TROLLOPE, *A VISIT TO ITALY*, VOLUME I.

7 JULY

A BORING OLD GEYSIR, 1856

The Earl of Dufferin's visit to Iceland included not only a sighting of winged rabbits (*see* 28 June), but also a more dutiful attendance on the Haukadalur Valley's world-famous Great Geysir. If he was baffled by the former he was not entirely awestruck by the latter. In Dufferin's defence it must be said that the geysir went through dormant periods and most Victorian travellers appear to have been charmed more by its reputation than its reality.

We had now been keeping watch for three days over the Geysir, in languid expectation of the eruption which was to set us free... when a cry from the guides made us start to our feet, and with one common impulse rush towards the basin. The usual subterranean thunders had already commenced. A violent agitation was disturbing the centre of the pool. Suddenly a dome of water lifted itself up to the height of eight or ten feet, – then burst, and fell; immediately after which a shining liquid column, or rather a sheaf of columns wreathed in robes of vapour, sprung into the air, and in a succession of jerking leaps, each higher than the last, flung their silver crests against the sky. For a few minutes the fountain held its own, then all at once appeared to lose its ascending energy. The unstable waters faltered, drooped, fell, 'like a broken purpose,' back upon themselves, and were immediately sucked down into the recesses of their pipe.

EARL OF DUFFERIN, *LETTERS FROM HIGH LATITUDES*.

8 JULY

RIO BY SUNSET, 1932

In 1932 the British explorer Peter Fleming (*see* 16 February) joined an expedition to ascertain the fate of Colonel Percival Harrison Fawcett, who had gone missing in the Mato Grosso several years before. Here he describes their arrival in Rio de Janeiro at the start of what would ultimately prove a futile quest.

We came to Rio at sunset. This must surely be the best time to do it.

For some hours Brazil had been in sight, a dark-green formidable outline, a coast (as far as we could see) almost unscathed by man. The huge cliffs slanted a little backwards, as if the land had been reined in sharply on the brink of salt perdition. The charging jungle stopped short only at the sea. I got the impression of a sub-continent with imperfect self-control.

We were passing a little island in the harbour's mouth. Against a tawny sunset the hills behind the city stood up fiercely. On their crests the tiny black silhouettes of trees showed with more than their share of detail and prominence. Some frigate birds went out past us to the darkening sea, flying low. The water front, still some way ahead of us, flaunted a solitary sky-scraper. All sky-scrapers look foolish and unnatural when isolated from their kind. It is only in the mass, huddled and strenuously craning, that they achieve a sort of crude dignity. Alone, cut off from their native background of competition and emergency, they appear gauche and rather forlorn. With this one it was particularly so. Ridiculously at variance with all that we could see, hopelessly irrelevant to all that we imagined, it had the pathos of the boor. It domineered without conviction, the totem of another tribe. It knew itself for a mistake, an oversight, an intrusion. It was like a bag of tools left behind, when the curtain rises, on a stage set for romance.

Later I was told that during the last revolution they threw a full-sized billiard table out of a window on its fourteenth floor. Then I forgave it. Where that sort of thing can happen to them, there is a place for sky-scrapers.

As we came closer the city evaded us. The hills drew in with the darkness, and Rio merged into her bodyguard. Between their shoulders we saw under a furled bank of cloud a strip of lemon-coloured sky, level and straight-edged like a wainscot. A little covey of rockets went up from somewhere in the town. They burst in a chorus of inoffensive popping noises and left surprised balls of smoke hanging in the air. There are always rockets in Brazil. The birth of a saint or the death of a patriot, the outbreak or suppression of revolt, the rise or fall of a government... Rockets are to the Brazilian calendar what exclamation marks are to the correspondence of a debutante.

In the twilight – yes, in the swift tropical twilight of which you have all read – the political exiles, no longer able to control their emotion, pointed out to us again and again the Sugar Loaf and Corcovado, those astonishing peaks. We duly marvelled. Our aesthetic susceptibilities were on their mettle. Two people were heard to say that the scene, if reproduced on canvas, would fail to command belief. The ship buzzed with ecstasy.

PETER FLEMING, *BRAZILIAN ADVENTURE*.

9 JULY

THE SOLITUDE OF SEASICKNESS, 1936

Returning from California aboard the *Pilgrim*, Richard Henry Dana (*see* 10 January) approached the notoriously volatile Cape Horn. He soon learnt that it was no time to feel seasick.

To be sick in a forecastle is miserable indeed. It is the worst part of a dog's life; especially in bad weather. The forecastle, shut up tight to keep out the water and cold air; – the watch either on deck, or asleep in their berths; – no one to speak to; – the pale light of the single lamp, swinging to and fro from the beam, so dim that one can scarcely see, much less read by it; – the water dropping from the beams and carlines, and running down the sides; and the forecastle so wet, and dark, and cheerless, and so lumbered up with chests and wet clothes, that sitting up is worse than lying in the berth! These are some of the evils. Fortunately, I needed no help from any one, and no medicine; and if I had needed help, I don't know where I should have found it. Sailors are willing enough, but it is true, as is often said – No one ships for nurse on board a vessel. Our merchant ships are always under-manned, and if one man is lost by sickness, they cannot spare another to take care of him. A sailor is always presumed to be well, and if he's sick, he's a poor dog. One has to stand his wheel, and another his look-out, and the sooner he gets on deck again, the better.

RICHARD HENRY DANA, *TWO YEARS BEFORE THE MAST*.

10 JULY

THE PERA PALAS, 1994

In 1994 the Scottish writer William Dalrymple (born 1965) journeyed through the realms of ancient Byzantium in search of the Middle East's remaining pockets of Christianity. Among his early stops was Istanbul's legendary Pera Palas hotel.

Arriving here is like stepping into a sensuous Orientalist fantasy by Delacroix, all mock-Iznik tiles and pseudo-Ottoman marble inlay. A hotel masquerading as a Turkish bath; you almost expect some voluptuous Turkish odalisque to appear and disrobe behind the reception desk.

I ate breakfast in a vast Viennese ballroom with a sprung wooden floor and dadoes dripping with recently reapplied gilt. The lift is a giant baroque birdcage, entered through a rainforest of potted palms. On the wall nearby, newly dusted, is a framed diploma from the 1932 Ideal Home Exhibition, signed by the Mayor of East Ham.

The Pera Palas was bought by the Turkish government last year, and attempts to renovate the old structure seem to have started manically, then been abruptly given up. In the dining room the gilt is so bright you have to wear sunglasses to look at it; but upstairs the carpets are as bald as the head of an Ottoman eunuch.

The hotel has a policy of naming its bedrooms after distinguished guests, which has unconsciously acted as a graph of its dramatic post-war decline: from before the war you can choose to sleep in Ataturk, Mata Hari or King Zog of Albania; after it there is nothing more exciting on offer than Julio Iglesias.

WILLIAM DALRYMPLE, *FROM THE HOLY MOUNTAIN*.

11 JULY

LONDON SMUG, 1971

The US satirist S.J. Perelman (*see* 2 February) was a fervent Anglophile until he actually spent some time in England. In a letter to his daughter Abby he let rip on the many defects to be found in the national character. Caustic remarks to one side, however, he managed to live in London for two years.

As regards the English and living among them, the honeymoon radiance in which I was bathed before I left on the journey has largely subsided and I see them with much more clarity. In many ways, they are the most supremely self-satisfied and smug bastards I've ever encountered. They consider that the world begins and ends here, and they're quick to let you know it. There is a phrase in the last chapter of Thoreau's *Walden* that describes their attitude perfectly: 'Consider the China pride and stagnant self-complacency of mankind.' For 'mankind,' just insert 'the middle- and upper-class Englishman or woman.' They all talk in a horrid sort of very fast mumble that is difficult to understand and that doesn't become easier to grasp the more you live here. This, of course, is due to the fact that they're so repressed: the males half or three-quarters fag from their schooling, the females because they've always been bludgeoned into silence. The expression 'It's not done' pretty well sums up not only the state of mind of the more solvent class, but the attitude of people in shops and businesses. If they haven't got some commonplace article, their response so often is 'Is that something you have in Ameddica?' accompanied by a vinegary smile. Or just a scornful 'No, I wouldn't know about that,' figuratively slapping you across the knuckles with a ruler like an algebra teacher.

S.J. PERELMAN, *DON'T TREAD ON ME*.

12 JULY

TO THE POLE BY BALLOON, 1897

In 1897 the Swedish explorers Salomon Andrée, Knut Fraenkel and Nils Strindberg attempted to reach the North Pole by balloon. The balloon left Spitzbergen on 11 July and came down on the 14th, stranding the three men on the polar pack-ice. They escaped across the floes to the desolate White Island, where they died of exhaustion and food poisoning. Their remains, along with their journals and camera films, were not discovered until 1930, when by pure chance a group of Norwegian scientists stopped at White Island to investigate the geology of this hitherto undocumented bit of rock. The following diary entry, written by Andrée two days into the flight, is one of the most poignant in the history of Arctic exploration.

It is not a little strange to be floating here above the Polar Sea. To be the first that have floated here in a balloon. How soon, I wonder, shall we have successors? Shall we be thought mad or will our example be followed? I cannot deny but that all three of us are dominated by a feeling of pride. We think we can well face death, having done what we have done. Is not the whole, perhaps, the expression of an extremely strong sense of individuality which cannot bear the thought of living and dying like a man in the ranks, forgotten by coming generations? Is this ambition? ... The rattling of the guide-lines in the snow are the only sounds heard, except the whining [of the wind] in the basket.

SALOMON ANDRÉE, *THE ANDRÉE DIARIES*.

13 JULY

THE DESICCATION OF YAZD, 1954

In June 1953, the Swiss travellers Nicolas Bouvier (1929–98) and Thierry Vernet (1927–93) left their homeland in an epic attempt to drive a Fiat Topolino from Geneva to the Khyber Pass. Bouvier once wrote, 'One thinks that one is going to make a journey, yet soon it is the journey that makes or unmakes you.' It was very nearly the latter when they reached the deserts of Iran.

In Yazd, most things arrive by truck from the west. Life is dear and the Yazdis – who are said to be the greatest cowards, the best gardeners and the finest businessmen in Iran – endeavour to make it dearer still. But at the beginning of July the heat is free, along with the thirst and the flies. A hat and dark glasses are not enough protection for the Yazd desert; you need to be muffled up like the Bedouins. But we drove bare-armed, our shirts unbuttoned, and in the course of the day the sun and wind relieved us of several litres of water. We thought we could re-establish the balance by drinking about twenty cups of mild tea at night – which were soon sweated off – and then we threw ourselves on to steamy beds in the hope of sleeping. As we slept, however, dryness was at work; it smouldered like a bush-fire; one's whole maddened organism cried out, and we found ourselves on our feet and panting, noses stuffed with hay, fingers like parchment, rooting round in the dark for any scrap of moisture – a drop of water, even old melon rinds to plunge our faces into. Three or four times a night this panic would hurl us out of bed, and when sleep finally came it was dawn, the flies were humming, and old men in pyjamas shouted to one another across the courtyard of the inn as they lit the first cigarettes of the day. Then the sun came up and began to pump us out again.

NICOLAS BOUVIER, *THE WAY OF THE WORLD*.

14 JULY

AN AMERICAN IN WALES, 1810

Writing from Glamorganshire, the American tourist Louis Simond (*see* 17 February) declared himself transfixed by the beauty and prosperity of Wales. Alas, the rural idyll would soon be transformed: Glamorgan was to become a hub of the Industrial Revolution.

———

Wales seems more inhabited, at least more strewed over with habitations of all sorts, scattered or in villages, than any part of England we have seen, and which are rendered more conspicuous by white-washing of the most resplendent whiteness. Every cottage too has its roses, and honeysuckles, and vines, and neat walk to the door; and this attention bestowed on objects of mere pleasurable comforts, is the surest indication of minds at ease, and not under the immediate pressure of poverty. It is impossible indeed to look round without the conviction, that this country is, upon the whole, one of the happiest, if not the happiest in the world. The women we see are certainly better looking than nearer London. The language of the inhabitants is quite unintelligible to us; at the inns, however, all is transacted in English. Having gone to see some ruins, while the horses were changing at Cardiff, we found the post-boy had driven away; and on inquiring the reason on his return, he said he was afraid the horses would catch cold standing – this is delightful for the middle of July, when the people of New York are dying with heat.

LOUIS SIMOND, *AN AMERICAN IN REGENCY ENGLAND*.

15 JULY

SPIRITS OF THE JAPANESE SEA, 1891

On the fifteenth day of the seventh month, according to the Japanese lunar calendar, the American Japanophile, Lafcadio Hearn (*see* 4 April), evoked the nautical spirits that roamed the Japanese Sea.

———•+•———

The blanched road winds along a coast of low cliffs, – the coast of the Japanese Sea. Always on the left, over a narrow strip of stony land, or a heaping of dunes, its vast expanse appears, blue-wrinkling to that pale horizon beyond which Korea lies, under the same white sun. Sometimes, through sudden gaps in the cliff's verge, there flashes to us the running of the surf. Always upon the right another sea, – a silent sea of green, reaching to far misty ranges of wooded hills, with huge pale peaks behind them, – a vast level of rice-fields, over whose surface soundless waves keep chasing each other under the same great breath that moves the blue to-day from Chōsen [Korea].

Though during a week the sky has remained unclouded, the sea has for several days been growing angrier; and now the muttering of its surf sounds far into the land. They say that it always roughens thus during the period of the Festival of the Dead, – the three days of the Bon, which are the thirteenth, fourteenth and fifteenth of the seventh month by the ancient calendar. And on the sixteenth day, after the shōryōbune, which are the Ships of Souls, have been launched, no one dares enter it: no boats can then be hired: all the fishermen remain at home. For on that day the sea is the highway of the dead, who must pass back over its waters to their mysterious home; and therefore upon that day is it called Hotoke-umi, – the Buddha Flood, – the Tide of the Returning Ghosts. And ever upon the night of that sixteenth day, – whether the sea be calm or tumultuous, – all its surface shimmers with faint lights gliding out to the open, – the dim fires of the dead; and there is heard a murmuring of voices, like the murmur of a city far-off, – the indistinguishable speech of souls.

But it may happen that some vessel, belated in spite of desperate effort to reach port, may find herself far out at sea upon the night of the sixteenth day. Then will the dead rise tall about the ship, and reach long hands and murmur: '*Tago, tago o-kure! – tago o-kure!*' ('A bucket honorably condescend to give'). Never may they be refused; but before the bucket is given, the bottom of it must be knocked out. Woe to all on board should an entire tago be suffered to fall even by accident into the sea! – for the dead would at once use it to fill and sink the ship.

Nor are the dead the only powers invisible dreaded in the time of the Hotoke-umi. Then there are the Ma most powerful, and the Kappa.

But in all times the swimmer fears the Kappa, the Ape of the Waters, hideous and obscene, who reaches up from the deeps to draw men down, and to devour their entrails.

Only their entrails.

The corpse of him who has been seized by the Kappa may be cast on shore after many days. Unless long battered against the rocks by heavy surf, or nibbled by fishes, it will show no outward wound. But it will be light and hollow – empty like a long-dried gourd.

Lafcadio Hearn, Glimpses of Unfamiliar Japan, Volume II.

16 JULY

RAILWAY WORK IN DAKOTA, 1887

In 1887 the Norwegian author Knut Hamsun (*see* 19 February) worked his way around the United States as a labourer. Newly arrived in North Dakota, he described the sweltering prospect in a letter to a friend.

We signed on in Minneapolis for work on the railway out here. In the course of the morning they set us down in the middle of the wide prairie. Three canvas tents stood nearby – that was all we saw. Huh! that was no place for us! So we threw our bags on our backs and went on foot to the nearest township. From there on to another town by train to get farm work. Got nothing. Then on to Fargo where we slept the night in an empty box car standing alone on the rails... It was a bit adventurous travelling like that as we did, but quite interesting. So here we are now in Dakota and will probably remain here until after the harvest. The pay, by the way, is not all that great.

What a place Dakota is! Like an ocean. It makes the same impression on me as the Atlantic does – precisely. The wagons along the road seem to swim, the houses float. It is inconsolably monotonous. And then, working during the day, under the glaring hot sun, white, shimmering, cruelly hot. Not a cloud above. The wind is hot rather than warm. Not a shadow for miles around. Here and there, on the so-called tree claims there might be a bush [sic]. A melancholy sight. The branches stretching up as though begging that rapacious heat on high for mercy. The trunk, the bark just a wretched, burnt husk. But the sunsets are absolutely beyond compare. Never anywhere else than here in America have I seen the sun shimmering so blood-red. Never in any painting, never in any poem. I do believe there are no words for it.

KNUT HAMSUN, *SELECTED LETTERS*, VOLUME I.

17 JULY

LOCUSTS IN MURMANSK

One summer day in 1922 the German artist George Grosz (1893–1959) gained entry to the Soviet Union via the port of Murmansk. Bewildered to find so many beggars, he tried to placate them with gifts of chocolate. Then he remembered a saying from the hunger years of the First World War: 'The Big Locust appears wherever people make war. It travels with the armies through the land and turns them into small locusts that have to eat and eat until nothing is left except the stripped trees, and the naked bare earth...'

She snatched it quickly with a gnarled, dirty hand, gave us a puzzled grin, put the basket down in front of her, and began to rub the chocolate between her hands, as if she were washing them. She had taken the chocolate for a bar of soap... I quickly pulled another slab of chocolate out of my pocket and bit off a piece. Then she understood and began contentedly to push the chocolate in and out of her toothless mouth, a ring of workers and peasants expectantly watching her every move. I can still see how one of them, a barefoot, parchment-coloured man with a thin little beard, freckles and sly eyes, suddenly grabbed the chocolate from the old woman's hand and started to suck it himself. The chocolate now travelled from mouth to mouth, people licking it like ice cream, while the old hag, robbed of her priceless treasure, set up a terrible wail... God alone knew how long it was since these people had had their last taste of chocolate or sugar...

Perhaps this was Locust Land; those mud-yellow barefoot insects crowding round the chocolate might suddenly fly up, rubbing their wings together and go buzzing in search of more chocolate... For God's sake, I thought, and felt things moving inside my pocket, as if insects were already crawling about.

GEORGE GROSZ, *A SMALL YES AND A BIG NO.*

18 JULY

RIO HIT-AND-RUN, 1949

Travelling through South America shortly after the Second World War, the French author Albert Camus (*see* 25 May) stopped in Rio de Janeiro. As he drove through its raucous sprawl, the city seemed to prefigure an urban dystopia.

We cross interminable suburbs in a bumpy streetcar. Sad and most of the time empty... but coagulating at long intervals around a center, a square brilliant with neon, with red and green lights... crammed with this multi-colored crowd at whom, from time to time, a loudspeaker screams the latest football scores. One thinks of these crowds of people, incessantly growing over the surface of the world, who will eventually cover everything and end up suffocating themselves. I understand Rio better like this, at any rate better than at the Copacabana – that aspect of it that's like an oil stain extending infinitely in every direction. Returning in a *lotacao*, a kind of group taxi, we see one of the numerous accidents that result from this unbelievable traffic. On an avenue shimmering with lights a speeding bus hits a poor, old black man, sends him flying like a tennis ball, drives round the body, and takes off. The driver flees because of the stupid law of *flagrante delicto*, which would send him to prison. So he takes off, there's no *flagrante delicto*, and he won't go to prison. Nobody comes to help the old black man. The shot he took would have killed a bull. Later on I learn that they'll put a white sheet over him – which will slowly turn red with his blood – set lit candles around him, and the traffic will continue to by-pass him until the authorities arrive.

ALBERT CAMUS, *AMERICAN JOURNALS*.

19 JULY

STEVENSON IN THE PACIFIC, 1890

In June 1888 Robert Louis Stevenson (*see* 2 June) and his family had set sail from San Francisco in a chartered yacht. Two years later, he described in a letter to the American publisher S.S. McClure how he and his family were faring after their time in the Pacific.

It may interest you to know (as it is the thing which most interests ourselves) that we have reached that stage in which all ship's food is revolting to the appetite and apparently no longer sustaining to the system, and are now waiting and longing for the harbour... Our clothes are falling from our bodies with filth, age, rot, and particularly from the effects of the last washing they received on the isle of Majuro in the Marshall Group where a reliable coloured man took them away and (after a due interval) brought them back thickly caked with soap but apparently quite innocent of water. The whole ship's company, owner, captain, engineer, supercargo and passengers are dressed like beggar men (and in the case of Mrs Stevenson like a beggar woman); all go with bare feet, all are in rags and many partly naked; in the midst of which, one German passenger sits serene in lawn, tussa [a rough silk], fine linen, shoes and socks and every refinement of civilisation... The ship wallows deep with barbaric trumpery collected by Mrs Stevenson, twopenny spears are triced up in the rigging; whenever the ship rolls, I look to have a shark's tooth scimitar discharged upon my dead head; and as I walk about the cabin dictating to Lloyd, my path is impeded by a Manihiki drum, vainly sprinkled on the outside with buhac powder [a natural insecticide], but supposed internally to be one clotted bolus of cockroaches.

ROBERT LOUIS STEVENSON, *LETTERS*, VOLUME VI.

20 JULY

A MICROCOSM IN TROUSERS, 1869

As he made his way through Yosemite with 2,500 sheep (*see* 7 June), John Muir became fascinated by the shepherd's trousers, which collected and preserved in fatty aspic the flora and fauna upon which he sat.

Following the sheep he carries a heavy six-shooter swung from a belt on one side and his luncheon on the other. The ancient cloth in which the meat, fresh from the frying pan, is tied serves as a filter through which the clear fat and gravy juices drip down his right hip and leg in clustering stalactites. This oleaginous formation is soon broken up, however, and diffused and rubbed evenly into his scanty apparel, by sitting down, rolling over, crossing his legs while resting on logs, etc., making shirt and trousers water-tight and shiny. His trousers, in particular, have become so adhesive with the mixed fat and resin that pine needles, thin flakes and fibres of bark, hair, mica scales and minute grains of quartz, hornblende, etc., feathers, seed wings, moth and butterfly wings, legs and antennae of innumerable insects, or even whole insects such as the small beetles, moths and mosquitoes, with flower petals, pollen dust and indeed bits of all plants, animals, and minerals of the region adhere to them and are safely imbedded, so that though far from being a naturalist he collects fragmentary specimens of everything and becomes richer than he knows. His specimens are kept passably fresh, too, by the purity of the air and the resiny bituminous beds into which they are pressed. Man is a microcosm, at least our shepherd is, or rather his trousers.

JOHN MUIR, *MY FIRST SUMMER IN THE SIERRA*.

21 JULY

THE MIKADO'S PALACE, 1885

On one of his many journeys to Japan the French naval officer Pierre Loti (*see* 15 March) visited Kyoto, the venerable city which until 1869 had been the imperial capital. Amidst the tumult of Japan's modernization the 16th-century palace of Toyotomi Hideyoshi offered a glimpse into a sterner, less accommodating world.

———•·•———

An enclosure of high walls. My rickshaw-men stop at the first gateway, built in an ancient severe and religious style: massive columns with bronze bases; a narrow frieze sculpted with outlandish figures; a heavy and enormous roof.

I walk into vast, deserted courtyards, planted with centuries-old trees whose boughs had been propped up, like old men with crutches. The immense palace buildings seem at first to be in disarray, without any semblance of unity. Everywhere these towering roofs, monumental and intimidating, whose corners turn up in the Chinese fashion and bristle with black ornaments.

Seeing nobody, I wander about at random.

This is where the incessant smile of modern Japan comes to a full stop. It is like entering the silence of an incomprehensible past, the dead splendour of a civilisation whose architecture, style and aesthetics are utterly alien to me.

A guardian monk spots me, comes over and, with a bow, asks for my name and passport. Everything is in order: he himself will guide me through the whole palace, provided I take off my shoes and hat. He brings me a pair of velvet slippers, which are kept for visitors. Thanks, but I would rather go barefoot like him, and so we begin our silent tour of an endless series of halls, covered in gold lacquer and decorated in a foreign style that is both delicate and exquisite... It is dark in this windowless palace; a semi-obscurity that lends itself to enchantments.

PIERRE LOTI, *VOYAGES*.

22 JULY

SHELLEY IN CHAMONIX, 1816

The conquest of Mont Blanc in 1786 opened the eyes of writers and artists to the beauty of the Alps. Among the many Romantics who rushed to the mountains were the English poet Percy Bysshe Shelley (1792–1822) and his wife Mary (1797–1851), author of *Frankenstein*. Here, Shelley describes his first view of Mont Blanc and its surrounding pinnacles and, subsequently, a visit to the Montenvers Glacier – the fabled Mer de Glace, the very sight of which sent early visitors into raptures.

Mont Blanc was before us – the Alps with their innumerable glaciers on high all around, closing in the complicated windings of the single vale – forests inexpressibly beautiful, but majestic in their beauty – intermingled beech and pine, and oak, overshadowed our road, or receded whilst lawns of such verdure as I have never seen before occupied these openings and gradually became darker in their recesses. Mont Blanc was before us, but it was covered with cloud; its base, furrowed with dreadful gaps, was seen above. Pinnacles of snow intolerably bright, part of the chain connected with Mont Blanc, shone through the clouds at intervals on high. I never knew – I never imagined what mountains were before. The immensity of these aerial summits excited, when they suddenly burst upon the sight, a sentiment of ecstatic wonder, not unallied to madness. And remember this was all one scene, it all pressed home to our regard and our imagination...

[At the Mer de Glace] On all sides precipitous mountains, the abodes of unrelenting frost, surround this vale; their sides are banked up with ice and snow, broken, heaped high, and exhibiting terrific chasms. The summits are sharp and naked pinnacles, whose overhanging steepness will not even permit snow to rest upon them. Lines of dazzling ice occupy here and there their perpendicular rifts, and shine through the driving vapours with inexpressible brilliance; they pierce the clouds like things not belonging to this earth. The vale itself is filled with a mass of undulating ice, and has an ascent sufficiently gradual even to the remotest abysses of these horrible deserts... It exhibits an appearance as if frost has suddenly bound up the waves and whirlpools of a mighty torrent... The waves are elevated about twelve or fifteen feet from the surface of the mass, which is intersected by long gaps of unfathomable depth, the ice of whose sides is more beautiful than the azure of the sky. In these regions everything changes, and is in motion... The echo of rocks, or of the ice and snow which fall from their overhanging precipices, or roll from their aerial summits, scarcely ceases for one moment. One would think that Mont Blanc, like the god of the Stoics, was a vast animal, and that the frozen blood for ever circulated through his stony veins.

PERCY BYSSHE SHELLEY, *HISTORY OF A SIX WEEKS' TOUR.*

23 JULY

THE TENT WAS GONE, 1911

In July 1911, before their attempt on the South Pole, three members of Robert Falcon Scott's Antarctic expedition (*see* 2 March) trudged across the Ross Ice Barrier to collect Emperor Penguin eggs which, it was hoped, might cast light on the process of evolution. In appalling winter conditions they managed to bring the eggs home but nearly lost their lives in the process. Apsley Cherry-Garrard (1886–1959) recorded the moment a blizzard snatched their tent.

There seemed not one chance in a million that we should ever see our tent again. We were 900 feet up on the mountain side, and the wind blew about as hard as a wind can blow straight out to sea. First there was a steep slope, so hard that a pick made little impression on it, so slippery that if you started down in finnesko [soft, insulated travelling boots] you never could stop: this ended in a great ice-cliff some hundreds of feet high, and then came miles of pressure ridges, crevassed and tumbled, in which you might as well look for a daisy as a tent: and after that the open sea. The chances, however, were that the tent had just been taken up into the air and dropped somewhere in this sea well on the way to New Zealand. Obviously the tent was gone.

Face to face with real death one does not think of the things that torment the bad people in the tracts, and fill the good people with bliss. I might have speculated on my chances of going to Heaven; but candidly I did not care. I could not have wept if I had tried. I had no wish to review the evils of my past. But the past did seem to have been a bit wasted. The road to Hell may be paved with good intentions: the road to Heaven is paved with lost opportunities.

APSLEY CHERRY-GARRARD, *THE WORST JOURNEY IN THE WORLD*.

24 JULY

BLACK DIANA, 1949

On his journey through South America (*see* 18 July) Albert Camus was touched by the power of *candomblé,* a Brazilian religious rite. Overall, though, he did not warm to Brazil: 'In this oversized land which has the sadness of large spaces, life is terribly banal.'

I learn nothing new until the entrance of a group of young black girls, semi-hypnotized, eyes almost closed, standing straight but swinging their feet forward and back. One of them, a tall thin girl, delights me. She's wearing a green dress and a blue huntress' hat with musketeer feathers and the brim turned up. In her hand she's holding a green and yellow bow loaded with an arrow at the end of which is a brooch representing a multicolored bird. The handsome, sleeping face reflects a smooth and innocent melancholy. This black Diana is infinitely graceful. And when she dances this extraordinary gracefulness remains undiminished. When the music stops, she totters. The rhythm alone lends her a kind of invisible guardian around which she spins her arabesques, uttering from time to time a strange, piercing but somehow melodious bird cry. All the rest isn't worth much. Mediocre dances expressing degenerated rituals. We leave with Catalao. But in this faraway neighborhood, as we stumble along the streets full of holes, through the heavy, aromatic night, the wounded bird's cry comes back to me and I recall my beautiful slumbering one.

ALBERT CAMUS, *AMERICAN JOURNALS.*

25 JULY

NO SWIMMING AT HEAVEN LAKE, 1981

The Indian author Vikram Seth (born 1952) was studying at Nanjing University when, on a July day, he visited the popular resort of Heaven Lake in China's western province of Xinjiang. He was preparing for a swim when a conversation made him think twice.

Mr Cao, with great offhandedness, addresses the air. 'People are often drowned here,' he says. After a pause, he continues. 'When was the last one?' This question is directed at the cook... 'Was it the Beijing athlete?' asks Mr Cao.

'Yes, yes, it was the Beijing athlete.'

'The Beijing athlete?' I quaver. The placidity of this water must be deceptive.

'Yes, I think so,' says Mr Cao to the cook. 'He'd swim across the lake and back every day...'

'Every day,' repeats the cook.

'And then one day he swam to the other side, and had just started on his way back when he simply disappeared. Drowned.'

'Drowned,' tolls the cook.

'Drowned? The Beijing athlete?' I ask, anxiously.

'Yes,' says Mr Cao. 'He was from an athletics college in Beijing. Or was it Tianjin?'

'Beijing,' says the cook, with authority.

'But... how did this happen?' I blurt out.

Mr Cao has gone back to his receipts. He looks up at the cook, who says, in a lugubrious tone, 'Well, no one knows. He might have had a heart attack.'

'Or he might have got cramp,' suggests Mr Cao.

'Or maybe the water was too cold,' adds the cook.

'Or maybe it was a current under the surface. No one knows. His body was never found.'

'Never found,' mutters the cook as he heads back for the kitchen.

I retie my shoe laces.

VIKRAM SETH, *FROM HEAVEN LAKE.*

26 JULY

CALABRESE LINGO, 1847

Edward Lear (*see* 17 June) crossed in 1847 from Sicily to Calabria, on the Italian mainland, where he found a guide whose incomprehensible dialect appealed to the nonsense poet within.

We had engaged a muleteer for an indefinite time, the expense for both guide and quadruped being six carlini daily; and if we sent him back from any point of our journey it was agreed that his charges should be defrayed until he reached Reggio.

Our man, a grave, tall fellow of more than fifty years of age, and with a good expression of countenance, was called Ciccio, and we explained to him that our plan was to do always just as we pleased – going straight ahead or stopping to sketch, without reference to any law but our own pleasure; to all of which he replied by a short sentence ending with 'Dogo: dighi, doghi, daghi, da' – a collection of sounds of frequent recurrence in Calabrese lingo, and the only definite portion of that speech that we could perfectly master. What the 'Dogo' was we never knew, though it was an object of our keenest search throughout the tour to ascertain if it were animal, mineral or vegetable. Afterwards, by constant habit, we arranged a sort of conversational communication with friend Ciccio, but we never got on well unless we said 'Dogi si' or 'Dogo no' several times as an ad libitum appoggiatura, winding up with 'Dighi, doghi, daghi, da,' which seemed to set all right.

EDWARD LEAR, *LEAR'S ITALY*.

27 JULY

ESQUIMAUX NIGHTS, 1823

During his two-year voyage in search of the North West Passage, Captain George Lyon (*see* 1 February) proved himself one of the era's more adventurous anthropologists. Here, in 1823, he journeyed by dog-sled – in which he was far ahead of his time – to spend the night with an Eskimo family.

We were joyfully welcomed to Ooyarra's abode, where the place of honour, the deer-skin seat, was cleared for my reception... The old mother, Now-kit-yoo, assisted the young women in pulling off our wet clothes and wringing our boots, which, being of Esquimaux manufacture, she afterwards soled and mended without any request on our parts, considering us as part of the family. Our knapsacks and clothes being all wet, we gladly turned into our blanket bags, which had been better guarded, before a dozen or two visitors of each sex. Dunn slept in the little tent to watch our goods, and I had a small portion of Ooyarra's screened off for me with seals' skins. Tired as I was, sleep was denied me, as I was obliged, on the arrival of each new set of people, to answer their questions, as to how I could possibly have got into the bag; the manner in which I had wrapped it round me for warmth leading them to suppose that I was sewed up in it.

My host and his wives having retired to another tent, and my visitors at length taking compassion on me, I went comfortably to sleep, but at midnight was awakened by a feeling of great warmth, and to my surprise found myself covered by a large deer skin, under which lay my friend, his two wives, and their favourite puppy, all fast asleep, and stark naked. Supposing this was all according to rule, I left them to repose in peace, and again resigned myself to rest.

GEORGE LYON, *PRIVATE JOURNAL.*

28 JULY

A RARE AND SAVAGE FEAST, 1855

Towards the end of his voyage in search of the Open Polar Sea (*see* 14 June), Elisha Kent Kane and his crew were forced to abandon ship and take to the boats. While heading for one of Greenland's few ports the starving men spotted a seal.

I would have ordered another shot, but no discipline could have controlled the men. With a wild yell, each vociferating according to his own impulse, they urged both boats upon the floes. A crowd of hands seized the seal and bore him up to safer ice. The men seemed half crazy: I had not realized how much we were reduced by absolute famine. They ran over the floe, crying and laughing and brandishing their knives. It was not five minutes before every man was sucking his bloody fingers or mouthing long strips of raw blubber.

Not an ounce of this seal was lost. The intestines found their way into the soup-kettles without any observance of the preliminary home-processes. The cartilaginous parts of the fore-flippers were cut off in the mêlée, and passed round to be chewed upon; and even the liver, warm and raw as it was, bade fair to be eaten before it had seen the pot. That night, on the large halting-floe, to which, in contempt of the dangers of drifting, we happy men had hauled our boats, two entire planks of the Red Eric were devoted to a grand cooking-fire, and we enjoyed a rare and savage feast.

ELISHA KENT KANE, *ARCTIC EXPLORATIONS*, VOLUME II.

29 JULY

SWIMMING IN TRIESTE, 1873

In 1872 Isabel Burton (*see* 8 January) accompanied her husband Richard to Trieste, where he had been appointed British consul. At that date the port still belonged to the Austro-Hungarian Empire, hence the Germanic commands in her account of their morning swimming rituals. (One wonders whether consuls keep the same impressively early hours today.)

Trieste was a beautiful place, especially the view round our bay. The hills were covered with woodland and verdure; the deep blue Adriatic was in the foreground dotted with lateen sails; and the town filled the valley and straggled up the slopes. The sky was softly blue on a balmy day; the bees and birds, the hum of insects, the flowers and fresh air, and the pretty, animated peasants, combined to form a picture which made one glad to live.

The charm of Trieste is that one can live exactly as one pleases. Richard and I drew out a line for ourselves when we first went to Trieste, and we always kept to it as closely as we could. We rose at 3 or 4 a.m. in summer and at 5 a.m. in winter... We took our daily exercise in the shape of an hour's swimming in the sea, or fencing at the school, according to weather...

The prettiest thing in Trieste was the swimming school. It was moored out at the entrance to the harbour. We used to reach it in a boat, and get hold of Tonina, the old woman who provided us with the *camerino*, or little stall to undress in, and who would grin from ear to ear at our chaff and the thought of her *bakshish*. The women's costumes were short trousers, with bodice or belt of blue serge or white alpaca trimmed with red. We plunged into the great *vasca*, or basin, an acre of sea, bottomless, but enclosed on all sides with a loaded net, to keep out the sharks. There were twelve soldiers to teach beginners. They used to begin with a pole and rope, like a fishing-rod and line, and at the end of the rope was a broad belt, which went round the waist of the beginner, and you heard the incessant 'Eins, zwei, drei' of the drill. Next they would lead the beginners round the edge of the basin with a rope, like pet dogs. But we adepts in swimming plunged in head first from a sort of trapeze, or from the roofs of the dressing-rooms, making a somersault on the way. The swimmers did the prettiest tricks in the water. Young married women met in the middle to shake hands and hold long conversations. Scores of young girls used to romp about, ducking each other under and climbing on each other's backs for support, and children of three or four used to swim about like whitebait, in and out, amongst us all. One stout old lady used to sit lazily in the water, like a blubber fish, knitting, occasionally moving her feet. We used to call her 'the buoy,' and hold on to her when we were tired.

ISABEL BURTON, *THE ROMANCE OF ISABEL LADY BURTON*, VOLUME II.

30 JULY

BEFORE THE THUNDERBOLT, 1914

The British journalist Philip Gibbs (1877–1962) visited Paris in the summer of 1914. One late-July day, he captured the atmosphere of that ominously sunny season. The French army would mobilize on 1 August.

Paris was beautiful in those last days of July under a hot sun. Outwardly its life seemed peaceful. In the Champs Elysées I heard the shrill squeak of Punch as the children laughed around the *Petit Guignol*. Down the rue de Rivoli strolled American tourists in panama hats, and English tourists in summer clothes, staring in the shop windows at the latest studies of nude women, and at night went in pursuit of adventure to Montmartre, where the orchestras of the Bal Tabarin were still fiddling mad tangos in a competition of shrieking melody, and where troops of painted ladies in the Folies Bergères still paraded in the *promenoir*, with langorous eyes, through wafts of sickly scent...

Then suddenly the thunderbolt fell with the signal of war, and in a few hours Paris was changed as though by a wizard's spell. Most of the children vanished from the Tuileries gardens with their white-capped nurses. Punch gave a final squawk of dismay and disappeared when the *Petit Guignol* packed up to make way for a more tragic drama. A hush fell upon Montmartre, and the musicians in the orchestra packed up their instruments and scurried with scared faces to Berlin, Vienna, and Budapest.

PHILIP GIBBS, *THE PAGEANT OF THE YEARS*.

31 JULY

AT LEAST THE TRAINS RUN ON TIME, 1923

The British journalist H.J. Greenwell visited Italy in July 1923 and was over-whelmed by its display of efficiency. As with many travellers to the heart of Fascism, he admired the discipline of dictatorship while preferring to ignore the means by which it was enforced. Still, his report would have cheered Agnes Castle (*see* 10 March).

There is something changed in the state of Italy. One feels it in the very air: travellers remark it, chat about it, forget it until they say to each other: 'Why, have you noticed? The train is on time.'

Not only is the train punctual now, but letters are delivered promptly, and the telegrams come to the hand with dispatch. Up and down the length and breadth of Italy there is not a murmur of a strike. What has brought about this remarkable condition of things?

The answer is: Benito Mussolini and his Fascists. From the Sicilian village children who hurl stones at your motor-car to the ragpickers of Naples who sweep down the Via Roma at nightfall all shout the Fascist greeting, 'Alala' to you.

Everywhere, too, friend greets friend with the right hand outstretched as in the days of ancient Rome. Sometimes, I think, the gesture and greetings are made with derision, but there is no doubt even those who mock recognise the renaissance of Italy under the dictatorship of Mussolini.

H.J. GREENWELL, QUOTED IN JAMES MCMILLAN (ED.), *THE WAY IT WAS*.

AUGUST

∞

1 AUGUST

FACING THE POLE, 1908

In 1908 Robert Peary left Cape York, on the northwest coast of Greenland, for a final stab at the North Pole (*see* 9 April). He was more than fifty years old and knew that, succeed or fail, this would be his last expedition to the Arctic.

Should I succeed? Should I return? Success in the attainment of 90° North would not inevitably carry with it the safe return... In the Arctic the chances are always against the explorer. The inscrutable guardians of the secret appear to have a well-nigh inexhaustible reserve of trump cards to play against the intruder who insists upon dropping into the game. The life is a dog's life, but the work is a man's work.

As we steamed northward from Cape York, on the first day of August, 1908, I felt that I was now in truth face to face with the final struggle. Everything in my life appeared to have led up to this day. All my years of work and all my former expeditions were merely preparations for this last and supreme effort. It has been said that well-directed labor towards a given end is an excellent kind of prayer for its attainment. If that be so, then prayer has been my portion for many years. Through all the seasons of disappointment and defeat I had never ceased to believe that the great white mystery of the North must eventually succumb to the insistence of human experience and will, and standing there with my back to the world and my face toward that mystery, I believed that I should win in spite of all the powers of darkness and of desolation.

ROBERT E. PEARY, *THE NORTH POLE*.

2 AUGUST

UPPING STICKS...

In 1935, at the age of ten, Gerald Durrell (1925–95) moved with his family from Britain to Corfu. It was the start of a life-long interest in nature that saw him become one of the world's leading conservationists and, along the way, a best-selling author. The relocation was largely at the instigation of his elder brother 'Larry' – the author Lawrence Durrell – who, as August began, was faintly irked by the rest of his family, under the weather in every sense.

July had been blown out like a candle by a biting wind that ushered in a leaden August sky. A sharp, stinging drizzle fell, billowing into opaque grey sheets when the wind caught it. Along the Bournemouth sea-front the beach-huts turned blank wooden faces towards a greeny-grey, froth-chained sea that leapt eagerly at the cement bulwark of the shore. The gulls had tumbled inland over the town, and they now drifted above the house-tops on taut wings, whining peevishly. It was the kind of weather calculated to try anyone's endurance.

Considered as a group my family was not a very prepossessing sight that afternoon, for the weather had brought with it the usual selection of ills to which we were prone. For me, lying on the floor, labelling my collection of shells, it had brought catarrh, pouring it into my skull like cement... For my brother Leslie, hunched dark and glowering by the fire, it had inflamed the convolutions of his ears so that they bled delicately but persistently. To my sister Margo it had delivered a fresh dappling of acne spots to a face that was already blotched like a red veil. For my mother there was a rich, bubbling cold, and a twinge of rheumatism to season it. Only my eldest brother, Larry, was untouched, but it was sufficient that he was irritated by our failings.

GERALD DURRELL, *My Family and Other Animals.*

3 AUGUST

...FOR CORFU, 1935

Larry Durrell (*see* 2 August) pressed his mother to pack up and leave Britain.

'I had a letter from George this morning – he says Corfu's wonderful. Why don't we pack up and go to Greece?'

'Very well, dear, if you like,' said Mother unguardedly.

Where Larry was concerned she was generally very careful not to commit herself.

'When?' asked Larry, rather surprised at this cooperation.

Mother, perceiving that she had made a tactical error, cautiously lowered *Easy Recipes from Rajputana*. 'Well, I think it would be a sensible idea if you were to go on ahead, dear, and arrange things. Then you can write and tell me if it's nice, and we can all follow,' she said cleverly.

Larry gave her a withering look. 'You said *that* when I suggested going to Spain,' he reminded her, 'and I sat for two interminable months in Seville, waiting for you to come out, while you did nothing except write me massive letters about drains and drinking-water, as though I was the Town Clerk or something. No, if we're going to Greece, let's all go together.'

'You do *exaggerate*, Larry,' said Mother plaintively; 'anyway, I can't go just like that. I have to arrange something about this house.'

'Arrange? Arrange what, for heaven's sake? Sell it.'

'I can't do that, dear,' said Mother, shocked.

'Why not?'

'But I've only just bought it'

'Sell it while it's still untarnished, then.'

'Don't be ridiculous, dear,' said Mother firmly; 'that's quite out of the question. It would be madness.'

So we sold the house and fled from the gloom of the English summer, like a flock of migrating swallows.

GERALD DURRELL, *My Family and Other Animals*.

4 AUGUST

CANADIAN LAKES, 1880

While the poet Walt Whitman (*see* 11 January) was travelling through Canada he wrote from Montreal to an American friend, Montgomery Stafford. He had come 500 miles from Ontario, where he had been laid up for several weeks, and was rejuvenated by the extent and beauty of Canada's lakes.

I am traveling mostly by water – and spent several days in 'the Lakes of the Thousand Islands' – that is what they call a part of the St Lawrence river, some 50 miles long & 10 to 20 wide, filled with the prettiest islands you ever see, all sizes, some big with fine farms on them, & some very moderate – others rocky hills like, of an acre or two covered with cedars – but *the water* every where I travel in this country is the best part – it is more beautiful and bright than you can conceive, very clean & pure, of a sky-blue color & there seems no end of it – I travel for days & days over it, from Lake Huron on through Lakes Erie and Ontario & down the St Lawrence to here (700 miles) & it is just as fascinating to me now as ever – I have been in sight of it or traveling on it ever since I have been in Canada – I never get tired of it – (We have nothing like it our way, so grand & bright & clear.)

WALT WHITMAN, *SELECTED LETTERS*.

5 AUGUST

SPIRITS OF THE HIMALAYA, 1921

The Englishman George Mallory (1886–1924), who fell to his death on Everest, was one of the most respected climbers of the age. On his first expedition to Everest, he sized up his nemesis and concluded (ironically, in the circumstances) that beautiful though the high tops were, there was a lot to be said for staying at the bottom.

———•••———

Perhaps the astonishing charm and beauty here lie in the complications half hidden behind a mask of apparent simplicity, so that one's eye never tires of following up the lines of the great arêtes, of following along the broken edge of the hanging glacier covering the upper half of this eastern face of Everest so as to determine at one point after another its relation with the buttresses below and with their abutments against the rock which it covers. But for me the most magnificent and sublime in mountain scenery can be made lovelier by some more tender touch; and that, too, is added here. When all is said about Chomolungma,* the Goddess Mother of the World, and about Chomo Uri,* the Goddess of the Turquoise Mountain, I come back to the valley, the valley bed itself, the broad pastures, where our tents lay, where cattle grazed and where butter was made, the little stream we followed up to the valley head, wandering along its well-turfed banks under the high moraine, the few rare plants, saxifrages, gentians and primulas, so well watered there, and a soft, familiar blueness in the air which even here may charm us. Though I bow to the goddesses I cannot forget at their feet a gentler spirit than theirs, a little shy perhaps, but constant in the changing winds and variable moods of mountains and always friendly.

GEORGE MALLORY, *CLIMBING EVEREST*.

* Two local names for Everest.

6 AUGUST

SUNSET ON MONT BLANC, 1873

In 1873 the Alpinist Leslie Stephen (*see* 19 June) climbed Mont Blanc with the painter Gabriel Loppé, so as to record the sunset from the summit of Europe's highest mountain.

A vast cone, with its apex pointing away from us, seemed to be suddenly cut out from the world beneath; night was within its borders and the twilight still round; the blue mists were quenched where it fell, and for the instant we could scarcely tell what was the origin of this strange appearance. Some unexpected change seemed to have taken place in the programme; as though a great fold in the curtain had suddenly given way and dropped on to part of the scenery... It is difficult to say how sharply marked was the outline and how startling was the contrast between this pyramid of darkness and the faintly-lighted spaces beyond its influence; a huge inky blot seemed to have suddenly fallen upon the landscape. As we gazed, we could see it move. It swallowed up ridge by ridge, and its sharp point crept steadily from one landmark to another... We were standing, in fact, on the point of the gnomon of a gigantic sun-dial, the face of which was formed by thousands of square miles of mountain and valley...

By some singular effect of perspective, rays of darkness seemed to be converging from above our heads to a point immediately above the apex of the shadowy cone. For a time it seemed that there was a kind of anti-sun in the east, pouring out not light, but deep shadow as it rose. The apex soon reached the horizon, and then to our surprise began climbing the distant sky. Would it never stop, and was Mont Blanc capable of overshadowing not only the earth but the sky?

LESLIE STEPHEN, *THE PLAYGROUND OF EUROPE*.

7 AUGUST

AUSTRIA BASKING, 1927

Driven by tuberculosis to swap the heat of Tuscany for the cool air of the Alps, D.H. Lawrence (*see* 4 January) settled briefly in the southern Austrian town of Villach. Fresh from the bustle and violence of Mussolini's Italy, he was amazed at the languor of diminished, post-Versailles Austria.

It's queer to be in a country with practically no government – a queer shabby kind of populace – quite nice – and no bosses or bossing at all – a queer empty sort of feeling, all the *forza* of Italy suddenly removed, and the *sforza* too. It is much more restful to the nerves... All the Viennese sunning their large and naked bodies like whitish seals on the shore – save for little bathing drawers – it is *de rigueur* to be naked all day long – and nobody making the slightest effort for anything – the slackest world you ever knew. In the evening was a Firework festa by the river – very funny – home-made fireworks, in this destitute country – pans of fire blazing and floating swiftly, very swiftly, away on the full icy river, one after another – squibby fountains of fire from damp powder, on moored rafts – and a few rockets that let out six red sparks – and crowds and crowds of queer amiable people in odd dress, and nobody to boss: dancing, beer-drinking, skittles etc. A queer world.

D.H. Lawrence, *Letters*, Volume VI.

8 AUGUST

THE CAULDRON OF THE WATERS, 2005

In 2005 Robert MacFarlane embarked on a journey of discovery to Britain's remaining areas of wilderness (*see* 28 March). Among the places he visited was Coruisk, on the Isle of Skye, whose Gaelic name translates as 'the cauldron of the waters'.

———•••———

The morning we left, the sky was a slurless blue. Before beginning the walk out, we took a last swim in the water of Loch Coruisk. We slipped into the loch from a warm tilted shore rock, having laid our clothes out on boulders to take up the sun's heat. The water was cool from the night, and still as stone. Its peaty colour gave my skin a goldfish lustre, the colour of old coin.

A hundred yards or so out across the loch was an island. Just a shallow hump of bare black rock, smoothed by the passage of the glaciers and no more than a foot above the water at its highest point. It looked like the back of a whale, and its form reminded me of the outline of my beechwood.

I swam across to it, clambered out and stood there, dripping, feeling the roughness of the rock beneath my feet, and the warmth it had already gathered from the sun. Then I lay down on my back, tucked my hands behind my head and looked into the sky.

After three or four minutes, I found myself struck by a sensation of inverted vertigo, of being on the point of falling upwards. The air was empty of indicators of space or time; empty, too, of markers of depth. There was no noise except the discreet lapping of the water against the island. Lying there, with no human trace except the rim of my own eyes, I could feel a silence that reached backwards to the Ice Age.

In the Basin I had come to imagine time differently, or at least to experience it differently. Time seemed to express itself in terms not of hours and minutes, but of shades and textures. After only a few days

I found it hard to think out of Coruisk: to the ongoing world of shops, colleges and cars, with its briskness and urgency, or even to my family, my city home and my garden, where the branches of the apple tree would be lolling with fruit.

The Basin kept many different kinds of time, and not all of them were slow. I had seen quickness there too: the sudden drop of a raven in flight, the veer of water round a rock, the darts of the damselflies, the midges who were born, danced and died in a single day. But it was the great chronologies of its making – the ice's intentless progress seawards, down the slope of time – which had worked upon my mind most powerfully.

To be in the Basin, even briefly, is to be reminded of the narrow limits of human perception, of the provisionality of your assumptions about the world. In such a place, your conventional units of chronology (the century, the life-span, the decade, the year, the day, the heartbeat) become all but imperceptible, and your individual gestures and impulses (the lift of a hand, the swimming stroke taken within water, the flash of anger, a turn of speech or thought) acquired an eerie quickness. The larger impulses of the human world – its wars, civilisations, eras – seem remote. Time in the Basin moves both too fast and too slowly for you to comprehend, and it has no interest in conforming to any human schedule. The Basin keeps wild time.

ROBERT MACFARLANE, *THE WILD PLACES*.

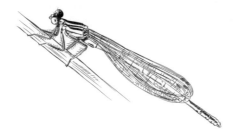

9 AUGUST

MAGICIANS IN DELHI, 1342

When the Moroccan traveller Ibn Battuta reached Delhi (*see* 15 September) he wasted no time in putting himself about. Soon, he had inveigled his way into the ruling Muslim hierarchy and had become a personal favourite of the sultan, Muhammad bin Tughluq. One August day his new royal friend invited him round to the palace for a magic show.

The Sultan sent for me once when I was at Delhi, and on entering I found him in a private apartment with some of his intimates and two of these *jugis*. One of them squatted on the ground, then rose into the air above our heads, still sitting. I was so astonished and frightened that I fell to the floor in a faint. A potion was administered to me, and I revived and sat up. Meantime this man remained in his sitting posture. His companion then took a sandal from his bag he had with him, and beat it on the ground like one infuriated. The sandal rose in the air until it came above the neck of the sitting man and then began hitting him on the neck while he descended little by little until he sat down alongside us. Then the sultan said, 'If I did not fear for your reason I would have ordered them to do stranger things than this you have seen.' I took my leave, but was affected with palpitations and fell ill, until he ordered me to be given a draught which removed it all.

IBN BATTUTA, *TRAVELS IN ASIA AND AFRICA.*

10 AUGUST

ARCTIC HIGHLANDERS, 1818

The Scottish naval officer and explorer John Ross (1777–1856) left Britain in 1818, under orders to find the North West Passage. He failed in his task but made several remarkable discoveries, among them a tribe he called the 'Arctic Highlanders'. The Etah Inuit were the northernmost community in the world, so isolated that they thought they were the only people in existence. They met Ross's interpreter Sacheuse on a sheet of ice, with some trepidation and a strip of clear water between them.

They first pointed to the ships, eagerly asking, 'What great creatures those were?' 'Do they come from the sun or the moon?' 'Do they give us light by night or by day?' Sacheuse told them that he was a man, that he had a father and mother like themselves; and, pointing to the south, said that he came from a distant country in that direction. To this they answered, 'That cannot be, there is nothing but ice there.' They again asked, 'What creatures these were?' pointing to the ships; to which Sacheuse replied, that 'they were houses made of wood.' This they seemed still to discredit, answering, 'No, they are alive, we have seen them move their wings.' Sacheuse now inquired of them, what they themselves were; to which they replied, they were men, and lived in that direction, pointing to the north; that there was much water there; and that they had come here to fish for sea unicorns. It was then agreed, that Sacheuse should pass the chasm to them, and he accordingly returned to the ship to make his report, and to ask for a plank.

JOHN ROSS, *A VOYAGE OF DISCOVERY*.

11 AUGUST

HALF MILE DOWN, 1934

Following his many diving expeditions (*see* 19 April) William Beebe teamed up with Otis Barton, a wealthy inventor, to probe the depths in their 'bathysphere'. Linked to a support ship, the *Ready,* by cables, oxygen tubes and a telephone line, they dropped into the sea off Bermuda and after several tries reached a record half-mile down (though on this particular descent they came 130 feet or so short of the mark). Added to the fear of the unknown, and the worry that their bathysphere might crumple under the water pressure, was the banal strain of having to talk non-stop into the telephone: a silence of more than five seconds was the emergency signal.

At 9.41 in the morning we splashed beneath the surface, and often as I have experienced it, the sudden shift from a golden yellow world to a green one was unexpected. After the foam and bubbles passed from the glass, we were bathed in green; our faces, the tanks, the trays, even the blackened walls were tinged. Yet seen from the deck, we apparently descended into sheer, deep ultramarine. The only hint of this change of colour vouchsafed those above was the increasing turquoise of the bathysphere as it approached the vanishing point, about 100 feet below the surface...

The sun was blazing over the ocean, the surface was unusually quiet; conditions were perfect for whatever the eye could carry to the brain. A question came over the phone, an answer went, and down we slipped through the water. As I have said, the first plunge erases, to the eye, all the comforting, warm rays of the spectrum. The red and the orange are as if they had never been, and soon the yellow is swallowed up in the green. We cherish all these on the surface of the earth and when they are winnowed out at 100 feet or more, although they are only one-sixth of the visible spectrum, yet, in our mind, all the rest belongs to chill and night and death. Even modern war bears this out; no more are red blood and scarlet flames its symbols, but the terrible greyness of gas, the ghastly blue of Very lights...

At 1,000 feet we took stock of our surroundings. The stuffing box and the door were dry, the noise of the blower did not interfere with the telephone conversation, the humidity was so well taken care of that I did not need a handkerchief over nose and mouth when talking close to the glass. The steel was becoming very cold. I tried to name the water; blackish-blue, dark grey-blue. It is strange that as the blue goes it is not replaced by violet – the end of the visible spectrum. That has apparently already been absorbed. The last hint of blue tapers into a nameless grey, and this finally into black, but from the present level down, the eye falters, and the mind refuses any articulate colour distinction. The sun is defeated and colour has gone for ever, until a human at last penetrates and flashes a yellow electric ray into what has been jet black for two billion years.

WILLIAM BEEBE, *HALF MILE DOWN*.

12 AUGUST

NEW YORK ALIGHT, 1939

Returning to Britain from a trip to Canada, the writer and social reformer Violet Markham (1872–1959) spent a few days in New York. Like most Europeans of the time she was struck by the city's vitality and its display of – and use of – energy.

It was more than thirty years since I had been in the U.S., and this time America and the Americans took my breath away. I was swept by the sense of youth and strength and vitality; by the marvel of this great continent, stretching three thousand miles westward, full of exciting men and women. As for New York, I thought it the most incredible and in its way the most marvellous city in the world. It was difficult to assess the values of anything so remote from European experience. The evening I arrived I found it impossible to go to bed and spent half the night hanging out of the window of my room high above the city watching the spectacle of the great buildings all lit up – a scene of such fantasy as my eyes had never previously beheld. What the Gothic is to the thirteenth century, the architecture of New York is to the twentieth. Each speaks the appropriate language of its epoch and each tries to storm heaven in its own way.

VIOLET MARKHAM, *RETURN PASSAGE.*

13 AUGUST

ROTTERDAM ZOO, 1641

When the diarist John Evelyn (*see* 3 June) took a tour of the Continent, Rotterdam was one of his first ports of call. There he observed a menagerie of marvels.

Here I first saw an Eliphant, who was so extreamely well disciplin'd and obedient that I did never wonder at anything more: It was a beast of a monstrous size, yet as flexible and nimble in the joynts (contrary to the vulgar tradition) as could be imagin'd from so prodigious a bulke, & strange fabrick; but I most of all admired at the dexterity, and strength of his proboscis, on which he was able to support two, or three men, and by which he tooke, and reached what ever was offer'd him; his teeth were but short being a female, and not old, as they told us. I was also shew'd a Pelican, or rather (as I conjectur'd) the Onocratulus of Pliny, having a large bill, tip'd with red, and pointing downewards a little reflected; but what is most prodigious, the under part, annex't to a gullet, so wide, and apt to extend; and would easily have swallowd, a little child: The plumage was white, wall eyd, the legge red and flatt footed; but in nothing resembling the picture, and description of the fabulous Pelican; which when I told the testy old-man who shew'd it; he was very wroth. There was also a Cock with 4 leggs; but what was most strange, with two rumps or vents, one whereof was at his breast; by which he likewise voyded dongue [voided dung], as they assur'd us; There was with this fowle an hen having two large Spurrs growing out at her sides, and penetrating through the feathers of her wings.

JOHN EVELYN, *DIARY*.

287

14 AUGUST

A BAD SUNDAY IN DUBLIN, 1949

The American humorist S.J. Perelman was in dyspeptic humour when he visited Ireland in 1949 with his wife Laura. Always even-handed in his range of targets, he was later just as condemning of England (*see* 11 July). He writes here to his scriptwriter friends Frances and Albert Hackett.

Dublin on a Sunday afternoon in mid-August is so close to being buried alive that I had better not chill your blood with any further description. There are 4,238 churches within one mile of where I'm sitting (sorry, where I'm *after* sitting), and that part of the population which isn't macerating itself inside them is closeted in the pubs. This morning the children and I walked miles through the slums... to find something called the Bird Market, which turned out to be a dozen louse-ridden canaries. That constitutes the total amusement facilities of this place. They don't even have the opportunity as they once did of sitting around and slandering the English, now that they have achieved their independence...

Well, girls... The kiddies are off seeing *Sorrowful Jones*, a Bob Hope epic, in some theater on O'Connell Street and if I stop now, Laura and I just have time to sneak down for afternoon tea in the lobby. That means bread-and-butter sandwiches, frosted cakes, and Irish county families muttering 'Divil a bit.'

S.J. PERELMAN, *DON'T TREAD ON ME.*

15 AUGUST

ECHOES OF ARMAGEDDON, 1916

During the First World War people living on the south coast of England gradually became accustomed to the thump of artillery from the trenches in Flanders. In an article published on this date in *The Times,* the author Virginia Woolf (1882–1941) described what it was like to take a walk on the South Downs of Sussex.

It sounds like the beating of gigantic carpets by gigantic women, at a distance. You may almost see them holding the carpets in their strong arms by the four corners, tossing them into the air, and bringing them down with a thud while the dust rises in a cloud above their heads. All walks on the Downs this summer are accompanied by this sinister sound of far-off beating, which is sometimes as faint as the ghost of an echo, and sometimes rises almost from the next fold of grey land. At all times strange volumes of sound roll across the bare uplands, and reverberate in those hollows in the Downside which seem to await the spectators of some Titanic drama. Often walking alone, with neither man nor animal in sight, you turn sharply to see who it is that gallops behind you. But there is no one. The phantom horseman dashes by with a thunder of hoofs, and suddenly his ride is over and the sound lapses, and you only hear the grasshoppers and the larks in the sky.

VIRGINIA WOOLF, *TRAVELS WITH VIRGINIA WOOLF.*

16 AUGUST

UPSETTING THE SCOTS, 1773

In August 1773 Dr Samuel Johnson (1709–84), general wit and compiler of the landmark *Dictionary of the English Language*, was persuaded by his friend James Boswell (1740–95) to make a tour of Scotland. They had been in Edinburgh barely two days before Johnson, a supremely opinionated man, told his hosts what he thought of the union between Scotland and England. Boswell, who recorded it all, was himself a Scot.

I here began to indulge old Scottish sentiments, and to express a warm regret, that, by our union with England, we were no more – our independent kingdom was lost.

JOHNSON: 'Sir, never talk of your independency, who could let your Queen [Mary, Queen of Scots] remain twenty years in captivity, and then be put to death, without even a pretence of justice, without your ever attempting to rescue her...

Worthy Mr JAMES KERR, Keeper of the Records: 'Half our nation was bribed by English money.'

JOHNSON: 'Sir, that is no defence: that makes you worse.'

Good Mr BROWN, Keeper of the Advocates' Library: 'We had better say nothing about it.'

BOSWELL: 'You would have been glad, however, to have had us last war, sir, to fight your battles!'

JOHNSON: 'We should have had you for the same price, though there had been no Union, as we might have had Swiss, or other troops. No, no, I shall agree to a separation. You have only to *go home*.'

Just as he had said this, I to divert the subject, shewed him the signed assurances of the three successive Kings of the Hanover family, to maintain the Presbyterian establishment in Scotland. 'We'll give you that,' said he, 'into the bargain.'

JAMES BOSWELL, *JOURNAL OF A TOUR TO THE HEBRIDES*.

17 AUGUST

WATER IN WADI RUM, 1967

While working as travel editor for the *Observer* newspaper, Eric Newby (*see* 18 February) visited Jordan. There, following in the tracks of T.E. Lawrence (*see* 18 May), he encountered a spring in Wadi Rum.

———•———

The way to the spring, which was called el Shellala, wound upwards among the rocks past fig trees brutally hacked by the Bedouin in their everlasting search for fuel, dwarf acacias and wild watermelon shrubs, the wild fruit of which lay among the rocks as light as ping-pong balls, dried out and filled with black seeds that rattled when one shook them. On the path big black beetles pushed doggedly at bits of goat dung, stashing them away.

Until the pipe had been put in to connect the spring to the fort the water had spouted into a basin cut in the rock, but now that the pipe had been cemented in, it only emerged as a trickle. Yet it was still an enchanting place, a rare place in the wilderness, overhung with fern and deliciously cool in the shadow of the cliffs...

From the top of the ledge above the spring, ravines a thousand feet deep that were like narrow trenches, led away into the mysterious heart of Jebel Rumm. Here and there the rain of centuries had worn cup-like depressions in the rocks. Someone, probably a Howeitat herdsboy, had baited them with seeds and then balanced flat stones above them on sticks, so that a bird touching one of them would bring the stone crashing down and be trapped.

But now there was not a bird or beast to be seen. The place was utterly silent. And there was no echo. I shouted up into the ravines and against the walls of the cliffs and the sounds died instantly. It was like shouting into a blanket or in a storm, when the wind whips the words away and they are gone.

ERIC NEWBY, *A TRAVELLER'S LIFE.*

18 AUGUST

INTO THE HELL GILL GORGE, 1996

The English nature-writer Roger Deakin (1943–2006) was inspired by John Cheever's short story 'The Swimmer' (1964) to explore Britain by swimming its waterways. On this day in August 1996, he plunged into the Hell Gill gorge near Ingleton in Yorkshire.

Courage up, I returned to the turbulent rim of the gorge and did what I knew might be an unwise thing. I couldn't help it. I began to slide into the mouth of the abyss itself. I found myself in the first of a series of smooth limestone cups four or five feet in diameter and anything between three and five feet deep, stepped at an acute angle down a flooded gulley of hollowed limestone that spiralled into the unknown. In the low light, the smooth, wet walls were a beautiful aquamarine, their shining surface intricately pock-marked like the surface of the moon. All my instincts were to hold on, but to what? The ice and water had polished everything perfectly. The torrent continually sought to sweep me with it, and so I slithered and climbed down Hell Gill's dim, glistening insides, through a succession of cold baths, in one long primal scream.

There is something atavistic about all swimming, but this was so intensely primitive it was visceral. I felt like Jonah inside the whale. Each time I dropped, or was swept, into a new cauldron, I thought it would be bottomless; the turbulence made the water opaque. Borne down this magical uterus, deafened by the rushing and boiling of the flood, with the sheer rock and just a crack of sky high above me, I felt at once apprehensive and exhilarated. Water was cupped, jugged, saucered, spooned, decanted, stirred and boiled. It was thrown up in a fine spray so you breathed it in, it splashed in your face, it stung you with its force, it bounced back off every curving surface, it worked unremittingly to sculpt the yielding limestone into the forms of its own well-ordered movement.

ROGER DEAKIN, *WATERLOG*.

19 AUGUST

HOLY ALHAMBRA, 1952

In the summer of 1952 the English novelist John Fowles (1926–2005) toured Spain with a group of friends. Disappointed in love, Fowles described it as 'a strange month, burning hot, black, sad, poignant for me; an experience I would not have missed for all its bitterness'. His visit to the Alhambra palace was part of the bitter-sweetness.

Far and away the holiest building I saw in Spain, and for me one of the supreme masterpieces of European architecture. To go with Chartres, and the Parthenon. There is in the Alhambra an atmosphere of serenity, of grace, of shade and discreet silences, which is overwhelmingly beautiful. Each room, each court, each pool, colonnade, fountain has a subtle air of mystery, an aristocratic enigma. This is the oriental paradise, the Persian park of wonders, the Old Man of the Mountain's hidden valley. Everywhere one glimpses the Ionian spirit of ancient Greece, delicate, smiling, faintly exotic and barbaric, feminine, above all graceful and profoundly enigmatic. The smile of the Caryatids of the great Erechtheion porch [on the Acropolis], the Da Vinci heads, the Gioconda strain in world art; one of the loveliest and most mystical of all the attitudes to the universe. Something Chinese also; silences and silent pools, peace and resignation, erotic sensations. The fountains work feebly in the Alhambra now; a pity, since the fountain is an important part of the architecture, animating, focusing the environment. I felt very sad, very moved by the past holiness. Related it to my own life and the absence of Monique...

JOHN FOWLES, *THE JOURNALS*, VOLUME I.

20 AUGUST

EATING ANOTHER MAN'S WORDS, 1796

On this day the Scottish explorer Mungo Park (*see* 8 December) discovered the object of his mission: 'the long sought for majestic Niger, glittering to the morning sun, as broad as the Thames at Westminster, and flowing slowly *to the eastward*'. All that remained was to get out of the country alive before the rains came. Having long since been stripped of all his possessions, he earned his board and lodging as best he could.

When [my landlord] heard that I was a Christian, he immediately thought of procuring a saphie [charm], and for this purpose brought out his *walha*, or writing-board, assuring me that he would dress me a supper of rice if I would write him a saphie to protect him from wicked men. The proposal was of too great consequence to me to be refused; I therefore wrote the board full from top to bottom on both sides; and my landlord, to be certain of having the whole force of the charm, washed the writing down from the board into a calabash with a little water, and having said a few prayers over it, drank this powerful draught: after which, lest a single word should escape, he licked the board until it was quite dry... When I had finished my supper of rice and salt, I laid myself down upon a bullock's hide, and slept very quietly until morning; this being the first good meal and refreshing sleep that I had enjoyed for a long time.

Mungo Park, The Travels of Mungo Park.

21 AUGUST

A HERD OF HUMANS, 1869

On his journey through Yosemite (*see* 7 June and 20 July) John Muir encountered a group of Native Americans. It was a salutary lesson for the outspoken nature-lover to find that humans could also be part of the natural world.

Just then I was startled by a lot of queer, hairy, muffled creatures coming shuffling, shambling, wallowing towards me as if they had no bones in their bodies. Had I discovered them while they were yet a good way off, I should have tried to avoid them. What a picture they made contrasted with the others I had just been admiring. When I came up to them, I found that they were only a band of Indians from Mono on their way to Yosemite for a load of acorns. They were wrapped in blankets made of the skins of sage-rabbits. The dirt on some of their faces seemed almost old enough and thick enough to have a geological significance; some were strangely blurred and divided into sections by seams and wrinkles that looked like cleavage joints, and had a worn abraded look as if they had been exposed to the weather for ages. I tried to pass them without stopping, but they wouldn't let me; forming a dismal circle about me, I was closely besieged while they begged whiskey or tobacco, and it was hard to convince them that I hadn't any. How glad I was to get away from the gray, grim crowd and see them vanish down the trail! Yet it seems sad to feel such desperate repulsion from one's fellow human beings, however degraded. To prefer the society of squirrels and woodchucks to that of our own species must surely be unnatural.

JOHN MUIR, *MY FIRST SUMMER IN THE SIERRA*.

22 AUGUST

LITTLE FINGERS OF TIBET, 1963

On a long-distance bicycle journey Dervla Murphy (*see* 9 March) was brought to a halt by the heat of Delhi. While waiting for the weather to change she found work at a Tibetan refugee camp in the north of India, an experience that involved multifarious unexpected duties.

No crises today – unless you like to so describe the cutting of the left-hand little finger-nails of all the adults in the camp. Tibetans keep the rest of their nails very short but this is worn about one inch long and used to dislodge nests of nits from each other's heads, to unwax the ears and to excavate the nostrils. Normally Oliver is all for preserving ancient Tibetan customs, but yesterday evening, when he went to the kitchen to photograph the colossal mud stove on which all the camp's food is cooked, he saw Chumba hanging over our dinner, excavating like mad. So this morning I was sent forth at dawn, armed with nail-clippers and instructions to go down fighting – which I very nearly did, as opposition was fierce. I found this a most distasteful chore, since the Tibetans are all absolutely devoted to that long, left, finger-nail – and now how can they cope with the nit-nests, etc.? I felt very tyrannical and without any real justification – after all, if one didn't *brood* on it a few consequences of excavation in the soup (thick veg.) would go unnoticed and do no harm.

DERVLA MURPHY, *TIBETAN FOOTHOLD*.

23 AUGUST

A DEATH ON MONTE MORO, 1845

The aesthete John Ruskin (*see* 28 May) was more comfortable admiring the beauties of the Alps than he was climbing them. Nevertheless, he had enough experience of low-lying passes and the easier peaks to boast a show of expertise, as with this encomium to a guide who perished on Monte Moro on the Swiss– Italian border.

———

You will perhaps see in the papers the loss of a guide on the Monte Moro – the Englishman who was with him came here yesterday. Poor fellow, the fresh snow which blinded Coutet, and half skinned me, was of worse effect to him, for being of Lucerne, not knowing the mountain, he went up what appeared the smoothest part of the glacier, but which he ought to have known, as anybody used to the Alps would have known in a moment, was cut by cross crevices. I saw the lines of them marked as if with the trace of a camel's hair pencil by the light indentation of snow – and even if I hadn't I should have known they must be there by the lie of the glacier. However, he wasn't minding what he was about – didn't even know he was off the road, the snow was so smooth – and down he went. The Englishman returned to Saas, being behind him, & got some people and ropes, but it was no good – there was 'no voice nor any that answered'. It is curious how stupid & rash the bad guides are – far better have none – the guide is often half-drunk, & the traveller is off his guard. Things of this kind can't happen if you keep your wits about you, but as Coutet says – *si vous marchez les yeux fermés – crac! – c'est fini.* ['If you walk with your eyes shut – crack! – it is all over.']

JOHN RUSKIN, *RUSKIN IN ITALY*.

24 AUGUST

RIDING THE RAILROADS, 1894

Shortly after his arrival in New York (*see* 20 June), W.H. Davies went north to visit a friend in Connecticut. Finding he had only ten dollars to his name, he fell in with a tramp called Brum. For the rest of the summer, as described here, they travelled the country as hoboes, hitching illegal rides on freight trains. They were by no means alone. The United States was undergoing a slump and huge parties of unemployed men roamed the land: when one coal train left the rails, killing everyone aboard, only four of the forty-four dead were railway employees; the rest were tramps. Derailings aside, the vagrants also faced perils ranging from irate guards to bad launchings and landings. Davies's own career came to an end five years later when his leg was pulled under the wheels as he tried to board a train.

———·•·———

Yes, I would see Chicago: and, suddenly becoming aware of a man occupying the other end of the seat, I enquired of him the way to Chicago, as though the distance was a paltry ten miles, instead of a hundred times greater. This man looked at me in astonishment, and at last asked me if I intended to beat my way. Seeing my lack of understanding, he enquired as to my financial resources. On shaking my head in the negative, implying that I had no money, he said: 'No more have I: and if you are agreeable we will both beat our way to Chicago...'

I was soon initiated into the mysteries of beating my way by train, which is so necessary in parts of that country, seeing the great distances between towns. Sometimes we were fortunate enough to get an empty car; sometimes we had to ride the bumpers; and often, when travelling through a hostile country, we rode on the roof of a car, so as not to give the brakesman an opportunity of striking us off the bumpers unawares. It is nothing unusual in some parts to find a man, always a stranger, lying dead on the track, often cut in many pieces. At the inquest they invariably bring a verdict of accidental death, but we know different. Therefore we rode the car's top, so as to be at no disadvantage in a struggle. The brakesman, knowing well that our fall would be his own, would not be too eager to commence hostilities. Sometimes we were desperate enough to ride the narrow iron rods, which were under the car, and only a few feet from the track. This required some nerve, for it was not only uncomfortable, but the train, being so near the line, seemed to be running at a reckless and uncontrollable speed, whereas, when riding on the car's roof, a much faster train seems to be running much slower and far more smooth and safe. Sometimes we were forced to jump off a moving train at the point of a revolver. At other times the brakesmen were friendly, and even offered assistance in the way of food, drink or tobacco. Again, when no firearm was in evidence, we had to threaten the brakesman with death if he interfered with us. In this way Brum and myself travelled the States of America, sleeping at night by camp fires, and taking temporary possession of empty houses.

WILLIAM HENRY DAVIES, *THE AUTOBIOGRAPHY OF A SUPER-TRAMP*.

25 AUGUST

BAD WATER IN PERSIA, 1880

The Irish war correspondent Edmond O'Donovan (1844–83) stayed in the Persian town of Meshed while reporting for Britain's *Daily News* on the advance of Russian troops into the region. His room was equipped with a rudimentary cooling system consisting of a large tank into which, now and then, a stone pipe spurted a mephitic jet of water.

The tank was nearly five feet deep, and on several occasions I narrowly escaped an involuntary bath as I entered my room in moments of abstraction. The water supply of Meshed is very bad and reeks with sulphuretted hydrogen [a poisonous gas], so that the presence of this tank in my bedroom was by no means an unmixed pleasure. Sometimes, indeed, when the water played at night from the jet and disturbed the lower depths of the pool, the stench was so unbearable that I used to have my bed carried out into the garden. Living fish were occasionally thrown in by the stream from the stone pipe, but they invariably died within a few hours, owing to the poisonous nature of the water. Besides the gases, which might readily be accounted for by the numerous cesspits through which the water supply passes in the town itself, the water seemed charged with mineral matters whose nature I could not determine. When I first arrived I wished to take a dose of Epsom salts, but on pouring the dose into half a tumbler of water it was almost instantly converted into a dirty white slag-mass like half-melted glass. The water had a thick and oily taste, and under normal circumstances would be quite undrinkable. This was all the more annoying, as hardly any other drink could be had in the place.

EDMOND O'DONOVAN, *MERV*.

26 AUGUST

THE RUINATION OF CONDOM, 1998

Alan Bennett (born 1934), the Yorkshire dramatist and keen observer of British foibles, visited the southwestern French town of Condom in 1998. His diary entry carried a tinge of familiar woe.

After years of sniggering English tourists having themselves photographed next to the town sign, the burghers of Condom have at last woken up to the fact that they are sitting on a gold mine. So now, though there is some doubt whether the town has any connection with prophylaxis at all, a Musée des Préservatifs has opened and the decent old-fashioned sepia postcards of this fairly ordinary provincial town have been banished in favour of highly coloured jokey views: a landscape in which the poplars are green condoms, the clouds white ones; monks have condoms as cowls and even the chaste tower of the twelfth-century cathedral has been sheathed in a condom.

None of which would matter much had not some enterprising mayor decided that the town could do other things besides exploiting its eponymous connection, so the decent little square in front of the cathedral now boasts half a dozen gleaming steel flagpoles, with the flags, I suppose, of all condom-using nations. Still, one must be grateful they are flags and not themselves condoms. Worse, there is a 'water feature', a pool from which water overflows down a ramp of artificial stone crossed by a shallow steel bridge which tourists are encouraged to think of as an ideal photo opportunity. In due course someone will throw a coin in the pool and all that will start. It's almost English in its vulgarity.

ALAN BENNETT, *UNTOLD STORIES*.

27 AUGUST

MRS BURTON BAGS A VULTURE, 1870

When Richard Burton was appointed British consul to Damascus, he had no hesitation in asking his wife Isabel to accompany him (*see* 8 January). She was made of stern stuff. On hearing talk of an uprising against Christians, she arranged her defence with precision and flair. In the end, the rumours proved false – just as well for the insurgents, one cannot help feeling.

Night was coming on, and of course I had not the slightest idea of what would happen, but feared the worst... I fully expected an attack, so I collected every available weapon and all the ammunition. I had five men in the house; to each one I gave a gun, a revolver, and a bowie-knife. I put one on the roof with a pair of elephant guns carrying four ounce balls, and a man to each of the four sides of the house, and I commanded the terrace myself. I planted the Union Jack on the flagstaff at the top of the house, and I turned my bull terriers into the garden to give notice of any approach...

During the three days we were in suspense a monster vulture kept hovering over our house. The people said it was a bad omen, and so I fetched my little gun, though I rather begrudged the cartridge just then; and when it was out of what they call reach, I had the good luck to bring it down. This gave them great comfort, and we hung the vulture on the top of the tallest tree.

Isabel Burton, *The Romance of Isabel Lady Burton*, Volume II.

28 AUGUST

NOT QUITE DEAD ON THE NILE, 1779

In 1779 the Englishwoman Eliza Fay (*c.* 1755–1816) sailed for India accompanied by her ineffectual lawyer husband. On the way they stopped at Cairo, where she gave a detailed description of one of many unidentified ailments to which European travellers were prone and which, in this case, was probably caused by its very 'cure': Nile water.

All of our Party, who have been in India, agree that they never felt the weather so oppressively hot as here; which proceeds from the terrible sandy deserts that surround the town, causing the air to smell like hot bricks. This however I could have borne, but just on our arrival there broke out a severe epidemical disease with violent symptoms. People are attacked at a moment's warning with dreadful pains in their limbs, a burning fever, with delirium and a total stoppage of perspiration. During two days it increases; on the third, there comes on uniformly a profound sweat (pardon the expression) with vomiting, which carries all off. – The only remedies prescribed are lying in bed and drinking plentifully, even two gallons a day, of Nile water: no nourishment, and not so much as gruel, is allowed until after the crisis; not one has died of the disease, nor, I believe, scarcely one escaped: even the beasts have been affected... It had every sign of the Plague, except that it was not mortal... and the general opinion is, that had it arrived in the month of February, the living would scarce have been sufficient to bury the dead.

ELIZA FAY, *ORIGINAL LETTERS FROM INDIA.*

29 AUGUST

VOODOO NIGHTS, 1954

In August 1954 author Graham Greene (*see* 4 May) was staying at the El Rancho Hotel in Port-au-Prince, Haiti. From there he wrote to his mistress, Catherine Walston, the day after he came face-to-face with a series of voodoo rituals. Greene was intrigued by the dark side of the Caribbean and portrayed it to good effect in his novels; his letter to Catherine carried the note: 'Will you keep this letter in case I need to refresh my mind?'

Last night we were at a Voodoo ceremony until 3 in the morning. One reads about such things but to see them is incredible & terrifying. The first two hours were spent in a kind of parody of Catholic rites – a choir of white-clothed girls jigging & singing & responding, holy banners – one marked St. Jacques, the portrait of a saint, the kissing of crosses & vestments, endless prayers from the Hongan or priest recited in a Catholic way, the 'fairy' motions of a server, a kind of Asperges with a jug of water – the horrible really began when the Agape began – a procession carrying fuel & food & dishes & a live hen. The man carrying the hen swung it like a censer, & then would dash to this & that member of the congregation & plaster his face & body with the live bird (you can imagine how I felt about that!). More interminable prayers & then the bird's feet were cracked off like cheese biscuits & the attendant put the live bird's head in his mouth & bit it off – the body of course went on flapping while he squeezed the blood out of the trunk...

The next startling thing was the initiations after the feast – the initiate wrapped in a sheet like a mummy was carried in on a man's back to the cooking pit flames (extraordinary shadows), & one hand & one foot were drawn out of the cerements [the shroud] & held for as much as a quarter of a minute in the flames while the drummers drummed & the women shrieked their sacred songs. Last of all & quite suddenly (the intervals were filled with a kind of bacchanalian dancing) came 'possession'. They believe that the various gods of war & love etc. start winging their way from Africa when the ceremony starts. They had taken about five hours to cross the Atlantic – & on this occasion it was the God of War. A man started staggering & falling & twisting. People held him up, twisted a scarlet cloth round his middle & put a rum bottle & panga [machete] in his hand. Then he began to whirl around the room, falling & tripping & brandishing the axe; we had to leap up on benches to get out of the way. Sometimes he pressed the blunt end of the panga in someone's stomach, & that man or woman fell on the ground before him & kissed it, while he sprayed them with rum out of his mouth. Two of those got possessed too, but were quietened by the priest. I was glad when the man gave a shriek & collapsed, & the God had started back to Africa & the party was over.

GRAHAM GREENE, *A LIFE IN LETTERS*.

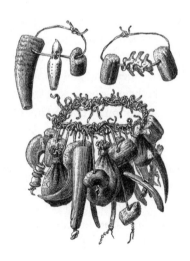

30 AUGUST

FISHING IN AMERICA, 1958

During his stay in the United States, the poet Ted Hughes never fully came to terms with the American way of life (*see* 25 June). Fishing, his favourite sport, was perhaps the area where he remained most obdurately Old World, as described in a late-August letter to his brother Gerald.

I meant to get some fishing over here, but I was a bit deflected by the fact that there is an air over all American sports, I don't know how to define it... In America a calendar picture, say, of a fishing episode, is of some bronzed pipe-smoking lawyer-cum-doctor-cum-truck-driver-cum-your-honest-neighbour plated and belted and buckled from head to foot in all those frontierish looking accessories, gaffs, nets, bowie-knives and the rest, healing over [sic] in a tarzan-tearing-the-arms-off-the-ape-stance as he surfaces some proud king of the deeps, and in the background, just on land will be shown the family beach-wagon in three colours drawn up with the back open showing the hams, steaks, squashes, and so on or perhaps they will all be actually laid out on a cloth on the pine-needles, while the R.K.O. [the Hollywood film studio] wife smiles at the five bouncing boys in their woodsy outfit. No I'm spoiling it. But that's the tendency. That is the image of the fisherman in the American mind. Now the same image in the English mind is of some clown sitting in pouring rain fishing in a pool that has a great notice 'Petrol Dump.' Something of that sort. But there's a difference. One can go fishing in England without feeling that you're taking part in some national Let's All Be Good Americans campaign, and be sure that any fish you catch won't have tattooed on its underside 'I'm an American too so treat me well and cook me with FRENCH'S HOTCHA SAUCE.' Something like that. So I haven't gone fishing.

TED HUGHES, *LETTERS*.

31 AUGUST

TROUBLE IN TRANSYLVANIA, 1866

The mountaineer Leslie Stephen (*see* 6 August) was on an excursion to Mount Bucsecs (Bucegi), in the Southern Carpathians – then part of Hungary, now in Romania – when he delivered a diatribe on the uselessness of the local guides. In the end he abandoned them and simply climbed the hill himself.

As I gradually discovered, the English and the Hungarian theories as to mountain climbing are radically divergent. To obviate, as far as possible, future misconceptions, I will endeavour to explain their characteristic differences. The English mountaineer holds that the problem before him is not fully solved until he has discovered the shortest practical route to the summit; and though he abhors the doctrine imputed to him by certain malingerers that it is right to climb against time, he yet takes a pardonable pleasure in a rapid ascent. The Hungarian, on the other hand, has a glorious indifference to all considerations of time. He has no objection to go a mile round to avoid such a slope as that of Holborn Hill [in London]. He cares very little about the precise summit, and looks upon the whole performance much as a Roman Catholic looks upon a pilgrimage. There are a certain number of stations to be visited, of which the top may or may not be one. Any amount of time may be spent on the excursion, and if possible, it must be done on horseback.

LESLIE STEPHEN, *THE PLAYGROUND OF EUROPE*.

SEPTEMBER

1 SEPTEMBER

A GARDENER IN THE DEVASTATED ZONE, 1919

While Britain and France pondered how best to commemorate the First World War, a London publisher called Newman Flower (1879–1964) came up with his own solution. One day in September, in the so-called Devastated Zone of the Western Front, he scoured the abandoned trenches for wild flower seeds. The memorial garden that he created at his home in Kent was so poignant that soon it was being replicated around the world.

In the Autumn of 1919 I went out to the battlefields to gather seeds before the trenches had been filled in, or the work of reconstruction begun.

The trenches on the Somme lay undisturbed. All they had done so far was to blow up ammunition dumps. The explosions were going on all day...

I gathered a large packet of poppy seeds from the trenches of the Somme – from the historic battlefields of La Boiselle and Pozières. In Fricourt I found some poppies that had grown round a patch of bandages stained russet now with blood, and I carefully took their seed.

In what remained of Delville Wood I found these lanky blue chicory flowers. In spite of the havoc of four years, their roots had come to life again. They had flowered as they were wont to do before the blast of shell-fire lay its poison upon the Earth.

I passed on to Vimy Ridge, and there in the untouched trenches the wild antirrhinum was flowering as if rejoicing that War had departed. Beneath the close trampling of men's feet on every inch of the Ridge their roots had still survived. Shells had flung these roots this way and that, but still they survived. They lived and blossomed in their season. Now, in the Autumn of 1919, they were heads of clustering seed where they bloomed their pageant of remembrance.

Very carefully I gathered these seeds, labelled them, and brought them home. I would make a War Garden...

NEWMAN FLOWER, *THROUGH MY GARDEN GATE*.

2 SEPTEMBER

A GATHERING STORM, 1939

The travel writer Norman Lewis (*see* 13 May) and his wife were in Cuba when a hurricane hit them. The violent weather seemed to be a portent, for when Lewis returned to Britain he found that it had been the last day of peace before the outbreak of war with Germany.

We found an open space, a hillock from which we could look down through the coloured clapboard houses to the sea. It had fallen slack, but something seemed to be on the move under its polished surface, as if a shoal of whales were about to surface. The sky curdled and darkened, throwing grey veils across the sun. There was not a flicker of breeze and the only sounds to be heard were the urgent tapping of hammers and shouts of the teamsters urging on their mules. Some miles out to sea a dark cloud, dense and fleshy as a negro's hand, pressed down on the water and was now rapidly expanding, and in a far corner of the field of vision the delicate wisp of a water spout joined sea and sky.

The small town of Nuevitas stretched into a promontory pointing at the great Cay of Sabinas and within minutes a wall of water charged into it. As it struck, the cay appeared to put up a crest of white water from one end to another, and we looked up to see thousands of sea-birds flying before the hurricane, like grey ash from a conflagration blown across the sky. As the shacks clustered on the headland caught the first lash of the wind, walls and thatches were snatched away. The next gust pelted us with airborne debris of all kinds, rocked the car on its springs and cracked a window. The moment had come for retreat.

NORMAN LEWIS, *JACKDAW CAKE*.

3 SEPTEMBER

A WEDDING IN WAR, 1939

Having fled Austria to escape the Nazis, the playwright Stefan Zweig (*see* 22 February) stopped in London *en route* to Brazil. He and his fiancée thought it as well to get married before catching their next ship. However, even as they were in the registrar's office, the news of war came through. Zweig was now an enemy alien and the ceremony would have to wait.

It was a strange morning. Silently we stepped back from the radio that had projected a message into the room which would outlast centuries, a message that was destined to change our world totally and the life of every single one of us. A message which meant death for thousands of those who had silently listened to it, sorrow and unhappiness, desperation and threat for every one of us, and perhaps only after years and years a creative significance. It was war again, a war, more terrible and far-reaching than ever before on earth any war had been. Once more an epoch came to an end, once more a new epoch began. Silently we stood in the room that had suddenly become deathly quiet and avoided looking at each other. From outside came the unconcerned twitter of the birds, frivolous in their love and subject to the gentle breeze, and in golden lustre the trees swayed as if their leaves, like lips, wished to touch one another tenderly.

STEFAN ZWEIG, *THE WORLD OF YESTERDAY*.

4 SEPTEMBER

MONUMENTS OF THE SULTANS, 1615

The Italian traveller Pietro Della Valle (*see* 25 January) was smitten by the architecture of Constantinople when he visited it in 1615. He left a description of the recently built Süleymaniye Mosque, one of the city's most striking edifices, and a work-in-progress that would eventually become the equally impressive Blue Mosque.

After leaving Santa Sophia, I went to take a last look, before going away, at the sepulchre of that great Emperor Suleyman; for surely though he was a Turk, the least I could do was to look at his coffin with feeling, for the valorous deeds he accomplished when alive. His mosque is smaller and I find it very pleasing, and in the modelling I should not perhaps lie if I said it exceeded Santa Sophia. And although there is not much coloured marble, since the greater part is white, all the same it seems to be solid work, with not one brick there by intention, but all stone from the foundations to the top. It can be seen that the emperor exercised great judgement in his affairs, for everything he left is well made. The mosque which is being built by today's Grand Signor, which I also went to see again this morning, is making gentle progress. It will look beautiful, with its white and mixed marble; but it is a fact that here the master is seen to have no spirit. I believe that the poor man is robbed of half what is spent, as well as another third that they get him to lay out wastefully, through the ignorance of the craftsmen, on tools and such things, of which far fewer are needed for the work. The best feature will be that the facade is on the Hippodrome, which is an imposing and beautiful piazza.

PIETRO DELLA VALLE, *THE PILGRIM*.

5 SEPTEMBER

GRIZZLIES IN THE WEST, 1850

One day in September 1850 the British traveller Frank Marryat (*see* 8 April) accepted an invitation to go bear-hunting in California. Although accompanied by his manservant, a pair of bloodhounds and a third dog of mixed descent but 'unfailing nose and great intelligence', he felt slightly nervous.

When we consider the weight of the grizzly, which often reaches fifteen hundred pounds, the enormous strength of which he is possessed, as evidenced by the limbs of trees which he will wrench from the trunk, and his extraordinary speed and activity, we have reason (speaking as one who lives in his vicinity) for congratulation that the animal is of inoffensive habits, and avoids the presence of man. The sole instance to the contrary is that in which you are unfortunate enough to invade the domestic circle of the she-bear when accompanied by her cubs: she invariably gives chase the instant she sees the intruder, who, if he is wise, will 'draw a bee-line' in an opposite direction. In running from a bear, the best plan is to turn around the side of a hill; for the bear having then, as it were, two short legs and two long ones, can't, under such circumstances, run very fast. There is but one sized tree that you can climb in safety in escaping from a bear, and you may run a long way before you find it. It must be just too small for your pursuer to climb up after you, and just too large for it to pull down – a nice point to hit.

FRANK MARRYAT, *MOUNTAINS AND MOLEHILLS*.

6 SEPTEMBER

THE ROAD TO MECCA, 1853

In this year the British explorer and orientalist Richard Burton (1821–90) embarked on an audacious voyage through Arabia. Disguised as a Muslim pilgrim from the far-flung Persian province of Khorasan, he joined a caravan whose destination was Islam's holy cities of Medina and Mecca – forbidden territory for a Christian such as himself.

This day's march was peculiarly Arabia. It was a desert peopled only with echoes, – a place of death for what little time there is to die in it, – a wilderness where, to use my companion's phrase, there is nothing but He. Nature scalped, flayed, discovered all her skeleton to the gazer's eye. The horizon was a sea of mirage; gigantic sand-columns whirled over the plain; and on both sides of our road were huge piles of bare rock, standing detached upon the surface of the sand and clay. Here they appeared in oval lumps, heaped up with a semblance of symmetry; there a single boulder stood, with its narrow foundation based upon a pedestal of low, dome-shaped rock. All were of a pink, coarse-grained granite, which flakes off in large crusts under the influence of the atmosphere...

At half-past ten that evening we heard the signal for departure, and, as the moon was still young, we prepared for a hard night's work... Darkness fell upon us like a pall. The camels tripped and stumbled, tossing their litters like cockboats in a short sea... It was a strange, wild scene. The black basaltic field was dotted with the huge and doubtful forms of the spongy-footed camels with silent tread, looming like phantoms in the midnight air; the hot wind moaned, and whirled from the torches flakes and sheets of flame and fiery smoke, whilst ever and anon a swift-travelling Takht-rawan [litter], drawn by mules, and surrounded by runners bearing gigantic mashlas or cressets [torches], threw a passing glow of red light upon the dark road and the dusky multitude.

RICHARD BURTON, *PERSONAL NARRATIVE OF A PILGRIMAGE TO AL-MADINAH & MECCAH*, VOLUME II.

7 SEPTEMBER

CONGO SUNRISE, 1926

The French writer André Gide (*see* 14 May) travelled to French Equatorial Africa in 1926 accompanied by his lover, the photographer (and future film director) Marc Allégret, with the aim of shooting a documentary. He didn't think much of French colonial policy but was impressed by the scenery.

The most magnificent spectacle greeted us on waking. The sun was rising as we entered the pool of Bolobo [on the Congo River]. Not a wrinkle was to be seen on the immense sheet of widening water, not even the slightest shiver to blur its surface; it lay, an intact and perfect shell, holding the pure and smiling reflection of the purest sky. In the east, the sun was crimsoning a few long, trailing clouds. Towards the west, sky and lake were the same pearl-colour, a delicate and tender grey; in this exquisite mother of pearl every blended colour lay dormant, yet already quivering with the promise of the day's glories. In the distance a few low-lying islands floated ethereally in a liquid haze... The enchantment of this mystic scene lasted only a few seconds; the outlines sharpened, grew definite; we were on common earth once more.

The air blows sometimes so light, so suave, so voluptuously soft, that one seems to be breathing deliciousness...

Tonight an admirable sunset was repeated impeccably in the smooth water. The horizon was dark with thick clouds, when a corner of the sky opened and showed an unknown star in the ineffable purity of its depths.

ANDRÉ GIDE, *TRAVELS IN THE CONGO*.

8 SEPTEMBER

DARKNESS IN THE CITY OF LIGHT, 1944

Martha Gellhorn's career as a reporter (*see* 22 January) brought her to Paris after its liberation from the Nazis. She filed this report one September day, coolly surveying the city's contrasts of luxury and deprivation.

Paris never had a war as we know it, an open war, and it has no war now. Paris is intact and beautiful and puzzling. Any day you can see men and women poking in garbage cans, looking for something to take home; by the way they do this sad work you realize that they have been doing it for a long time. You can then walk down the street and eat a splendid luncheon in a black-market restaurant for ten dollars. You can buy what will always be the most beautiful dresses in the world, at any of the great dressmaking houses, for a mere three hundred dollars or so, and you can walk ten blocks to a working-class district and see women who have had no new clothes at all for four years and have been cold for four winters in the same threadbare cheap coat.

You can buy as many orchids as your heart desires, in the great flower market of the Halles, but you could not buy a pound of coal to keep warm. In fact you could more easily take a bath in champagne than in hot water, and whether you live in a dismal peeling room in a slum or in the lovely high-ceilinged rooms of the fine houses on the Avenue Foch, you would be equally cold. The city of light has practically no electricity, and if you want to be amused you can go to a freezing theatre and watch actors rehearsing a new play, with a few electric bulbs burning dimly in the footlights, and behind them and before them the cold darkness of the empty house, and they tell you they will open as soon as there is enough current. Since dancing was forbidden during the occupation, the few night clubs now operating are human sardine cans. The Boeuf sur le Toit was always very chic and very expensive; now it is not very chic and twice as expensive and outside the door every night there is a thicket, a wilderness, of bicycles on which the clientele have arrived.

The main emotion in Paris is the relief of people who for four years have lived in silence, with fear and disgust in their hearts. But there must be and there will be emotions greater than relief. That aristocracy which resisted the Germans inside France, those faithful ones who fought as Free French outside their country, those millions who have suffered in German concentration and forced-labor camps, will have to guide in rebuilding their country and a Paris which is materially unharmed. Meanwhile people who have never been to Paris before go on saying that Paris is the same as it always was.

Martha Gellhorn, *The Face of War.*

9 SEPTEMBER

THE SHOCK OF THE GALLIC, 1783

Edward Nares (1762–1841), a twenty-one-year-old Briton, arrived in Calais on a September day in 1783 at the start of his Great Tour. It was the biggest shock of his life.

Nothing could exceed my astonishment to be awakened out of my first sleep, by three armed men at my bedside, enquiring in the French tongue, who I was, whence I came, whither I was going, and what my business might be in France... The short sleep I had taken had been just sufficient to obliterate all traces of my journey, and all recollection of my sudden change of abode; so that I thought I was still at my father's, and the appearances around me, seemed totally inexplicable – what account I gave of myself I know not, but their behaviour was civil, though their figures were so alarming, and I was soon rid of their company. This was not the first surprize I had been in – The moment we disembarked on the pier head at Calais, we seemed to be in a New World – nothing could be greater than the contrast between the English and the French shores. And we looked back at Dover Castle, scarcely capable of persuading ourselves that England could really be at so small a distance... Monks were to be seen in all the streets, in the habits of their order, with their feet bare or in sandals... The carriages, carts, horses and even dogs were different, so that the scene altogether was particularly striking... my brother... declared... that considering all things, particularly its near neighbourhood to England, he was very much more struck with the differences of manners, persons, customs, etc. etc. than upon his first interview with the American Indians.

QUOTED IN JEREMY BLACK, *THE BRITISH ABROAD*.

10 SEPTEMBER

POISONING IN MOROCCO, 1959

The American author Paul Bowles (*see* 30 January) described a doleful experience as recounted by his Moroccan friend Mohammed Larbi. While staying with his family in the Rif Mountains, Larbi had been poisoned to within an inch of his life. The culprit was his father's youngest wife, whose advances he had rejected and who, in revenge, had cooked him a deadly tagine.

He ripped open the meat with his fingers, to find that a small inner pocket of meat enclosing various powders and other things had been sewn into the larger piece. He also discovered that he had eaten a certain amount of that pocket and its contents. He said nothing, scrambled up off the floor and ran out of the house, and to this day he has never been back there, although subsequently he did manage to persuade his father to get rid of that particular wife.

The 'other things' in the food, in addition to the assorted drugs, were, by his reluctant admission, powdered fingernails and finely cut hair – pubic hair, he maintains – along with bits of excrement from various small creatures. 'Like what?' I wanted to know. 'Like bats, mice, lizards, owls... how should I know what women find to feed to men?' he cried aggrievedly. At the end of a month his skin began to slough off, and one arm turned bluish purple. That is usual; I have seen it on occasion. It is also considered a good sign; it means that the poison is 'coming out.' The consensus of opinion is that if it stays in, there is not much that anyone can do in the way of finding an antidote. The poisons are provided by professionals; Larache is said to be a good place to go if you are interested in working magic on somebody. You are certain to come back with something efficacious.

PAUL BOWLES, *TRAVELS*.

11 SEPTEMBER

AFLOAT IN UMBRIA, 1908

Despite her periodic bouts of depression, the author Virginia Woolf (*see* 15 August) never failed to have a good word for Italy, as expressed in a journal entry written in Perugia one September day.

When you walk out of the front door here you find yourself apparently upon a parade, with the sea beneath. A blue vapour fills in the spaces between the white columns of the parapet; & the people are leaning & looking over, as they do at the sea side. But in truth it is dry land beneath, dropped down some distance; there are curved vineyards, groves of olives, & the hills which rise against the sky seem about on the level of our heads. At sunset, of course, there is a tremendous display; clouds of flamingo & scarlet, & of the shape of curled feathers; spaces of crimson, with bars upon them; hills laid against the furnace so that their little fringe of trees is visible; but I like the foreground best with its soft green & brown, & its highest light the dull white enamel of the road...

It is perhaps because I compare Umbrian vineyards with English fields that I am slow to come at any picture of this place. The divisions at first seemed to me perplexing: I found no solitude & no wildness; there were no deep clumps of shade, no fields with long grasses. The ground is singularly bare, & stony; brittle looking granaries of old pink brick, are dotted here & there, & perhaps there is an archway where women sit, handling maize. The snug circle of our farmyard does not exist. But the place is beautiful; the twisted little trees, now green, now black against the sky, are full of lines; lovely are the peaks in the distance, like a great encampment of tents of all sizes; here before is Perugia on its hill, with all its long towers & square blocks massed out in line; there is no softness, nothing indistinct, but I begin to see that there is a character in this land, with its gnarled little trees, & its sharp outlines, which would soon make all other scenery insipid.

VIRGINIA WOOLF, *TRAVELS WITH VIRGINIA WOOLF.*

12 SEPTEMBER

NIGHT TRAIN TO DENVER, 1879

In mid-September Walt Whitman (*see* 11 January) went on a long jaunt west – from Philadelphia to Denver, Colorado, 'penetrating the Rocky Mountain region enough to get a good notion of it all'. He took patriotic pride in the sleeper car that hurtled him to his destination in the course of two glorious nights.

What a fierce, weird pleasure to lie in my berth at night in the luxurious palace-car, drawn by the mighty Baldwin [locomotive] – embodying, and filling me, too, full of the swiftest motion, and most resistless strength! It is late, perhaps midnight or after – distances join'd like magic – as we speed through Harrisburg, Columbus, Indianapolis. The element of danger adds zest to it all. On we go, rumbling and flashing, with our loud whinnies thrown out from time to time, or trumpet-blasts, into the darkness. Passing the homes of men, the farms, barns, cattle – the silent villages. And the car itself, the sleeper, with curtains drawn and lights turn'd down – in the berths the slumberers, many of them women and children – as on, on, on, we fly like lightning through the night – how strangely sound and sweet they sleep! (They say the French Voltaire in his time designated the grand opera and a ship of war the most signal illustrations of the growth of humanity's and art's advance beyond primitive barbarism. Perhaps if the witty philosopher were here these days, and went in the same car with perfect bedding and feed from New York to San Francisco, he would shift his type and sample to one of our American sleepers.)

WALT WHITMAN, *SPECIMEN DAYS IN AMERICA*.

13 SEPTEMBER

THE HERETIC OF KHORASAN, 1853

Having accomplished his incognito mission to visit Islam's most sacred site, the Kaaba in Mecca, Richard Burton (*see* 6 September) returned to his guest house, where he amused himself at the expense of his fellow residents.

I had scarcely composed myself upon the carpeted Mastabah [stone ledge], when the remainder was suddenly invaded by the Turkish, or rather, the Slavo-Turk pilgrims inhabiting the house, and a host of their visitors. They were large, hairy men, with gruff voices and square figures; they did not take the least notice of me, although feeling the intrusion, I stretched out my legs with provoking *nonchalance*. At last one of them addressed me in Turkish, to which I replied by shaking my head. His question being interpreted to me in Arabic, I drawled out, 'My native place is the land of Khorasan.' This provoked a stern and stony stare from the Turks, and an 'ugh!' which said plainly enough, 'Then you are a pestilent heretic.' I surveyed them with a self-satisfied simper, stretched my legs a trifle farther, and conversed with my water-pipe. Presently, when they all departed for a time, the boy Mohammed raised, by request, my green box of medicines, and deposited it upon the Mastabah; thus defining, as it were, a line of demarcation and asserting my privilege to it before the Turks... My acquaintance with them began roughly enough, but afterwards, with some exceptions, who were gruff as an English butcher when accosted by a lean foreigner, they proved to be kind-hearted and not unsociable men. It often happens to the traveller, as the charming Mrs. Malaprop observes, to find intercourse all the better by beginning with a little aversion.

RICHARD BURTON, *PERSONAL NARRATIVE OF A PILGRIMAGE TO AL-MADINAH & MECCAH*, VOLUME II.

14 SEPTEMBER

BIG HAIR IN VIENNA, 1716

Lady Mary Wortley Montagu (*see* 27 March) was travelling overland with her husband to Constantinople in 1716 when she paused for a moment to denigrate hairstyles in Vienna.

I cannot forbear in this place giving you some description of the fashions here, which are more monstrous and contrary to all common sense and reason than 'tis possible to imagine. They build certain fabrics of gauze on their heads, about a yard high, consisting of three or four storeys, fortified with numberless yards of heavy ribbon. The foundation of this structure is a thing they call a bourle, which is exactly of the same shape and kind, but about four times as big as those rolls our prudent milk-maids make use of to fix their pails upon. This machine they cover with their own hair, which they mix with a great deal of false, it being a particular beauty to have their heads too large to go into a moderate tub. Their hair is prodigiously powdered to conceal the mixture and set out with three or four rows of bodkins (wonderfully large, that stick out two or three inches from their hair) made of diamonds, pearls, red, green and yellow stones, that it certainly requires as much art and experience to carry the load upright as to dance upon May day with the garland. Their whalebone petticoats out-do ours by several yards' circumference and cover some acres of ground. You may easily suppose how much this extraordinary dress sets off and improves the natural ugliness with which God Almighty has been pleased to endow them all generally.

LADY MARY WORTLEY MONTAGU, *THE COMPLETE LETTERS*, VOLUME I.

15 SEPTEMBER

INDIAN POST, 1333

By September 1333 the Moroccan traveller Ibn Battuta (*see* 25 April) had been on the road for more than eight years. His original plan, to make a pilgrimage to Mecca, had long since been superseded by a grander ambition – to continue eastwards until he felt he had seen and done enough. Now he was poised on the border of India, a land freshly annexed by Muslim invaders and something of a New World compared to the older kingdoms to the west.

From Sind to the capital of Dihli [Delhi], the sultan's capital, it is fifty days' march, but when the intelligence officers write to the sultan from Sind the letter reaches him in five days by the postal service. In India the postal service is of two kinds. The mounted couriers travel on horses belonging to the sultan with relays every four miles. The service of couriers on foot is organized in the following manner. At every third of a mile there is an inhabited village, outside which there are three pavilions. In these sit men girded up ready to move off, each of whom has a rod a yard and a half long with brass bells at the top. When a courier leaves the town he takes the letter in the fingers of one hand and the rod with the bells in the other, and runs with all his might. The men in the pavilions, on hearing the sound of the bells, prepare to meet him, and when he reaches them one of them takes the letter in his hand and passes on, running with all his might and shaking his rod until he reaches its destination. This post is quicker than the mounted post. It is sometimes used to transport fruits from [the northern Persian region of] Kurasan which are highly valued in India; they are put on plates and carried with great speed to the sultan. In the same way they transport the principal criminals; they are each placed on a stretcher and the couriers run carrying the stretcher on their heads. The sultan's drinking water is brought to him by the same means, when he resides at Dawlat Abad, from the river Kank [Ganges], to which the Hindus go on pilgrimage and which is at a distance of forty days' journey from there.

When the intelligence officials write to the sultan informing him of those who arrive in the country, he studies the report very minutely. They take the utmost care in this matter, telling him that a certain man has arrived of such-and-such an appearance and dress, and noting the number of his party, slaves and servants and beasts, his behaviour both in action and at rest, and all his doings, omitting no details. When the new arrival reaches the town of Multan, which is the capital of Sind, he stays there until an order is received from the sultan regarding his entry and the degree of hospitality to be extended to him. A man is honoured in that country according to what may be seen of his actions, conduct, and zeal, since no one knows anything of his family or lineage. The king of India, Sultan Muhammad Shah, makes a practice of honouring strangers and distinguishing them by governorships or high dignities of State. The majority of his courtiers, palace officials, ministers of state, judges, and relatives by marriage are foreigners, and he has issued a decree that foreigners are to be given in his country the title of *Aziz* [Honourable], so that this becomes a proper name for them.

IBN BATTUTA, *TRAVELS IN ASIA AND AFRICA*.

16 SEPTEMBER

THE SOOTY CITY OF PITTSBURGH, 1861

The Times of London's war correspondent W.H. Russell (*see* 14 February) stopped for a night at Pittsburgh on his way to cover the American Civil War. In common with most commentators of the time, he found the city an industrial hell-hole, almost worse than the 'Black Country' in the English Midlands.

Pittsburgh, where we halted next night on the Ohio, is certainly, with the exception of Birmingham, the most intensely sooty, busy, squalid, foul-housed, and vile-suburbed city I have ever seen. Under its perpetual canopy of smoke, pierced by a forest of blackened chimneys, the ill-paved streets swarm with a streaky population whose white faces are smudged with soot-streaks – the noise of vans and drays which shake the houses as they pass, the turbulent life in the thoroughfares, the wretched brick tenements – built in waste places on squalid mounds, surrounded by heaps of slag and broken brick – all these give the stranger the idea of some vast manufacturing city of the Inferno; and yet a few miles beyond, the country is studded with beautiful villas, and the great river, bearing innumerable barges and steamers on its broad bosom, rolls its turbid waters between banks rich with cultivated crops.

WILLIAM HOWARD RUSSELL, *MY DIARY NORTH AND SOUTH*.

17 SEPTEMBER

SAINT LENIN, 1932

In 1932, Malcolm Muggeridge (*see* 19 March) went to Moscow as correspondent for the *Manchester Guardian*. Convinced that the Great Depression heralded the collapse of capitalism, the then left-leaning Muggeridge saw the Soviet regime as 'the only convincing alternative, and I had a great longing to go to Russia, not just to look round, but to stay there and bring up my family there'. His enthusiasm didn't last long, as his diary entry for his second day in the city suggests.

Lenin's tomb is remarkable. For the two hours that it is open daily a constant procession of people file past the embalmed body. They take their hats off when they go in and do not talk; otherwise there is no ceremonial. No one kisses the glass around him, or makes the sign of the Hammer and Sickle, or anything like that. They just stare. And there he is – a little man with a neat beard and a determined mouth and a well-shaped, but not memorable head. Altogether the effect is austere, at the same time theatrical.

What do the thousands upon thousands of Russians who wait, sometimes a considerable time, to see him, make of the spectacle, I wondered. Their faces, quite blank, give away nothing. Here, I thought, is the one successful, even convincing, piece of ceremony devised in modern times. But I had a queer conviction that one day an enraged mob would tear him from his place and trample him under foot. Lenin did not look a fanatic, but, as far as appearances are concerned, is quite in the Russian saintly tradition.

Coming away from the tomb I looked into a church and saw four or five old crones and a half-witted priest blessing one another indiscriminately. Christianity at least is over in Russia, and it is difficult to see how it will ever be revived.

MALCOLM MUGGERIDGE, *LIKE IT WAS*.

18 SEPTEMBER

REFLECTIONS ON THE RIVER CONCORD, 1842

Rail travel (*see* 5 May) was not the only form of transportation that interested Nathaniel Hawthorne. In 1842 he bought a canoe from fellow author Henry David Thoreau with which he explored the waterways of New England. Having newly mastered the art, he now embarked on navigating the Concord River in eastern Massachusetts.

———

I toiled onward stoutly, and, entering the North Branch, soon found myself floating quietly along a tranquil stream, sheltered from the breeze by the woods and a lofty hill. The current, likewise, lingered along so gently that it was merely a pleasure to propel the boat against it... I scarcely remember a scene of more complete and lovely seclusion than the passage of the river through this wood. Even an Indian canoe, in olden times, could not have floated onward in deeper solitude than my boat. I have never elsewhere had such an opportunity to observe how much more beautiful reflection is than what we call reality. The sky, and the clustering foliage on either hand, and the effect of sunlight as it found its way through the shade, giving lightsome hues in contrast with the quiet depth of the prevailing tints, – all these seemed unsurpassably beautiful when beheld in the upper air. But on gazing downward, there they were, the same even to the minutest particular, yet arrayed in ideal beauty, which satisfied the spirit incomparably more than the actual scene. I am half convinced that the reflection is indeed the reality, the real thing which Nature imperfectly images to our grosser sense. At any rate, the disembodied shadow is nearest to the soul.

NATHANIEL HAWTHORNE, *COMPLETE WORKS*, VOLUME IX.

19 SEPTEMBER

THE MARVEL OF LONDON, 1599

Thomas Platter was a Swiss medical student who visited Elizabethan England in 1599 'to see Her Majesty and the country', and also to write a report for his fellow Swiss on how this martial nation was developing. He paused on arrival to note the remains of the Spanish Armada, still scattered along the coast after eleven years, then continued to London where he was flabbergasted by the Thames and London Bridge.

The wherries are charmingly upholstered and embroidered cushions laid across the seats, very comfortable to lean against, and generally speaking the benches only seat two people next to one another; many of them are covered in, particularly in rainy weather or fierce sunshine They are extremely pleasant to travel in... Much salmon and sturgeon are caught with lines in this river.

The bridge, across the river is of squared stone, very long and with twenty arches, and on it are built very splendid, finely constructed dwelling houses of prosperous merchants, makes the appearance of a very fine street.

At the top of one tower almost in the centre of the bridge, were stuck on tall stakes more than thirty skulls of noble men who had been executed and beheaded for treason and for other reasons. And their descendants are accustomed to boast of this, themselves even pointing out to one their ancestors' heads on this same bridge, believing that they will be esteemed the more because their antecedents were of such high descent that they could even covet the crown, but being too weak to attain it were executed for rebels; thus they make an honour for themselves of what was set up to be a disgrace and an example.

THOMAS PLATTER AND HORATIO BURSINO, *THE JOURNALS OF TWO TRAVELLERS*.

20 SEPTEMBER

A WORLD BROKEN LOOSE, 1874

In the late summer of 1874 Robert Louis Stevenson (*see* 2 June) found himself in North Wales. There, in a letter to his inamorata, Frances Sitwell, he described an otherworldly experience during a night-time walk outside the town of Llandudno.

I took my usual walk before turning in last night, and dallied over it a little. It was a cool, dark, solemn night, starry, but the sky charged with big black clouds. The lights in the house windows you could see; but the houses themselves were lost in the general blackness. A church clock struck eleven as I went past, and rather startled me. The whiteness of the road was all I had to go by. I heard an express train roaring away down the coast into the night, and dying away sharply in the distance; it was like the noise of an enormous rocket, or a shot world, rather one would fancy. I suppose the darkness made me a little fanciful; but when at first I was puzzled by this great sound in the night, between sea and hills, I thought half seriously that it might be a world broken loose – this world, to wit. I stood for, I suppose, five seconds with this looking-for of destruction in my head, not exactly frightened but put out; and I wanted badly not to be overwhelmed where I was, unless I could cry out a farewell with a great voice over the ruin and make myself heard. Good-bye, dear friend.

ROBERT LOUIS STEVENSON, *LETTERS*, VOLUME II.

21 SEPTEMBER

NICE TO BE BACK, 1888

At the conclusion to his US travels (*see* 16 July), Knut Hamsun caught a steamer back to Denmark in September 1888. In the same month he wrote to a friend in Minneapolis, Ingvar Laws, to say how pleased he was to be home.

How comfortable I feel in this country! I do assure you, the whole nature of things, the way of life here is essentially in harmony with my mind and my nature! This is Europe, and I am a European – God be praised! One has time to live here – one finds the time – one even takes time to stop outside bookshop windows and read the book titles – and not just your book-worms like me, either – no, also old hussars and fat ladies with half-dead eyes and people from the country with heavy irons on their heels – they find time for it – it interests them! And then the European way of greeting! That appeals to me – it is noble and beautiful – with a deep sweep of the hat – without saying anything – as, with bared head, one walks past the person one is greeting. In America they said: '*How do you do?*' and walked on by; and before I had time to answer, the person who had spoken was ten paces behind me; so that my reply, when it finally came, encountered the chest of the next man I met – probably a butcher from Chicago or some flat-chested reformist woman from Philadelphia! In parenthesis, Laws, what kind of a question is that to put to anybody? *How do you do?* Throwing a meaningless question like that in my face in the middle of the street – a question which I cannot manage to answer without running after him – asking me in everybody's hearing how I 'do'! Considering that I left home with the firm intention of not getting mixed up in people's affairs – damn it, it's civilized barbarity.

KNUT HAMSUN, *SELECTED LETTERS*, VOLUME I.

22 SEPTEMBER

A BAPTISM OF FEAR IN THE HIMALAYA, 1887

On about this date in 1887 the British soldier, spy, mountaineer and mystic Francis Younghusband (1863–1942) made his first crossing of the Himalaya. It was a journey that involved the terrifying Mustagh Pass and which he later dubbed his 'baptism of fear'.

———•——

We now had our first taste of real cold. We were about fifteen thousand feet above the sea-level, and as soon as the sun set one could almost see the cold stealing over the mountains – a cold grey creeps over them, the running streams become coated with ice, and as soon as we had had our dinner... we took up our beddings... and hurried off to deposit them behind any rock which would shelter us from the icy wind which blew down from the mountains. It is a curious fact, but when real difficulties seem to be closing around, one's spirits rise. As long as you have health – that is the main point to look after, but it is easily attained in mountain travel – and provided that you take plenty of food, difficulties seem only to make you more and more cheery. Instead of depressing you, they only serve to brace up all your faculties to their highest pitch; and though as I lay down that night, I felt that for the next two or three weeks we should have harder and harder work before us, I recollect that evening as one of those in all my life in which I have felt in keenest spirits.

At the first dawn of day on the following morning we were astir... The going was good. I left the ponies, and in my eagerness hurried on rapidly in front of them, straining to see the top of the pass, and the 'other side' – that will-o'-the-wisp which ever attracts explorers and never satisfies them, for there is ever another side beyond. The height was beginning to tell, and the pass seemed to recede the nearer I approached it. One rise after another I surmounted, thinking it would prove the summit, but there was always another beyond. The valley was wide and open, and the going perfectly easy, leading sometimes over round boulders, but more often loose soil. At length I reached a small lake, about a quarter of a mile in length, and a small rise above it at the further end was the summit of the pass. I rushed up it, and there before me lay the 'other side,' and surely no view which man has ever seen can excel that. To describe the scene in words would be impossible. There are no words with which to do so, and to attempt it with those that are at our disposal would but stain its simple grandeur and magnificence.

Before me rose tier after tier of stately mountains, among the highest in the world – peaks of untainted snow, whose summits reached to heights of twenty-five thousand, twenty-six thousand, and, in one supreme case, twenty-eight thousand feet above sea level. There was this wonderful array of mountain majesty set out before me across a deep rock-bound valley, and away in the distance, filling up the head of this, could be seen a vast glacier, the outpourings of the mountain masses which give it birth. It was a scene which, as I viewed it, and realized that this seemingly impregnable array must be pierced and overcome, seemed to put the iron into my soul and stiffen all my energies for the task before me.

FRANCIS YOUNGHUSBAND, *THE HEART OF A CONTINENT*.

23 SEPTEMBER

ONCE A BUM, ALWAYS A BUM, 1961

On this date in 1961, the author John Steinbeck (*see* 20 March) left his home in Sag Harbor, Massachusetts, on a road trip to the other side of America. He was fifty-eight years old and accompanied by his poodle, Charley; together they travelled in a purpose-built truck named *Rocinante*, named after Don Quixote's horse. 'When the virus of restlessness begins to take possession of a wayward man,' Steinbeck wrote, 'the victim must first find in himself a good and sufficient reason for going.' This was it.

When I was very young and the urge to be someplace else was on me, I was assured by mature people that maturity would cure this itch. When years described me as mature, the remedy prescribed was middle age. In middle age I was assured that greater age would calm my fever and now that I am fifty-eight perhaps senility will do the job. Nothing has worked. Four hoarse blasts on a ship's whistle still raise the hair on my neck and set my feet to tapping. The sound of a jet, an engine warming up, even the clopping of shod hooves on pavement brings on the ancient shudder, the dry mouth and vacant eye, the hot palms and the churn of stomach high up under the rib cage. In other words, I don't improve; in further words, once a bum always a bum. I fear the disease is incurable. I set this matter down not to instruct others but to inform myself.

JOHN STEINBECK, *TRAVELS WITH CHARLEY.*

24 SEPTEMBER

MISERY ON MOUNT CAMEROON, 1895

The English traveller Mary Kingsley (1862–1900) was a woman determined to defy the world. In 1893, bucking all convention, she travelled on her own from Sierra Leone to Angola, and later she returned for further adventures. (When hailed as a 'New Woman' she protested that she had never once worn trousers.) At one point she scaled the 13,255-foot-high Mount Cameroon, taking a route unknown to European explorers.

The ground, bestrewn with leaves and dried wood, is a mass of large flies, rather like our common houseflies, but both butterflies and beetles seem scarce; but I confess I do not feel up to hunting much after yesterday's work, and deem it advisable to rest.

My face and particularly my lips are a misery to me, having been blistered all over by yesterday's sun, and last night I inadvertently whipped the skin all off one cheek with the blanket, and it keeps on bleeding, and, horror of horrors, there is no tea until that water comes.

I wish I had got the mountaineering spirit, for then I could say, 'I'll never come to this sort of place again, for you can get all you want in the Alps.' I have been told this by my mountaineering friends – I have never been there – and that you can go and do all sorts of stupendous things all day, and come back in the evening to the *table d'hôte* at an hotel; but as I have not got the mountaineering spirit, I suppose I shall come fooling into some such place as this as soon as I get the next chance.

MARY KINGSLEY, *TRAVELS IN WEST AFRICA*.

25 SEPTEMBER

THE MIDNIGHT ROADS OF VERDUN, 1916

While visiting Verdun in 1916, during the notoriously bloody battle in that sector of the Western Front, Britain's Poet Laureate John Masefield (*see* 18 March) caught a glimpse of the constant movement of men and animals that allowed the French positions to keep fighting. In a letter to his wife he described the midnight *ravitaillement,* or resupply.

When we went on again, we came out into open rolling plains, with the glimmer of flashes, & the rising and falling of starshells, just as before. The moon came out now, & the night cleared up, & we could see the whole great battlefield, for miles & miles... All that debateable land lives a strange life at midnight. The harvesters (mostly German prisoners) were gathering harvest on both sides of the road; carts were bringing up cracked stones for the shell holes, & engineers were filling the shell holes, & the ravitaillement went on & on, going up to the famous forts. They went on just the same, in the days of the attack, night after night, & the wreck of their carts & the bones of their horses lay in heaps all along the road on both sides. I don't think any soldiering comes up to the ravitaillement. In a trench, you have comrades, & bombs to fling & a gun to fire, & a parapet to hide you; but out on these open roads the drivers were alone on their horses, & the roads were like rivers of fire, & they had to go on & on, as though they were carrying the host; and they saved Verdun; nobody else.

JOHN MASEFIELD, *LETTERS FROM THE FRONT.*

26 SEPTEMBER

IN THE HEART OF DARKNESS, 1890

The novelist Joseph Conrad had had forebodings when he left for the Congo (*see* 22 May), and once he reached it his nightmares came true. In a letter to his aunt, written from Kinshasa, he yearned to be shot of both the country and its colonial management.

Decidedly I regret having come here. I even regret it bitterly... Everything here is repellent to me. Men and things, but men above all. And I am repellent to them. From the manager in Africa who has taken the trouble to tell one and all that I offend him supremely, down to the lowest mechanic, they all have the gift of irritating my nerves – so that I am not so agreeable to them perhaps as I should be... As crowning joy, my health is far from good. Keep it a secret for me – but the truth is that in going up the river I suffered from fever four times in two months, and then at the Falls (which is its home territory), I suffered an attack of dysentery lasting five days. I feel somewhat weak physically and not a little demoralized; and then, really, I believe that I feel homesick for the sea, the desire to look again on the level expanse of salt water which has so often lulled me, which has smiled at me frequently under the sparkling sunshine of a lovely day, which many times too has hurled the threat of death in my face with a swirl of white foam whipped by the wind under the dark December sky. I regret all that.

JOSEPH CONRAD, *COLLECTED LETTERS*, VOLUME I.

27 SEPTEMBER

MESOPOTAMIA, LAND OF MUD, 1933

When Robert Byron (*see* 2 May) visited Baghdad his admiration for Iraq – more traditionally, Mesopotamia – was waning. Whatever its antiquity, he had lost patience with it as a land through which to travel. He was keen to move on to Persia and beyond.

It is little solace to recall that Mesopotamia was *once* so rich, so fertile of art and invention, so hospitable... The prime fact of Mesopotamian history is that in the XIIIth century Hulagu [the Mongol conqueror] destroyed the irrigation system; and from that day to this Mesopotamia has remained a land of mud deprived of mud's only possible advantage, vegetable fertility. It is a mud plain, so flat that a single heron reposing on one leg beside some rare trickle of water in a ditch, looks as tall as a wireless aerial. From this plain rise villages of mud and cities of mud. The river flows with liquid mud. The air is composed of mud refined into a gas. The people are mud-coloured; they wear mud-coloured clothes and their national hat is nothing more than a formalised mud-pie. Baghdad is the capital one would expect of this divinely favoured land. It lurks in a mud fog; when the temperature drops below 110, the residents complain of the chill and get out their furs. For only one thing is it now justly famous: a kind of boil which takes nine months to heal, and leaves a scar.

ROBERT BYRON, *THE ROAD TO OXIANA.*

28 SEPTEMBER

THE DERVISH NEXT DOOR, 1848

The Albanian city of Tirana was a horrible spot as far as Edward Lear (*see* 3 May) was concerned. The accommodation was primitive and whenever he tried to paint the scenery he was menaced by a dervish. On the night of 28 September his sleep was disturbed by curious sounds from the next room.

No sooner, after retiring to my pigsty dormitory, had I put out my candle and was preparing to sleep, than the sound of a key turning in the lock of the next door to that of my garret disturbed me, and lo! broad rays of light illumined my detestable lodging from a large hole a foot in diameter, besides from two or three others, just above my bed; at the same time a whirring, humming sound, followed by strange whizzings and mumblings, began to pervade the apartment. Desirous to know what was going on, I crawled to the smallest chink, without encountering the rays from the great hiatus, and what did I see? My friend of the morning – the maniac dervish – performing the most wonderful evolutions and gyrations; spinning round and round for his own private diversion, first on his legs, and then pivot-wise, *sur son seant* [on his backside], and indulging in numerous other pious gymnastic feats. Not quite easy at my vicinity to this very eccentric neighbour, and half anticipating a twitch from his brass-hooked stick, I sat watching the event, whatever it might be. It was simple. The old creature pulled forth some grapes and ate them, after which he gradually relaxed in his twirlings and fell asleep.

EDWARD LEAR, *EDWARD LEAR IN GREECE*.

29 SEPTEMBER

ORWELL IN MARRAKESH, 1938

Shortly before the Second World War, the English author and social commentator George Orwell (1903–50) repaired to Marrakesh in the hope that its dry climate would cure his tuberculosis. In a letter to his friend Jack Common, he bemoaned his inability to make contact with the average Moroccan. Previously, in his travels through Britain, France and Spain, he had prided himself on finding common cause with like-minded locals; but here the gulf was too great.

It makes me sad to hear you say you've never been out of England, especially when I think of the bastards who do travel, simply going from hotel to hotel and never seeing any difference anywhere except in the temperature. At the same time I'm not sure how much good travel does to anyone. One thing I have always believed, and that is that one really learns nothing from a foreign country unless one works in it, or does something that really involves one with the inhabitants. This trip is something quite new to me, because for the first time I am in the position of a tourist. The result is that it is quite impossible, at any rate at present, to make any contact with the Arabs, whereas if I were here, say, on a gun-running expedition, I should immediately have the entrée to all kinds of interesting society, in spite of the language difficulty. I have often been struck by how easy it is to get people to take you for granted if you and they are really in the same boat, and how difficult otherwise. For instance, when I was with the tramps, merely because they assumed that I was on the bum it didn't make a damn's worth of difference to them that I had a middle-class accent and they were willing to be actually more informative than I wanted. Whereas if, say, you brought a tramp into the house and tried to get him to talk to you it would just be a patron–client relationship and quite meaningless. I am as usual taking careful notes of everything I see, but am not sure what use I shall be able to make of them afterwards. Here in Marrakech it is in some ways harder to find out about conditions in Morocco than it would be in a less typical Arab town. In a town like Casablanca you have a huge French population and a white proletariat, and consequently local branches of the Socialist Party and so forth. Here with not very important differences it is very like Anglo-Indian society and you are more or less obliged to be a pukka sahib or suffer the consequences... [The state of things in Marrakech is] pretty frightful, wages generally work out at about 1d or 2d an hour and it's the first place I've seen where beggars do literally beg for bread and eat it greedily when given it.

George Orwell, A Life in Letters.

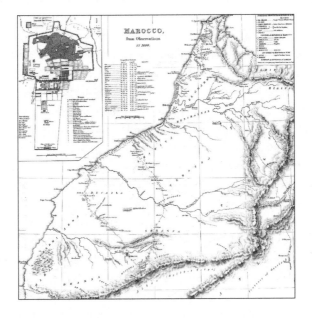

30 SEPTEMBER

IN A SPANISH VALLEY, 1936

When Laurie Lee left his rural English home in midsummer (*see* 5 June) his goal was far-distant Spain. By September he was there and, it would seem, relishing every bucolic minute.

I'd been almost a month on the road; a month of vintage September weather; travelling in easy stages through autumnal landscapes which seemed to be moistly wrapped in fruit-skins... There were purple evenings, juicy as grapes, the thin moon cutting a cloud like a knife; and dawns of quick sudden thunder when I'd wake in the dark to splashes of rain pouring from cracks of lightning, then walk on to the village to sit cold and alone, waiting for it to wake and sell me some bread, watching the grey light lifting, a man opening a stable, the first girls coming to the square for water.

Out in the open country it grew dark early, and then there was nothing to do but sleep. As the sun went down, I'd turn into a field and curl up like a roosting bird, then wake in the morning, soaked with dew, before the first farmer or the sun was up, and take to the road to get warm, through a smell of damp herbs, with the bent dawn moon still shining.

In the valley of the Guadiana I saw herds of black bulls grazing in fields of orange dust, and square white farms, like desert strongholds, protected by packs of savage dogs. Somewhere here, in a barn, under a roof crusted with swallows' nests, a mother and daughter cooked me a supper of eggs, while a horse watched me eating, chickens walked on the table, and an old man in the hay lay dying.

LAURIE LEE, *As I Walked Out One Midsummer Morning*.

OCTOBER

1 OCTOBER

RAPPING ON THE HIBACHI, 1890

While working in a Japanese school, Lafcadio Hearn (*see* 4 April) described the small rituals of the staffroom. As was often remarked among Western professors, the pace of modernization in Meiji Japan was enough to age a man prematurely. Here, Hearn and his fellow teachers catch a few moments of respite from their busy schedule.

On the walls there are maps, crowded with Japanese ideographs; a few large charts representing zoological facts in the light of evolutional science; and an immense frame filled with little black lacquered wooden tablets, so neatly fitted together that the entire surface is uniform as that of a blackboard. On these are written, or rather painted, in white, names of teachers, subjects, classes, and order of teaching hours; and by the ingenious tablet arrangement any change of hours can be represented by simply changing the places of the tablets...

On every teacher's desk there is a small hibachi of glazed blue-and-white ware, containing a few lumps of glowing charcoal in a bed of ashes. During the brief intervals between classes each teacher smokes his tiny Japanese pipe of brass, iron, or silver. The hibachi and a cup of hot tea are our consolations for the fatigues of the class-room.

Nishida and one or two other teachers know a good deal of English, and we chat together sometimes between classes. But more often no one speaks. All are tired after the teaching hour, and prefer to smoke in silence. At such times the only sounds within the room are the ticking of the clock, and the sharp clang of the little pipes being rapped upon the edges of the hibachi to empty out the ashes.

LAFCADIO HEARN, *GLIMPSES OF UNFAMILIAR JAPAN*, VOLUME II.

2 OCTOBER

DEATH ON SAKHALIN, 1890

While visiting the Russian penal island of Sakhalin in 1890 (*see* 27 June), Anton Chekhov was told by a local official of the execution of nine men who had been found guilty of murder.

It was an early October morning, grey, cold and dark. The faces of the prisoners were yellow with fear and their hair was waving lightly. An official read out the death sentence, trembling with nervousness and stuttering because he could not see well. The priest, dressed in black vestments, presented the Cross for all nine to kiss, and then turned to the district commander, whispering:

'For God's sake, let me go, I can't...'

The procedure is a long one. Each man must be dressed in a shroud and led to the scaffold. When they finally hanged the nine men, there was an 'entire bouquet' hanging in the air – these were the words of the district commander as he described the execution to me. When the bodies were lifted down the doctors found that one was still alive.

This incident had a peculiar significance. Everyone in the prison, all those who knew the innermost secrets of the crimes committed by the inmates, the hangman and his assistants – all of them knew he was alive because he was innocent of the crime for which he was being hanged.

'They hanged him a second time,' the district commissioner concluded his story. 'Later I could not sleep for a whole month.'

ANTON CHEKHOV, *A JOURNEY TO THE END OF THE RUSSIAN EMPIRE.*

3 OCTOBER

UNDULATING IN VENICE, 1851

In 1851 John Ruskin (*see* 28 May) was studying in Venice – at that time governed from Vienna – when an imperial visit was announced. Like most Venetians he hired a gondola and jostled with the crush of boats, waiting in suspense until the Austrian emperor made his appearance.

Everyone on the Grand Canal was requested by the municipality to illuminate their house *inside*: and the Rialto was done at the public expense. They spent altogether – in Bengal lights and other lamps about 300 pounds – a large sum for Venice in these days – but I never saw the Rialto look so lovely: There were no devices or letters or nonsense on it – only the lines of its *architecture* traced in chains of fire – and two lines of ruby lamps set along its arch underneath – so as to light the vault of it; all streaming down in bright reflection on the canal... [The canal] was literally as full of boats as it could hold – They were jammed against each other as tight as they could be – leaving just room for each boatman to get his oar down into the water at the side – and so we waited for some half-hour. It was a strange sight in the darkness, the crowd fixed, yet with a kind of undulation in it which could not have been had upon land, every gondolier at his stern, balanced, ready for the slightest movement of the boats at his side – lest they should oust him out of his place – and the figures standing up on the lower level, in the open part of the boats – from one side of the canal to the other – one could not see on what they stood – only here and there the flashing of the tide beneath, as it flowed fiercely in the torchlight – and beside and among the figures the innumerable beaks of the Gondolas, reared up with their strange curving crests like a whole field full of dragons.

JOHN RUSKIN, *LETTERS FROM VENICE*.

4 OCTOBER

LUNARDI'S LADIES OF SCOTLAND, 1785

Vincenzo Lunardi, secretary to the Neapolitan ambassador since 1783, was the most flamboyant balloonist Britain had ever seen. His letters, written to an Italian sponsor, were spattered with italics and capitals and display an endearing combination of *braggadocio*, self-doubt and unrequited lust – in this case directed at the LADIES of Edinburgh, as he quivered in anticipation of an ascent from Herriot Gardens.

———

I have endeavoured to give you some faint idea of their *personal charms*; but their *mental ones* are far more striking! *Grace* without *affectation*, *frankness* without *levity*, *good-humour* without *folly*, and *dignity* without *pride*, are their distinguishing characteristics. Do you not think this is a fiery ardeal [sic] for my heart? – I assure you no: they are all so very *amiable*, that I cannot attach myself to *any* ONE in *particular*: I love them all; and shall court their general approbation with as much ardour as the most empassioned lover would that of his mistress. Ah! what glory to ascend my AERIAL CHARIOT in their view! to be the object of *their* admiration! to have all their eyes turned towards me! and to hear their united acclamations! Oh Heaven! my very brain turns giddy with the thought, and my whole soul anticipates the happy moment!

I have just received letters from *three* LADIES, expressing their wishes to accompany me in my voyage; but I must of necessity refuse myself that gratification. How unfortonate [sic] that the Balloon should be too small to ascend with more than one person! and I have not time to enlarge it, or else – I am interrupted:– Good God! a message from HERRIOT'S GARDEN, requiring my immediate attendance! What can be the matter? How I tremble! Perhaps some unforeseen accident, – but I will not torment myself with conjectures; – Adieu.

VINCENZO LUNARDI, *AN ACCOUNT OF FIVE AERIAL VOYAGES IN SCOTLAND*.

5 OCTOBER

THIRST IN TRIPOLI, 1792

Miss Tully (*see* 12 January) had been stationed in Tripoli long enough to have become accustomed to its relentless bouts of plague, famine and drought. But she was still shocked by the effect of a desert wind on an already parched city.

The seasons have been particularly dry at Tripoli for the past two years; but the fatal effects of the want of rain have never struck us so forcibly as to-day. Owing to a strong land-wind, which has blown incessantly with increasing heat for the last five days, several Moors coming off the sands into the town have perished, who might have been saved could they have obtained in time a draught of water. Four people died to-day literally of thirst: they were with a caravan just arrived from the deserts, and expired a few minutes before they reached town. Not a drop of rain has descended from the atmosphere for several months, and such a dearth of water occasions the intense heat of the air to become in many instances fatal. The air here is heated to that degree at present, that the insects cannot resist it. Scorched to death, they drop in numbers from the burning atmosphere. It is not usual for these extraordinary winds to blow here successively for more than three or four days; if they do, the heat, which is then dreadful, increasing rapidly to the ninth, sometimes to the tenth day, renders respiration so difficult as to occasion death.

Miss Tully, *Narrative of a Ten Years' Residence at Tripoli in Africa.*

6 OCTOBER

SHOTS IN SAMARKAND, 1934

On or about this date, Peter Fleming (*see* 16 February) had a remarkable encounter with a Soviet pilot in a Samarkand hotel. Having blasted a few shots into the air, just for the hell of it, the airman turned his attentions to the blonde receptionist.

As I came down for the last of my suitcases a beggar appeared in the hotel entrance and stood peering not very hopefully into the lighted lounge. Nikolai, who was making little headway with the blonde, saw this apparition and for one reason or another took a pot-shot at it. He missed, the beggar vanished with a howl of dismay, the blonde screamed, Nikolai slapped her face and in the resulting confusion I managed to grab the pistol and withdraw to my room.

The hotel was now in a state of some tumult. Doors were opening, bells were ringing, feet were pounding along the corridor. All this gradually died down as I undressed, and peace would have reigned once more over Samarkand if I hadn't started to worry about the safety-catch on Nikolai's automatic. Was it cocked or wasn't it? It was a Russian pistol and I had no means of telling. In the matter of firearms my upbringing was a strict one, and I decided that, rather than risk leaving a cocked pistol lying about my bedroom, I had better find out whether it was on safe or not. So I opened the window, pointed the pistol at the sky and pulled the trigger.

There was a deafening explosion. Once more doors opened, bells rang, feet pounded down the corridors. And I, as I got into bed and fell into a dreamless sleep, reflected that life in Samarkand seemed from my brief experience of it to have a rather unusual flavour.

PETER FLEMING, QUOTED IN DUFF HART-DAVIS, *PETER FLEMING*.

7 OCTOBER

RUMINATIONS ON THE ICE, 1894

Fridtjof Nansen was on the second year of his Arctic drift on the *Fram* (*see* 2 January) when he wrote this journal entry. He was the most mystical of all polar explorers and, in terms of distance gained and lives not lost, undoubtedly the most successful.

Thoughts come and thoughts go. I cannot forget and I cannot sleep. Everything is still; all are asleep. I only hear the quiet step of the watch on deck; the wind rustling in the rigging and the canvas, and the clock gently hacking the time in pieces there on the wall. If I go on deck there is black night, stars sparkling high overhead, and faint aurora flickering across the gloomy vault, and out in the darkness I can see the glimmer of the great monotonous plain of the ice; it is all so inexpressibly forlorn, so far, far removed from the noise and unrest of men and all their striving. What is life thus isolated? A strange, aimless process; and man a machine which eats, sleeps, awakes; eats and sleeps again, dreams dreams but never lives. Or is life really nothing else? And is it just one more phase of the eternal martyrdom, a new mistake of the erring human soul, this banishing of one's self to the hopeless wilderness, only to long there for what one has left behind? Am I a coward? Am I afraid of death? Oh, no! but in these nights such longing can come over one for all beauty, for that which is contained in a single word, and the soul flees from this interminable and rigid world of ice.

FRIDTJOF NANSEN, *FARTHEST NORTH*, VOLUME II.

8 OCTOBER

TURKEYS IN THE WISCONSIN DELLS, 1961

One day in early October, during their transcontinental road trip (*see* 23 September), John Steinbeck and his poodle Charley stopped in Wisconsin. For Steinbeck, who bemoaned the commercial desecration of wild America, Wisconsin was simultaneously a nightmare and a land of surprises.

———

Beside the road I saw a very large establishment, the greatest distributor of sea shells in the world – and this in Wisconsin, which hasn't known a sea since pre-Cambrian times. But Wisconsin is loaded with surprises. I had heard of the Wisconsin Dells but was not prepared for the weird country sculptured by the Ice Age, a strange, gleaming country of water and carved rock, black and green. To awaken here might make one believe it a dream of some other planet, for it has a non-earthly quality, or else the engraved record of a time when the world was much younger and much different. Clinging to the sides of the dreamlike waterways was the litter of our times, the motels, the hot-dog stands, the merchants of the cheap and mediocre and tawdry so loved by summer tourists, but these incrustations were closed and boarded against the winter and, even open, I doubt that they would dispel the enchantment of the Wisconsin Dells.

I stopped that night on a hilltop that was a truckers' place but of a special kind. Here the gigantic cattle trucks rested and scraped out the residue left by their recent cargoes. There were mountains of manure and over them mushroom clouds of flies. Charley moved about smiling and sniffing ecstatically like an American woman in a French perfume shop. I can't bring myself to criticize his taste. Some people like one thing and some another. The odors were rich and earthy, but not disgusting.

As the evening deepened, I walked with Charley among his mountains of delight to the brow of a hill and looked down on the little valley below. It was a disturbing sight. I thought too much driving had distorted my vision or addled my judgement, for the dark earth below seemed to move and pulse and breathe. It was not water but it rippled like a black liquid. I walked quickly down the hill to iron out the distortion. The valley floor was carpeted with turkeys, it seemed like millions of them, so densely packed that they covered the earth. It was a great relief. Of course, this was a reservoir for Thanksgiving.

To mill so close together is in the nature of turkeys in the evening. I remembered how on the ranch in my youth the turkeys gathered and roosted in clots in the cypress trees, out of reach of wildcats and coyotes, the only indication I know of that turkeys have any intelligence at all. To know them is not to admire them, for they are vain and hysterical. They gather in vulnerable groups and then panic at rumours. They are subject to all the sicknesses of other fowl, together with some they have invented. Turkeys seem to be manic-depressive types, gobbling with blushing wattles, spread tails and scraping wings in amorous bravado at one moment and huddled in craven cowardice the next. It is hard to see how they can be related to their wild, clever, suspicious cousins. But here in their thousands they carpeted the earth waiting to lie on their backs on the platters of America.

JOHN STEINBECK, TRAVELS WITH CHARLEY.

9 OCTOBER

MANHATTAN FROM THE SEA, 1988

Around this date the British writer Jonathan Raban (born 1942) arrived in New York aboard the freight ship *Atlantic Conveyor*. His aim in making the crossing was to retrace the steps of the immigrants who, in such large numbers, had travelled between the British Isles and the United States.

The city was hiding behind the low hills of Brooklyn and the thick weather – a distant glow of ruddy smoke, like a forest fire in another county. It took an age to reach the Verrazano Bridge and enter the Narrows, from where New York was suddenly on top of us. Manhattan was a dozen glittering sticks of light, through which livid storm clouds were rolling, lit from below, sooty-orange in colour, as they swirled past the middling-and upper-storeys of the buildings. The choppy sea in the harbour was like a lake of troubled mercury, and the water glared so fiercely that it was almost impossible to find the tiny red and green sparks of the buoys marking the deepwater channel. Then one's eye adjusted and the city's famous icons began to emerge from the general dazzle of things. *There* was Brooklyn Bridge, a sweeping curve of white lights to the north; *there*, on her rock was Liberty, weirdly floodlit in leprechaun green. Manhattan's freakish height and narrowness, rising in front of the low dark industrial sprawl of the Jersey shore, defied gravity, proportion, nature. It was brazen in its disdain for the ordinary limits of human enterprise. I watched the storm and the city battling it out, high in the sky. For a few moments, the sailing clouds exposed a large, low moon. It was drifting over the Boroughs like a huge corroded gilt medallion. Given the air of high melodrama in the surrounding landscape, I would have been only mildly surprised to see the moon come crashing out of heaven and set the whole of Queens on fire.

JONATHAN RABAN, *HUNTING MISTER HEARTBREAK*.

10 OCTOBER

THE GOLDEN HORN FROM A WINDOW, 1906

Virginia Woolf (*see* 15 August) was much taken by Constantinople when she visited it in 1906, after a trip to Greece. She went to Turkey only twice in her life, and each time the experience was spoiled by an illness in her group. But on this occasion, one October evening, the holiday still had hopes.

Remembering Athens, you felt yourself in a metropolis; a place where life was being lived successfully. And that did seem strange, & – if I have time to say so – a little uncomfortable. For you also realised that life was not lived after the European pattern, that it was not even a debased copy of Paris or Berlin or London, & that, you thought was the ambition of towns which could not actually be Paris or any of those inner capitals. As the lights came out in clusters all over the land, & the water was busy with lamps, you knew yourself to be the spectator of a vigorous drama, acting itself out with no thought or need of certain great countries yonder to the west. And in all this opulence there was something ominous, & something ignominious – for an English lady at her bedroom window. At any rate, it was a stirring sight to look upon; & if I may use the shorthand of a hack writer, a most beautiful one into the bargain.

The Golden Horn drives a broad blue wedge between two high banks of houses; so that, as some one says, a battle ship rides at anchor in the street before your door. Then the sunset in long bars of flame & scarlet with a border of chimneys & mosques drawn black upon their lowest margin; the blue waters were lit up & golden lights were sprinkled upon them. Up in the air, & deep down in the earth the lamps burnt; & then the moon, a crescent, swung slowly up in the sky, & a pure drop of light, the evening star, turned the innumerable lamps to gold.

VIRGINIA WOOLF, *TRAVELS WITH VIRGINIA WOOLF*.

11 OCTOBER

ORCHARDS OF CAPE COD, 1849

For the US literary luminary Henry David Thoreau (1817–62), to visit Cape Cod, Massachusetts, was to enter a landscape where none of the usual rules applied. The trees, the mists, the weather – even the atmosphere – seemed different. 'To an inlander,' he wrote, 'the Cape landscape is a constant mirage.'

Everything told of the sea, even when we did not see its waste or hear its roar. For birds there were gulls, and for carts in the fields, boats turned bottom upward against the houses, and sometimes the rib of a whale woven into the fence by the road-side. The trees were, if possible, rarer than the houses, excepting apple-trees, of which there were a few small orchards in the hollows. These were either narrow and high, with flat tops, having lost their side branches, like huge plum-bushes growing in exposed situations, or else dwarfed and branching at the ground, like quince-bushes... I afterward saw on the Cape many full-grown apple-trees not higher than a man's head; one whole orchard, indeed, where all the fruit could have been gathered by a man standing on the ground; but you could hardly creep beneath the trees. Some, which the owners told me were twenty years old, were only three and a half feet high, spreading at six inches from the ground five feet each way, and being withal surrounded with boxes of tar to catch the cankerworms; they looked like plants in flower-pots, and as if they might be taken into the house in winter. In another place, I saw some not much larger than currant-bushes; yet the owner told me they had borne a barrel and a half of apples that fall. If they had been placed close together I could have cleared them all at a jump.

HENRY DAVID THOREAU, *CAPE COD*.

12 OCTOBER

ON SKID ROW, 1952

From a Skid Row flophouse in San Francisco, Jack Kerouac wrote to his friend John Clellon Holmes, describing in typical style yet another trip west across America (*see* 10 June). His first novel, *The Town and The City*, had been a success but his second, *On the Road,* had just been rejected. He was living the life of a wanderer, and Holmes (with whom he had coined the term 'Beat Generation') had just sent him a welcome $50.

The days of *The Town and The City* are all forgotten – I start West in the train – John, you think I'm a self-made martyr? I go 3,000 motherfucking miles, sleep on railroad porches, in Salvation flops, drink, eat out of cans – in Hickey, N.C. I stand in the drizzle exhausted, one saves me – I stay at Ed White's in Beverly's backyard – we cook weenies, drink Tokay – I make love to big Swedish student-girl Edeltrude – Mrs. White motherly packs me lunch, I hitch to Salt Lake (after a day spent sketching Neal's entire Denver area) and sleep in motel garage, hitch straight to Neal's [Neal Cassady's] door via wild trips, including Australian history professor anxiously from top of oil pole, in Nevada desert, scanning horizon for swimming hole – 'nothing I like better than swimming, ya know?' – we end up on little slimy rocks of Tuckee River... I was bored with the job in Rocky Mount, with $5 in my pocket I lifted my seabag up and walked out my sister's backdoor ('Never mind presents from China, just mail me $50 room & board for the month of August.')... If it wasn't for the railroad now, people would instantly recognize me as a true hobo – the bo's on Third St. all do – A HOBO LIVES LIKE AN INDIAN.

JACK KEROUAC, *SELECTED LETTERS*.

13 OCTOBER

COLUMBUS AND THE CARIBS, 1492

The day after he discovered America – or, rather, landed on an unidentified island in the Bahamas – the Genoese adventurer Christopher Columbus (1451–1506) greeted the natives. They were a coffee-coloured people, soon to be extinguished by white men's diseases. Columbus provided this first description of the vanished Carib race.

As soon as day broke, there came to the shore many of these men, all youths, as I have said, and all of a good height, very handsome people. Their hair is not curly, but loose and coarse as the hair of a horse; all have very broad foreheads and heads, more so than any people that I have seen up to now. Their eyes are very lovely and not small. They are not at all black, but the colour of Canarians, and nothing else could be expected, since this is one line from east to west with the island of Hierro in the Canaries. Their legs are very straight, all alike; they have no bellies but very good figures. They came to the ship in boats, which are made of a tree-trunk like a long boat and all of one piece. They are wonderfully carved, considering the country, and large, so that in some forty or forty-five men came. Others are smaller, so that in some only a solitary man came. They row them with a paddle, like a baker's peel, and they travel wonderfully fast. If one capsizes, all at once begin to swim and right it, baling it out with gourds which they carry with them. They brought balls of spun cotton and parrots and spears and other trifles, which it would be tedious to write down, and they gave them all for anything that was given to them. And I was attentive and laboured to know if they had gold...

CHRISTOPHER COLUMBUS, *THE JOURNAL OF CHRISTOPHER COLUMBUS*.

14 OCTOBER

KNOCKING ON THE TURKISH PLAIN, 1953

Driving from Switzerland to Afghanistan, Nicolas Bouvier and Thierry Vernet (*see* 13 July) were plagued by the fear of breaking down in the middle of nowhere. On a plain in Turkey, in 1953, it seemed as if their nightmare was coming true.

The afternoon was getting on, the sky was clear, we were crossing an absolutely deserted plain. The atmosphere was so transparent that you could make out a lone tree standing twenty miles away. And suddenly... tock... tocktock... tack... a hail of light knocks sounding louder as we went on, clear and irritating. A bit like the crackling of dry twigs in a fire, or metal at white-heat expanding and contracting. Thierry stopped the car, going pale, and I shared his fear: we must have lost oil, overheated and stripped the differentials. But we were mistaken, because the noise didn't stop. In fact it increased, just on our left. We went over to look: just across the bank which ran along one side of the road the plain was black with tortoises, who were rapt in their autumn amours and were knocking their shells together. The male used his like a ram to poke his companion and push her towards a stone or tuft of dry grass, where she was cornered. They were a little bit smaller than the females. At the moment of coupling the males would be standing straight up to reach them, stretching out their necks, opening their bright red mouths and letting out strident cries. As we left, we could see tortoises in all directions hastening slowly over the plain to their rendezvous. Night fell, and they were no longer to be heard.

NICOLAS BOUVIER, *THE WAY OF THE WORLD*.

15 OCTOBER

AN AFTERNOON IN MEXICO, 1908

On a lazy October day (too somnolent to be granted the urgency of a precise date), the wealthy US idler Charles Macomb Flandrau (1871–1938) admired his brother's Mexican coffee plantation, which he had adopted as his temporary residence.

It is a cloudless, burning day, the best kind of day for coffee, and the asoleadero [terrace] is covered with it. Through the house there is a slight stir of air, and the fact that the house-boy has just swept the floor with tea leaves left over from several breakfasts, makes the breeze for the moment seem cool – which it isn't. On such a day one is grateful for the bareness of a room – the smooth, unadorned walls, the hard, cool chairs. From the asoleadero comes without ceasing the harsh, hollow sound of the wooden hoes as they turn the coffee over in the sun and scrape against the cement. It is a hot and drowsy sound; the Mexican equivalent of the sound made by a lawn mower in an American 'front yard' in August. It would send me to sleep, I think, if it were not counteracted by the peculiar rustling of a clump of banana trees outside the window. The slightest breath of air puts their torn ribbons into motion that is a prolonged patter, indistinguishable usually from the patter of rain. To-day it is more like the plashing of a fountain – a fountain that, on account of the goldfish, plashes gently. Whenever we need rain – and in the middle of the night I wake up and seem to hear it – it turns out to be the banana trees; but when 'too much water has fallen,' as they say here, and I persuade myself that this time it is only a fluttering in the banana trees, it is always rain. The whole landscape is suspended in heat haze ('swooning' is the word I should like to use, but I shan't), from the bamboo trees nodding against the sky on the crest of the hill behind the house, through the cafetal [plantation] in front of it, down, down the long valley between extinct, woolly looking volcanoes – thirty miles away to the sea. The sea, for some reason, never looks from this distance like the sea; it is not flat but perpendicular. I should have thought it a pale-blue wall across the valley's lower end. In an untiled corner of the piazza some chickens are taking dust baths and talking scandal in low tones; the burro, near by, has curled up in the shade like a dog and gone to sleep. I used to think I should never allow chickens to take dust baths or burros to doze on my piazza. It seemed dreadfully squalid to permit it. Yet I have long since come to it. What can one do? Es el costumbre del pais. So, also, is the custom of letting a few fastidious hens lay eggs in one's bed. But I have always been very firm about that.

CHARLES FLANDRAU, VIVA MEXICO!

16 OCTOBER

PASSING STROMBOLI, 1894

Hubert Lyautey (1854–1934) was a mere staff officer in the French army when he passed through the Mediterranean *en route* to French Indochina (modern Vietnam). Later, as Resident-General of Morocco on behalf of France, his taste for the dramatic would become notorious: he adopted a gold and purple cloak, wore pistols upholstered in tiger skin and lived in a tent complete with oriental carpets and a scarlet ceiling.

It is 8 a.m.; in the bathroom where a Somali Masseur has prepared my bath I dress slowly, enjoying the beautiful weather, the temperature of 78 degrees Fahr., the rippling water, the absence of responsibility, the realization that there will be 'no uniform and no reports,' when suddenly through the open porthole, rising from the sea, there appears a blue and rose-coloured cone. It is Stromboli, youngest of volcanoes, born almost yesterday! Quick, on deck! We are in the Lipari archipelago, passing between Panaria and Salina, and already the great walls of Calabria and Sicily are visible on the horizon, though as yet one cannot see the gap between them.

While awaiting the thrilling passage of the Straits of Messina, all our attention is given to the Lipari islands. Six aquatic volcanoes, but only Vulcan and Stromboli still active. The others are mere craters, crevassed, with jets of lava congealed in their liquid shape. Life has attached itself to their flanks, houses smile, bell-towers point upwards, vines grow on terraces, and our glasses never weary of searching out those unknown members of the human race who accomplish their orbits like ours, like yours.

HUBERT LYAUTEY, *INTIMATE LETTERS FROM TONQUIN*.

17 OCTOBER

A DINNER PARTY IN TANGIERS, 1963

In an October 1963 magazine article, Paul Bowles (*see* 30 January) described a surreal assembly of expatriates at a dinner party in Tangiers. The dotty Miss Higginbotham was a model of normality set against characters such as Sir Malcolm, who had a fetish for whipping his dancing girls at dinner, and Mr Black, who kept a fridge full of blood, each half-pint from a different person. 'Will you have some?' he liked to ask. 'It's delicious chilled, you know.'

Not at all sinister is Miss Higginbotham, who, like so many of the older residents, came to Tangier for a short vacation and never again managed to leave. Since it was all of forty years ago that she arrived, one can assume that she will be staying on a while longer. She calls everyone 'Ducks', including the members of the large company of animals and fowls that have come her way over the years. You go into her kitchen and find it bustling with hens and roosters. You pass by the door of her bedroom and hear the fierce barking of many dogs. The screams that issue from her dining room are only some cockatoos and a macaw conversing, but the door from there into the sitting room must be kept shut, or the spider monkey will get in and tease the birds. And if you are unfortunate enough to go into her bathroom you will be met by an irate goat that resents even Miss Higginbotham's intrusions. 'I tried to tether the poor dear in the garden,' she explains. 'But those beastly Spaniards who live downstairs tormented him night and day. Sooner or later they'd have eaten him. They're Communists, you know.'

PAUL BOWLES, *TRAVELS*.

18 OCTOBER

STUCK IN A DHOW, 1988

In his role as traveller and writer, the comedian Michael Palin (born 1943) undertook a Phileas Fogg-like circumnavigation of the world in eighty days. The journey involved catching a dhow from Arabia to India but, unlike in Fogg's time, the dhow was motorized and any romance the journey may have held evaporated soon after leaving Dubai.

An air of anticlimax hangs over the boat. The elation of the first few days has been replaced by impatience and now resignation. At one time on the dhow I wanted time to stand still; now that it is, I just feel frustrated.

Our speed has been cut to four knots, a pervasive odour of fish hangs over the boat, for most of yesterday's catch is being dried for the return voyage home... As I'm not eating I feel my energy reserves dwindling. Nowhere on the boat is comfortable any more. The clear bright skies are gone and it's cloudier, humid and very still. Even the weather seems to be waiting for something to happen.

The captain is less relaxed the nearer we get to Bombay. An Indian navy vessel passes slowly and he eyes it unhappily. Apparently they occasionally come aboard and ask awkward questions about gold wristwatches, especially if they know you are from Dubai.

The navy boat disappears over the horizon. The captain has a new stomach-cure for me today, 7-Up and black pepper. Kishoor, the slim dark engineer with big sensuous eyes, erects a screen in the bows before having a shower. This occasions the only real guffaws of the day. Apparently, he is going to shave his entire body. When I ask why, I'm told, with much giggling, that his wife prefers him that way. At dusk more oil platforms sprout on the horizon, flaming away like mini-sunsets.

MICHAEL PALIN, *AROUND THE WORLD IN 80 DAYS*.

19 OCTOBER

THE BEAT HOTEL, 1957

The US poet Allen Ginsberg (1926–97) moved to Paris in 1957 with his companion Peter Orlovsky. They took rooms in a rundown building whose romantic setting and cheap rates attracted so many like-minded Americans that it became known as 'The Beat Hotel'. One of its *habitués* was fellow poet Gregory Corso, whose rent-dodging antics Ginsberg described in this letter to his father.

It's a small furnished room size place, rather damp in rain, leaks in fact, with paper thin walls so I can't talk after 10 pm on account of next door working couple, one weak yellow light bulb, a small sink with hot water Thurs, Fri & Sat., discolored plaster, charming view of roofs and chimneys & small round table covered with oilcloth. Big sagging bed, all three of us, me Peter & Gregory sack out in it, Gregory looking for a room or a girl with a room... All in all a typical Paris *vie de foreign boheme.* Not uncomfortable, a little crowded... – awful housing shortage, everybody huddled like rats in rotting old picturesque buildings without hot water. Day we arrived back there was strike, no gas or electric, metros not running, candles selling for 35c ea... [35 centimes each] out of my window I can see the river, down the side of the street, & the booksellers stalls in the rain, & I'm 10 minutes walk from the Louvre, and 10 min. in other direction to St. Germain, the place where all the hip & existentialist & foreign intellectuals have their cafe area – Sartre lives upstairs from Cafe Bonaparte – on the corner, the celebrated Cafe Deux Magots & Cafe de Flore, hundreds of tables full of odd respectable looking literary & theatrical types. Landlady just burst into the room looking for secret radios adding to her electric bills – fortunately it was people next door, & Gregory was gone.

ALLEN AND LOUIS GINSBERG, *FAMILY BUSINESS.*

20 OCTOBER

A PASSAGE TO JAPAN, 1955

Two years after his encounter with amorous tortoises (*see* 14 October), Nicolas Bouvier disembarked at Yokohama, having worked his way east in the galley of a cruise ship. He found a postwar society that was desperate for foreign contact and even welcomed such threadbare specimens as himself.

I didn't even hear the ship berth and the gangway descend. For three days, in a torrid hold under the kitchen, I had used a knife and a steam jet to remove fat from serving platters and dripping-pans the size of coffins, assisted by Alceste and Francis, two black men from Martinique who kept up a dialogue all day in a flowery, nicely antiquated French that was riddled with nursery rhymes, proverbs, rustic images, and devoted exclusively to the penis's penetration of the vagina. These charming, erotic litanies made the time pass quickly. To think incessantly of lovemaking, like this, in the middle of this grease, seemed truly the sign of natural happiness. All the more since the stink and the heat made the work so hard that it was often necessary to pause and vomit the 'Turbot suprême' or the 'Marengo soufflé' that we had taken from the ovens of the huge kitchen. In the yellow haze and grease of our cabin, I just barely recognized the stripes of the commissioner who came to find me...

Captain Cook had a sword and saluted the Maori chiefs with a cocked hat as brilliant as the sun. La Perouse randomly distributed iron axes and blue glass pearls. Phileas Fogg kept a pigskin suitcase stuffed with bank notes by his side. I arrived on the sooty bridge like a tallow candle with nothing to offer but the dishcloth I had in my hand. Travelling had changed.

Nicolas Bouvier, *The Japanese Chronicles*.

21 OCTOBER

A LAND OF STONE AND WATER, 1773

Samuel Johnson (*see* 16 August) and his biographer James Boswell were touring Scotland in 1773 when they alighted on the island of Mull. Boswell was keen to show Johnson just how beautiful Scotland was. Johnson, an avowed Londoner, had his own opinions, which he aired one evening at dinner. Their unfortunate host was a man named McLeod.

Sir Allan M'Lean bragged, that Scotland had the advantage of England, by its having more water. JOHNSON: 'Sir, we would not have your water, to take the vile bogs that produced it. You have too much! A man who is drowned has more water than either of us'; and then he laughed. (But this was surely robust sophistry: for the people of taste in England, who have seen Scotland, own that its variety of rivers and lakes makes it naturally more beautiful than England, in that respect.) Pursuing his victory over Sir Allan, he proceeded: 'Your country consists of two things, stone and water. There is, indeed, a little earth above the stone in some places, but a very little; and the stone is always appearing. It is like a man in rags; the naked skin is still peeping out.'

He took leave of Mr M'Leod, saying, 'Sir, I thank you for your entertainment and for your conversation.'

JAMES BOSWELL, *JOURNAL OF A TOUR TO THE HEBRIDES*.

22 OCTOBER

AN EXISTENTIALIST IN IRELAND, 1959

The French intellectual Jean-Paul Sartre (1905–80) was, in 1959, staying with the US film director John Huston, who had settled in Ireland for tax reasons. His house, in which Sartre and many other guests found themselves, was a cold and sepulchral mansion which Sartre likened to the state of Ireland as a whole.

What madness! What sheer madness! Such a barrage of incoherent fleeting thoughts! Everyone's got a complex, all the way from masochism to brutality. Still, I don't want to give the impression we're in hell. It's more like a big cemetery: everyone dead, with their complexes frozen. There's very, very little life here... They're unbelievable, these imperial or regal rooms, all opening onto an imposing landscape, each room with its small human creature inside, which feels it is dying. As a matter of fact, there's an incontestable correlation between the extraordinary Irish countryside and the soul of the master of this house. Here's what I mean: 8 to 9 million Irish in 1900; today 3 million. The others have emigrated to America, from where they support the Irish who stayed behind. In addition, the Church and convention delay marriages (the women get married *after* thirty, the men after forty). Of course as soon as possible they produce six offspring of middle-aged parents, who proceed to die or emigrate. No misery, simply poverty and above all *death*. Just think: in the past 50 years 2 out of 3 men have left. You can just imagine the abandoned heath. Everywhere stubborn little walls enclose plots of land that still show signs of life while others are completely dead, repossessed by nature. Everywhere you go, ruins, which range with no warning from the 6th century to the 20th. A house in ruins (generally from the last century or the 18th) beside two lowly little houses painted with American money. The ruins are impressive, the facades usually remain standing, but you'd think a bomb had blown out the roof and insides. You can see the sky through the windows. Mostly they're small houses, but sometimes they turn out huge and quite overwhelm the little one-storey huts, mirroring the character of the countryside, where the dead overpowers the living. Add to that, strange round towers beside a dark and lifeless body of water, like a saltwater lake (Galway Bay) and other tall towers (which are naturally considered phallic) near churches in ruins and cemeteries (they are said to have been built by Scandinavian invaders in the 6th century); and then everywhere those stubborn, gray, useless little walls (the tallest were built as public works to employ the locals in bad times). You really get the feeling of a *dead* landscape: only the presence of grass proves that an atom bomb wasn't dropped there, killing all life with its radiation. The weird part is that the countryside seems profoundly *human* (with all these vestiges) and for that very reason in its death throes... So there you have it: one step away from lunar. Which is precisely the interior landscape of my boss, the great Huston.

Jean-Paul Sartre, Quiet Moments in a War.

23 OCTOBER

A WALK IN THE PARK, 1923

Among the many things the Austrian writer Joseph Roth pondered while in Berlin (*see* 23 April) was the nature of its parks and the lives of those who frequented them.

———•+•———

I have long been curious as to what park wardens do in the winter. It's scarcely credible that they should ever leave their parks to share a kitchen with wives and children. Much more likely that they wrap themselves in straw and rags, and passersby take them for rose trees or bits of statuary, or that they dig in for the winter, and come out in the spring along with the violets and primulas. With my own eyes I have seen them feeding off hips and haws, in the manner of shy forest creatures...

Even in Schiller Park the leaves drop from the trees in a timely fashion, in the autumn, but they are not left to lie. In the Tiergarten, for instance, a melancholy walker can positively wade through foliage. This sets up a highly poetic rustling and fills the spirit with mournfulness and a sense of transience. But in Schiller Park, the locals from the working-class district of Wedding gather up the leaves every evening, and dry them, and use them for winter fuel.

Rustling is strictly a luxury, as if poetry without central heating were unnatural.

The rosehips look like fat red little liqueur bottles, distributed for promotional purposes. They fall from the trees free of charge, and are collected by the children. The park wardens look on, feeling no alarm. For they have placed their trust in the Lord, who feeds the wardens in the fields, and arrays them in local-authority caps.

JOSEPH ROTH, *WHAT I SAW.*

24 OCTOBER

AN ALPINE CROSSING, 1783

For many early travellers the Alps were a source of unmitigated terror. In 1783, however, Thomas Brand, a Briton who was making his way to Italy on the Grand Tour, pooh-poohed their frightfulness in a letter to his friend Robert Wharton.

We passed Mt. Cenis after bad weather and it was covered with snow six or eight inches deep but even in that state we could not help shrugging our shoulders and shaking our heads at the extravagant exaggerations of danger which most travellers indulge themselves in describing that famous passage. It was indeed a little cold in going up but once on the plain the air was temperate enough and at the descent it was mild beyond expectation. We rode up upon mules and were carried down by porters: you sit in a kind of chair carried on poles like a sedan with a piece of wood or a cord to press your feet against and a little elbow to rest your arms on. In this manner with your legs and thighs in a straight horizontal position and in the plane of the poles the porters whisk you with incredible strength and celerity down a steep stony road with sharp angles at each turn. Perhaps for the first five or six minutes I was under some fright but the firmness of their steps soon set me at ease and the beautiful cascades that present themselves on every side and the majesty of the hoary mountains that surrounded me furnished me with sufficient matter of admiration and astonishment. The porters are fond of conversing with you.

THOMAS BRAND, QUOTED IN JEREMY BLACK, *THE BRITISH ABROAD*.

25 OCTOBER

THE MARIA THERESA THALER, 1930

Evelyn Waugh (*see* 5 January) had just arrived in Addis Ababa to attend the coronation of Haile Selassie, Emperor of Abyssinia. Around this date, he included in his account the following disquisition on the Maria Theresa thaler, a silver bullion coin minted in Austria in 1751 and named after the Austrian empress – and since then used continuously in world trade.

———•••———

The Marie Therese thaler, ousted elsewhere in Africa by the meagre rupee or the sordid East African shilling, is still the basic coin of Abyssinia. It is not the most commodious form of currency. It varies in value with the price of silver, and gives opportunity for a great deal of rather shady speculation. Notes are issued by the Bank of Abyssinia against a silver deposit. Even at Dirre-Dowa, two stations down the line from Addis, the local branch of the bank charges a three per cent discount in cashing them, and except in the capital or on the railway they are quite valueless. I saw a small caravan setting out for three months in the interior which carried two mule-loads of dollars for current expenses. It is the coin which the people are used to, and they insist on having it. The Menelik dollar went out of circulation because no one wanted it. The half and quarter dollar are accepted after prolonged scrutiny. There are two issues, in one of which the lion's tail is straight, while in the other it curls back at the tip; both are of equally pure silver, but the second is usually refused, even as a tip. A hundred years ago the Marie Therese thaler was the coin of the Arab trader from Tangier to Manchuria. Now its general use survives only in Arabia and Ethiopia. It is still minted in Vienna from the 1780 die; a gracious survival which forms, however, a very deceptive introduction to Ethiopian manners.

EVELYN WAUGH, REMOTE PEOPLE.

26 OCTOBER

A GILDED CITY, 1925

In the eyes of Joseph Roth (*see* 23 April), the playground that was Nice in the Roaring Twenties seemed to be populated by a cast of literary characters made flesh. His description of the hedonistic city appeared in a piece written for the *Frankfurter Zeitung*.

The town of Nice looks as if it had been dreamed up by society novelists and populated by their heroes. Most of the characters you see on the promenade and the beach come straight out of the lending library and the dreams of little country girls. God can't have created such people. They aren't made of common clay, but of high-end pulp. Writers spent so long writing about them that they came to life. Their movements, their walk, their clothes, their talk, their thoughts, their ambitions, their desires, their pain, their experiences have all been put through a literary filter, and all are exquisite and extraordinary. Here, for the first time, we have the opposite of the usual process: here are people who were originally a literary creation, and were then copied out in flesh and blood. An author dictated a world into a typewriter – and lo! – it appeared, here it is, it walks and talks, it plays roulette, dances the Java, and goes sea-bathing.

A whole season in this novelettish world would probably pall. But three days are restful. You get over the stresses and strains of normal terrestrial life, of contact with our common worries… In the society of the sons of Adam, we are caught up in the ordinary whiff of ordinary tragedy. Here in Nice, though, there is the incense of literary tragedy. Here there are only luxury lives. Here are noble creations. Well-paid domestics stood by their golden cradles. Their whole youth was a *comme il faut* nursery, personally aired by physicians. Their marriage was an extraordinarily shrewd investment. Even when they die, they won't leave a gap but an inheritance.

JOSEPH ROTH, *THE WHITE CITIES*.

27 OCTOBER

DR LIVINGSTONE, I PRESUME, 1871

This was the celebrated moment, as recorded by David Livingstone (1813–73) himself, when Henry Morton Stanley 'rescued' the Scottish explorer. Livingstone had no particular wish to be rescued, detested the *New York Herald* – and wasn't that impressed by Stanley (whose name he misspelled).

When my spirits were at their lowest ebb, the good Samaritan was close at hand, for one morning Susi came running at the top of his speed and gasped out, 'An Englishman! I see him!' and off he darted to meet him. The American flag at the head of a caravan told of the nationality of the stranger. Bales of goods, baths of tin, huge kettles, cooking pots, tents &c., made me think 'This must be a luxurious traveller, and not one at his wits' end like me.'... It was Henry Moreland Stanley, the travelling correspondent of the *New York Herald*, sent by James Gordon Bennett, junior, at an expense of more than 4000*l.*, to obtain accurate information about Dr. Livingstone if living, and if dead to bring home my bones... I really do feel extremely grateful, and at the same time I am a little ashamed at not being more worthy of the generosity. Mr. Stanley has done his part with untiring energy; good judgement in the teeth of very serious obstacles. His helpmates turned out depraved blackguards, who, by their excesses at Zanzibar and elsewhere, had ruined their constitutions, and prepared their systems to be fit provender for the grave. They had used up their strength by wickedness, and were next to no service, but rather downdrafts and unbearable drags to progress.

DAVID LIVINGSTONE, *THE LAST JOURNALS OF DAVID LIVINGSTONE*, VOLUME II.

28 OCTOBER

THE TASTE OF THE DESERT, 1946

The explorer Wilfred Thesiger (*see* 27 May) was the first European to cross the Rub' al Khali, or Empty Quarter, a stretch of emptiness in Saudi Arabia that daunted even the Bedouin tribesmen who knew its paths. Here he stands on its brink, marvelling at the sense of adventure carried by the wind. He visited the region regularly between 1945 and 1949, sharing and recording the Bedouin way of life and, with sadness, charting its gradual decline.

To the south, grassy downs, green jungles, and shadowy gorges fell away to the plain of Jarbib and to the Indian Ocean which opened on to another world, whereas immediately to the north a landscape of black rocks and yellow sand sloped down to the Empty Quarter. I looked out over the desert. It stretched away unbroken for fifteen hundred miles to the orchards round Damascus and the red cliffs of Rum. A desert breeze blew round me. I thought of that ruined castle in distant Syria which Lawrence had visited. The Arabs believed that it had been built by a prince of the border as a desert palace for his queen, and declared that its clay had been kneaded with the juice of flowers. Lawrence was taken by his guides from room to crumbling room. Sniffing like dogs, they said, 'This is jasmine, this violet, this rose'; but at last one of them had called, 'Come and smell the very sweetest smell of all', and had led him to a gaping window where the empty wind of the desert went throbbing past. 'This', they told him, 'is the best: it has no taste.'

WILFRED THESIGER, *ARABIAN SANDS*.

29 OCTOBER

A NURSE IN MALTA, 1916

When her fiancé Roland Leighton was killed in the trenches of the Western Front, Vera Brittain (1893–1970) enrolled as an army medic. Her first posting was Malta, where she arrived on 7 October suffering from an illness so severe (possibly food-poisoning) that for most of the month she was a patient rather than a nurse.

Almost the end of October had come before I was able to drag myself to a chair on the stone balcony outside my ward, and look across a deep, rocky valley to the domes and towers of Citta Vecchia, the old Maltese capital, drowsing in a heat more radiant and profound than the warmest English midsummer.

In those first normal hours I fell in love with the island; a secret rapture which the years have not dimmed made me thank heaven that I had defied the nightmare sea and bidden farewell to melancholy, tragic England. It was all so different from Buxton, and so infinitely different from Camberwell! At the end of the summer the grass all over the island was parched and withered; from a distance the surface of the uplands resembled the stretched skin of a great tawny lion. A macabre fascination, such as I had realised in Mudros, seemed to radiate from the dazzling light which drenched this treeless barrenness, making black and sharp-edged the tiny shadows cast by the clumps of tropical shrubs – cactus and prickly pear and eucalyptus – that fringed the dusty white roads or leaned against the ubiquitous stone walls. In the hospital gardens immediately below the balcony, pastel-blue plumbago and pink geranium foamed with luscious generosity over sulphur-hued balustrades.

It's just like the illustrations to [the Rubaiyat of] Omar Khayyam, I thought.

> They say the lion and the lizard keep
> The Courts where Jamshyd gloried and drank deep.

That's what it reminds me of. But it's like the Bible too. That rough track dipping steeply down into the valley and then winding up to walled Citta Vecchia might be the road from Bethany to Capernaum.

Whenever I could escape from my fellow-patients in the stone-floored ward with its wide-open doors and windows, I sat alone on the balcony, happy and at peace in this strange, new country as I had never been since the War began. Occasionally, as strength returned to insecure legs, another patient and I made expeditions in a *carrozza* [carriage] to Citta Vecchia across the valley, where we encountered the characteristic Maltese odour of unwashed humanity, centuries-old mud, and goats. We debated quite hotly which were the more numerous and which smelt worse, the monks or the goats, without coming to any permanent conclusion.

Never before had I realised the sense of spiritual freedom which comes with southern warmth and colour and beauty. Night after night the sun set exuberantly all over the sky. Beneath its glories of orange and violet, of emerald and coral and aquamarine, the dusty flats surrounding Imtarfa turned into purple moorlands. I began to understand why Roland, hating the grey abnegations of Protestantism, had turned from mud and horror and desolation to the rich, colourful glamour of the Catholic Church.

VERA BRITTAIN, TESTAMENT OF YOUTH.

30 OCTOBER

STREET PEOPLE AND AIR PEOPLE, 1988

After a few weeks in New York (*see* 9 October), Jonathan Raban discovered that Manhattan society was riven by a deep gulf. The divide, as he saw it, was not so much a matter of class or money but of altitude.

There were Street People and there were Air People. Air People levitated like fakirs. Large portions of their day were spent waiting for, and travelling in, the elevators that were as fundamental to the middle-class culture of New York as gondolas had been to Venice in the Renaissance. It was the big distinction – to be able to press a button and take wing to your apartment. It didn't matter that you lived on the sixth, the 16th or 60th floor: access to the elevator was proof that your life had the buoyancy that was needed to stay afloat in a city where the ground was seen as the realm of failure and menace...

Everyone I knew lived like this. Their New York consisted of a series of high-altitude interiors, each one guarded, triple-locked, electronically surveilled. They kept in touch by flying from one interior to the next, like sociable gulls swooping from cliff to cliff. For them, the old New York of streets, squares, neighbourhoods, was rapidly turning into a vague and distant memory. It was the place where TV thrillers were filmed. It was where the Street People lived.

JONATHAN RABAN, *HUNTING MISTER HEARTBREAK*.

31 OCTOBER

A WELCOME HOMECOMING, 1718

When Lady Mary Wortley Montagu returned to England from Constantinople (*see* 27 March), she wrote to her friend, the Abbé Conti, reviewing her transcontinental travels in a patriotic, yet wistful, vein.

I cannot help looking with partial eyes on my native land. That partiality was certainly given us by nature to prevent rambling, the effect of an ambitious thirst after knowledge which we are not formed to enjoy. All we get by it is fruitless desire of mixing the different pleasures and conveniences which are given to different parts of the world and cannot meet in any one of them. After having read all that is to be found in the languages I am mistress of, and having decayed my sight by midnight studies, I envy the peace of mind of a ruddy milk maid who, undisturbed by doubt, hears the sermon with humility every Sunday, having not confused the sentiments of natural duty in her head by the vain enquiries of the schools, who may be more learned, yet after all must remain as ignorant. And after having seen part of Asia and Africa and almost made the tour of Europe, I think the honest English squire more happy who verily believes the Greek wines less delicious than March beer, that the African fruits have not so fine a flavour as golden pippins, and the becafiguas of Italy are not so well tasted as a rump of beef, and that, in short, there is no perfect enjoyment of this life out of Old England. I pray God I may think so for the rest of my life, and since I must be contented with our scanty allowance of daylight, that I may forget the enlivening sun of Constantinople.

LADY MARY WORTLEY MONTAGU, *THE COMPLETE LETTERS*, VOLUME I.

NOVEMBER

∞

1 NOVEMBER

THE WEEPING ORPHANS OF NAPLES, 1943

While dining in Naples (*see* 1 May), Norman Lewis was horrified to see a line of children enter the restaurant. They were on a half-day outing from a nearby orphanage and their overseer had been either 'unable or unwilling to stop them from being lured away by the smell of food'.

———••———

Suddenly five or six little girls between the ages of nine and twelve appeared in the doorway. They wore hideous straight black uniforms buttoned under their chins, and black boots and stockings, and their hair had been shorn short, prison-style. They were all weeping, and as they clung to each other and groped their way towards us, bumping into chairs and tables, I realized they were all blind. Tragedy and despair had been thrust upon us, and would not be shut out. I expected the indifferent diners to push back their plates, to get up and hold out their arms, but nobody moved. Forkfuls of food were thrust into open mouths, the rattle of conversation continued, nobody saw the tears...

The experience changed my outlook. Until now I had clung to the comforting belief that human beings eventually come to terms with pain and sorrow. Now I understood that I was wrong, and like Paul I suffered a conversion – but to pessimism. These little girls, any one of whom could be my daughter, came into the restaurant weeping, and they were weeping when they were led away. I knew that, condemned to everlasting darkness, hunger and loss, they would weep on incessantly. They would never recover from their pain, and I would never recover from the memory of it.

NORMAN LEWIS, *NAPLES '44.*

2 NOVEMBER

AROUND THE WORLD BY B.O.A.C., 1959

In 1959 Ian Fleming (*see* 16 March) was asked by the *Sunday Times* to visit his thirteen favourite destinations. A few hours out of London, aboard his de Havilland Comet G/ADOK, he started his round-the-world trip.

Zürich came and the banal beauty of Switzerland, then the jagged sugar-icing of the Alps, the blue puddles of the Italian lakes and the snow melting down towards the baked terrazza of the Italian plains... Below us Venice was an irregular brown biscuit surrounded by the crumbs of her islands. A straggling crack in the biscuit was the Grand Canal. At six hundred miles an hour, the Adriatic and the distant jagged line of Yugoslavia were gone in thirty minutes. Greece was blanketed in cloud and we were out over the Eastern Mediterranean in the time it took to consume a cupful of B.O.A.C. fruit salad...

It was now two o'clock in the afternoon G.M.T., but we were hastening towards the night and dusk came to meet us. An hour more of slow, spectacular sunset and blue-black night and then Beirut showed up ahead – a sprawl of twinkling hundreds-and-thousands under an Arabian Nights new moon that dived down into the oil lands as the Comet banked to make her landing. Beirut is a crooked town and, when we came to rest, I advised my neighbour to leave nothing small on his seat, and particularly not his extremely expensive camera. I said that we were now entering the thieving areas of the world. Someone would get it. The hatch clanged open and the first sticky fingers of the East reached in.

IAN FLEMING, *THRILLING CITIES*.

3 NOVEMBER

A COUNTRY HOUSE ON ASCENSION, 1982

The British diarist and politician Alan Clark (1928–99) was returning from Port Stanley, in the aftermath of the Falklands War, when his plane stopped to refuel at Ascension Island.

The mini-buses climbed away from the airfield into the foothills of the Green Mountain and the beginnings of vegetation could be detected. Dried-up, burnt-out stalks, without colour or leaf, except in little gullies where shelter from the sun had kept them green, rather like an [David] Attenborough film of a desert awaiting the seasonal flood. But gradually, as we climbed, the vegetation became greener and thicker, brilliant and towering banks of hibiscus and bougainvillea crowded up to the edge of the roadside; dense greenery with fleshy leaves, nameless white and yellow blooms and petals and voluptuous curving ferns...

Then, quite suddenly, in this equatorial jungle, we drew up beside a perfect English vicarage of the Regency period. Everything was flawless, from the Georgian window panes, to the gutterings, to the broken pediment over the arch that led into the separate kitchen garden. The lay-out of lodges and stables was precisely the same as the architect would have arranged on a hillside in Dorset in 1820. But of course the foliage that pressed around it was entirely different. And when I walked into the yard at the back to say hello to the pigs in their teak and granite sties, clouds of tropical birds flew up from the troughs.

This was the dwelling built for the Commander of the Marine Garrison that had been stationed on Ascension to help defend St Helena after Napoleon had been exiled there. All the materials and craftsmen had been brought out from Britain and the result was the most perfect country house south of the Tropic of Capricorn.

ALAN CLARK, *DIARIES: INTO POLITICS*.

4 NOVEMBER

A CANADA OF CONTRASTS, 1928

Her father having settled in Canada, Freya Stark decided to visit the country in 1928, the same year as her Syrian excursion (*see* 14 January). Montreal was fine, and so were the forests and lakes, but when she reached the plains she began to have doubts. 'The towns are springing up like mushrooms,' she wrote, 'and more hideous than one can easily imagine... While they are fighting to tear a living out of the unknown, these people have something very attractive, free and self-reliant and keen: but when it gets to money and comfort, it is not so pleasant any longer.'

There is really no means of describing this great lovely country. This is comparatively uninhabited, and Montreal is a very fine city, with handsome buildings. It is all beautifully organised so as to rest the jaded city-mind and avoid unnecessary trouble. Then your train starts and soon you are out in the endless flat stretches of woods and lakes, solitary as anything you can imagine. The train slips along for two days, and it is always the same: the long stretches of water where the ice is now forming at the edge: the thick pines and white birches, and here and there a sandy road with perhaps two lonely little square boxes of three or four rooms, or some shanty by the water's edge with a canoe drawn up for the winter. People get lost in these woods and can never find the way out again. They go to shoot moose, or fish in the lakes. The monotony of it adds extraordinarily to the sense of remoteness and of the valiancy of men's efforts who live here and make the land habitable.

FREYA STARK, *OVER THE RIM OF THE WORLD*.

5 NOVEMBER

STARS ABOVE THE *CORINTHIC*, 1906

Having spent several years studying music in London, Katherine Mansfield (*see* 23 January) was on her way back to New Zealand. One November night she lay on the deck of SS *Corinthic* and sought meaning in the stars. It was around this time that she decided to give up music and try writing instead.

————•+•————

Swiftly the night came. Like a great white bird the ship sped onward – onward into the unknown. Through the darkness the stars shone; yet the sky was a garden of golden flowers, heavy with colour. I lay on the deck of the vessel, my hands clasped behind my head, and watching them I felt a curious complex emotion – a swift realisation that they were shining steadily and ever more powerfully into the very soul of my soul. I felt their still light permeating the very depths, and fear and ecstasy held me still – shuddering. There is some fearful magic in their shining, I thought. As the power of the sunlight causes the firelight to become pale and wasted, so is the flame of my life as a little, little candle flickering fearfully and fancifully, and I thought before long it will go out; and then even as I thought I saw there where it had shone darkness remained.. Then I was drifting, drifting – where, whence, whither? I was drifting in a great boundless purple sea. I was being tossed to and fro by the power of the waves, and the confused sound of many voices floated to me. A sense of unutterable loneliness pervaded my spirit. I knew this sea was eternal. I was eternal. This crying was eternal.

KATHERINE MANSFIELD, *JOURNAL*.

6 NOVEMBER

AN ENGLISHMAN ABROAD, 1873

In 1873, on a solo trip to the Rockies, Isabella Bird (*see* 3 January) endured many vicissitudes. Among the most irksome of them was an encounter with one of her own countrymen.

I sat in the chimney corner, speculating on the reason why many of the upper class of my countrymen – 'High Toners,' as they are called out here – make themselves so ludicrously absurd. They neither know how to hold their tongues or to carry their personal pretensions. An American is nationally assumptive, an Englishman personally so. He took no notice of me till something passed which showed him I was English, when his manner at once changed into courtesy, and his drawl was shortened by a half. He took great pains to let me know that he was an officer in the Guards, of good family, on four months' leave, which he was spending in slaying buffalo and elk, and also that he had a profound contempt for everything American. I cannot think why Englishmen put on these broad, mouthing tones, and give so many personal details.

Isabella Bird, A Lady's Life in the Rocky Mountains.

7 NOVEMBER

IDLING IN ITALY, 1844

In 1844 Charles Dickens made a tour of Italy. At times an ungenerous traveller (*see* 1 April), he appears to have resented not only the slow pace of Italian life but also the fact that he had gone there at all. His jaded attitude contrasts starkly with the euphoria of John Ruskin just one year later (*see* 28 May).

What a strange, half-sorrowful and half-delicious doze it is, to ramble through these places gone to sleep and basking in the sun! Each, in its turn, appears to be, of all the mouldy, dreary, God-forgotten towns in the wide world, the chief. Sitting on this hillock, where a bastion used to be, and where a noisy fortress was, in the time of the old Roman station here, I became aware that I have never known till now, what it is to be lazy. A dormouse must surely be in very much the same condition before he retires under the wool in his cage; or a tortoise before he buries himself. I feel that I am getting rusty. That any attempt to think, would be accompanied with a creaking noise. That there is nothing, anywhere, to be done, or needing to be done. That there is no more human progress, motion, effort, or advancement of any kind beyond this. That the whole scheme stopped here centuries ago, and laid down to rest until the Day of Judgement.

CHARLES DICKENS, *AMERICAN NOTES AND PICTURES FROM ITALY*.

8 NOVEMBER

LONDON FILTH, 1617

When Horatio Bursino was appointed chaplain to the Venetian ambassador in London he greeted the post with mixed feelings. In a series of letters written to a colleague back home between October 1617 and September 1618, he described the city's bustle, vigour and prosperity; but he also bemoaned its squalor, ruffianly populace, xenophobia and (following the establishment of the breakaway Church of England) the general lack of good Catholic values. In this letter, written some time in November, he described the raucous celebrations that surrounded the appointment of a new lord mayor. Needless to say, following the Spanish Armada's attempt to invade Britain in 1588, any Spaniards spotted on the streets were given a good drubbing.

On looking into the street we saw a surging mass of people moving in search of some resting place which a fresh mass of sightseers grouped higgledy piggledy rendered impossible. It was a fine medley: there were old men in their dotage; insolent youths and boys, especially the apprentices alluded to; painted wenches and women of the lower classes carrying their children, all anxious to see the show. We noticed but few coaches and still fewer horsemen; only a few gentlewomen coming in their carriages for a view at some house in the Row belonging to their friends or relations, for the insolence of the mob is extreme. They cling behind the coaches and should the coachman use his whip, they jump down and pelt him with mud. In this way we saw them bedaub the smart livery of one coachman who was obliged to put up with it. In these great uproars no sword is ever unsheathed, everything ends in kicks, fisty cuffs and muddy faces...

Foreigners are ill regarded not to say detested in London, so sensible people dress in the English fashion, or in that of France, which is adopted by nearly the whole court, and thus mishaps are avoided or passed over in silence. The Spaniards alone maintain the prerogative of wearing their own costume, so they are easily recognised and most mortally hated. Some of our party saw a wicked woman in a rage with an individual supposing him to belong to the Spanish embassy. She urged the crowd to mob him, setting the example by belabouring him herself with a cabbage stalk and calling him a Spanish rogue, and although in very brave array his garments were foully smeared with a sort of soft and very stinking mud, which abounds here at all seasons, so that the place better deserves to be called Lorda (filth) than Londra (London). Had not the don saved himself in a shop they would assuredly have torn his eyes out, so hateful are the airs assumed here by the Spanish, whom the people of England consider harpies...

THOMAS PLATTER AND HORATIO BURSINO, *THE JOURNALS OF TWO TRAVELLERS*.

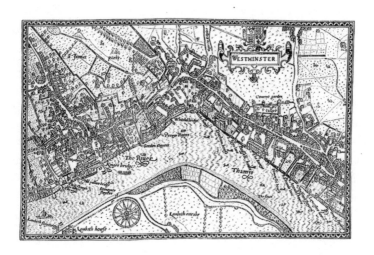

9 NOVEMBER

PACIFIC MIGHT, 1914

In 1914 the Australian journalist Charles Bean (1879–1968), on attachment with Australian troops, sailed from Sydney to report on the new European war. A few days into the journey he witnessed the impressive sight of a Japanese battleship moving into action. With such might at the Entente Powers' disposal, he reckoned that the conflict would be over in months. The timescale fitted nicely with his plan to take a walking tour of the Rhineland in 1915.

The Japanese ship was moving up on the other side of us, where she was stationed, in order to cross our bows and get on the port side of us also. She was stoking up; the smoke was pouring from her funnels thicker than ever – the wind carried it away from us so that the ship appeared nestled into the black masses of it. She passed us a few minutes later – prepared for action. Her decks were naked – a few white figures were clearing away or fastening down the last few encumbrances. Her upperworks – both bridges, and I think, the fire control stations – were neatly padded with rolled hammocks. One huge Japanese ensign was flying at the peak planted fair against the black smoke cloud. And just as she passed us she broke from the mainmast head a second great ensign of the rising sun – her battle flag. She was moving fast by this time – punching great masses of white out of the rich dark sea, spreading the seas wide on either side of her bluff bows as she went.

CHARLES BEAN, *BEAN'S GALLIPOLI.*

10 NOVEMBER

WORSE THAN A SHIP, 1848

During its voyage of discovery and surveying, HMS *Rattlesnake* stopped in 1848 for supplies at Port Essington, on the north coast of Australia. This much-detested outpost had been founded as a 'southern Singapore', to prosper from passing trade. But the trade never came, nobody settled and it was abandoned in 1849. The English biologist T.H. Huxley (*see* 7 February) loathed life aboard ship, but was faintly cheered to find conditions were even nastier in Port Essington.

As to the place itself it deserves all the abuse that has ever been heaped upon it. It is fit for neither man nor beast. Day and night there is the same fearful damp and depressing heat, producing an unconquerable languor and rendering the unhappy resident prey to ennui and cold brandy-and-water.

Vile as the climate is, however, it does not seem positively unhealthy. That is to say there are very few endemic diseases, no predominant fever and not overmuch dysentery, yet many of the men have spent a third of their time on the sick list, and as I have said there were but ten of the whole party fit for duty...

There are just five officers in the place, to wit one captain and two lieuts. of marines, one surgeon and one asst. surgeon, and there is as much petty intrigue, caballing and mutual hatred as if it were the court of the Great Khan.

We had not been two days in the settlement before we were masters of all the scandal of the place. Each man seemed to hate the other with a delightful cordiality and the only thing in which they were united was in the most unqualified abuse of the whole settlement.

I can't say more for Port Essington than that it is worse than a ship, and it is no small comfort to know that this is possible.

THOMAS HENRY HUXLEY, *DIARY OF THE VOYAGE OF H.M.S. RATTLESNAKE.*

11 NOVEMBER

NAPOLEON'S TRAVEL TIPS, 1803

Writing to his younger sister Pauline, who had just married her second husband, the wealthy Prince Camillo Borghese, Napoleon Bonaparte (1769–1821) offered some useful advice as to how she should deport herself in Italy.

The season for travelling is nearly past, and the Alps will soon be icebound. So set off for Rome. Make yourself remarked for your gentleness, your politeness to everyone, and an extreme regard for the ladies who are friends or relations of your mother's side of the family. More is expected of you than anyone. Above all, conform to the customs of the country; never run down anything; find everything splendid; and don't say, 'We do this better in Paris.' Show great attachment and respect for the Holy Father, of whom I am very fond, and whose simple manners make him worthy of the post he holds. Whatever I am told about you, nothing will please me more than to hear that you are good-tempered. The only foreigners you must never receive at your house, as long as we are at war with them, are the English – indeed, you must never allow them to be in your company. Love your husband, make your household happy, and above all don't be frivolous or capricious. You are 24 and it is time you were mature and sensible. I love you and shall always be pleased to hear that you are happy.

NAPOLEON BONAPARTE, *NAPOLEON'S LETTERS*.

12 NOVEMBER

STORM IN THE DRAKENSBERG, 1994

Dervla Murphy (*see* 9 March) was bicycling through South Africa when she was caught by a rainstorm near the town of Colenso in Natal. The *apartheid* regime had recently fallen, and in some parts of the country fearful whites were checking their armaments. Most vociferous among them was the AWB, the Afrikaner Weerstandsbeweging, the right-wing nationalist movement led by Eugène Terre'Blanche that sought – in the face of black-majority rule – the creation of a separate Boer state within South Africa.

Crossing to the other side of this narrow bridge, I caught my breath. Towers of inky clouds stood immobile over Grobbelaar's Mountain and Mount Hlangwane while beneath them stretched a wide band of rosiness – and the river, reflecting that strange radiance, shone mushroom pink between dark green, densely bushy banks. Then without warning a gale banished the day's torpid stillness, pulling a curtain of rain across the scene. As I sprinted back to the hotel – everyone in sight was sprinting somewhere – a premature twilight fell, thunder crashed continuously overhead, blue sheet lightning danced above the veld and the first huge raindrops splashed me.

Here the barman is an alarmingly thin Afrikaner youth with a pallid spotty face, pale blue eyes, a crew-cut and what I have come to think of as an AWB expression. He ignored my greeting, didn't trouble to open my Castle [beer], then resumed reading something under the counter. When he was summoned to the black bar I peered at his reading matter, a glossy *Guns & Other Weapons* periodical costing R8.50.

DERVLA MURPHY, *SOUTH FROM THE LIMPOPO*.

13 NOVEMBER

BLUE SHEEP AT SUNSET, 1973

A decade after his white-water rafting adventure (*see* 18 April), Peter Matthiessen journeyed to the Himalaya, accompanied by the zoologist George Schaller, to study a species of wild blue sheep – and, with luck, to catch a glimpse of the rare and near mythical snow leopard. For Matthiessen, a student of Zen Buddhism, it was also a voyage to his inner self.

—————

I descend the mountain to the Saldang path, turn west towards Shey. Already the path lies in twilight shadow, but the rocks on which the blue sheep stand, not thirty yards above, are in full sun. And now these creatures give a wild sunset display, the early rut that I had waited for all day. Old males spring off their rocks to challenge other males, and chase them off, and young males do as much for the females and young, and even the females butt at one another. Unlike the true sheep, which forges straight ahead, the bharal, in its confrontations, rears up and runs on its hind legs before crashing down into the impact, as true goats do – just the sort of evidence that GS had come so far to find. The whole herd of thirty-one joins in the mêlée, and in their quick springs from rock to rock, the goat in them is plain. Then one kicks loose a large stone from the crest, scattering the animals below, and in an instant, the whole herd is still.

Gold-eyed horned heads peer down out of the Himalayan blue as, in the silence, a last pebble bounces down the slope and comes to rest at my feet.

The bharal await me with the calm regard of ages.

Have you seen us now? Have you perceived us?

PETER MATTHIESSEN, *THE SNOW LEOPARD*.

14 NOVEMBER

A HUMAN ANT-HILL, 1850

Writing from Constantinople to his friend Louis Bouilhet, the French novelist Gustave Flaubert – having worked his way from Egypt (*see* 13 March) through Syria and Lebanon – was struck, like most Westerners, by his first encounter with the city. Unusually, though, the dead as much as the living contributed to his enjoyment.

———•———

Of Constantinople, where I arrived yesterday morning, I shall tell you nothing today, except to say that I have been struck by the idea of Fourier, that some day it will be the capital of the world. It is really fantastic as a human ant-hill. You know that feeling of being crushed and overwhelmed that one has on a first visit to Paris: here you are penetrated by that feeling, elbowing so many unknown men, from the Persian and the Indian to the American and the Englishman, so many separate individualities which, in their frightening total, humble your own. And then, the city is immense. One gets lost in the streets, which seem to have no beginning or end. The cemeteries are like forests in the middle of the city...

The oriental cemetery is one of the most beautiful things about the East. It does not have that profoundly exasperating quality of cemeteries at home – no wall, no ditch, no separation or enclosure of any kind. It is situated anywhere, in the country or in a town, here and there and everywhere, like death itself alongside of life, and given no attention whatever. You walk through a cemetery as you would walk through a bazaar. All the graves are alike; they differ only in age, and as they grow old they sink and disappear, like one's memory of the dead. The cypresses planted in the cemeteries are gigantic, and give the places a green light full of peace.

GUSTAVE FLAUBERT, *SELECTED LETTERS*.

15 NOVEMBER

ANOTHER SMALL COUNTRY IN THE MIDDLE EAST, 1961

The American 'Beat' poet Allen Ginsberg (*see* 19 October) was underwhelmed by the experience of visiting Israel in the early 1960s. The nation was less than fifteen years old and was still forging an identity. Writing to his father (also a poet), Ginsberg explained how he was torn between racial obligation, political approval, aesthetic disappointment and the fact that despite his Jewish background he was, in the end, from a completely different country.

The main beauty of Israel (aside from democracy as I mentioned) is that it is a haven for persecuted Jews. Many are here by necessity and not all are happy to be here just by necessity – after that it is another thing, to live for future. And living for future is not necessarily fun here as it's not for some people as interesting a place as N.Y. or Paris or even Mexico City or Athens. I don't personally feel much historical connection in my bones after all – I feel it more in the *Idea* or *Ideal* than I do in the reality while I'm here – that is to say, this place is just another small country while & when you're here for real – unless you have a pronounced tendency to be Yiddish which I don't – as a matter of fact I feel a more pronounced tendency to feel at home among Indians & Arabs in Mexico or Tangier – and that *Oriental* atmosphere is slowly disappearing here, to the dismay of many Sabras [native-born Israeli Jews] – disappearing to be replaced by a materialistic polyglot modern second rate industrial country. That is the significance that's attached to the slow decay of the idealistic socialist kibbutz scene – which now has a minority place & in a sense is no longer the soul of the new nation. All I'm saying is that unless you have a pronounced single-minded dedication to an *exclusive Jewish* frame of reference in life, this place is not so exciting. Granted it's fine as a refuge for the persecuted, and granted also that the persecuted themselves are not so kindly to their own Arab minority. But it's like being in a Chinese place where all the Chinamen are hung up on being Chinese and that's all they talk about – can be maddening too. It demands an *exclusively* Jewish mentality, whatever that is (everybody here's always arguing that) and I find that a definite limitation on my own mentality which is Jewish enough but a lot more than that. This is XX Century and I still say the old order of Identity is a big nationalistic hang up on every side. It would be something if there were any folk songs to preserve, but here they *invent* second rate folk songs so they can 'cherish tradition'.

ALLEN AND LOUIS GINSBERG, FAMILY BUSINESS.

16 NOVEMBER

MR CLARK'S FEAR OF FLYING, 1987

Alan Clark (*see* 3 November), the British minister of trade from 1986 to 1989, disliked flying. It was unfortunate therefore that his job involved lengthy bouts of air travel. His nerves – and hypochondria – are apparent in this diary entry describing a flight from Vancouver to San Francisco.

How very *dry* and flushed one becomes on these great long-distance flights. My Harold Acton death-spots gleam reproachfully in the lights of the silent, stainless steel lavabos. Round me, my fellow travellers who, some eight hours ago, boarded groomed and confident with their Etienne Aigner luggage, are now pinched and watery-eyed... Below, the Canadian tundra slips past. Many lakes. Skirting the Northern Ice-cap was deeply frightening – more so even than the Andean Desert. So *utterly* lifeless and bleak... Oh these hateful flights!...

If one is nurturing cancer, pre-cancerous, which I often think I am, these hideous great flights must be the very worst thing.

I long, I physically long for a great long walk, to breathe deep gulps and to stretch the spine. We have been in the air eight and a half hours, yet the clock has advanced less than twenty minutes since take-off.

We are almost keeping pace with the sun.

ALAN CLARK, *DIARIES*.

17 NOVEMBER

THE END OF THE DESERT, 1845

By November 1845 Charles Sturt (*see* 13 January) had spent more than a year exploring the desolate stretch of Australia that would later bear his name – the Sturt Stony Desert – and was at the end of his tether. Within a month he would be back home with his wife Charlotte, the 'Dearest' to whom he wrote his weekly journal entries.

I dismounted, Dearest, having ridden 917 miles in five weeks and three days. When I got off my horse I felt as if the old dog had put his head between my legs as is his wont in welcoming any one and was pushing me forward. I turned round therefore to chide him but no dog was there. It was the jerking of the muscles of my thighs, and was the forerunner of something worse My two journeys combined made up 1878 miles that I had travelled since the 14th of August... I had tired and worn out every man in the party and started on my last journey with entirely new hands. I had been exposed from sunrise to sunset to a scorching sun and at night had slept under the canopy of heaven alone. No wonder then that I was at length reduced, but the object I had in view made me reckless alike of exposure and privation. The day after I arrived in the camp, I lost the use of my left leg, the main muscles contracted and I lost all power of straightening the limb. Gradually my right leg became affected until at length I am stretched on my mattress a helpless and prostrate being. However, Dearest, I complain not.

CHARLES STURT, *JOURNAL OF THE CENTRAL AUSTRALIAN EXPEDITION, 1844–5.*

18 NOVEMBER

AN ARSONIST IN MONTEREY, 1879

From August 1879 to August 1880 Robert Louis Stevenson (*see* 2 June) spent a year travelling through America, from which he emerged with a wife and several books' worth of memories. In the November 1880 issue of *Fraser's Magazine*, he recounted a spot of arson during a forest fire in Monterey, California.

I have an interest of my own in these forest fires, for I came so near to lynching on one occasion, that a braver man might have retained a thrill from the experience. I wished to be certain whether it was the moss, that quaint funereal ornament of Californian forests, which blazed up so rapidly when the flame first touched the tree. I suppose I must have been under the influence of Satan, for instead of plucking off a piece for my experiment, what should I do but walk up to a great pine tree in a portion of the wood which had escaped so much as scorching, strike a match, and apply the flame gingerly to one of the tassels. The tree went off simply like a rocket; in three seconds it was a roaring pillar of fire. Close by I could hear the shouts of those who were at work combating the original conflagration. I could see the waggon that had brought them tied to a live oak in a piece of open; I could even catch the flash of an axe as it swung up through the undergrowth into the sunlight. Had any one observed the result of my experiment my neck was not worth a pinch of snuff; after a few minutes of passionate expostulation I should have been run up to a convenient bough... I have run repeatedly, but never as I ran that day. At night I went out of town, and there was my own particular fire, quite distinct from the other, and burning, as I thought, with even greater vigour.

ROBERT LOUIS STEVENSON, *FROM SCOTLAND TO SILVERADO*.

19 NOVEMBER

A DEATH ON THE OCEAN, 1834

In the same year that he left Boston aboard the *Pilgrim* (*see* 10 January), Richard Henry Dana witnessed his first death at sea.

The lost man is seldom mentioned, or is dismissed with a sailor's rude eulogy – 'Well, poor George is gone! His cruise is up soon! He knew his work, and did his duty, and was a good shipmate.' Then usually follows some allusion to another world for sailors are almost all believers; but their notions and opinions are unfixed and at loose ends. They say, – 'God won't be hard upon the poor fellow,' and seldom get beyond the common phrase which seems to imply that their sufferings and hard treatment here will excuse them hereafter, – *'To work hard, live hard, die hard, and go to hell after all, would be hard indeed!'* Our cook, a simple-hearted old African, who had been through a good deal in his day, and was rather seriously inclined, always going to church twice a day when on shore, and reading his Bible on a Sunday in the galley, talked to the crew about spending their Sabbaths badly, and told them that they might go as suddenly as George had, and be as little prepared.

Yet a sailor's life is at best but a mixture of a little good with much evil, and a little pleasure with much pain. The beautiful is linked with the revolting, the sublime with the commonplace, and the solemn with the ludicrous.

RICHARD HENRY DANA, *TWO YEARS BEFORE THE MAST.*

20 NOVEMBER

ACROSS THE STEPPE TO TASHKENT, 1893

The Swedish explorer Sven Hedin (*see* 16 April) travelled by sledge and cart across the Kirghiz steppe to Tashkent, arriving on 4 December. He was impressed by the numbers. 'Thus,' he wrote, 'in nineteen days, I had traversed eleven and a half degrees of latitude, passed thirty thousand telegraph poles, employed one hundred and eleven drivers, used three hundred and seventeen horses and twenty-one camels and had passed from a Siberian winter to a temperature that, in daytime, rose to 54°.'

The wheels creaked on the frozen snow. The horses trotted and galloped, and the *troika* burnt up the road. The constant jolting nearly bumped me to pieces. We continued hour after hour, yet the *tarantass* [a horse-drawn carriage] remained the centre of a never-changing circle of plain-land. Now and then the driver stopped for a spell to let the perspiring horses get their breath. Occasionally he pointed his whip in the direction we were going and said: 'After a while we'll meet a *tarantass* from the south.'

With my field-glasses I scanned the horizon, and discovered nothing more than a tiny speck. But the driver could even make out the colour of the approaching horses. Their outdoor life on the steppe has sharpened the senses of the Kirghiz incredibly. In the middle of the night, when it is pitch-dark and cloudy, they find their way. Nothing but the blizzards baffles their sense of locality. Of course, the telegraph-poles mark the road to a certain extent; but in heavy blizzards one can lose one's way between two poles, leaving no choice but to wait for the dawn. During such nights it behoves one to beware of the wolves.

SVEN HEDIN, *MY LIFE AS AN EXPLORER*.

21 NOVEMBER

A SECRET GARDEN IN ROME, 1978

In 1978 the ageing British conservationist James Lees-Milne (1908–97) visited Rome to examine monuments and statues by the 18th-century sculptor Joseph Nollekens. Some less cerebral aspects of the Eternal City caught his eye too.

Rome is a curiously sexy city. I watched at nightfall men and women wandering aimlessly and furtively in an enclosed garden at the top of steep steps in front of the Museum of Modern Art. I went inside to have a look around. Against one stone wall of the south boundary was a long hedge of evergreens. In the hedge at intervals were openings. Between the openings and the wall were couples, some with their trousers down and skirts up, blatantly having sex. No one seemed to be the least disturbed or perturbed by my intrusion. They went on with the job unabashed. And when satisfied strolled away, without a word being spoken. I did not see any money passing. And the total silence sinister.

JAMES LEES-MILNE, *THROUGH WOOD AND DALE*.

22 NOVEMBER

FAREWELL MARJORIBANKS, 1933

At Herat, Robert Byron was delighted to quit the Western influences of Persia (*see* 2 May) for the more independent, if more backward, world of tribal Afghanistan. One of his great bugbears in Persia had been its dictatorial shah, whom he referred to in his journal as 'Marjoribanks' in case it should be read by the authorities.

———•••———

Engrossed by the contrast with Persia, I return the people's stare. The appearance of the ordinary Persian, as dressed by Marjoribanks's sumptuary laws, is a slur on human dignity; impossible, one thinks, for this swarm of seedy mongrels to be really the race that have endeared themselves to countless travellers with their manners, gardens, horsemanship, and love of literature. How the Afghans may endear themselves remains to be seen. Their clothes and their walk are credential enough to begin with. A few, the officials, wear European suits, surmounted by a dashing lambskin hat. The townsmen too sport an occasional waistcoat in the Victorian style, or the high-collared frock-coat of the Indian Mussulman. But these importations, when accompanied by a turban as big as a heap of bedclothes, a cloak of parti-coloured blanket, and loose white peg-top trousers reaching down to gold-embroidered shoes of gondola shape, have an exotic gaiety, like an Indian shawl at the Opera. This is the southern fashion, favoured by the Afghans proper. The Tajiks, or Persian element, prefer the quilted gown of Turkestan. Turcomans wear high black boots, long red coats, and busbies of silky black goats' curls. The most singular costume is that of the neighbouring highlanders, who sail through the streets in surtouts of stiff white serge, dangling false sleeves, almost wings, that stretch to the back of the knee and are pierced in patterns like a stencil. Now and then a calico bee-hive with a window at the top flits across the scene. This is a woman.

Hawk-eyed and eagle-beaked, the swarthy loose-knit men swing through the dark bazaar with a devil-may-care self-confidence. They carry rifles to go shopping as Londoners carry umbrellas. Such ferocity is purely histrionic. The rifles may not go off... Even the glare of the eyes is often due to make-up. But it is a tradition; in a country where the law runs uncertainly, the mere appearance of force is half the battle of ordinary business. It may be an inconvenient tradition, from the point of view of the government. But at least it has preserved the people's poise and their belief in themselves. They expect the European to conform to their standards, instead of themselves to his, a fact which came home to me this morning when I tried to buy some arak; there is not a drop of alcohol to be had in the whole town. Here at last is Asia without an inferiority complex.

ROBERT BYRON, *THE ROAD TO OXIANA*.

23 NOVEMBER

LUNARDI, COME DOWN, 1785

Following his success in Edinburgh (*see* 4 October), Vincenzo Lunardi took his balloon to Glasgow, where once again he astonished the natives. Shortly after the following surreal conversation, Lunardi landed and succeeded in one of his most heartfelt desires – to entice a LADY into the basket.

The water generated by the inflammable air came down converted into icicles: I tasted a piece of it, and found it was similar to that of a long Scotch turnip. I passed horizontally through the clouds for about eight minutes: when I came in sight of the healthy hills again, I heard a voice call, *'Lunardi, come down,'* quite plain, and I knew not who it was; – I saw at a distance sheep feeding, but could not see a human being; and I was greatly surprised to hear my name pronounced by any shepherd that might have been there with his sheep; and I could perceive no house, nor even huts in the neighbourhood. I called aloud several times through the hill and after one third of a minute, or 19 seconds, I could hear the echo of my words returned as loud as they were pronounced; but I never had repeated *Lunardi, come down*, though I heard these words several times repeated, on which I answered through the trumpet, *Hallow, hallow*, with a great voice; – I heard the words, *Lunardi, hallow,* repeated; and being now quite free from any interruption from clouds, I could see distinctly some people on horseback.

VINCENZO LUNARDI, *AN ACCOUNT OF FIVE AERIAL VOYAGES*.

24 NOVEMBER

AN OLYMPIAN IN JODHPUR, 1925

The English author Aldous Huxley (1894–1963) – grandson of T.H. Huxley (*see* 7 February) – was travelling through India when, in late November, he reached the celebrated city of Jodhpur. For all Jodhpur's wonder, he didn't much like getting there: 'An interesting and picturesque country,' he wrote, 'but unfortunately traversed by railways on which trains never average more than fourteen miles an hour.'

Standing on the ramparts of Jodhpur fort – on a level with the highest wheelings of the vultures, whose nests are on the ledges of the precipices beneath the walls – one looks down on the roofs of the city, hundreds of feet below. And every noise from the streets and houses comes floating up, diminished but incredibly definite and clear, a multitudinous chorus, in which, however, one can distinguish all the separate component sounds – crying and laughter, articulate speech, brayings and bellowings and bleatings, the creak and rumble of wheels, the hoarse hooting of a conch, the pulsing of drums. I have stood on high places above many cities, but never on one from which the separate sounds making up the great counterpoint of a city's roaring could be so clearly heard, so precisely sifted by the listening ear. From the bastions of Jodhpur fort one hears as the gods must hear from their Olympus – the gods to whom each separate word uttered in the innumerably peopled world below comes up distinct and individual to be recorded in the books of omniscience.

ALDOUS HUXLEY, *PILATE JESTING: THE DIARY OF A JOURNEY.*

25 NOVEMBER

TRANSCENDENT IN NEPAL, 1973

Towards the end of his Himalayan journey (*see* 13 November) Peter Matthiessen was rewarded by a moment of sublimity. Five days later, on returning to the relative luxury of India, he looked in a mirror and wrote: 'this is the face of a man I do not know'.

———•·•———

We climb onward, towards the sky, and with every step my spirits rise. As I walk along, my stave striking the ground, I leave the tragic sense of things behind; I begin to smile, infused with a sense of my own foolishness, with an acceptance of the failures of this journey as well as of its wonders, acceptance of all that I might meet upon my path. I know that this transcendence will be fleeting, but while it lasts, I spring along the path as if set free; so light do I feel that I might be back in the celestial snows.

This clear and silent light of the Himalaya is intensified by the lack of smoke and noise. The myriad high peaks, piercing the atmosphere, let pass a light of heaven – the light on stones that makes them ring, the sun roaring and the silverness that flows in lichens and the wings of crows, the silverness in the round tinkle of a pony's bell, and in the scent of snows...

Below the track, an old woman in wild black rags flails barley heaps on the flat roof of her hut; the wood blade cuts the mountain sky as she rears to strike. Under a walnut tree, a hangman's limb, a black cow awaits the dusk; its bell is still.

PETER MATTHIESSEN, *THE SNOW LEOPARD*.

26 NOVEMBER

AN AFRICAN ARMAGEDDON, 2004

In 2004 the British Labour politician Chris Mullin (born 1947), then a minister in the Foreign Office, travelled to Liberia on a fact-finding mission. He found that the capital, Monrovia, still bore the imprint of half a decade of civil war.

To see Monrovia is to glimpse Armageddon. A million people here live without running water or electricity. This is a place where, until the coming of the UN, the Lords of Chaos had free rein. Where youths armed to the teeth and drugged to the eyeballs rampaged at will, looting, raping, murdering. Much of the city is derelict, shop fronts peppered with bullet holes, houses (still inhabited) half demolished or half built; roofless, windowless, burnt-out buildings in every street. And in every street a church. Can there be any place on earth that has as many churches as Liberia? So many Christians and so little Christianity. God is everything. 'The blood of Jesus prevails over his enemies,' says a slogan on a billboard outside the Church of the God of Prophecy. 'Oh God, please give us your choice of leader for Liberia,' says another (divine guidance may well be required: so far more than 40 presidential candidates have been declared – the latest an international footballer who has every chance of winning). A sign on the road from the airport reads: 'Time is running out for Liberia.' You can say that again.

CHRIS MULLIN, *A VIEW FROM THE FOOTHILLS*.

27 NOVEMBER

NEVER ALONE IN THE DESERT, 1946

During his first journey through the Empty Quarter (*see* 28 October), Wilfred Thesiger paused above a desert well to contemplate life. It was his first moment of solitude during the journey.

I climbed to the summit of the dune and lay peacefully in the sun, four hundred feet above the well. A craving for privacy is something which Bedu will never understand; something which they will always instinctively mistrust. I have often been asked by Englishmen if I was never lonely in the desert, and I have wondered how many minutes I have spent by myself in the years that I have lived there. It is true that the worst loneliness is to be lonely in a crowd. I have been lonely at school and in European towns where I knew nobody, but I have never been lonely among Arabs. I have arrived in their towns where I was unknown, and I have walked into the bazaar and greeted a shopkeeper. He has invited me to sit beside him in his shop and has sent for tea. Other people have come along and joined us. They have asked me who I was, where I came from, and innumerable questions which we should never ask a stranger. Then one of them has said, 'Come and lunch', and at lunch I have met other Arabs, and someone else has asked me to dinner. I have wondered sadly what Arabs brought up in this tradition have thought when they visited England; and I have hoped that they realised that we are as unfriendly to each other as we must appear to be to them.

WILFRED THESIGER, *ARABIAN SANDS*.

28 NOVEMBER

MOROCCAN CHARM, 1960

The author Paul Bowles (*see* 30 January) was approached by a Californian publisher seeking unusual and magical Moroccan recipes for a forthcoming cookery book. He wrote the following reply.

Thank you for your letter of November twenty-eighth. I can see that the collecting of the sort of recipes I should like to send you is going to take a good deal more work than I had imagined. Since you have a deadline of February first, perhaps it would be more practical if I renounced the project and sent you the one recipe I have been able to get for you... One Marrakechi was kind enough to give me the following information (which can scarcely be considered a recipe for anything), and I give it to you merely to show you the sort of thing they are willing to give. It's called BEID EL BEITA F'KERR EL HMAR, and requires three nights to prepare. 'Buy an egg. Find a dead donkey, and the first night lodge the egg in its anus. The second night the egg must be put into a mousehole on top of a Moslem tomb. The third night it must be wrapped in a handkerchief and tied around the chest of the person desiring to perform the magic. The following day it must be given for breakfast, prepared in any fashion, to the other individual, who immediately upon eating it discovers that the bestower is necessary for his happiness.' (Or her happiness; the sex of the two people seems to have nothing to do with the charm's efficacy.)

PAUL BOWLES, *In Touch*.

29 NOVEMBER

THE DESERT WIND TO ASPEN, 1988

By this date, Michael Palin was on the sixty-sixth day of his Phileas Fogg-inspired circumnavigation (*see* 18 October). With his camera crew as companion – replacing the French valet Passepartout of Jules Verne's novel – he was now in the United States, on the Desert Wind train from Los Angeles to Aspen, Colorado.

The sun spills into the train as we set off again alongside the Colorado River. It's about 25 yards wide here, and on its flat banks, protected from the winds, grow orchards of apple, pear and peach. Halfway down the train is an observation car. It's filling up fast on this clear and sunny afternoon.

There's a lady of late middle-age calling herself Mar-Mer, who became a clown two years ago. She sparkles with the delight of it all and bursts into song and jokes with the zeal of a new convert. How does her husband cope with her new profession, I ask. 'Oh... he's kind of an introvert,' she reveals, as if describing an incurable illness. There's a man travelling with his son simply because he prefers trains: 'Sure knocks hell outta driving.' His wife is a cellist with the gloriously named Mile High Orchestra in Denver. But I get the feeling that these are not average Americans. They're people who care about their environment, who despise and fear what big business is doing to it and who are immensely knowledgeable about where they live and determined to protect it from unnecessary development.

MICHAEL PALIN, *AROUND THE WORLD IN 80 DAYS*.

30 NOVEMBER

CURZON IN KUWAIT, 1903

George Nathaniel Curzon (1859–1925) was coming up to his fifth year as Viceroy of India, a position that made him one of the most powerful individuals in the world. In this role he visited Kuwait in November 1903, where his superiority was given a casual – or perhaps deliberate – shake.

As I sat there, bandying civilities with my host, a sound of violent rending and tearing, accompanied by loud shouts and plunging of horse-hoofs broke the solemn hush of our palaver. Not a word was said on the subject. But when the interview was over and I descended to the street, only the fragments of the Bombay Victoria [a carriage], reduced to matchwood, littered the ground, and the steeds had vanished! It appeared that these animals, who had never before been harnessed to a vehicle, had made up for their orderly behaviour, while conducting the Sheikh and myself from the landing-place to the town, by kicking the somewhat flimsy construction to pieces as soon as they were left alone. I doubt if a Victoria has been seen in Koweit since.

We had to feel our way very gingerly on foot over heaps of ordure and amid indescribable filth to a nearer point of embarkation for our vessel, which was lying at anchor at a considerable distance in the shallow waters of the Gulf. Thus began and thus ignobly ended my Viceregal entry into Koweit.

GEORGE CURZON, *TRAVELS WITH A SUPERIOR PERSON*.

DECEMBER

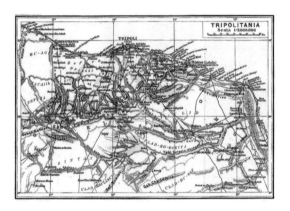

1 DECEMBER

A PUDDING IN THE JUNGLE, 1899

Some years before her husband's débâcle in the Middle East (*see* 30 November), Lady Mary Curzon, wife of Indian Viceroy Lord Curzon, caught her husband in the act of hurling a plum cake to a fellow gun during a tiger hunt.

After breakfast we drove 3 miles further, and then went over rough ground on elephants to a deep gully where the tiger drive was to be. There we got into a castellated tower... [and the other guns] in two little round towers on the other side of the [ravine]. We waited for hours and no tiger came. We did not make a sound and the expectation was very great; and when my Camera cracked & the chair I was sitting on collapsed it sounded like the earthquake in a china factory, and my whole soul apologised for the outrageous action of the furniture & I was seized with a *fou rire*. We had food in our little tower but the opposite party had none & after 8 hours of famine showed signs of emaciation so with wonderful aim George threw a fine plum cake across the chasm which was caught in silent gratitude... A tiger broke back and the beat began anew, and about 5 there was a crunching and a growl, and a flash of yellow dashed before us, and George fired and missed him: the fraction of a second, and as the tiger galloped past, George shot him in the back and Captain Baker-Carr fired, and all was over and the tiger *gone*! It was so sudden and thrilling that my eyes were falling out and my tongue tied.

MARY CURZON, *LADY CURZON'S INDIA*.

2 DECEMBER

FIRING SQUAD IN SPAIN, 1937

In December 1937 Laurie Lee returned to Spain to fight in the Civil War on the Republican side. Having crossed the Pyrenees he was promptly arrested as a spy, thrown into a cellar for a fortnight, and then taken away, as he supposed, to be shot. Instead he was later released and sent on his way to Madrid (see 7 January).

As the sun rose higher and whitened the rocks, the landscape turned blank, as though over-exposed. And with the whistling guards on either side of me, and the bully-shouldered officer up front, I was sure I was on the road to my doom. As my eyes grew used to the light – after all, I'd been two weeks in darkness – I saw the landscape shudder into shape, grow even more desolate and brutal. Yet never more precious as it floated past me, the worn-out skin of this irreplaceable world, marked here and there by the scribbled signs of man, a broken thatched cabin, or a terraced slope. Every breath I took now seemed rich and stolen, in spite of the oil-fumed heat in the car...

We'd been driving, I guessed, for about an hour, when the officer suddenly straightened up and snapped his fingers, and we pulled off the road and stopped. The dead icy tableland crept with yellow mist, and seemed quite empty, save for a clump of trees in the distance. I was ordered out of the car, one of the guards stuck a gun in my back, pointed to the trees and said, 'March!'...

I saw the vast cold sky and the stony plain and I began to walk towards the distant trees. I heard the soldiers behind me slip the bolts on their rifles. This then, of course, could be the chosen place – the plateau ringed by rock, the late dawn on our breath, the empty silence around us, the little wood ahead, all set for quiet execution or murder. I felt the sharp edges of the stones under my thin-soled shoes. The guards behind me shuttled the bolts of their guns.

LAURIE LEE, *A MOMENT OF WAR.*

3 DECEMBER

A TIGER FIGHT IN JAVA, 1866

The Marquis de Beauvoir (*see* 2 April) was approaching Australia when he and his aristocratic companions stopped in Java, where they learned of the sultan's various entertainments.

When we left the harem, we went to see the tigers, which are shut up in great wooden buildings and reserved for fights on the Sultan's fête day. It must be a very fine sight. The army is formed in four rows in the largest court belonging to the palace, and six young princes called 'the six heroes of the sun,' with golden helmets and naked to the waist, bravely cut the cords which fasten the door of the great cage, and show their courage by not retreating before the tiger, except in a kind of dance of death to the sound of cymbals. Then the fierce-eyed beast rushes against the wall of men bristling with lances, and finally falls howling and pierced through. Sometimes a wild buffalo is let in against the tiger; then the fight becomes desperate and the struggles are awful. At the last fête the most fearful moment was also rather ludicrous. Attacked and conquered by the buffalo, the tiger bounded some twenty feet into the air above the lances into a cocoa-nut tree. There, according to custom on the first night in the tropics, some thirty natives were in an elevated position amongst the branches of this tree; in one and the same moment they let themselves fall, like ripe fruit from a tree that is shaken...

MARQUIS DE BEAUVOIR, *A VOYAGE ROUND THE WORLD*, VOLUME II.

4 DECEMBER

A PHANTOM CASTLE IN DENMARK, 1904

The poet Rainer Maria Rilke was staying at Charlottenlund, near Copenhagen, when he undertook an excursion to a once-majestic castle. Having become bored by the climate of Rome (*see* 12 May), he was pleased to report that Denmark had seasons in abundance: 'a quintessence of summer... a festival of autumn... and, now, a proper deep winter'.

And once there was a complete journey, white through white, seven hours by train into Småland, followed by a swift sleigh-run through a silently snowing afternoon, and finally arriving in early dusk at a lonely estate. Amid the jangling of ten small bells we drove down a long, old avenue of linden trees, – the sleigh swung out and there was the forecourt, flanked by the small side wings of the castle. But where four stairs climbed heavily and laboriously out of the snow of the courtyard up to the terrace, and where this terrace, bordered by a balustrade with ornamental vases, thought itself a preparation for the castle, – there was nothing, nothing but a few bushes sunk in snow and sky, gray, trembling sky out of whose scattered twilight flakes were falling. One had to tell oneself, no, there is no castle here, and then one remembered having heard that it had burned down long ago, but one felt nevertheless that something was there, that somehow the air behind that terrace had not yet merged with the rest of the air, that it was still divided into passages and rooms and in the middle it still formed a hall, a high, empty, abandoned dining-hall. – But then from the side wing on the left the lord of the manor stepped out, tall, thick-set, with a blond moustache, and admonished the four long dachshunds to stop barking.

RAINER MARIA RILKE, *RAINER MARIA RILKE AND
LOU ANDREAS SALOMÉ: THE CORRESPONDENCE.*

5 DECEMBER

COLD COMFORT IN KABUL, 1956

Returning to Warsaw from a trip through India, the Polish journalist Ryszard Kapuściński (*see* 12 April) was issued with a typically tortuous Cold War ticket, involving changes in both Kabul and Moscow. On a December day, having been detained for not having a transit visa, he described the capital of Afghanistan with little warmth.

I landed in Kabul just as the sun was setting. An intensely pink, almost violet sky cast its light onto the dark navy-blue mountains surrounding the valley. The day was dying, sinking into a total and profound silence – it was the hush of a landscape, a region, a world that could be disturbed neither by the bell on a donkey's neck nor by the fine patter of a flock of sheep passing the airport barracks...

Kabul is dust upon dust. Winds blow through the valley where the city lies, carrying clouds of sand from the nearby deserts. A pale brown, grayish particulate matter hangs in the air, coating everything, pushing its way in everywhere, settling only when the winds die down. And then the air grows transparent, crystal clear.

Every evening the streets looked as if a spontaneous, improvised mystery play were being staged on them. The all-pervasive darkness is pierced only by oil lamps and torches burning on the street stalls, whose feeble and wavering flames illuminate the cheap and meagre goods laid out by the vendors directly on the ground, on patches of road, on the thresholds of houses. Between these rows of lights people pass silently – hunched, covered figures whipped on by the cold and the wind.

RYSZARD KAPUŚCIŃSKI, *TRAVELS WITH HERODOTUS*.

6 DECEMBER

VOICES OF THE *BOUNTY*, 1825

En route to the Arctic aboard HMS *Blossom*, Captain Frederick William Beechey (1796–1856) stopped at Pitcairn Island in the South Pacific. It was to this tiny dot – circumference seven miles – that Fletcher Christian and his companions had fled following the *Bounty* mutiny of 1789. By now, the mutineers' descendants numbered almost sixty and they had developed a unique method of communication.

It was dark when we reached the houses, but we found by a whoop that echoed through the woods that we were not the last from home. This whoop, peculiar to the place, is so shrill, that it may be heard half over the island, and the ear of the natives is so quick, that they will catch it when we could distinguish nothing of the kind. By the tone in which it is delivered they also know the wants of the person, and who it is. These shrill sounds, which we had just heard, informed us, and those who were at the village, that a party had lost their way in the woods. A blazing beacon was immediately made, which, together with a few more whoops to direct the party, soon brought the absentees home.

F.W. Beechey, *Narrative of a Voyage to the Pacific and Bering's Strait*, Volume I.

7 DECEMBER

RIO BY NIGHT, 1768

While sailing down the coast of South America the *Endeavour* stopped at Rio de Janeiro – to the delight of the naturalist Joseph Banks (*see* 29 May), who wasted no time recording the religious practices of those parts. The reason for the processions, he discovered, was that a church needed rebuilding: to raise the funds, all boys beneath a certain age were given permission to beg by candlelight one night a week.

———

Each of these were dressd in a Black cassock with a short red Cloak reaching half way down their shoulders, and carried in his hand a Lanthorn hung on the End of a pole about 6 or 7 feet long, the light caused by this (for there were always at least 200 Lights) is greater than can be imagined; I myself who saw it out of the cabbin windows calld together my mess mates and shewd it to them imagining that the town was on fire.

Besides this traveling religion a man who walks the streets has opportunity enough to shew his attachment to any saint in the Calendar, for every corner and almost every house has before it a little cupboard in which some Saint or other keeps his Residence, and lest he should not see his votaries in the night he is furnished with a small lamp which hangs before his little glass window: to these it is very customary to pray and sing hymns with all the vociferation imaginable, as may be imagind when I say that I and every one Else in the Ship heard it very distinctly every night tho we lay at least half a mile from the town.

JOSEPH BANKS, *The 'Endeavour' Journal.*

8 DECEMBER

MUMBO JUMBO, 1795

When the Scottish explorer Mungo Park (1771–1806) left Britain in 1795 in search of the course of the Niger (*see* 20 August), his aim was as much to investigate the people and nations he encountered along the way as to chart the river. By early December he had already followed the River Gambia hundreds of miles into the African interior. To make life easier he learned the language of the region's Mandingo (Mandinka) people – and was rewarded for his trouble with a phrase that has since spread across the English-speaking world.

About noon, I arrived at Kolor, a considerable town, near the entrance into which I observed, hanging upon a tree, a sort of masquerade habit, made of the bark of trees, which I was told on inquiry belonged to MUMBO JUMBO. This is a strange bugbear, common to all the Mandingo towns, and much employed by the Pagan natives in keeping their women in subjection; for as the Kafirs are not restricted in the number of their wives, every one marries as many as he can conveniently maintain; and as it frequently happens that the ladies disagree among themselves, family quarrels sometimes rise to such a height that the authority of the husband can no longer preserve peace in his household. In such cases, the interposition of Mumbo Jumbo is called on, and is always decisive.

This strange minister of justice (who is supposed to be either the husband himself, or some person instructed by him), disguised in the dress that has been mentioned, and armed with the rod of public authority, announces his coming (whenever his services are required) by loud and dismal screams in the woods near the town. He begins the pantomime at the approach of night; and as soon as it is dark he enters the town, and proceeds to the Bentang [stage], at which all the inhabitants immediately assemble.

It may easily be supposed that this exhibition is not much relished by the women; for as the person in disguise is entirely unknown to them, every married female suspects that the visit may possibly be intended for herself; but they dare not refuse to appear when they are summoned; and the ceremony commences with songs and dances, which continue till midnight, about which time Mumbo fixes on the offender. The unfortunate victim being thereupon immediately seized, is stripped naked, tied to a post, and severely scourged with Mumbo's rod, amidst the shouts and derision of the whole assembly; and it is remarkable, that the rest of the women are the loudest in their exclamations on this occasion against their unhappy sister. Daylight puts an end to this indecent and unmanly revel.

MUNGO PARK, *THE TRAVELS OF MUNGO PARK*.

9 DECEMBER

A RAINY FAREWELL TO LONDON, 1933

In 1933, the teenaged Patrick Leigh Fermor (*see* 15 January) set out to cross Europe on foot, in an epic journey that took him from the Hook of Holland to Istanbul and occupied more than two years. (The writing up of it, however, took him another forty years.) The point of departure was London, but as that involved cab rides and ferries he preferred to think of his trek starting the other side of the Channel – and given the drear and sodden day he had chosen to leave, who can blame him?

'A splendid afternoon to set out!' said one of the friends who was seeing me off, peering at the rain and rolling up a window.

The other two agreed. Sheltering under the Curzon Street arch of Shepherd Market, we found a taxi rank at last. In Half Moon Street, all collars were up. A thousand glistening umbrellas were tilted over a thousand bowler hats in Piccadilly; the Jermyn Street shops, distorted by streaming water, had become a submarine arcade; and the clubmen of Pall Mall, with china tea and anchovy toast in mind, were scuttling for sanctuary up the steps of their clubs. Blown askew, the Trafalgar Square fountains twirled like mops, and our taxi, delayed by a horde of Charing Cross commuters reeling and stampeding under a cloudburst, crept into The Strand. The vehicle threaded its way through a flux of traffic. We splashed up Ludgate Hill and the dome of St. Paul's sank deeper in its pillared shoulders. The tyres slewed away from the drowning cathedral and a minute later the silhouette of The Monument, descried through veils of rain, seemed so convincingly liquefied out of the perpendicular that the tilting thoroughfare might have been forty fathoms down. The driver, as he swerved wetly into Upper Thames Street, leaned back and said: 'Nice weather for young ducks.'

PATRICK LEIGH FERMOR, *A TIME OF GIFTS*.

10 DECEMBER

THE RUBBISH TIP OF OXYRHYNCHUS, 1994

On the trail of Byzantine Christianity, William Dalrymple (*see* 10 July) ran it to earth – almost literally – on the rubbish dump of an ancient Egyptian town. It was Oxyrhynchus, an extraordinary archaeological site that had yielded a treasure trove of papyri dating to the first century AD.

It was while walking back from the tomb, baffled by the total absence of any visible remains, that I noticed for the first time what I was standing on. Every time my foot touched the ground, the sand appeared to crunch beneath my weight. Bending down I looked more closely at the surface. The dunes all around were littered with pot shards: handles of amphorae, small roundels of red Samian-ware dishes, the decorated bases of cups, jugs, mugs and bowls. But it was not just pieces of pottery: fragments of brilliant aquamarine Byzantine glass glinted in the winter sun; beside them lay small lumps of slag and smelting clinker, fragments of jet, amber and garnet, pieces of bone and the shells of mussels and oysters.

I walked and walked for the rest of the morning, but the soft crunch underfoot did not stop: the midden extended for many miles. The town of Oxyrhynchus had clearly disappeared, destroyed – presumably – by generations of Nile floods and the robbing of the villagers of Behnasa; but its middens remained: epic drifts of Pharaonic, Graeco-Roman and Byzantine rubbish, left where it had been dropped by the street cleaners nearly two thousand years ago. I was standing on one of the great rubbish dumps of the ancient world.

Pulling at an amphora handle jutting out of the ground, I broke a Byzantine pot, and its contents, a pile of chaff winnowed, perhaps, while Justinian still ruled the Empire, floated away in the winter breeze.

WILLIAM DALRYMPLE, *FROM THE HOLY MOUNTAIN.*

11 DECEMBER

FADING RAJ, 1921

By 1921 the cracks in Britain's empire were already beginning to show. But in Hyderabad, the novelist E.M. Forster (*see* 9 January) managed to locate a town where the imperial presence had long since faded, and whose ruins were a premonition of what was to come throughout the sub-continent.

Hyderabad is as big as France and as populous as Egypt. Lingsugur is in S.W. corner of same – an unknown place, but head of a District. Once it was a British Cantonment, but we cleared out in 1860, and our relics have a curious effect on me. A civilisation, however silly, is touching as soon as it passes away, and I sit on the stucco curve of what was once a bandstand, or wander through ruined halls of bungalows that once smelt of whisky and echoed to giggles, or read on the tombs in the cemetery that the 'dearly beloved sweet gentle wife of Captain Pedley' has 'gone before'. No English now, no English spoken, no soldiers, no music, railway station sixty miles away. Only an exquisite lake where the British once bathed and rowed, and where a few black Canarese now squat fishing.

E.M. Forster, *The Hill of Devi and Other Indian Writings*.

12 DECEMBER

SEA-PRAIRIES OF THE JERSEY SHORE, 1876

While recuperating from a stroke, Walt Whitman (*see* 11 January) moved to New Jersey where, one December day, he took a walk along the long, flat expanses of its shoreline.

Five or six miles at the last, our track enter'd a broad region of salt grass meadows, intersected by lagoons, and cut up everywhere by watery runs... I could have journeyed contentedly till night through these flat and odorous sea-prairies. From half past 11 till 2 I was nearly all the time along the beach, or in sight of the ocean, listening to its hoarse murmurs, and inhaling the bracing and welcome breeze... Then after dinner ...I walk'd off in another direction, (hardly met or saw a person) and taking possession of what appear'd to have been the reception room of an old bath-house range, had a broad expanse of view all to myself – quaint, refreshing, unimpeded – a dry area of sedge and Indian grass immediately before and around me – space, simple, unornamented space. Distant vessels, and the far-off, just visible trailing smoke of an inward-bound steamer; more plainly, ships, brigs, schooners, in sight, most of them with every sail set to the firm and steady wind.

The attractions, fascinations there are in sea and shore! How one dwells on their simplicity, even vacuity! What is it in us, arous'd by those indirections and directions? That spread of waves and gray-white beach, salt, monotonous, senseless – such an entire absense of art, books, talk, elegance – so indescribably comforting, even this winter day – grim, yet so delicate-looking, so spiritual – striking, emotional, impalpable depths, subtler than all the poems, paintings, music I have ever read, seen, heard. (Yet let me be fair, perhaps it is because I have read those poems and heard that music.)

WALT WHITMAN, *SPECIMEN DAYS IN AMERICA*.

13 DECEMBER

A WARTIME CHRISTMAS IN BERLIN, 1939

December 1939 was the first wartime Christmas in Berlin since 1917, and rationing had already been in place for several months. The US radio correspondent William Shirer (*see* 23 June) described in his diary the lengths to which people went to make life seem normal.

The Christmas trees are in and being snapped up. No matter how tough or rough or pagan a German may be, he has a childish passion for Christmas trees. People everywhere trying to make this Christmas seem like the old ones in the time of peace. I did a little Christmas shopping to-day, and it was a bit sad. There were so many nice things in the windows which you couldn't buy because they were only there for show, on the orders of the authorities. Germans usually give wearing apparel and soaps and perfumes and candy to one another on Christmas, but this year, with these articles rationed, they must find something else. In the shops, which were crowded, they were buying to-day mostly books, radios, gramophones, records, and jewellery. I tried to buy some gramophone records for the four girl secretaries at the *Rundfunk* [radio station] who have been most friendly and helpful to me, but found you could only buy new records if you turned in your old ones. Having none, I was out of luck. The government is loosening up a little on rations over Christmas. Everyone will get a quarter of a pound of butter and a hundred grams of meat extra, and four eggs Christmas week instead of one.

WILLIAM SHIRER, *BERLIN DIARY*.

14 DECEMBER

FARTHEST SOUTH, 1911

On this day in 1911, Roald Amundsen and his four companions planted the Norwegian flag at the South Pole. He was to be heartily condemned by the British public for having beaten Robert Falcon Scott (*see* 2 March) and thereby having cheated in some indefinable manner. To which Amundsen retorted: 'By and large, the British are a race of very bad losers.'

On the morning of December 14 the weather was of the finest, just as if it had been made for arriving at the Pole... We advanced that day in the same mechanical way as before; not much was said, but eyes were used all the more. [Helmer] Hanssen's neck grew twice as long as before in his endeavour to see a few inches farther... But, however keenly he stared, he could not descry anything but the endless flat plain ahead of us... At three in the afternoon a simultaneous 'Halt!' rang out from the drivers. They had carefully examined their sledge-meters and they all showed the full distance – our Pole by reckoning. The goal was reached, the journey ended. I cannot say – though I know it would sound much more effective – that the object of my life was attained. That would be romancing rather too bare-facedly. I had better be honest and admit straight out that I have never known any man be placed in such a diametrically opposite position to the goal of his desires as I was at that moment. The regions around the North Pole – well, yes, the North Pole itself – had attracted me since childhood, and here I was at the South Pole. Can anything more topsy-turvy be imagined?

ROALD AMUNDSEN, *THE SOUTH POLE*.

15 DECEMBER

GOODBYE TO JAVA, 1866

In 1866 the Marquis de Beauvoir (*see* 2 April) was on the first year of his trans-global voyage and had reached the infamous port of Batavia, in Java (*see also* 24 December). He didn't think much of it.

Then the conjuror-priest called some children of about ten or twelve years old, who crawled up to his feet; he took a box of steel needles about twenty inches long, and thrust one into each child's face. The needle penetrated the flesh in the middle of one cheek and came out in the middle of the other; then he opened their mouths to show that it crossed them like a bit between the tongue and the palate. Thus spitted through, they came in a row to show themselves to us; the operator then drew out the steel with a sharp pull, licked over the holes with his tongue, and the children, looking perfectly happy, showed no trace of this piercing. But I can tell you that the sight curdled my blood. The last act of this burlesque of fanatics was acted by 'tjagogs,' or Chinese singers with their faces thickly painted with yellow; and it all finished like Punch or a fight. Naked wrestlers beat one another about with sticks and clubs, to the great delight of the enchanted populace, who rallied the vanquished. The combatants gave such terrible blows, owing to their great muscular strength, and so excited themselves with wild shrieks, that the police were sometimes obliged to interfere to prevent their being killed. All this time an intoxicated orchestra beat bamboo drums with all their strength, and the enthusiastic crowd wandered about beneath the feathery branches of the lighted up banana and tulip trees; Bengal fires illuminated the luxuriant clusters of the avenues at intervals. It is one o'clock in the morning, and in five hours we shall have bade farewell to Java.

MARQUIS DE BEAUVOIR, *A VOYAGE ROUND THE WORLD*.

16 DECEMBER

BETTER HANG ON GRASS, 1947

At the end of the Second World War the author Ian Fleming (*see* 16 March) bought a plot, sight unseen, on the north shore of Jamaica where he built his house Goldeneye. It was the start of a life-long relationship with the island. In a 1947 *Horizon* article he introduced a war-weary British readership to Jamaica's attractions.

Bad or indecent language is almost absent from the native vocabulary. Thief, liar, badman are about the strongest words you will hear and these will mean real hate or rage. 'Will you do me a rudeness?' means 'will you sleep with me?', to which a brazen girl will reply 'you better hang on grass, I goin' move so much.'

Despite your visits to Milk River [a spa], you would be very ill-advised to try any 'rudeness' with the local beauties. It would be unpopular with both coloured people and whites. For other reasons I would advise you to give a miss to the stews of Kingston although they would provide you with every known amorous constellation and permutation. One of the reasons why our Atlantic Squadron is based on Bermuda instead of Kingston (the Americans wanted us to contribute to the defence of Panama) was the veto of our naval health and welfare officers. Kingston is a tough town – tough and dirty – despite all the exhortations of *The Daily Gleaner* (my favourite newspaper above all others in the world) and the exertions of the quite admirable Jamaican police force.

IAN FLEMING, *TALK OF THE DEVIL*.

17 DECEMBER

SWEAT IN ZANZIBAR, 1930

On his semi-accidental traverse of Africa (*see* 10 February), Evelyn Waugh stopped at Zanzibar. He had been warned that the place was hot, but its intense humidity came as a surprise all the same. In defence of the place, it could be said that Waugh's expectations were perhaps higher than those of the average tourist.

Throughout my stay I am obsessed by heat; I see everything through a mist, vilely distorted like those gross figures that loom at one through the steam of a Turkish bath.

I live at the English Club. Every day, soon after dawn, I am awakened by the heat; I lie there under my mosquito-net streaming with sweat, utterly exhausted; I take time summoning enough resolution to turn the pillow dry side up; a boy comes in with tea and a mango; I lie there uncovered for a little while, dreading the day. Everything has to be done very slowly. Presently I sit limply in a hip-bath of cold water; I know that before I am dry of the water I shall again be damp with sweat. I dress gradually. One wears long trousers, coat, shirt, socks, suspenders, bow tie, buckskin shoes, everything in this town. Halfway through dressing I cover my head with eau-de-quinine and sit under the electric fan. I do this several times a day. They are the only tolerable moments.

EVELYN WAUGH, *REMOTE PEOPLE*.

18 DECEMBER

A SURREALIST AT THE SORBONNE, 1955

When the ineffably self-satisfied Salvador Dalí (*see* **29** June) gave a lecture at the Sorbonne, he made sure his audience knew exactly what he thought of the French national character.

Dalinian apotheosis last night in the Temple of Knowledge before a fascinated crowd. I had barely arrived in my Rolls Royce stuffed full of cauliflowers, when I was greeted by thousands of exploding flashbulbs. I took the floor in the great amphitheatre of the Sorbonne. The tremulous audience were expecting some decisive words. They got them. I had decided to communicate in Paris the most intoxicating intelligence of my life, because France is the most intelligent country in the world, the most rational country in the world. Whereas I, Salvador Dalí, come from Spain, which is the most irrational and the most mystical country in the world... Frantic applause received these first words, for no one is more sensitive to compliments than a Frenchman. Intelligence, I said, merely leads us into the fog of scepticism's nuances, and its principal effect is to reduce things for us to the coefficients of a gastronomic and super-gelatinous, Proustian and spoiled incertitude. For these reasons it is good and necessary that from time to time Spaniards like Picasso and me should come to Paris to set before the eyes of the French a raw and bloody hunk of truth.

At this, there were various stirrings, as I had expected.

SALVADOR DALÍ, *DIARY OF A GENIUS*.

19 DECEMBER

SOCIAL LIFE IN CALCUTTA, 1780

In a letter home, the Englishwoman Eliza Fay (*see* 28 August) described a typical afternoon in Calcutta as spent by the employees of the East India Company and hangers-on such as herself and her husband.

The custom of reposing, if not of sleeping after dinner is so general that the streets of Calcutta are from four to five in the afternoon almost as empty of Europeans as if it were midnight – Next come the evening airings to the Course, every one goes, though sure of being half-suffocated with dust. On returning from thence tea is served and universally drank here even during the extreme heats. After tea, either cards or music fill up the space 'till ten, when supper is generally announced. Five card loo is the usual game and they play a rupee a fish limited to ten. This will strike you as being enormously high but it is thought nothing of here...

Formal visits are paid in the evening; they are generally very short, as perhaps each lady has a dozen to make a party waiting for her at home besides. Gentlemen also call to offer their respects and if asked to put down their hat, it is considered as an invitation to supper. Many a hat have I seen vainly dangling in its owner's hand for half an hour, who at last has been compelled to withdraw without any one's offering to relieve him from the burthen.

ELIZA FAY, *ORIGINAL LETTERS FROM INDIA*.

20 DECEMBER

FAT ANKLES IN THE VALAIS, 1921

Katherine Mansfield (*see* 23 January) was staying at Montana-sur-Sierre, in the Valais region of Switzerland, when she wrote this letter to the Bloomsbury Group swell, Lady Ottoline Morrell. For several years Mansfield had changed homes in an attempt to halt the progress of her tuberculosis. Montana fitted the bill as far as climate and scenery went, but she was less sure about the locals.

If climate were everything, then Montana must be very near Heaven. The sun shines and shines. Its [sic] cold in the shade, but out of it it is hot enough for a hat and a parasol – far and away hotter than the S. of France, and windless. All the streams are solid little streams of ice, there are thin patches of snow, like linen drying, on the fields. The sky is high, transparent, with marvellous sunsets. And when the moon rises & I look out of my window down into the valley full of clouds its like looking out of the Ark while it bobbed above the flood.

But all the same I shall never get over my first hatred of the *Swiss*. They are the same everywhere. Ugly, dull, solid lumps, with a passion divided between pigs and foreigners. Foreigners are what they prefer to gorge themselves with but pigs will serve. As to their ankles – they fill me with a kind of anguish. I should have an ankle complex if I lived in Switzerland long. But one never lives anywhere *long*...

KATHERINE MANSFIELD, *COLLECTED LETTERS*, VOLUME IV.

21 DECEMBER

DRIVING ACROSS THE GOBI DESERT, 1933

The Swedish explorer Sven Hedin (*see* 16 April) was nearing the end of his career when he travelled along the Silk Road – or the most difficult part of it. Hedin had a tireless fascination with the Gobi, probably due to the fact that he had lost several men – and nearly died himself – during his various attempts to traverse it. This time, though, he had a motor car.

A motor-drive across the Gobi, over that endless desert with its scraggy little ridges, its low hills where cairns sit enthroned like fossilized wizards, its vast plains crossed by countless shallow dried-up watercourses, and its dunes with their waves of drifting sand, formed by the wind on a regular system – may to a certain degree be monotonous, but has also an indescribable fascination. You pitch camp every evening by a spring or in a place where there is fuel; you have lovely dreams in your sleeping-bag on the ground, you breathe fresh air day and night, live simply and have only two meals a day. And between the camping-grounds the desert or steppe unfolds day after day this flat, desolate scenery. And one never gets tired of it. One can never have enough of it. The boundless space alone fascinates by its majestic grandeur as the sea does.

The mountains that grow blue in the distance offer magnificent scenery, and the low undulations of the ground follow one another like the ocean swell. One must be very tired even to go to sleep in the car. And if one does, one is woken in a few minutes by a jolt, an uneven place caused by erosion, a tussock, or the sound of bells from an approaching caravan. The objects of our attention changed continually – lightly bounding antelopes, an eagle, a hare, sometimes a wolf. The only test of our patience was the road-mapping, but that was necessary, and we were soon reconciled to the delay it caused us.

SVEN HEDIN, *THE SILK ROAD.*

22 DECEMBER

UNDER FIRE IN VENICE, 1849

While in Venice, Effie Ruskin (1828–97), the disappointed wife of John Ruskin (*see* 28 May), found a friend in the long-time British resident Rawdon Brown. Until recently the city had been bombarded by Austrian artillery, an action that caused Venetians who lived at a safe remove not only to sleep on their roofs but to build turrets and cupolas to see the explosions better. Brown took the more dangerous recourse of making an observation-nest in the much-shelled Botanical Gardens.

Mr Brown took us to a place we had never heard of being in Venice, the Botanical Gardens close to where the Railway Bridge is. You will see the position from being [sic] so exposed to the Austrian Lines several shells fell in the Gardens and we saw one which had not exploded, 900 lbs. weight. The gardens are therefore not in good order at present... Mr Brown used to go very often to this garden to view the siege operations and had a kind of seat made for himself in one of the high trees, and when the shot & shells were falling about, he took the best care of himself he could, but it must have been a very dangerous pastime but he seemed to have seen a great deal & got no harm.

EFFIE RUSKIN, *EFFIE IN VENICE*.

23 DECEMBER

SUNSET IN ADEN, 1934

In December 1934 Freya Stark (*see* 14 January) made her first journey through Arabia, a region that would exert a lifelong fascination – as well as, four years later, impress upon her a tattoo (*see* 9 February). What impressed her now were the colours and a primordial landscape.

You can have no idea of what a sunset is in Aden. Imagine one half of the sky a luminous green. I can't tell you how luminous, like green water when you are in it and looking through it to the sun: and this green shoots up fanlike in rays towards the other half of the sky where night is lying already, deep blue. Above the sea along the horizon are pink ripples of cloud; the sea heaves with the sweep of the coast past the mouth of Aden bay, with flat lights on it as it catches the west. And half-bathed in the light, half-black in their own volcanic shadows, the rocks of Aden stand up like the Dolomites, so jagged and old. M[onsieur] Besse took me for a long walk over these jagged ridges; they are all lava, spongy and unsafe; we came down to the sea where the beach is undercut and a coating of barnacle shells makes the edge quite delicate pink: here the launch met us and we came back towards the sunset, and the full moon came up behind the great natural rampart of Aden. There is a feeling of gigantic and naked force about it all – and one thinks what it was when these hills were boiling out their streams of fire, hissing them into the sea – and wonders at anything so fragile as man living on these ancient desolations.

FREYA STARK, *OVER THE RIM OF THE WORLD*.

24 DECEMBER

THE SEWERS OF BATAVIA, 1770

Batavia (now Jakarta), the main port in the Dutch colony of Java, was famed for the wealth of its exports and its appalling mortality rate. Having recently discovered (and run his ship onto) the Great Barrier Reef, Captain James Cook was forced to stop there for repairs in 1770. By the time he left, after little more than two months, his crew were dropping like flies. This description by the naturalist Joseph Banks (*see* 29 May) helps explain why.

Few streets in the town are without canals of a considerable breadth running through, or rather stagnating in them... [In] the dry season these stink most intolerably, and in the wet many of them overflow their banks, filling the lower stories of the houses near them with water. Add to this that when they clean them, which is pretty often as some are not more than 3 or 4 feet deep, the black mud taken out is sufferd to lie upon their banks, that is in the middle of the street, till it has acquird a sufficient hardness to be conveniently laden into boats; this mud stinks most intolerably, as indeed it must, being cheifly [sic] formed from human ordure of which (as there is not a necessary house in the whole town) the Canals every morning receive their regular quota, and the more filthy recrements of housekeeping, which the uncommon police of the countrey suffers every body to throw into them. Add to this that the running ones, which are in some measure free from the former inconveniences, have every now and then a dead horse or hog stranded in the shallow parts of them, a nuisance which as I was inform'd no particular person was appointed to remove – which account I am inclind to believe, as I remember a Dead Buffaloe laying in one of the principal streets of thoroughfare for more than a week, which was at last carried away by a flood...

JOSEPH BANKS, *THE 'ENDEAVOUR' JOURNAL*, VOLUME I.

25 DECEMBER

A CHRISTMAS IN OMAN, 1955

In 1955 Said bin Taimur, the Sultan of Muscat and Oman since 1932, toured the outlying parts of his rebellious realm, checking on local rulers whose loyalty might be swayed by gifts from neighbouring states. With the sultan came the British writer James – now Jan – Morris (born 1926), who recorded the homage paid by the particularly notable Sheikh Suleiman. Far away, in Morris's homeland, Christmas turkeys were being roasted and crackers pulled. It was an irony he did not ignore.

———•••———

The Sultan's slaves, trim in their blue sweaters, ran light-footed to meet the visitors and asked them to wait; and I walked across to greet them. I shall always remember the moment, for the old sheikh rose to his feet with an expression that I can only describe as being of unfathomable foxiness, suggesting to me some infinitely clever beast in Aesop, about to hoodwink a lion, goat, or slow-witted bird... Suleiman was a big man with a powerful face, rather Dickensian in concept, and a triangular grey beard. On his head was a twisted blue and white turban. His *aba* [robe] was blue, gold-edged and filmy. In his hand was a cane with a carved end, and in his belt a curved Omani dagger of splendid ostentation, which I greatly coveted. The old rogue seemed keen to have his picture taken, but as he was prepared to pose, word arrived that the Sultan was waiting for him; hastily assuming an expression of unutterable innocence, Suleiman followed the slaves to the presence. My own instinct told me that this fine scoundrel should be decapitated, for the good of the Sultan and the sterling area, if so ill-matched a pair of causes might be placed in partnership; but I was rather glad, all the same, when he reappeared from the interview intact, and drove away into the mountains with only minor (and I am sure temporary) modifications of his manner.

So Christmas Day came.

JAMES MORRIS, *SULTAN IN OMAN*.

26 DECEMBER

THE JADE-GREEN INDUS, 1974

By December 1974 Dervla Murphy, along with her daughter Rachel, was a month into her journey up the Indus (*see* 9 March) and finding the vertiginous ravines hypnotically fascinating.

None of the adjectives usually applied to mountain scenery is adequate here – indeed, the very word 'scenery' is comically inappropriate. 'Splendour' or 'grandeur' are useless to give a feeling of this tremendous ravine that twists narrow and dark and bleak and deep for mile after mile after mile, with never a single blade of grass, or weed, or tiny bush to remind one that the vegetable kingdom exists. Only the jade-green Indus – sometimes tumbling into a dazzle of white foam – relieves the grey-brown of crags and sheer precipices and steep slopes. Many of these slopes are strewn with sharp, massive hunks of rock, often the size of a cathedral yet seeming mere boulders. Soon the river begins to have a hypnotic effect and, appalled as one is by the sight, one peers down constantly at that beautifully untouchable green serpent which is usually so far below it looks no more than a stream. We passed two of those steel rope 'bridges' across which the locals propel themselves in small wooden boxes and glimpsed one man so occupied. Rather him than me...

Naturally most of this area is uninhabited. But at rare intervals, where the gradient permits terracing, or a ledge of rock has allowed some soil to defy erosion, clusters of rectangular stone hovels stand amidst apricot, mulberry, plane and poplar trees. In summer these oases must look very lovely. Now, observed in the fearful sterility of mid-winter, they simply seem improbable. One wonders why and how people ever came to settle in such a violently inhospitable region, where climate and terrain are equally opposed to human survival.

DERVLA MURPHY, *WHERE THE INDUS IS YOUNG*.

27 DECEMBER

MEXICAN REVERIES, 1950

In December 1950, Jack Kerouac (*see* 10 June) wrote to his road-trip companion Neal Cassady, urging him to escape to Mexico. It would be just the two of them, their wives, their typewriters, their drugs and a bizarre dreamworld.

We'd live on same street and meet in dusty alley and go down to teafields to see José and hang around sun. Night, write. I'd have me wife and me near friend nearby, and you too. $500 a year, I say. No foolishness like La Vie Parisienne... We'd hang on to every cent, give the Mexes no quarter, let them get sullen at the cheap Americans and stand side by side in defense, and make friends in the end when they saw we was poor too. Comes another Mex revolution, we stands them off with our Burroughsian arsenal bought cheap on Madero St. and dash to big city in car for safety shooting and pissing as we go; whole Mex army follows hi on weed; now no worries any more. Just sit on roof hi enjoying hot dry sun and sound of kids yelling and have us wives & American talk of our own as well as exotic kicks and regular old honest Indian kicks. Become Indians... Wow. How's about it? Hurry to N.Y. so we can plan and all take off in big flying boat '32 Chandler across crazy land. Bring juke, bop records, mambo records and dixieland records; typewriters, clothes, toasters, percolators, etc.

JACK KEROUAC, *SELECTED LETTERS*.

28 DECEMBER

MEXICAN GOLD, 1908

In the Mexican city of Puebla, Charles Macomb Flandrau (*see* 15 October) felt compelled to invent a new word to describe the profusion of gold leaf that encrusted the cathedral.

The use of gold leaf in decoration is like money. A little is pleasant, merely too much is vulgar; but a positively staggering amount of it seems to justify itself... Gold – polished, glittering, shameless gold – blazes down and up and across at one; from the stone rosettes in the vaulting overhead, from the grilles in front of the chapels, from the railings between which the priests walk to the altar and choir, from the onyx pulpit and the barricade of gigantic candlesticks in front of the altar, from the altar itself – one of those carefully insane eighteenth-century affairs, in which a frankly pagan tiem polito and great lumps of Christian symbolism have become gloriously muddled for all time. Gold flashes in the long straight sun shafts overhead, twinkles in the candle flames, glitters from the censers and the chains of the censers. The back of the priest at the altar is incrusted with gold, and to-day – for Christmas lingers – all the pillars from capital to base are swathed in the finest of crimson velvet, fringed with gold. It isn't vulgar, it isn't even gaudy. It has surpassed all that and entered into the realm of the bewildering – the flabbergastric.

Charles Flandrau, Viva Mexico!

29 DECEMBER

THE SKY AT NIGHT, 1935

In 1935 the French pilot Antoine de Saint-Exupéry (1900–44) took to the air in an attempt to break the record between Paris and Saigon. He got no farther than Tripolitania (Libya, as it now is). Shortly after recording these thoughts he crashed in the desert and nearly died of thirst, before eventually making his way back to civilization. His friend and fellow aviator Jean Mermoz, whom he quotes here so enthusiastically, would die in the Atlantic the following year.

———

Off to Benghazi! We still have two hours of daylight. Before we crossed into Tripolitania I took off my glare glasses. The sands were golden under the slanting rays of the sun. How empty of life is this planet of ours! Once again it struck me that its rivers, its woods, its human habitations were the product of chance, of fortuitous conjunctions of circumstance. What a deal of the earth's surface is given over to rock and sand!

But all this was not my affair. My world was the world of flight. Already I could feel the oncoming night within which I should be enclosed as in the precincts of a temple – enclosed in the temple of night for the accomplishment of secret rites and absorption in inviolable contemplation.

Already this profane world was beginning to fade out: soon it would vanish altogether. This landscape was still laved [washed] in golden sunlight, but already something was evaporating out of it. I know nothing, nothing in the world, equal to the wonder of nightfall in the air.

Those who have been enthralled by the witchery of flying will know what I mean – and I do not speak of the men who, among other sports, enjoy taking a turn in a plane. I speak of those who fly professionally and have sacrificed much to their craft. Mermoz said once: 'It's worth it. It's worth the final smash-up.'

No question about it; but the reason is hard to formulate. A novice taking orders could appreciate this ascension towards the essence of things, since his profession too is one of renunciation: he renounces the world; he renounces riches; he renounces the love of woman. And by renunciation he discovers his hidden god.

I, too, in this flight, am renouncing things. I am giving up the broad golden surfaces that would befriend me if my engines were to fail. I am giving up the landmarks by which I might be taking my bearings. I am giving up the profiles of mountains against the sky that would warn me of pitfalls. I am plunging into the night. I am navigating. I have on my side only the stars.

The diurnal death of the world is a slow death. It is only little by little that the divine beacon of daylight recedes from me. Earth and sky begin to merge into each other. The earth rises and seems to spread like a mist. The first stars tremble as if shimmering in green water. Hours must pass before their glimmer hardens into the frozen glitter of diamonds. I shall have a long wait before I witness the soundless frolic of the shooting stars. In the profound darkness of certain nights I have seen the sky streaked with so many trailing sparks that it seemed to me a great gale must be blowing through the outer heavens.

ANTOINE DE SAINT-EXUPÉRY, *WIND, SAND AND STARS*.

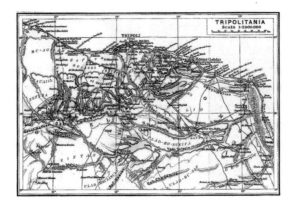

30 DECEMBER

REFLECTIONS ABOVE THE CLOUDS, 1945

Returning by plane from India to Britain at the end of 1945, E.M. Forster (see 9 January) fell prey to dejection. His mother had recently died, he was two days off his sixty-seventh birthday, and he felt his literary powers were waning. Little wonder that he slipped into a *tristesse* as he gazed through the aeroplane window.

Between Africa and Malta, above the clouds. The sun rose on us about half an hour ago. The sea travels with us, the clouds seeming to lie beneath it, foam passes over their flocks. Sometimes two sets of clouds, one travelling with us, the other which must [be] lower down, going contrary under the impact of the wind. Difficult to reconstruct realities from appearances. I have thought how the Greeks would have liked to be in this plane, also Ruskin. I have thought how Man has not yet conquered the world in the sense of knowing its beauty, and how – my powers of imagination now spent – I have failed to do what I might. The only first-class thing about me now is my grief...

O lovely world, teach others to expound you as I have not been able to do! O untroubled spaces, seldom looked upon by men's eyes, and unmarked by their activities! These clouds over the Mediterranean which will keep moving when I have passed, those deserts in Arabia which I flew over coming out, and again the other night in the dark. You remain pure and unconquered, and the imagination of others shall conquer you.

E.M. FORSTER, *THE HILL OF DEVI AND OTHER INDIAN WRITINGS*.

31 DECEMBER

NEW YEAR'S EVE ON THE YARDARM, 1938

At the year's end, Eric Newby was working on the grain ship *Moshulu* (*see* 25 March) when he and the Scandinavian crew were called aloft to gather sail. They were in the southern Atlantic, a famously rough piece of sea.

All that evening squalls of gale force bore down on the ship. At eleven the glass fell rapidly and there was continuous lightning. All hands were called and I found myself with Kroner sent to furl the main upper topgallant. Going aloft was horrible, the atmosphere illuminated by the incandescent glare of electricity burning on the steel yards.

At the main top, playing for time and hoping that these phenomena would disperse, I clutched Kroner's jacket. Only after trying several times could I make myself heard above the din.

'What is it?' I shouted.

'St Elmo's fire. Götterbloodydämmerung. Nice, isn't it?'

'It's horrible.' Then, as an afterthought I wished him a Happy New Year.

'Let's get on,' shouted Kroner. 'You can push 1939 right up.'

The sail was wild and untameable because someone had made up the gaskets in such a way that they could not be released. Holding the sail on the yard in a damp huge mass, we struggled to loose them while the masthead careered across the sky and the yard arms pointed at one moment into the sea and the next into the upper air. All around us the overcharged atmosphere crackled and hummed with electricity. At midnight our watch, while clewing-up the mainsail on deck, wished each other a Happy New Year.

'You noh,' said Sedelquist with more than usually happy inspiration, '1939 is going to be focking no good year.'

ERIC NEWBY, *THE LAST GRAIN RACE*.

SOURCES AND ACKNOWLEDGEMENTS

Amundsen, Roald (trans. A.G. Chater), *The South Pole*, London: John Murray, 1912.

Andrée, Salomon, Nils Strindberg and K. Fraenkel (trans. E. Adams-Ray), *The Andrée Diaries, Being the Diaries and Records of S.A. Andrée, Nils Strindberg and Knut Fraenkel Written during their Balloon Expedition to the North Pole in 1897 and Discovered on White Island in 1930, Together with a Complete Record of the Expedition*, London: John Lane, 1931.

Auden, W.H. and Christopher Isherwood, *Journey to a War*, London: Faber & Faber, 1939. *Journey to a War* © 1939, 1990 by W.H. Auden and Christopher Isherwood. Used by permission of The Wylie Agency (UK) Limited and The Wylie Agency LLC on behalf of the Isherwood Estate.

Baker, Samuel, *The Albert N'yanza, Great Basin of the Nile*, 2 vols, London: Macmillan, 1867.

Banks, Joseph (ed. J. Beaglehole), *The 'Endeavour' Journal of Joseph Banks 1768–1771*, 2 vols, Sydney: Angus & Robertson, 1962.

Bean, Charles (ed. K. Fewster), *Bean's Gallipoli: The Diaries of Australia's Official War Correspondent*, Crows Nest, New South Wales: Allen & Unwin, 2007.

Beauvoir, Marquis de, *A Voyage Round the World*, 2 vols, London: John Murray, 1870.

— (trans. A. and H. Stephenson), *The Conclusion of a Voyage Round the World*, London: John Murray, 1872.

Beauvoir, Simone de (trans. C. Cosman), *America Day by Day*, London: Gollancz, 1998. © Editions Gallimard. English translation reprinted by permission of the Orion Publishing Group, London.

Beckford, William (ed. G. Chapman), *The Travel-Diaries of William Beckford of Fonthill*, 2 vols, London: Constable, 1928.

Beebe, William, *Beneath Tropic Seas*, New York: Putnam's Sons, 1928. By permission of ICM.

—, *Half Mile Down*, London: John Lane, 1935. By permission of ICM.

Beechey, F.W., *Narrative of a Voyage to the Pacific and Bering's Strait to Co-operate with the Polar Expeditions Performed on His Majesty's Ship 'Blossom' under the Command of Captain F.W. Beechey, R.N., F.R.S. &c. in the Years 1825, '26, '27, '28*, 2 vols, London: Colburn & Bentley, 1831.

Bell, Gertrude, *The Desert and the Sown*, London: Heinemann, London, 1907.

— (ed. Lady Bell), *The Letters of Gertrude Bell*, 2 vols, London: Ernest Benn, 1927.

Belzoni, Giovanni, *Narrative of the Operations and Recent Discoveries in Egypt and Nubia*, 2 vols, London: John Murray, 1822.

Bennett, Alan, *Untold Stories*, London: Faber & Faber/Profile Books, 2005. Reprinted by permission of Faber and Faber Ltd and used by permission of United Agents (www.unitedagents.co.uk) on behalf of Forelake Ltd (© Forelake Ltd 2005).

Bird, Isabella, *A Lady's Life in the Rocky Mountains*, London: John Murray, 1879.

— (ed. K. Chubbuck), *Letters to Henrietta*, London: John Murray, 2002.

Black, Jeremy, *The British Abroad: The Grand Tour in the Eighteenth Century*, New York: St Martin's Press, 1992.

Blumenfeld, Ralph, *R.D.B.'s Diary, 1887–1914*, London: Heinemann, 1930.

Blunt, Wilfrid Scawen, *My Diaries: Being a Personal Narrative of Events 1888–1914*, 2 vols, London: Martin Secker, 1919.

Bonaparte, Napoleon (trans. and ed. J. Thompson), *Napoleon's Letters*, London: Prion, 1998.

Boswell, James, *Journal of a Tour to the Hebrides with Samuel Johnson, LL.D*, Dublin: White, Byrne & Cash, 1785.

Bougainville, Louis de (trans. J. Forster), *A Voyage Round the World in the Years 1766, 1767, 1768 and 1769*, London: Nourse & Davies, 1772.

Bouvier, Nicolas (trans. A. Dickerson), *The Japanese Chronicles*, Edinburgh: Polygon, 1995. Reprinted by permission of Eland Publishing Ltd. Text © 1989, 1991 Editions Payot © 2001 Éditions Payot & Rivages. English translation © 1992 Mercury House, Incorporated.

— (trans. R. Marsack), *The Way of the World*, London: Eland, 2007. Reprinted by permission of Eland Publishing Ltd and Robyn Marsack. Text © Editions *La Découverte*, Paris, France, 1963, 1985. English translation © Robyn Marsack, 1992.

Bowles, Paul (ed. J. Miller), *In Touch: The Letters of Paul Bowles*, New York: Farrar, Straus & Giroux, 1994. Copyright © 1994 by Paul Bowles. Reprinted by permission of Farrar, Straus and Giroux, LLC.

— *Travels: Collected Writings 1950–93*, London: Sort Of Books, 2010. Copyright © 2010, The Estate of Paul Bowles.

Brittain, Vera, *Testament of Youth*, London: Gollancz, 1933. Used by permission of Gollancz, an imprint of the Orion Publishing Group, London.

Brooke, R. (ed. G. Keynes), *The Letters of Rupert Brooke*, London: Faber and Faber, 1968.

Bryson, Bill, *Notes from a Small Island*, London: Doubleday, 1995. Copyright © Bill Bryson, 1995. Reprinted by permission of The Random House Group Ltd.

Burckhardt, 'John Lewis' (i.e. Johann Ludwig), *Travels in Syria and the Holy Land*, London: John Murray, 1822.

Burroughs, William and Allen Ginsberg, *The Yage Letters*, San Francisco: City Lights Books, 2006. Copyright © William S. Burroughs and Allen Ginsberg, 1963, 1975, copyright © The William Burroughs Trust, 2006, copyright © The Allen Ginsberg Trust, 2006. All rights reserved. Used by permission of The Wylie Agency (UK) Limited.

Burton, Isabel, *The Romance of Isabel Lady Burton*, 2 vols, London: Hutchinson, 1897.

Burton, (Sir) Richard (ed. I. Burton), *Personal Narrative of a Pilgrimage to Al-Madinah & Meccah,* 2 vols, London: Tylston & Edwards, 1893.

Byrd, Richard, *Alone*, London: Putnam, 1938.

Byron, Lord (ed. P. Quennell), *Byron: A Self-Portrait – Letters and Diaries 1798 to 1824*, 2 vols, London: John Murray, 1950.

Byron, Robert (ed. L. Butler), *Robert Byron: Letters Home*, London: John Murray, 1991.

—, *The Road to Oxiana*, London: Jonathan Cape, 1937.

Calderón de la Barca, Frances, *Life in Mexico, During a Residence of Two Years in That Country*, London: Chapman & Hall, 1843.

Camus, Albert (trans. H. Levick), *American Journals*, London: Hamish Hamilton, 1989. © Editions Gallimard.

Chateaubriand, Vicomte de, *The Memoirs of Chateaubriand*, London: Henry Colburn, 1848.

Chekhov, Anton (trans. R. Bartlett, A. Philips and L. and M. Terpak), *A Journey to the End of the Russian Empire*, London: Penguin, 2007.

— (ed. A. Yarmolinsky), *Letters of Anton Chekhov*, London: Jonathan Cape, 1974.

Cherry-Garrard, Apsley, *The Worst Journey in the World*, London: Chatto & Windus, 1937. Reprinted by permission of The Random House Group Ltd.

Churchill, Clementine and Winston (ed. M. Soames), *Speaking For Themselves: The Personal Letters of Winston and Clementine Churchill*, London: Doubleday, 1998. Reproduced by permission of Curtis Brown Ltd, London, on behalf of the Master and Fellows of Churchill College, Cambridge. Copyright © Clementine Churchill.

Clark, Alan, *Diaries*, London: Weidenfeld and Nicolson, 1993. By permission of the Orion Publishing Group, London.

—, *Diaries: Into Politics 1972–1982,* London: Weidenfeld & Nicolson, 2000. By permission of the Orion Publishing Group, London.

Cocteau, Jean (trans. W. J. Strachan), *My Journey Round the World*, London: Peter Owen, 1958. Reproduced courtesy of Peter Owen Ltd. By permission of Editions Gallimard.

Coleridge, Samuel Taylor, *Letters of Samuel Taylor Coleridge*, 2 vols, London: Heinemann, 1895.

Columbus, Christopher (trans. C. Jane), *The Journal of Christopher Columbus*, London: Anthony Blond, 1968.

Conrad, Joseph (eds F. Karl and L. Davies), *The Collected Letters of Joseph Conrad*, vol. I, Cambridge and New York: Cambridge University Press, 1983.

Cook, Frederick, *My Attainment of the Pole*, New York: Polar Publishing, 1911.

Cooke, Alistair, *Reporting America: The Life of the Nation 1946–2004*, London: Allen Lane, 2008. Introduction and all 'Letters from America' copyright © The Estate of Alistair Cooke, 2008. Published in the USA in 2008 by The Overlook Press, Peter Mayer Publishers, Inc. All rights reserved.

Coward, Noël (ed. B. Day), *The Letters of Noël Coward*, London: Methuen, 2007. Copyright © NC Aventales AG and Barry Day 2007 by permission of Alan Brodie Representation Ltd. www.alanbrodie.com.

Crouch, Archer, *On a Surf-Bound Coast; or, Cable-laying in the African Tropics*, London: Sampson Low, Marston, Searle & Rivington, 1887.

Curzon, George (ed. P. King), *Travels with a Superior Person*, London: Sidgwick & Jackson, 1985.

Curzon, Mary (ed. J. Bradley), *Lady Curzon's India: Letters of a Vicereine*, London: Weidenfeld & Nicolson, 1985.

Dalí, Salvador (trans. R. Howard), *Diary of a Genius*, London: Hutchinson, 1966. © Salvador Dali, Fundació Gala-Salvador Dali, Figueres, 2011.

— (trans. H. Chevalier), *The Secret Life of Salvador Dalí*, London: Vision, 1973. © Salvador Dali, Fundació Gala-Salvador Dali, Figueres, 2011.

Dalrymple, William, *From the Holy Mountain: A Journey in the Shadow of Byzantium*, London: HarperCollins, 1997. Reprinted by permission of HarperCollins Publishers Ltd © 1997, William Dalrymple.

Dana, Richard Henry, *Two Years Before the Mast*, New York: Macmillan, 1916.

Darwin, Charles, (ed. F. Burkhardt), *The 'Beagle' Letters*, Cambridge and New York: Cambridge University Press, 2008.

Davies, W(illiam) H(enry), *The Autobiography of a Super-Tramp*, London: Jonathan Cape, 1968.

Deakin, Roger, *Waterlog*, London: Chatto & Windus, 1999. Published by Vintage Books. Reprinted by permission of The Random House Group and courtesy of Jane Turnbull.

Della Valle, Pietro (trans. G. Bull), *The Pilgrim: The Travels of Pietro Della Valle*, London: Hutchinson, 1990.

Delmer, Sefton, *Trail Sinister*, London: Secker & Warburg, 1961. Courtesy of the Estate of Sefton Delmer.

Dickens, Charles, *American Notes and Pictures from Italy*, London: Chapman & Hall, 1898.

Dorfman, Ariel, *Desert Memories: Journeys Through the Chilean North*, Seattle, WA: National Geographic Society, 2004. Reprinted with permission of the National Geographic Society. Copyright © 2004 Ariel Dorfman.

Dufferin, Earl of, *Letters from High Latitudes*, Leipzig: Bernhard Tauchnitz, 1891.

Durrell, Gerald, *My Family and Other Animals*, London: Rupert Hart-Davis, 1956. Reproduced by permission of Curtis Brown Ltd on behalf of the Estate of Gerald Durrell.

Eberhardt, Isabelle (trans. N. de Voogd, ed. R. Kabbani), *The Passionate Nomad: The Diary of Isabelle Eberhardt*, London: Virago, 1987.

Evelyn, John (ed. G. de la Bédoyère), *The Diary of John Evelyn*, Woodbridge, Suffolk: Boydell Press, 1995.

Fay, Eliza, *Original Letters from India*, London: Hogarth Press, 1925.

Fermor, Patrick Leigh, *A Time of Gifts*, London: John Murray, 1977. Copyright © Patrick Leigh Fermor. Reproduced by permission of John Murray (Publishers) Limited.

—, *Three Letters from the Andes*, London: John Murray, 1991. Copyright © Patrick Leigh Fermor. Reproduced by permission of John Murray (Publishers) Limited.

Flandrau, Charles (Macomb), *Viva Mexico!*, London: Eland, 1982.

Flaubert, Gustave (trans. and ed. F. Steegmuller), *The Selected Letters of Gustave Flaubert*, London: Hamish Hamilton, 1954.

Fleming, Ian, *Talk of the Devil*, London: Queen Anne Press, 2008. Copyright: Ian Fleming Will Trust.

—, *Thrilling Cities*, London: Jonathan Cape, 1963. Reproduced with permission of Ian Fleming Publications Ltd, London. Copyright © Ian Fleming Publications Ltd 1963. www.ianfleming.com.

Fleming, Peter, *Brazilian Adventure*, London: Jonathan Cape, 1933. Copyright: Estate of Peter Fleming.

—, *News from Tartary*, London: Jonathan Cape, 1936. Copyright: Estate of Peter Fleming.

Flower, Newman, *Through My Garden Gate*, London: Cassell, 1945.

Forster, E.M., *The Hill of Devi and Other Indian Writings*, London: Edward Arnold, 1983. Copyright © E. M. Forster. Reproduced by permission of Hodder Education.

—, *Selected Letters*, 2 vols, London: Collins, 1985.

Fowles, John (ed. C. Drazin), *The Journals*, 2 vols, London: Jonathan Cape, 2003. Copyright © J.R. Fowles Ltd.

Gellhorn, Martha, *The Face of War*, London: Rupert Hart-Davis, 1959. Copyright © the Estate of Martha Gellhorn.

Gibbs, Philip, *Pageant of the Years*, London: Heinemann, 1946.

Gide, André (trans. J. O'Brien), *The Journals of André Gide 1939–1949*, London: Secker & Warburg, 1951. Reproduced courtesy of Random House Ltd.

— (trans. D. Bussy), *Travels in the Congo*, New York: Alfred Knopf, 1930. Translated by Dorothy Bussy, translation copyright 1929 and renewed 1957 by Alfred A. Knopf, a division of Random House, Inc. Used by permission of Alfred A. Knopf, a division of Random House, Inc.

Ginsberg, Allen and Louis, *Family Business: Selected Letters Between a Father and a Son*, London: Bloomsbury, 2002. Copyright © 2001 by Allen Ginsberg and Louis Ginsberg. Reprinted by permission of Bloomsbury USA.

Goethe, Johann Wolfgang von (trans. W.H. Auden and E. Mayer), *Italian Journey*, London: Collins, 1962. Copyright © 1962, 1970, The Estate of W.H. Auden.

Greene, Graham (ed. R. Greene), *Graham Greene: A Life in Letters*, London: Little, Brown, 2007. Reproduced courtesy of David Higham Associates.

—, *Journey Without Maps*, London: Heinemann & The Bodley Head, 1978. Reproduced courtesy of Random House Ltd.

Grey, (Sir) George, *Journals of Two Expeditions of Discovery in North-West and Western Australia*, 2 vols, London: T. & W. Boone, 1841.

Grosz, George (trans. A. Pomerans), *A Small Yes and a Big No*, London: Allison & Busby, 1982. The Estate of George Grosz, Princeton, New Jersey. Text © Estate of George Grosz/Licensed by VAGA, New York, NY.

Hamsun, Knut (ed. H. Noess and J. McFarlane), *Selected Letters*, Vol. I: *1879–98*, Norwich: Norvik Press, 1990. By permission of Norvik Press.

Hart-Davis, Duff, *Peter Fleming*, London: Jonathan Cape, 1974.

Hawthorne, Nathaniel, *Passages from the French and Italian Note-books of Nathaniel Hawthorne*, 2 vols, London: Strahan, 1871.

—, *The Complete Works of Nathaniel Hawthorne,* 13 vols, London: Kegan Paul, Trench, Trubner, 1894.

Hearn, Lafcadio, *Glimpses of Unfamiliar Japan*, 2 vols, Boston: Houghton, Mifflin, 1900.

Hedin, Sven, *My Life as an Explorer*, London: Cassell, 1926.

—, *The Silk Road*, London: Macmillan, 1938.

Heyerdahl, Thor, *The Kon-Tiki Expedition* (trans. F. H. Lyon), London: Allen & Unwin, 1950. © Gyldendal Norsk Forlag AS, Oslo, 1948.

Hornby, Lady, *Constantinople during the Crimean War*, London: Richard Bentley, 1863.

Hughes, Ted (ed. C. Reid), *Letters of Ted Hughes*, London: Faber & Faber, 2007. Reprinted by permission of Faber and Faber Ltd.

Humboldt, Alexander von (trans. J. Wilson), *Jaguars and Electric Eels*, London: Penguin, 2007.

Huxley, Aldous, *Jesting Pilate: The Diary of a Journey*, London: Chatto & Windus, 1926. Copyright © 1926, 1953 by Aldous Huxley. Reprinted by permission of Georges Borchardt, Inc. for the Estate of Aldous Huxley.

Huxley, Thomas Henry (ed. J. Huxley), *T.H. Huxley's Diary of the Voyage of H.M.S. Rattlesnake*, London: Chatto & Windus, 1935. Copyright © 1926, 1953 by Aldous Huxley. Reprinted by permission of Georges Borchardt, Inc. for the Estate of Aldous Huxley.

Hyslop, Donald, Alastair Forsyth and Sheila Jemima (eds), *Titanic Voices: Memories from the Fateful Voyage*, Southampton: Southampton City Publishing, 1994.

Ibn Battuta (trans. H. Gibb), *Travels in Asia and Africa 1325–1354*, London: Routledge & Sons, 1929.

Judson, Ann (ed. J. Knowles), *Memoir of Ann H. Judson, Late Missionary to Burmah*, Boston: Gould, Kendall & Lincoln, 1831.

Kane, Elisha Kent, *Arctic Explorations in the Years 1853, '54, '55*, 2 vols, Philadelphia: Childs & Peterson, 1856.

—, *The U.S. Grinnell Expedition in Search of Sir John Franklin*, New York: Harper & Bros, 1854.

Kapuściński, Ryszard (trans. K. Glowczewska), *Imperium*, London: Granta Books, 1994. Reprinted by permission of Granta Publications. Reprinted by permission of SLL/Sterling Lord Literistic, Inc. Copyright © 1994 by Klara Glowczewska.

— (trans. W. Brand), *The Soccer War*, London: Granta Books, 1990. Reprinted by permission of Granta Publications. Reprinted by permission of SLL/Sterling Lord Literistic, Inc. Copyright © 1986, 1990 by Ryszard Kapuściński.

— (trans. K. Glowczewska), *Travels With Herodotus*, London: Penguin Books, 2007. Copyright © Ryszard Kapuściński, 2007.

Kerouac, Jack (ed. A. Charters), *Selected Letters 1940–1956*, New York: Viking, 1995. Copyright © Jack Kerouac. Reproduced by permission of PFD (www.pfd.co.uk) on behalf of the Estate of Jack Kerouac.

Kingsley, Mary, *Travels in West Africa*, London: Macmillan, 1897.

Kipling, R. *Letters of Travel (1892–1913)*, London: Macmillan, 1920.

—, Unpublished letter, RIBA archive, London.

Lawrence, D.H. (eds S. De Filippis, P. Eggert and M. Kalnins), *D.H. Lawrence and Italy*, London: Penguin, 2007.

—, *The Letters of D.H. Lawrence*, Cambridge and New York: Cambridge University Press, 1987.

Lawrence, T.E. (ed. D. Garnett), *The Letters of T.E. Lawrence*, London: Jonathan Cape, 1938.

Lear, Edward, *Edward Lear in Greece: Journals of a Landscape Painter in Greece and Albania*, London: William Kimber, 1965.

— (ed. M. Montgomery), *Lear's Italy: In the Footsteps of Edward Lear*, London: Cadogan, 2005.

Leblich, Domingo Badia y, *Travels of Ali Bey, in Morocco, Tripoli, Cyprus, Egypt, Arabia, Syria, and Turkey between the years 1803 and 1807*, 2 vols, London: Longman, 1816.

Lee, Laurie, *A Moment of War: A Memoir of the Spanish Civil War*, London: Penguin Books, London, 1991, 1992. Copyright © 1991 by Laurie Lee. Reproduced by permission of Penguin Books Ltd. Reprinted by permission of The New Press. www.thenewpress.com.

—, *As I Walked Out One Midsummer Morning*, London: André Deutsch, 1969. Reproduced by permission of Penguin Books Ltd.

Lees-Milne, James, *Through Wood and Dale: Diaries 1975–1978*, Norwich: Michael Russell, 2007.

Lewis, Norman, *Jackdaw Cake*, London: Hamish Hamilton, 1985. Copyright © Estate of Norman Lewis. Reproduced by permission of the Estate of Norman Lewis, c/o Rogers, Coleridge & White Ltd, 20 Powis Mews, London, W11 1TN.

—, *Naples '44*, London: Collins, 1978. Reprinted courtesy of the Perseus Books Group.

Livingstone, David, *The Last Journals of David Livingstone in Central Africa from 1865 to His Death, Continued by a Narrative of His Last Moments and Sufferings Obtained from His Faithful Servants Chuma and Susi*, 2 vols, London: John Murray, 1880.

Lothian, Alan, Private correspondence from the author's collection.

Loti, P, *Voyages (1872–1913)*. Robert Laffont, Paris, 1991. Extracts translated by the author.

Lunardi, Vincenzo, *An Account of Five Aerial Voyages in Scotland*, Edinburgh: Drummond Books, 1976.

Lyautey, Hubert (trans. A. Le Blond), *Intimate Letters from Tonquin*, London: John Lane, 1932.

Lyon, George, *The Private Journal of Captain G. Lyon, of H.M.S. Hecla, During the Recent Voyage of Discovery under Captain Parry*, London: John Murray, 1824.

MacFarlane, Robert, *The Wild Places*, London: Granta, 2007. Copyright © 2007 by Robert MacFarlane. Reprinted by permission of Granta Publications. Used by permission of Viking Penguin, a division of Penguin Group (USA) Inc.

McMillan, James (ed.), *The Way It Was, 1914–1934*, London: Kimber, 1979.

Mallory, George, *Climbing Everest*, London: Gibson Square, 2010.

Mansfield, Katherine (ed. J. Middleton Murry), *Journal of Katherine Mansfield*, London: Constable, 1954.

— (ed. V. O'Sullivan and M. Scott), *The Collected Letters of Katherine Mansfield*, 5 vols, Oxford: Clarendon Press, 1984–2008.

Markham, Violet, *Return Passage*, London: Oxford University Press, 1953. Copyright © Violet Markham. Reproduced courtesy of Oxford University Press.

Marryat, Frank, *Mountains and Molehills*, London: Longmans, Brown, Green & Longmans, 1855.

Masefield, John (ed. P. Vansittart), *Letters from the Front 1915–1917*, London: Constable, 1984. Courtesy of The Society of Authors as the Literary Representative of the Estate of John Masefield.

— (ed. D. Stanford), *Letters to Margaret Bridges (1915–1919)*, Manchester: Carcanet, 1984. Courtesy of The Society of Authors as the Literary Representative of the Estate of John Masefield.

Matthiessen, Peter, *The Cloud Forest: A Chronicle of the South American Wilderness*, London: André Deutsch, 1962. Copyright © 1961 by Peter Matthiessen. Published by Harvill, reprinted by permission of The Random House Group Ltd. Used by permission of Viking Penguin, a division of Penguin Group (USA) Inc.

—, *The Snow Leopard*, London: Chatto & Windus, 1979. Published by Chatto & Windus. Copyright © 1978 by Peter Matthiessen. Reprinted by permission of The Random House Group Ltd and by permission of Viking Penguin, a division of Penguin Group (USA) Inc.

Mawson, Douglas, *Home of the Blizzard*, 2 vols, London: Heinemann, 1915.

Mendelssohn, F. (trans. Lady Wallace), *Letters from Italy and Switzerland*, London: Green, Longman, Roberts and Green, 1862.

Mermod, Michel (trans. J. Hoare), *The Voyage of the Genève: Five Years Around the World*, London: John Murray, 1973.

Montagu, Lady Mary Wortley, *The Complete Letters of Lady Mary Wortley Montagu*, 3 vols, Oxford: Clarendon Press, 1965.

Morris, Jan, *Sultan in Oman*, London: Eland Books, 2008. Reprinted by permission of Eland Publishing Ltd © Jan Morris 1957 and by permission of A.P. Watt Ltd on behalf of Jan Morris.

Morris, William, *Icelandic Journals*, London: Mare's Nest, 1996.

Muggeridge, Malcolm (ed. J. Bright-Holmes), *Like It Was*, London: Collins, 1981. Courtesy of The Malcolm Muggeridge Society.

Muir, John, *My First Summer in the Sierra*, London: Constable, 1911.

Mullin, Chris, *A View from the Foothills*, London: Profile Books, 2009. Reproduced courtesy of Profile Books Ltd.

Murphy, Dervla, *South from the Limpopo: Travels Through South Africa*, London: John Murray, 1997. © Dervla Murphy.

—, *Tibetan Foothold*, London: John Murray, 1966. © Dervla Murphy.

—, *Where the Indus is Young: Walking to Baltistan*, London: John Murray, 1977. © Dervla Murphy.

Nansen, Fridtjof, *Farthest North, Being the Record of a Voyage of Exploration of the Ship 'Fram' 1893–96 and of a Fifteen Months' Sleigh Journey by Dr. Nansen and Lieut. Johansen*, 2 vols, New York: Harper, 1897.

Newby, Eric, *A Traveller's Life*, London: Picador, 1982. By permission of Sonia Ashmore.

—, *The Last Grain Race*, London: Secker & Warburg, 1956. By permission of Sonia Ashmore.

O'Donovan, Edmond, *Merv: A Story of Adventures and Captivity*, London: Smith, Elder, 1883.

Nightingale, Florence, *Letters from Egypt*, London: Barrie & Jenkins, 1987

Orwell, George, *A Life in Letters*, London: Harvill Secker, 2010. Copyright © George Orwell, 1937 by permission of Bill Hamilton as the Literary Executor of the Estate of the Late Sonia Brownell Orwell and Secker & Warburg Ltd. Excerpt from *The Collected Essays, Journalism and Letters of George Orwell, Volume I: An Age Like This, 1920–1940*, edited by Sonia Orwell and Ian Angus, copyright © 1968 by Sonia Brownell Orwell and renewed 1996 by Mark Hamilton, reprinted by permission of Houghton Mifflin Harcourt Publishing Company.

Palin, Michael, *Around the World in 80 Days*, London: BBC Books, 1989. By permission of the Orion Publishing Group, London.

Park, Mungo, *The Travels of Mungo Park*, London: Dent, 1907.

Peary, Robert E., *The North Pole: Its Discovery in 1909 under the Auspices of the Peary Arctic Club*, New York: Frederick A. Stokes, 1910.

Perelman, S.J. (ed. P. Crowther), *Don't Tread On Me: The Selected Letters of S.J. Perelman*, New York: Viking, 1987. Reprinted by permission of PFD (www.pfd.co.uk) on behalf of the Estate of S.J. Perelman.

Platter, Thomas and Horatio Bursino, *The Journals of Two Travellers in Elizabethan and Early Stuart England*, London: Caliban Books, 1995.

Prokofiev, Sergei (trans. A. Phillips), *Sergey Prokofiev, Diaries: 1915–1923: Behind the Mask*, London: Faber & Faber, 2008. Reprinted by permission of Faber and Faber Ltd and Cornell University Press.

Raban, Jonathan, *Hunting Mister Heartbreak*, London: Collins Harvill, 1990. Reprinted by permission of The Random House Group Ltd. Copyright © Jonathan Raban, 1990.

Rilke, Rainer Maria (trans. E. Snow and M. Winkler), *Rainer Maria Rilke and Lou Andreas Salomé: The Correspondence*, New York: Norton, 2006.

— (trans. R. Hull), *Selected Letters of Rainer Maria Rilke 1902–1926*, London: Macmillan, 1946.

Ross, John, *A Voyage of Discovery*, London: John Murray, 1819.

Roth, Joseph, *The White Cities: Reports from France 1925–39*, London: Granta Books, 2004.

— (trans. M. Hofmann), *What I Saw: Reports from Berlin 1920–33*, London: Granta Books, 2003.

Ruskin, Effie (ed. M. Lutyens), *Effie in Venice: Unpublished Letters of Mrs John Ruskin Written from Venice Between 1849–1852*, London: John Murray, 1965.

Ruskin, John (ed. H. Shapiro), *Ruskin in Italy: Letters to His Parents 1845*, Oxford: Clarendon Press, 1972.

— (ed. J. Bradley), *Ruskin's Letters from Venice 1851–1852*, Wesport, CT: Greenwood Press, 1978.

Russell, W(illiam) H(oward), *My Diary North and South,* London: Bradbury & Evans, 1863.

—, *My Indian Mutiny Diary*, London: Cassell, 1957.

Saint-Exupéry, Antoine de (trans. L. Galantière), *Wind, Sand and Stars*, London: Heinemann, London, 1939.

Sartre, Jean-Paul (ed. S. de Beauvoir), *Quiet Moments in a War: The Letters of Jean-Paul Sartre to Simone de Beauvoir 1940–1963*, London: Hamish Hamilton, 1994. Copyright © Editions Gallimard 1983. Reproduced by permission of Penguin Books Ltd.

Scott, Robert Falcon (ed. M. Jones), *Journals: Captain Scott's Last Expedition*, Oxford and New York: Oxford University Press, 2005.

Seth, Vikram, *From Heaven Lake: Travels Through Sinkiang and Tibet*, London: Chatto & Windus, 1983. Reprinted by permission of The Random House Group Ltd.

Shackleton, Ernest, *South*, London: Heinemann, 1919.

Shelley, Percy Bysshe, *History of a Six Weeks' Tour Through a Part of France, Switzerland, Germany, and Holland*, London: Hookham, 1817.

Shirer, William, *Berlin Diary: The Journal of a Foreign Correspondent 1934–1941*, London: Hamish Hamilton, 1941. Reprinted by permission of Don Congdon Associates, Inc. © 1941, renewed 1968 by William L. Shirer.

Simond, Louis (ed. C. Hibbert), *An American in Regency England: The Journal of a Tour in 1810–1811*, London: History Book Club, 1968.

Slocum, Joshua, *Sailing Alone Around the World*, London: Sampson Low, Marston, 1900.

Smollett, T., *Travels through France and Italy*, London: Oxford University Press, 1907.

Stanley, Henry Morton, *Through the Dark Continent*, 2 vols, London: Sampson Low, Marston, Searle & Rivington, 1878.

Stark, Freya (ed. C. Moorehead), *Over the Rim of the World: Freya Stark, Selected Letters*, London: John Murray, 1988. Reprinted by permission of John Murray, part of the Hachette UK Group.

Steinbeck, John, *Travels with Charley: In Search of America*, London: Penguin Books, 1992. Copyright © The Curtis Publishing Company Inc., 1961, 1962. Copyright © John Steinbeck, 1962. Copyright renewed Elaine Steinbeck, Thom Steinbeck and John Steinbeck IV, 1989, 1990. Reproduced by permission of Penguin Books Ltd. Used by permission of Viking Penguin, a division of Penguin Group (USA) Inc.

Steinbeck, John and Edward Ricketts, *Sea of Cortez: A Leisurely Journal of Travel and Research*, New York: Viking, 1941. Copyright 1941, 1951 by John Steinbeck and Edward F. Ricketts. Copyright renewed © 1969 by John Steinbeck and Edward F. Ricketts, Jr. Reproduced by permission of Penguin Books Ltd. Used by permission of Viking Penguin, a division of Penguin Group (USA) Inc.

Stephen, Leslie (ed. J. Bicknell), *The Letters of Leslie Stephen*, 2 vols, London: Macmillan, 1996.

—, *The Playground of Europe*, London: Longmans, Green, 1871.

Stevenson, Robert Louis (ed. B. Booth and E. Mehew), *The Letters of Robert Louis Stevenson*, 8 vols, New Haven, CT: Yale University Press, 1994–5.

— (ed. J. Hart), *From Scotland to Silverado*, Cambridge, MA: Harvard University Press, 1966.

Sturt, Charles (ed. J. Waterhouse), *Journal of the Central Australian Expedition 1844–5*, London: Caliban Books, 1984.

Thesiger, Wilfred, *Arabian Sands*, London: Longmans, Green, 1959. Copyright © 1959, 1983, renewed © 1987 by Wilfred Thesiger. Used by permission of Viking Penguin, a division of Penguin Group (USA) Inc. Reproduced by permission of Curtis Brown Group Ltd, London on behalf of The Estate of Wilfred Thesiger. Copyright © The Estate of Wilfred Thesiger, 1959.

Thomas, Dylan (ed. P. Ferris), *Dylan Thomas: The Collected Letters*, London: Dent, 2000. Courtesy of David Higham Associates.

Thoreau, Henry David, *Cape Cod*, London: Sampson Low, 1865.

Trollope, Frances, *A Visit to Italy*, 2 vols, London: Richard Bentley, 1842.

Tully family, *Narrative of a Ten Years' Residence at Tripoli in Africa: From the Original Correspondence in the Possession of the Family of the Late Richard Tully, Esq., Comprising Authentic Memoirs and Anecdotes*, London: Henry Colburn, 1816.

—, *Letters Written During a Ten Years' Residence at the Court of Tripoli*, London: Henry Colburn, 1819.

Twain, Mark, *The Innocents Abroad*, New York: Library of America, 1984.

Waugh, Evelyn, *Ninety-Two Days*, London: Duckworth, 1943, Penguin Classics 2011. Copyright © Evelyn Waugh, 1934. Reproduced by permission of Penguin Books Ltd. Used in the United States of America by permission of The Wylie Agency (UK) Limited.

—, *Remote People*, London: Duckworth, 1931, Penguin Books 1985, Penguin Classics 2002. Copyright by Evelyn Waugh, 1931. Reproduced by permission of Penguin Books Ltd. Used in the United States of America by permission of The Wylie Agency (UK) Limited.

Whitman, Sidney, *Turkish Memories*, London: William Heinemann, 1914.

Whitman, Walt (ed. E. Miller), *Selected Letters of Walt Whitman*, Iowa City: University of Iowa Press, 1990.

—, *Specimen Days in America*, London: Walter Scott Publishing, 1888.

Whymper, Edward, *Travels Amongst the Great Andes of the Equator*, London: Lehmann, 1949.

Woolf, Virginia (ed. J. Morris), *Travels with Virginia Woolf*, New York: Random House, 1993.

Younghusband, Francis, *The Heart of a Continent*, London: John Murray, 1896.

Zweig, Stefan, *The World of Yesterday*, London: Cassell, 1943. © Williams-Verlag, Zürich.

INDEX

Page numbers in **bold** denotes a person or written source quoted.

Abadan, Persia (later Iran) 28
Accra, Ghana 238
Acropolis, Athens 293
Acton, Harold 402
Addis Ababa, Ethiopia 374
Adelaide 24
Adélie Land, Antarctica 108–9
Aden 58, 444
Advance (ship) 73
Afghanistan 160, 408–9, 425
Alcobaca, Portugal 208
Algiers 204–5
Alhambra palace, Granada, Spain 293
Ali, Muhammad 41*n*
Allégret, Marc 317
Alps 89, 218, 258, 279, 297, 373, 386, 396
America 21, 22, 42–43, 69, 78–79, 123, 125, 130, 193, 209, 221–22, 225, 252, 286, 295, 298–99, 306, 315, 323, 328, 330, 336, 354–55, 356, 358, 359, 380, 390, 404, 416, 433
American Civil War (1861–5) 328
Amundsen, Roald 86
The South Pole **435**
Amur Valley, Siberia 227
Anacapri 179
Anatolia 166
Andes 89, 92, 220

Andrée, Salomon: *The Andrée Diaries* **247**
Anglo-Persian Oil (now BP) 28
Antarctica 81, 86, 96, 108, 117, 136, 145, 187, 260
Antisana, Mt., Ecuador 89
Arabia 53, 58, 178, 316, 444
Arctic 12, 64–65, 73, 113, 247, 273, 353
Ascension Island 387
Aspen, Colorado 416
Athens 119
Atlantic Conveyor (ship) 356
Atlantic Ocean 167, 186, 219, 450, 453
Auden, W.H. and Isherwood, Christopher: *Journey to a War* **88, 90, 156, 202**
August Wilhelm, Prince of Prussia 127
Australia 24, 30, 395, 403
Austria 110, 279, 313
AWB (Afrikaner Weerstandsbeweging) 397

Baghdad, Iraq 340
Bagni di Lucca, Italy 240
Bahamas 360
Bahrain 188
Baikonur, Kazakhstan 152
Baker, Florence 77
Baker, Herbert 71
Baker, Samuel: *The Albert N'yanza*, Volume II **77, 99**
Baker-Carr, Captain 421
Ballets Russes 74

Banda Islands, eastern Indonesia 111
Banks, Joseph
The 'Endeavour' Journal 427
The 'Endeavour' Journal, Volume I **191, 445**
The 'Endeavour' Journal, Volume II **239**
Barbados 31
Barcelona 118
Bartin, Otis 284
Batavia (now Jakarta), Java 436, 445
Beagle, HMS 134
Bean, Charles: *Bean's Gallipoli* **394**
Beckford, William: *The Travel-Diaries* **208**
Beebe, William
Beneath Tropic Seas 52, 143
Half Mile Down **284–85**
Beechey, F.W.: *Narrative of a Voyage to the Pacific and Bering's Strait*, Volume I **426**
'Beer Hall Putsch' (Munich, 1923) **26**
Beirut, Lebanon 386
Belgium 217
Bell, Gertrude
The Desert and the Sown 53
The Letters of Gertrude Bell, Volume I **166**
Belzoni, Giovanni: *Narrative of the Operations and Recent Discoveries in Egypt and Nubia* **27, 97**
Belzoni, Sarah 27

Benares, India 20
Bennett, Alan: *Untold Stories* 301
Bennett, James Gordon, junior 376
Berlin 19, 147, 372, 434
Bermuda 284, 437
Bernese Oberland, Switzerland 218
Bird, Isabella
  A Lady's Life in the Rocky Mountains 390
  Letters to Henrietta 13
Birmingham 328
Black, Jeremy: *The British Abroad* 320, 373
Bloomsbury Group 441
Blossom, HMS 426
Blue Mosque, Constantinople 314
Blumenfeld, Ralph: *R.D.B.'s Diary* 224, 226
Blunt, Sir Wilfrid Scawen: *My Diaries*, Volume I 32
Boiling Advance Base, Ross Ice Shelf 136, 145
Bordeaux 229
Borghese, Prince Camillo 396
Borghese, Princess Pauline Bonaparte 396
Bosphorus 236
Boston, Massachusetts 148
Boston & Maine Railroad 163
Boswell, James: *Journal of a Tour of the Hebrides* 290, 369
Bougainville, Louis de: *A Voyage Round the World* 128–29
Bouilhet, Louis 98, 399
Bounty mutiny (1789) 426
Bournemouth 274
Bouvier, Nicolas
  The Japanese Chronicles 368
  The Way of the World 248, 361

Bowers, Henry 'Birdie' 117
Bowles, Paul
  In Touch 415
  Travels 44, 321, 365
Brand, Thomas 373
Brazil 55, 72, 242–43, 261
Bridges, Margaret 104
Bridges, Robert 104
British Empire 31, 167, 432
British Guiana 16
British Intelligence Corps 172
Brittain, Vera: *Testament of Youth* 378–79
Brooke, Rupert: *The Letters of Rupert Brooke* 62
Brown, Rawdon 443
Brownshirts 26
Bryson, Bill: *Notes from a Small Island* 107
Buchs, Switzerland 164–65
Bucsecs (Bucegi), Mt., Southern Carpathians 307
Buran (space shuttle) 152
Burckhardt, Johann: *Travels in Syria and the Holy Land* 169
Burma 174–75
Burroughs, William: *The Yagé Letters* 92–93
Bursino, Horatio 331, 392–93
Burton, Isabel: *The Romance of Isabel Lady Burton*, Volume II 19, 266–67, 302
Burton, Richard 19, 266, 302
  Personal Narrative of a Pilgrimage to Al-Madinah & Meccah, Volume II 316, 324
Buttermere, Lake District 116
Byrd, Richard: *Alone* 136, 145
Byron, Lord: *A Self-Portrait*, Volume II 76, 192

Byron, Robert
  Letters Home 160
  The Road to Oxiana 160, 340, 408–9

Caesar, Julius 99
  Commentaries 217
Cairo 38, 303
Calabria, Italy 263
Calais 320
Calcutta 440
Calderón de La Barca, Frances: *Life in Mexico* 182, 213
California 21, 131, 315, 404
Calthrop, Gladys 137
Cameroon, Mt. 337
Camus, Albert: *American Journals* 186, 254, 261
Canada 276, 388
Canadian Lakes 276
Canton, China 15, 88, 90
Cape Cod, Massachusetts 358
Cape Horn 112, 244
Cape York, Greenland 273
Capri 74–75, 179
Carchemish, Turkey 178
Carib people 360
Casablanca, Morocco 343
Cassady, Neal 359, 448
Castle, Agnes 95, 269
Cawnpore (Kanpur), India 63, 80
Cenis, Mt. 373
Ceylon (now Sri Lanka) 133
Charlottenlund, near Copenhagen 424
Chartres Cathedral 200, 293
Chateaubriand, Vicomte de: *The Memoirs of Chateaubriand* 217
Cheever, John: 'The Swimmer' 292
Chekhov, Anton
  A Journey to the End of the Russian Empire 180–81, 227, 348
  Letters 170

Cherry-Garrard, Apsley:
  *The Worst Journey in
  the World* 260
Chiang Kai-shek 88, 156
Chicago 69, 78
Chile 176
China 13, 66, 88, 90, 124,
  168, 200, 202, 235, 262
China National Aviation
  Corporation (CNAC) 34
Christian, Fletcher 426
Chungking, China 34
Churchill, Clementine and
  Winston: *Speaking for
  Themselves* 31
Clark, Alan
  Diaries 402
  Diaries: Into Politics 387
Cliveden 226
Cocteau, Jean: *My Journey
  Round the World* 119,
  146, 168, 193
Cold War 425
Colenso, Natal 397
Coleridge, Samuel Taylor 116
  Letters, Volume II 214
Coleridge, Sara 214
Colette 79
Collyer, Charlotte 138–39
Collyer, Harvey 138
Colorado River 416
Columbus, Christopher:
  *The Journal of
  Christopher Columbus*
  360
Common, Jack 342
Concord Railroad 163
Concord River 330
Condom, France 301
Congo 153, 173, 183, 339
Congo River 51, 317
Connecticut River 17
Conrad, Joseph
  Collected Letters, Volume
  I 183, 339
  Heart of Darkness 183
Constantinople (later
  Istanbul) 114, 236, 245,
  314, 357, 381, 399
Conti, Abbé 381

Cook, Frederick: *My
  Attainment of the Pole*
  144
Cook, Captain James 445
Cooke, Alistair
  Letter from America
  broadcasts 45
  Reporting America 45
Corfu 274, 275
Corinthic, SS 389
Corso, Gregory 367
Côte d'Azur, France 71
Coutet, Joseph 297
Coward, Noël: *Letters* 61,
  137
Crouch, Archer: *On a Surf-
  Bound Coast* 206
Cuba 312
Curzon, Lord George 421
  *Travels with a Superior
  Person* 417
Curzon, Lady Mary: *Lady
  Curzon's India* 421

Dalí, Salvador
  Diary of a Genius 439
  *The Secret Life of
  Salvador Dalí* 229–30
Dalrymple, William: *From
  the Holy Mountain* 245,
  431
Damascus 302, 377
Dana, Richard Henry: *Two
  Years Before the Mast*
  21, 244, 405
Darwin, Charles 55
  The Beagle Letters 134
Davies, William Henry:
  *The Autobiography of
  a Super-Tramp* 219,
  298–99
de Beauvoir, Marquis
  *The Conclusion of a
  Voyage Round the World*
  124, 150–51, 209, 423
  *A Voyage Round the
  World* 436
de Beauvoir, Simone:
  America Day by Day
  42–43, 78–79, 125

Dead Sea 137
Deakin, Roger: *Waterlog*
  292
Delaware River 22
Delhi 282, 296, 326
Della Valle, Pietro: *The
  Pilgrim* 38, 314
Delmer, Sefton: *Trail
  Sinister* 127
Denmark 333, 424
Denver, Colorado 207, 323,
  416
Desert Wind train 416
Diaghilev, Sergei 74, 75
Dickens, Charles: *American
  Notes and Pictures from
  Italy* 123, 391
Dorfman, Ariel: *Desert
  Memories* 176
Dover, Kent 107, 320
Druse people 25
Dubai 366
Dublin 288
Dufferin, Earl of: *Letters
  from High Latitudes*
  228, 241
Durrell, Gerald: *My Family
  and Other Animals* 274,
  275
Durrell, Lawrence 274, 275
Durrell, Leslie 274
Durrell, Margo 274

East India Company 440
Eberhardt, Isabelle: *The
  Passionate Nomad* 11,
  204–5
Ecuador 89, 154, 220
Edinburgh 290, 350, 410
Egypt 27, 32, 38, 41, 68, 97,
  98, 137, 303, 431
Elephant Island 187
Elizabethville (now
  Lubumbashi,
  Democratic Republic of
  the Congo) 59
Empty Quarter (Rub' al
  Khali) 188, 189, 377, 414
Endeavour, HMS 191, 239,
  427

English Civil War (1642-51) 199
Eskimos (Inuit) 49, 132, 187, 264, 283
Esopus, New York State 221
Ethiopia 59, 374
Etna, Mt. 215–16
European Space Agency 152
Evans, Edgar 102–3
Evelyn, John: *Diary* 199, 287
Everest, Mt. 188, 277

Fakir of Benares 20
Falklands War (1982) *387*
Fascists 269
Fay, Eliza: *Original Letters from India* 303, **440**
Fermor, Patrick Leigh: *A Time of Gifts* 26, **430**
First World War 95, 104, 110, 164–65, 268, 289, 311, 338, 378, 394
Fitzroy, Captain Robert 134
Flandrau, Charles Macomb: *Viva Mexico!* 362–63, **449**
Flaubert, Gustave: *Selected Letters* 98, 399
Fleming, Ian
Dr No 101
Talk of the Devil 101, 141, 437
Thrilling Cities 386
Fleming, Peter 352
Brazilian Adventure 242–43
News from Tartary 66, 235
Florence 240
Flower, Newman: *Through My Garden Gate* 311
Forster, E.M.: *The Hill of Devi and other Indian Writings* 20, 432, 452
Fourier, Charles 399
Fowles, John: *The Journals*, Volume I 293

Foxe Basin, Canada 49
Fraenkel, Knut 247
Fram (ship) 12, 113, 353
France 19, 210–11, 223, 268, 318–19, 320, 367, 375, 392, 439
Franco, General Francisco 18
Franco-Prussian War (1870–1) 19
Franklin, Sir John 73
Franz-Josef Land, Russia 64–65
Freetown, Sierra Leone 162, 183
French Equatorial Africa 317

Gambia 206
Gambia River 206, 428
Ganges River 20, 326
Garden of Eden 141
Gebel-el-Teir, Egypt 98
Gellhorn, Martha: *The Face of War* 34–35, 56–57, 118, 318–19
Genève (boat) 33
Germany 19, 147, 372
Gervase, Mr (a portrait painter) 115
Ghana 238
Ghent, Belgium 217
Gibbs, Philip: *The Pageant of the Years* 268
Gide, André: *Travels in the Congo* 173, 317
Ginsberg, Allen 207
Ginsberg, Allen and Louis: *Family Business* 367, 400–401
Glamorgan, Wales 249
Glasgow 410
Gobi desert 442
Goebbels, Joseph 127
Goethe, Johann Wolfgang von: *Italian Journey* 85, 197
Gogol, Nikolai 170
Golden Horn, Constantinople 357

Gondokoro, Sudan 77
Great Barrier Reef 445
Great Depression *329*
Great Geysir, Haukadalur Valley, Iceland 241
Great Southern Ocean 112
Greece 166, 386
Greek War of Independence (1821-32) *76*
Greene, Barbara 39, 87
Greene, Graham
Journey Without Maps **39**, 87
A Life in Letters 162, 304–5
Greenland 265
Greenwell, H.J. 269
Grey, George: *Journals of two Expeditions of Discovery*, Volume II **177**
Grinnell, Henry 73
Grosz, George: *A Small Yes and a Big No* 253
Gulf of California, Mexico 106

Hackett, Frances and Albert 288
Hadley, Leila 50, 111
Haile Selassie, Emperor 59, 374
Haiti 52, 143, 304–5
Hamel, northern France 104
Hamsun, Knut: *Selected Letters*, Volume I **69**, 252, 333
Hankow, China 90
Hanssen, Helmer 435
Happy Days (raft) 142
Harris, Joseph 24
Hart-Davis, Duff: *Peter Fleming* 352
Hawthorne, Nathaniel: *Complete Works*, Volume IX **163**, 330
Hearn, Lafcadio: *Glimpses of Unfamiliar Japan*, Volume II **126**, 250–51, 347

Heaven Lake, Xinjiang, China 262
Hecla, HMS 49
Hedin, Sven
  My Life as an Explorer **140, 406**
  The Silk Road **442**
Hell Gill gorge, near Ingleton, Yorkshire 292
Henley, William 198
Henslow, J.S. 134
Henson, Matthew 132
Herat, Afghanistan 408
Heyerdahl, Thor: *The Kon-Tiki Expedition* **154–55, 184, 185**
Hierro, Canary Islands 360
Himalaya 334–35, 398, 412
Hitler, Adolf 26, 127
Hofbrauhaus, Munich 26
Hollywood 78
Holmes, John Clellon 359
Holmes, Oliver Wendell 218
Holy Land 100, 137, 231
Hong Kong 34, 61, 168
Hopei, China 66
Hornby, Lady:
  Constantinople During the Crimean War **236**
Hughes, Gerald 225, 306
Hughes, Ted: *Letters* **225, 306**
Hulah 340
Humboldt, Alexander von: *Jaguars and Electric Eels* **60**
Huston, John 370
Huxley, Aldous: *Pilate Jesting: The Diary of a Journey* **411**
Huxley, Thomas Henry 411
  Diary of the Voyage of H.M.S. Rattlesnake **55, 395**
Hyderabad, India 432
Hyslop, D., *et al*: *Titanic Voices* **138–39**

Ibn Battuta: *Travels in Asia and Africa* **149, 282, 326–27**
Ibraham Pasha 41
Iceland 228, 241
Inagua, Bahama islands 101
India 20, 63, 80, 282, 296, 326–27, 411, 412, 421, 432, 440
Indian Mutiny (1857-9) 63, 80
Indus Gorge, Pakistan 94
Indus River 447
Industrial Revolution 249
Iran 248
Ireland 288, 370–71
Isherwood, Christopher **88, 90, 156, 202**
Israel 53, 137, 400–401
Istanbul *see* Constantinople
Italy 56–57, 74–75, 85, 95, 161, 190, 197, 240, 263, 269, 279, 322, 349, 364, 385, 386, 391, 396, 407, 443
Iwalatan (Walata), Mauretania 149

Jamaica 437
Jamestown, St Helena 167
Japan 126, 150–51, 257, 347, 368
Japanese Sea 250–51
Java 423, 436, 445
Jerusalem 53, 137
Jodhpur, India 411
Johanssen, Hjalmar 64
Johnson, Dr Samuel 290, 369
Jordan 100, 291
Judson, Adoniram 174
Judson, Ann: *Memoir* **174–75**
Justinian, Emperor 68

Kabul, Afghanistan 425
Kafka, Franz **116**
Kailahun, Sierra Leone 39
Kane, Elisha Kent

Arctic Explorations, Volume I **212**
Arctic Explorations, Volume II **265**
The U.S. Grinnell Expedition **73**
Kapuściński, Ryszard
  Imperium **135**
  The Soccer War **238**
  Travels with Herodotus **425**
Karakoram Mountains, Pakistan 94
Keriya oasis, Sinkiang province, China 235
Kerouac, Jack
  On the Road **359**
  Selected Letters **207, 359, 448**
  The Town and The City **359**
Khill, Marcel 119
Kingsley, Mary: *Travels in West Africa* **337**
Kingston, Jamaica 437
Kinshasa, Democratic Republic of the Congo 339
Kipling, Rudyard
  Letters of Travel **17**
  unpublished letter, RIBA Archive (London) **71**
Kirghiz steppe, Kazakhstan 406
Kléber, General Jean-Baptiste 68
Kon-Tiki (raft) 154, 155, 184, 185
Kuling, China 156
Kung, Imperial Regent Prince 124
Kuwait 417
Kyoto, Japan 257
Kyseth, Torger 69

Lake Albert N'yanza 77, 99
Lake Bey-Sheher (Beysehir) 166
Lake District 116
Larache, Morocco 321

473

Larbi, Mohammed 321
Larissa, Greece 76
Lawrence, D.H.
   D.H. Lawrence and Italy
   14–15
   Letters, Volume IV **91**,
   133
   Letters, Volume VI **279**
Lawrence, T.E. (Lawrence of
   Arabia) 291, 377
   Letters **178**
Laws, Ingvar 333
Lear, Edward
   Edward Lear in Greece
   341
   Lear's Italy **161**, 215–16,
   263
Lebanon 53, 386
Leblich, Domingo: *Travels
   of Ali Bey*, Volume II 37
Lee, Laurie
   *As I Walked Out One
   Midsummer Morning*
   201, 344
   A Moment of War **18**,
   422
Lees-Milne, James: *Through
   the Wood and Dale*
   407
Leighton, Roland 378, 379
Lenin, Vladimir 329
Leopold II, King of the
   Belgians 183
Letter from America (radio
   broadcasts) 45
Lewis, Norman
   Jackdaw Cake **172**, 312
   Naples '44 **159**, 385
Liberia 39, 87, 413
Libya 23, 450
Lima, Peru 92–93
Lipari islands 364
Lisbon 105, 229–30
Livingstone, David 51
   *The Last Journals of
   David Livingstone*,
   Volume II **376**
Llandudno 332
Loch Coruisk, Isle of Skye
   280–81

London 28, 36, 40, 67, 218,
   224, 246, 313, 331, 389,
   392–93, 430
Loppé, Gabriel 278
Los Angeles 78–79, 416
Lothian, Alan: private
   correspondence 152
Loti, Pierre: *Voyages* **100**,
   257
Lualaba River 51
Lunardi, Vincenzo: *An
   Account of Five Aerial
   Voyages in Scotland*
   350, 410
Lyautey, Hubert: *Intimate
   Letters from Tonquin*
   364
Lyon, George: *Private
   Journal* **49**, 264

McAuliffe, Christa 45
McClure, S.S. 255
MacFarlane, Robert: *The
   Wild Places* **116**, 280–81
MacGillivray, John 55
Machiguenga people 142
McMillan, James, ed.: *The
   Way It Was* **95**, 269
Madrid 18, 118, 422
Maillart, Ella 66, 235
Majuro isle, Marshall
   Group 255
Mallory, George: *Climbing
   Everest* **277**
Malta 214, 378–79
Mandingo (Mandinka)
   people 428–29
Manhattan, New York 356
Mansfield, Katherine
   Collected Letters, Volume
   IV **441**
   Journal **36**, 389
Mao Zedong 88
Marinetti, Filippo:
   Manifesto of Futurism
   70
Markham, Violet: *Return
   Passage* **286**
Marquesas Islands, French
   Polynesia 54

Marrakesh, Morocco
   342–43
Marryat, Frank: *Mountains
   and Molehills* **131**, 315
Mary Queen of Scots 290
Masefield, John
   Letters from the Front **338**
   *Letters to Margaret
   Bridges* **104**
Massachusetts 225, 330,
   358
Massine, Léonide 74, 75
Matthiessen, Peter
   The Cloud Forest **142**
   The Snow Leopard **398**,
   412
Matveyevna, Claudia 135
Mawson, Douglas: *Home
   of the Blizzard*, Volume
   I 108–9
Mecca, Saudi Arabia 37,
   149, 316, 324, 326
Medina, Saudi Arabia 316
Meiji Restoration 126
Mendelssohn, Felix:
   *Letters from Italy and
   Switzerland* **179**
Mer de Glace, France
   (Montenvers Glacier)
   258
Mermod, Michel, *The
   Voyage of the Genève*
   33, 54, 167
Mermoz, Jean **450**
Meshed, Persia 300
Mesopotamia (later Iraq)
   40, 340
Mexico 182, 213, 362–63,
   448, 449
Mile High Orchestra 416
Mirgorod, Ukraine 170
Missolonghi, Greece 76
M'Lean, Sir Allan 369
Monrovia, Liberia 87, 413
Mont Blanc 216, 258–59,
   278
Montagu, Lady Mary
   Wortley: *The Complete
   Letters*, Volume I
   114–15, **325**, **381**

Montana-sur-Sierre, Switzerland 441
Monte Moro 297
Monterey, California 404
Montreal, Canada 276, 388
Morocco 231, 321, 342–43, 365, 415
Morrell, Lady Ottoline 441
Morris, James: *Sultan in Oman* 446
Moscow 329
Moshulu (ship) 112, 453
Muggeridge, Malcolm: *Like It Was* 105, 200, 329
Muhammed, Prophet 68
Muir, John: *My First Summer in the Sierra* 203, 256, 295
Mull, Scotland 369
Mullin, Chris: *A View from the Foothills* 413
Multan, Sind 327
Murmansk, Soviet Union 253
Murphy, Dervla
South from the Limpopo 397
Tibetan Foothold 296
Where the Indus is Young 94, 447
Murphy, Rachel 447
Murray, John 76, 192
Mussolini, Benito 269
Mustagh Pass 334

Nansen, Fridtjof
Farthest North, Volume I 113
Farthest North, Volume II 12, 64–65, 353
Naples 75, 85, 159, 197, 269, 385
Napoleon Bonaparte 25, 68, 167, 217, 387
Napoleon's Letters 396
Nares, Edward 320
NASA 45
Native Americans 295
Nazis 26, 72, 223, 229, 313, 318

Nepal 412
Nesbitt, Cathleen 62
New England 17
New Jersey 433
New York 69, 78, 125, 286, 356, 380
New York Zoological Society 52
New Zealand 36
Newby, Eric
The Last Grain Race 112, 453
A Traveller's Life 68, 291
Nice, France 375
Niger River 294, 428
Nightingale, Florence: *Letters from Egypt* 41
Nile River 38, 41, 77, 98, 99, 303, 431
Nollekens, Joseph 407
North Dakota 252
North Pole 12, 132, 144, 247, 273, 435
North-West Passage 49, 73, 264, 283
Nuevitas, Cuba 312

Oates, Captain Laurence 'Titus' 86, 96, 102, 102, 103
O'Donovan, Edmond: *Merv* 300
Ohio River 123
Oman 446
Open Polar Sea 212, 265
Orde-Lees, Thomas 81
Orlovsky, Peter 367
Orwell, George: *A Life in Letters* 342–43
Ottoman Empire 23, 53
Oudh, India 80
Oxyrhynchus, Egypt 431

Pacific Ocean 54, 111, 130, 184, 255
Paddington Station, London 226
Pakistan 94
Palestine 53, 137

Palin, Michael: *Around the World in 80 Days* 366, 416
Pampa Union, Chile 176
Panama 131, 437
Paris 19, 223, 268, 318–19, 367, 399, 439
Paris Commune (1871) 19
Park, Mungo: *The Travels of Mungo Park* 294, 428–29
Parthenon, Athens 119, 293
Peary, Robert E. 144
The North Pole 132, 273
Peking (Beijing) 124, 200
Peking-Hankow Railway 66
Pera Palas hotel, Istanbul 245
Perelman, Abby 246
Perelman, Laura 288
Perelman, S.J.: *Don't Tread on Me* 50, 111, 246, 288
Persia (later Iran) 28–29, 340, 408
Peru 92–93, 131, 142, 154, 155
Perugia, Italy 322
Petra, Jordan 169
Petropolis, Brazil 72
Philadelphia 323
Picasso, Pablo 439
Pilgrim (ship) 244, 405
Pistoia, Italy 190
Pitcairn Island 426
Pittsburgh 328
Plath, Sylvia 225
Platter, Thomas and Bursino, Horatio:
The Journals of Two Travellers 331, 392–93
Pocock, Frank 153
Polaris (North Star) 132
Polynesia 154, 191
Pompeii 74
Pongo de Mainique, Peru 142
Port Essington, Australia 395
Port-au-Prince, Haiti 304
Portugal 105

Praslin Island, Seychelles
141
President Cleveland, SS 50
Proby, Hon. John 215
Prokofiev, Sergei: *Diaries*
74–75
Pucallpa, Peru 93
Puebla, Mexico 449
Pyrenees 18, 118, 422

Quito, Ecuador 220

Raban, Jonathan: *Hunting
Mister Heartbreak* 356,
380
Rameses II 97
Rangoon, Burma 146,
174–75
Rattlesnake, HMS 55, 395
Ready (supply ship) 284
Rebolledo, Señor 89
Red Sea 91
Richthofen, Frieda von 14
Ricketts, Edward **106**
Rilke, Rainer Maria
*Rainer Maria Rilke and
Lou Andreas Salomé:
The Correspondence*
424
Selected Letters 171
Rio de Janeiro, Brazil 55,
242–43, 254, 427
Rocky Mountains 390
Rome 74, 75, 161, 171, 192,
407, 424
Rosetta, Egypt 27
Ross, John: *A Voyage of
Discovery* **283**
Ross Ice Shelf (Barrier) 136,
260
Roth, Joseph
What I Saw **147**, 372
The White Cities 375
Rothenstein, William **20**
Rotterdam 287
Royal Navy 239
Royal Society 199
Royat, France 198
*Rubaiyat of Omar
Khayyam* 378

Rum, Wadi, Jordan 377
Ruskin, Effie: *Effie in
Venice* **443**
Ruskin, John **40**, 391, 443,
452
Letters from Venice 349
Ruskin in Italy 190, **297**
Russell, William Howard
*My Diary North and
South* **328**
My Indian Mutiny Diary
63, **80**
Russia 135

S-Bahn, Berlin 147
Sacheuse (interpreter) 283
Sahara 11, 44, 149, 204
Sahel 11
St Catherine's Monastery,
Sinai Peninsula 68
St Helena 167, 387
Saint-Exupéry, Antoine de
450–51
Sakhalin, Russian Far East
180, 227, 348
Salisbury Cathedral 200
Samarkand, Uzbekistan 352
San Agustin, Mexico 213
San Francisco 130, 193, 209,
359
Santa Barbara, California 21
Sardinia 11
Sartre, Jean-Paul 42
Quiet Moments in a War
370–71
Saudi Arabia 37, 149, 316,
324, 326, 377
Savannah, Georgia 125
Schaller, George 398
Schaub, Julius 127
Scobee, Commander Dick
45
Scotland 203, 290, 350,
369, 410
Scott, Robert Falcon 108,
188, 260, 435
Journals 86, 96, **102–3**,
117
Second Sino-Japanese War
(1937-45) *90*

Second World War *34–35,
56–57, 105, 159, 162,
172, 223, 229, 312, 313,
434*
Secret Intelligence Service
(MI6) 105, 162
Seth, Vikram: *From Heaven
Lake* **262**
Seychelles 141
Shackleton, Ernest: *South*
81, **187**
Shah, Sultan Muhammad
327
Shanghai 202
Shaw, George Bernard 219
Shelley, Mary 258
Shelley, Percy Bysshe:
*History of a Six Weeks'
Tour* 258–59
Sheykh Obeyd, Egypt 32
Shirer, William: *Berlin
Diary* **223**, 434
Siberia 135
Sicily 14–15, 215–16, 269
Sierra Leone 162
Sikhs 146
Silk Road 442
Simond, Louis: *An
American in Regency
England* 67, 249
Sinai, Mt. 91, 169
Sinai Peninsula 68
Sind 326, 327
Sino-Japanese War (1937-45)
34, 156, 202
Sirocco 179
Sitwell, Frances 332
Slad, Gloucestershire 201
Slavyansk, Ukraine 170
Slocum, Joshua: *Sailing
Alone Around the World*
148
Smith, Frederick 177
Smollett, Tobias: *Travels
Through France and
Italy* 210–11
Sofia, Bulgaria 114–15
Somme, Battle of the (1917)
104, 311
Sorrento 75

South Africa 397
South America 16, 60, 89, 92–93, 131, 134, 154–55, 177, 261, 427
South Downs, Sussex 289
South Georgia 187
South Pacific 128, 426
South Pole 86, 102, 108, 188, 260, 435
Southern Cross 50
Soviet Union 329
  collapse of (1991) 135
Space Shuttle *Challenger* 45
Spain 18, 118, 293, 344, 422
Spanish Armada (1588) 331, 392
Spanish Civil War (1936-9) 18, 118, 201, 422
Spray (ship) 148
S.S. 26
Stafford, Montgomery 276
Stanley, Henry Morton 39, 376
  Through the Dark Continent, Volume II **51**, 153
Stark, Freya: *Over the Rim of the World* 25, 58, **388**, **444**
Steinbeck, John: *Travels with Charley* 336, 354–55
Steinbeck, John and Ricketts, Edward: *Sea of Cortez* **106**
Stephen, Leslie
  Letters, Volume I **218**
  The Playground of Europe 278, 307
Stevenson, Robert Louis
  From Scotland to Silverado **404**
  Letters, Volume II **332**
  Letters, Volume IV **198**
  Letters, Volume VI **255**
Storm Troopers 26
Strindberg, Nils 247
Stromboli. Mt. 364

Sturt, Charles: *Journal of the Central Australian Expedition, 1844-5* 24, 30, **403**
Sturt, Charlotte 24, 403
Suez Canal 91
Suleiman, Sheikh 446
Süleymaniye Mosque, Constantinople 314
Svyatogorsk, Ukraine 170
Switzerland 164–65, 218, 386, 441
Syria 25, 53, 377

Tahiti 62, 128–29, 191, 239
Taimur, Said bin, Sultan of Muscat and Oman 446
Tajiks 408
Tangier 231, 365
Taormina, Sicily 133
Tashkent, Uzbekistan 406
Tempelhof airport, Berlin 127
Terre'Blanche, Eugène 397
Thackeray, Minny 218
Thames River 331
Thebes, Egypt 97
Thesiger, Wilfred: *Arabian Sands* **188–89**, 377, **414**
Thomas, Caitlin 130
Thomas, Dylan: *Collected Letters* 28–29, 130
Thoreau, Henry David 330
  Cape Cod 358
  Walden 246
Tibet 140
Tierra del Fuego 134
Tirana, Albania 341
Titanic, RMS 138–39
Tomsk, Siberia 180–81
Toyotomi Hideyoshi palace, Kyoto, Japan 257
Trans-Siberian Express 135
Transjordan 200
Trieste 266–67
Tripoli, Libya 23, 237, 351
Trollope, Frances: *A Visit to Italy*, Volume I 240
Tughluq, Muhammad bin 282

Tully, Miss
  Letters Written During a Ten Years' Residence at the Court of Tripoli 237
  Narrative of a Ten Years' Residence at Tripoli in Africa 23, **351**
Tunis 172
Tunisia 11
Turkey 114, 166, 236, 245, 314, 357, 361, 381
Twain, Mark: *The Innocents Abroad* 231

University of California at Berkeley 130
Urubamba, Rio 142
US Air Force 52

Valetta, Malta 214
Venezuela 60
Venice 349, 386, 443
Verdun, Battle of (1916) 338
Vermont 17
Verne, Jules 416
Vernet, Thierry 248, 361
Vesuvius, Mt. 197
Vienna 325
Villach, Austria 279
Voltaire 323
Vulcan, Mt. 364

Wales 249, 332
Walston, Catherine 304
Warrup (an Aborigine) 177
Waterloo, Battle of (1815) 217
Waugh, Evelyn
  Ninety-Two Days 16
  Remote People 59, 374, **438**
Weddell Sea 81
Westminster, Duke of 226
Wharton, Robert 373
White Island, Canadian Arctic 247
Whitman, Mannahatta 221
Whitman, Sidney: *Turkish Memories* **40**

Whitman, Walt
  Selected Letters 221–22,
    276
  *Specimen Days in
    America* 22, 221, 323,
    433
Whymper, Edward: *Travels
  Amongst the Great
  Andes of the Equator*
  89, 220

Wilson, Edward 103, 117
Wisconsin Dells 354–55

Woolf, Virginia: *Travels
  with Virginia Woolf* 289,
  322, 357

Yakutsk, Russia 135
Yangtze River 90
Yazd, Iran 248
Yokohama, Japan 150–51,
  368
Yosemite, California 203,
  256, 295
Younghusband, Francis:
  *The Heart of a
  Continent* 334–35

Zagorski, Karol 183
Zanzibar 438
Zemzem, sacred well of,
  Mecca, Saudi Arabia 37
Zürich 386
Zweig, Elizabeth 72
Zweig, Stefan
  Jeremiah 164
  The World of Yesterday
  72, 110, 164–65, 313